FROM THE SIDELINES TO THE HEADLINES

Volleyball team celebrates 2021 conference championship.

FROM THE SIDELINES TO THE HEADLINES

The Legacy of Women's Sports at Trinity University

BETSY GERHARDT PASLEY

Foreword by
JODY CONRADT

Maverick Books, an imprint of
Trinity University Press
San Antonio, Texas

Trinity University Press
San Antonio, Texas 78212

Book design by BookMatters, Berkeley
Cover design by Anne Richmond, Boston
Cover photograph, copyright © Diana Mara Henry

ISBN 978-1-59534-983-5 paper
ISBN 978-1-59534-984-2 ebook

Trinity University Press strives to produce its books using methods and materials in an environmentally sensitive manner. We favor working with manufacturers that practice sustainable management of all natural resources, produce paper using recycled stock, and manage forests with the best possible practices for people, biodiversity, and sustainability. The press is a member of the Green Press Initiative, a nonprofit program dedicated to supporting publishers in their efforts to reduce their impacts on endangered forests, climate change, and forest-dependent communities.

The paper used in this publication meets the minimum requirements of the American National Standard for Information Sciences—Permanence of Paper for Printed Library Materials, ansi 39.48–1992.

CIP data on file at the Library of Congress

27 26 25 24 23 | 5 4 3 2 1

For Professor Emeritus Douglas Brackenridge, whose love for Trinity led not only to this book but also to an enduring (and endearing) influence on students, colleagues, and fellow joggers through his long and exemplary life

CONTENTS

FOREWORD

JODY CONRADT

In 2022, as the historic date of June 23 approached, faculty, staff, students, and constituents of institutions of higher education across the United States engaged in a near simultaneous review of the past fifty years since Title IX was signed.

> No person in the United States shall, on the basis of sex, be excluded from participation in, be denied the benefits of, or be subjected to discrimination under any education program or activity receiving Federal financial assistance.

Not a word referred to sports or athletics, but this law indeed was the change agent for initiating participation opportunities for girls and women. However, much work had been done prior to 1972.

Trinity University and other institutions in our great state of Texas were fortunate to have dedicated and visionary leaders who formed the foundation for what would become the Association of Intercollegiate Athletics for Women and the National Collegiate Athletic Association divisional programs. They were educators first, administrators and coaches second. They often labored in obscurity and viewed the small steps of progress in scholarship dollars, facility access, and provision of equipment and uniforms as huge victories. After all, they also were working in a social environment where women often were not expected to pursue professions or passions where men were predominant.

Trinity was acclaimed for its nationally competitive tennis participants, among other standout student-athletes, and its coaches are part of the institution's long-honored athletics lore.

While the framework of men's athletics at Trinity was forever transformed by the loss of athletic scholarships, women's athletics continued to emerge and flourish as undergraduate enrollment blossomed with females pursuing both an education and cocurricular activities like sports.

These two elements—access to education and the opportunity to train and compete—helped alter the path of acceptance for women far beyond gyms and courts. They utilized their education and team experiences to become more marketable employees in areas of business, science, law, teaching, and engineering. Soon, they also became prominent coaches and athletics administrators.

We celebrate not only fifty years of Title IX influence but also the lives impacted by those who made the tenets of the law come to life. Trinity University has proudly carried a banner for change and opportunity over many decades leading to Title IX and afterward.

This book chronicles the influencers and courageous participants in a personal and colorful way that we all can appreciate, especially those of us who had the privilege of knowing and working alongside them in similar roles at our own institutions. It is a sisterhood that will live forever.

Introduction

One May evening in 2014, former Trinity University athlete Peggy Kokernot Kaplan ('75) clicked "send" on an email to the school's athletic department. Under the subject line, "Founder of the Trinity women's track team 1975," she asked the school to post statistics from the team's inaugural season—especially her national qualifying 880-yard time at the state collegiate meet. Kaplan had started her investigation even earlier, as her email referenced similar appeals to prior Tiger coaches. It's no surprise that they couldn't fulfill her request; Trinity had sparse records from the 1970s—not just for track and field but for most performances by female athletes before 1991, when Trinity joined an NCAA Division III conference. A renowned student activist, Kaplan wanted recognition for these early athletes. "Just as Baseball, Tennis, and Football share their history on the website, I think it is important for the Women's Track team to be given its place as well," she wrote from her home office in Columbus, Ohio.

Once again disappointed with the official response, Kaplan reached out to Shirley Rushing, the retired professor who had inspired the drama major to start that team almost forty years earlier. Rushing, who spent thirty-five years in Trinity's physical education department, made a call to former religion professor Douglas Brackenridge. The university historian and author recruited school archivist Jes Neal and me—as a former athlete—to form a small committee to follow up on Kaplan's story and research other gaps in the history of Trinity's women's sports. Thus, the Trinity University Women's Intercollegiate Athletics history project began in earnest. While the original intent was to capture the significant changes sparked by Title IX in the 1970s, the group's research expanded into the next formative decades, and eventually incorporated the school's first hundred years as well.

Eight years later, what began as a humble email request culminated not only in this book but also in a growing oral history archive and companion website to honor the past contributions of the women who played and persevered through these challenging decades. It's fitting that this book was completed the same year as the fiftieth anniversary of Title IX, the legislation that opened doors to women far beyond college campuses.

In these pages you'll hear from students and coaches who were principal actors in this unfolding drama, amid national and state-level events that provided the backdrop for sportswomen of the day. The progress of women in US sports falls into three general time periods.[1]

1. Around the turn of the twentieth century, a pivot was made away from Victorian ideals that considered physical exercise not "womanly." More enlightened experts began to see the benefits of physical activity for women in respectable social encounters. Educators gradually added sports to the curriculum during this period.

2. The golden decade from 1925 to 1935 not only followed voting rights for women but also introduced cultural changes that extended female physical engagement beyond the upper class. It became more acceptable for female students to engage in intramural and limited extramural activities. In the next few unsettled decades, overseers of women's sports experimented with nonthreatening recreational approaches within this restrictive framework, including competition between classes (e.g., sophomore vs. freshman) and low-key contests with students from other schools.

3. The contemporary era began in the 1970s, as women formerly forced to the sidelines were allowed entry into the world of official school-sponsored sports. While the evolution of national governance models helped, the true catalyst was the game-changing legislation

> of Title IX. The resulting grassroots activism and institutional leadership in the following three decades specifically moved all Trinity teams away from a win-at-all-costs attitude toward a more balanced academic and athletic approach.

Note the large gaps in the historical overview. Many false starts were interrupted by cultural shifts, economic depressions, and world wars, which women had to repeatedly rebound from.

Trinity's story unfolds along these general lines, as it moved its way around central Texas before settling in San Antonio on the abandoned quarry site it still occupies seventy years later. For example, the school's relocation to San Antonio's Woodlawn campus in the first years of World War II coincided with the unprecedented entry of women into the workforce. Its 1952 move to the Skyline campus took place in the shadow of society forcing women back to homemaker status. And Trinity's 1969 centennial celebration was held amid tumultuous protests, both for civil rights and against a foreign war, soon to be followed by transformational cultural and legislative change that finally—and permanently—opened doors for female students and athletes. Evident throughout these eras are the fingerprints of characters who overcame obstacles to ensure those doors remained open.

The most active years of progress were between 1970 and 2000, when Division III finally stabilized. According to Shirley Rushing, the three events that ensured advancement for the university's female athletes in this period were the 1972 passage of Title IX, the hiring of Libby Johnson, and the 1979 arrival of President Ron Calgaard. In his twenty-year term, Calgaard successfully realigned the university culture to a balance of academic and athletic excellence. He was also a vocal advocate for the school's female athletes and responsible for many organizational and facility changes needed to accommodate their new opportunities. The twentieth century concludes with a dual celebration of tennis titles, and the final chapter offers a brief overview of the new century and the continuing successes of Trinity women's sports from 2000 to the present.

Some stories in this book are male-centric out of necessity. For example, the 1971 elimination of men's athletic scholarships at Trinity opened the door for the noncommercial Division III philosophy that would eventually benefit the fledgling female teams. Other deep dives include ongoing debates related to Title IX and the unique status of Trinity women's tennis. But the characters and events all lead to Trinity's current status as both a highly ranked academic leader and conference sports powerhouse.

That said, this book is by no means a comprehensive account of every seminal event during this timeframe. As with any large project, there were obstacles and limitations.

The primary obstacle in researching for this project was the lack of adequate documentation of female athletes' accomplishments, which of course was the catalyst for this effort in the first place. Unlike the male teams—which had trainers, scorekeepers, and the preponderance of attention from the public relations department and local media—women's teams had little coverage and almost no record keeping. As an assistant to the sports information director in 1976–77, I compiled statistics for a number of women's games, but those seem to have been relegated to the dustbin of history.

The lack of documentation at Trinity was exacerbated by the school's relocations to four Texas campuses in its first eighty-three years: Tehuacana (1869–1902), Waxahachie (1902–42), and San Antonio (1942–52 on the Woodlawn campus, and 1952–present on the Skyline campus). Each move resulted in the loss of records and artifacts; some had to be stored in various offices and departments due to the lack of adequate archival facilities, and others were inadvertently misplaced, discarded, or destroyed.

This wasn't just a Trinity problem. Prior to 1982, when NCAA assumed control, much of the story of US women's intercollegiate athletics had not been well preserved. In doing research for *Before Brittney: A Legacy of Champions*, a book about women's athletics at Baylor University, Nancy Goodloe described her own experiences: "The records of their [female intercollegiate athletes] accomplishments may or may not be filed away in libraries across this country. There are no websites or media guides with information from that era. Some of these records may be gathering dust stashed away in storage rooms and closets, in private homes or university archives. These names and their team accomplishments are not easy to find."[2]

Fortunately, some primary sources have survived and are supplemented by microfilm and digital copies from other archives and personal collections. This project was further brought to life through dozens of oral history interviews with former athletes, faculty, administrators, and trustees under the helpful guidance of Trinity's archivist.

Unfortunately, the most common resources weren't always the most helpful. A quick glance at the endnotes of this book shows that the majority of citations are from the weekly student newspaper, *Trinitonian*, and the annual *Mirage* yearbook. However earnest, student reporters were not always accurate. (As one of those sportswriters, I speak from experience.) Although our committee of researchers tried our best to find outside attribution for important points, these student publications had to function as the most definitive sources.

Unlike today's photo-saturated landscape, many time periods highlighted in this book lacked visual documentation. Some of the best photographs were posed team pictures found sprinkled throughout the glossy pages of yearbooks from the early 1900s. Camera technology at that time precluded action shots, and the hand-held Instamatic cameras of the 1960s and 1970s produced snapshots that were often blurry and brown. The occasional photos of sportswomen in the *Trinitonian* and *Mirage* were rarely of the quality needed for a book.

Nor is there space for team recaps of the formative and fulfilling years between 1970 and 2000, as the project originally intended. Trinity's publication archives provided season-by-season accomplishments of the major women's sports programs, unearthing many compelling personal stories in the process. Highlights of those are in this narrative, but those interested in more detailed sport summaries and personal profiles can find them in Trinity's online archives located at the student-created Playing Field (https://playingfield.coateslibrary.com).

Finally, the limitations of a printed book preclude a comprehensive view of substantive cultural challenges that continue to this day. One example is the lack of African American representation on women's teams. Trinity's southern roots meant it was late to the desegregation game, as aptly summarized in Douglas Brackenridge's *Trinity University: A Tale of Three Cities.*[3] Although residence halls were finally opened to all in the 1960s, the percentage of minority students in the overall student population remained minuscule, and the committee found few detailed records or photographs of individual African American athletes until the 1990s. These students attempted to create community through organizations such as Black Efforts at Trinity in the 1970s and the establishment of the Black Student Union in 1989. But their recruitment to Trinity sports was often thwarted by larger schools dangling athletic scholarships and strong academic support systems, making it difficult for Division III institutions such as Trinity to compete.

In addition, the admittedly inadequate coverage of LGBTQ rights isn't intended to dismiss the likely presence of homosexual players and coaches during this era. Their struggles were difficult to document for different reasons. A player who came out to the public as a lesbian in the 1970s or 1980s in such a small community would rarely be welcomed or accepted, and a coach could lose her job in those days of legal discrimination. Trinity women (and men) typically kept their sexual orientation under the radar.

A curious reader can find more information about these and other related issues in the bibliography. The exponential nature of these sources means that many of the articles and papers have their own helpful bibliographies. Also, filling these information gaps is a priority for Trinity, which in 2022 initiated programs to better understand the undergraduate experiences and subsequent careers of African American and LGBTQ student athletes. Those wanting to help Trinity expand on these stories are invited to do so on the Playing Field website home page.

On a technical note, to reduce confusion, former students are referred to by their maiden names, even if they later married and changed their last names. The rare exceptions are those who married while attending Trinity. In the acknowledgments is a list of women and men interviewed for this book. Married names are included there when appropriate.

Finally, there's a proverbial elephant in the room I feel I must address. When the project committee asked me to turn its extensive research notes, drafts, and oral history interviews into a book, much had been included about a feisty young runner named Betsy Gerhardt—me. My humility told me to cut the passages, but my desire for a diverse retelling convinced me to keep some of them in the book. Please excuse my hubris; I hope you see how it fits together.

But enough about what could and couldn't be covered in this retrospective; the story of this journey will provide readers a history of how an institution that chose a Division III path helped its female students advance in education, athletics, and life.

I hope you enjoy this book, learn from it, and are inspired by it.

A CENTURY

ON THE SIDELINES

The John Boyd residence, the original home of Trinity University

CHAPTER 1

No Time for Sports

1869–1902

The moral atmosphere at Tehuacana, Texas is excellent. The faculty is able. Students are required to study—can find nothing else in Tehuacana to do but study, since the place is devoid of all the disadvantages of cities.

—BENJAMIN D. COCKRILL, PRESIDENT OF TRINITY UNIVERSITY, 1890[1]

The story of Trinity University begins in 1869, when the Cumberland Presbyterian Synods in Texas founded the institution in Tehuacana (ta-WA-ka-na), a rural town ninety miles south of the still-young city of Dallas.

At this time, perceptions of the role of American women in the Victorian Age—which reigned over the second half of the century—presented immovable obstacles on a female's societal path. According to historians, the ideal of delicacy over vigor spoke to the ultimate Victorian goal: "the twin functions of attracting a man and bearing a child."[2] These views were perpetuated at the highest judicial level in 1873. Just four years after Trinity's founding, the US Supreme Court denied a married woman the right to practice law in Illinois. In *Bradwell v. Illinois*, the male justices articulated their view of a woman's place in society, writing: "Man is, or should be, woman's protector and defender. The natural and proper timidity and delicacy which belongs to the female sex evidently unfits it for many of the occupations of civil life. The

Trinity women relax in traditional poses and attire in the 1890s.

paramount destiny and mission of woman are to fulfill the noble and benign offices of wife and mother. This is the law of the Creator."[3]

Photographs from the period effectively portray the formal dress and deportment of the few women who did compete in the more genteel activities.

Coed from the Beginning

For Texas women, there was good news about Trinity University's founding: it welcomed women, a rarity among institutions of higher education in 1869. Prior to the Civil War, no coeducational colleges or universities existed in Texas due to longstanding social resistance to "mixing the sexes," attitudes that persisted well into the nineteenth century.

This trend put Trinity at the forefront of change. Despite opposition from some trustees and parents, the school's faculty unanimously endorsed coeducation as pedagogically sound and already practiced by

Trinity University,

FOR BOTH SEXES.

◆◆◆◆

L. A. JOHNSON, A.M., President.
D. S. BODENHAMER, Professor of Mathematics.

◆◆◆◆

TEHUACANA, TEXAS.

Advertisement in an 1888 issue of *Cumberland Presbyterian* magazine

some of the best schools outside of Texas. Church officials also found nothing in the university charter to preclude such a move and recognized the financial necessity that mandated the decision to enroll men and women. To quell parental concerns, officials did promise to enforce rules regulating the social interaction of male and female students. The 1871 university catalog reinforced this notion with the note that "Trinity is absolutely free from the temptations of vice abounding in the various towns of the country."[4]

To historians, this maternalistic view made sense in the nineteenth century, when educators believed women would have more difficulty withstanding the "physiological and psychological rigors of four years of a classical education."[5] This opinion is reflected in the minutes of an 1884 trustees meeting: "Trinity needs a good competent male teacher at the head of the musical department. This does not demean the ability of the present instructor [female] but we are grounded solely in the belief that the labors of said department is too much for a lady."[6]

Accordingly, the presence of female students on Trinity's campus didn't mean they were expected (or encouraged) to enter the male-dominated workforce after graduation. While women were allowed to take the same classes as men in Trinity's classical curriculum and earn baccalaureate degrees, most parents wanted their daughters to enroll in more "ornamental" courses like sewing, drawing, music, and art. As a result, many women left Trinity after only two years of study, earning certificates or diplomas rather than degrees.

The subject of womanhood was addressed in Trinity publications,

A survey class in 1901. The lone female student is Eula McCain.

repeating these opinions about a woman's limitations for intellectual and physical activities. One story in the *Trinity Exponent* (a precursor to the *Trinitonian*) was titled "A Letter to the Girls" and offered advice to young women preparing for future careers. In wording that seemed to acknowledge progress while also echoing the Supreme Court's wording, the author wrote:

> Around us we see evidences showing that the age in which a woman was expected to spend her life as an ornament is past. She has now wide fields of praiseworthy labor open to her. Yet nowhere is her work more demanded or in greater need than in her own family. Who wields a more lasting influence than mother, sister, or daughter? She can call the son from the haunts of wickedness, lead the brother to Jesus, turn the husband from destruction, or send them deeper into the ways of sin. Determined to obtain a thorough, practical education, to cultivate an amiable disposition and a pure heart.... An excessive love of dress, light literature and society must be avoided before studies habits can be formed. It will profit you by far more to form studies, punctual and honest habits, though you fail to finish the college curriculum than to do so without acquiring such habits.[7]

School-sponsored athletics wouldn't appear on US campuses until the end of the century. Until that time, educators leaned on the country's Puritan roots, which deemed athletics as frivolous activities that distracted students from academic pursuits and negatively affected the formation of moral and spiritual character. Another dominant theory of the day was that each human had a fixed amount of energy, and that combining physical exercise with intellectual pursuits could be hazardous.[8]

This accepted "science" convinced medical experts that women should not engage in physical activity, especially during menstruation. One historian wrote that physicians on both sides of the Atlantic promoted a theory of menstrual disability that "contributed substantially to a deepening stereotyping of women as both the weaker and a periodically weakened sex."[9] Another concern was that the prospect of damage to female reproductive organs through physical activity contributed to defective offspring. It's important to note that virtually all of these recorded medical opinions concerning a female's physical abilities come from male professionals. At the turn of the century, only about five percent of practicing physicians were women, and that minuscule representation persisted for more than a half century.[10]

There were a few exceptions to these rules: women's intramural teams had become a staple on some of the original female-only campuses. But the seemingly progressive offerings were mitigated by activities supporting the accepted norms. One such 1837 requirement at Mount Holyoke encouraged students to participate not only in calisthenics but also in domestic work (i.e., housework) for exercise.[11] Smith College touted its physical education curriculum in its 1875 prospectus: "In addition to lectures on Physiology and Hygiene, regular exercises in the gymnasium and open air will be prescribed under the direction of an educated lady physician. These exercises will be designed not merely to secure health, but also a graceful carriage and well-formed bodies."[12]

Established four years after the end of the Civil War, Trinity offered a coeducational education but no intercollegiate sports during its first three decades. This was not due to lack of student interest or financial resources. Instead, like most other nineteenth-century educators, Trinity faculty and trustees thought sports did not merit a place in university curricula. While these attitudes may sound foreign to contemporary readers, they were widely held in higher education circles throughout the century.

So Trinity offered no competitive outlet to either its male or female

A female Trinity student "in uniform"

students, and even informal sport activities were quickly quashed. William Beeson, Trinity's first president, "ferreted out clandestine sports of the boys" when their penchant for recreation encroached on study hours. Students referred to Beeson as Jack for his jackrabbit speed in chasing players and confiscating their equipment. Note that only "the boys" are mentioned since women of the 1870s were considered anatomically and emotionally incapable of sustained exertion and prohibited from participating in such activities.[13]

To discourage students from participating in athletics and other "sinful" activities—such as dancing, smoking, and drinking—university officials closely monitored their behavior and kept them occupied from dawn to dark. Trinity faculty specified a daily routine for students that left little time for anything more than eating and sleeping. Their week-days began with morning prayers, followed by classroom recitations, chapel services, and extended afternoon and evening study hours. Sundays were filled with mandatory Sunday school and church attendance as well as private time for spiritual reflection. Strict observance of the Holy Day precluded any exercise other than a quiet stroll around town. Women who ventured out for a walk had to be properly chaperoned.[14] The 1886–87 catalog provides clear instructions:

> Study Hours are from 8:30 in the morning until noon; from 1:30 to 4:00 in the afternoon; from nightfall until time for retiring; and from early rising in the morning until breakfast. Students must not leave their rooms during these hours except to attend their duties at the college. Students must not engage in any diversion, amusement, or correspondence which will be detrimental to the acquisition of knowledge.[15]

As another alternative to athletics, Trinity and other colleges encouraged the formation of male and female literary societies. Members held weekly meetings to conduct debates, discussions, and other public speaking events, and the organizations often competed in friendly rivalries. These continued into the 1920s, eventually supplanted by athletics and other social activities.[16]

Cracks in the Victorian Veneer

In the last few years of the nineteenth century, prospects for both male and female sports participants began to brighten. New physiological and psychological research about exercise showed that physical activity not only improved the general health of young people but also developed positive personality traits like courage, resolution, and endurance. This enlightened view contributed to a proliferation of physical education courses. In addition, intramural and intercollegiate sports gradually became campus fixtures. Not surprisingly, the primary beneficiaries of these new scientific findings were male, since researchers still considered them better suited to cope with the rigors and stress of intercollegiate athletics.

At Trinity, these changes were spearheaded by a new generation of progressive young faculty who advocated for giving students more responsibility for their behavior and providing a more relaxed social atmo-

A 1902 column head. ...Sporting News...

sphere. Although Trinity's founders had viewed organized athletics as an intrusion into the academic routine, these younger professors considered exercise and athletic competition as critical to improving physical health, developing individual discipline, and promoting school spirit.[17]

Students at the Tehuacana campus also supported the shift—at least for the men. Members of Trinity's Young Men's Christian Association helped spark interest in athletics by raising money for exercise equipment. As a result of their efforts, two rooms on campus were furnished with parallel and horizontal bars, a punching bag, hand weights, Indian clubs, and tumbling mats.[18] The male students also formed an athletic association consisting of fifty members who had "some money on hand for expenses" and hoped to expand efforts already in place to facilitate "this necessary branch of college life."[19] Numerous articles and editorials in the *Trinitonian* urged faculty and administrators to support these student efforts to bring Trinity in line with peer institutions regarding physical education and athletics: "Much interest is being manifested by the various leading schools in the North and East over the out-of-door sports. The schools are beginning to realize more and more the necessity of developing the physical as well as the mental and moral faculties, and it is right they should. We hope to find Trinity is in the lead to this important characteristic, as she is, and has been, a leader in intellectual development."[20]

Men's team sports began appearing on Trinity's first campus during the 1890s, featuring occasional baseball games, foot races, and friendly contests with local amateur teams but mostly led by students. That changed when young faculty member B. Eugene Looney attended the University of Chicago for a graduate degree, where he observed how the school's students derived physical and social benefits from university-sponsored intercollegiate athletic competition. He also forged a friendship with legendary football coach Amos Alonzo Stagg, who encouraged Looney to initiate intercollegiate sports at Trinity.[21] On his 1898 return to Tehuacana Looney founded a thirteen-member tennis club. The sport became a favorite pastime and started a legacy that continued throughout Trinity's history. Considered a "gentleman's game," tennis meshed well with the university's standards of decorum and was the only one in which coeducational recreational play was permitted. One early team member, Frank L. Wear, later became president of Trinity.

Two years later Looney further implemented Stagg's advice, becoming faculty manager for the school's first intercollegiate football team and accompanying the Trinity Warriors to a scrimmage in Waco on November 17, 1900. Although they lost 17–0 to Baylor in that inaugural intercollegiate contest, their performance inspired student interest in football and other intercollegiate sports.[22]

On the other hand, the primary reason for a woman to exercise continued to be the reproduction and raising of healthy children. These more enlightened physicians suggested women could safely engage in limited activities, such as moderate bicycling, tennis, and walking. Compared to earlier Victorian standards, these were revolutionary concepts.[23]

This incremental acceptance created opportunities and inspired new organizations for oversight of female athletes. The Women's Athletic Association (WAA), the first sports-focused governing body for college women, was formed at Bryn Mawr College in 1891. And when Smith College's physical education director Senda Berenson introduced her own version of the new game called basketball, the sport spread quickly to other colleges and spurred the desire for intercollegiate play. "The mother of women's basketball" Berenson modified James Naismith's original rules, restricting handling of the basketball to three dribbles and three seconds, and she posted nine players per side in a restricted zone to prevent fast breaks and reduce the strain of a full-court contest.[24]

Unfortunately, organizers like Berenson frequently encountered physical educators who opposed intercollegiate competition, based on fresh fears that women athletes would fall under the win-at-all-costs philosophy seen emerging in men's sports.[25] Another common concern was the risk of overexcitement for female athletes, who might develop qualities deemed "not womanly" when competing against other schools.[26] In fact, after Berenson introduced basketball to Smith College, her faculty peers delayed the start of interschool competition because they were afraid of losing control of their women's programs.

In a similar situation, Bryn Mawr challenged Vassar College to a tennis match in 1894, but the Vassar faculty withheld permission for their players to compete. This denied the schools a place in history; had

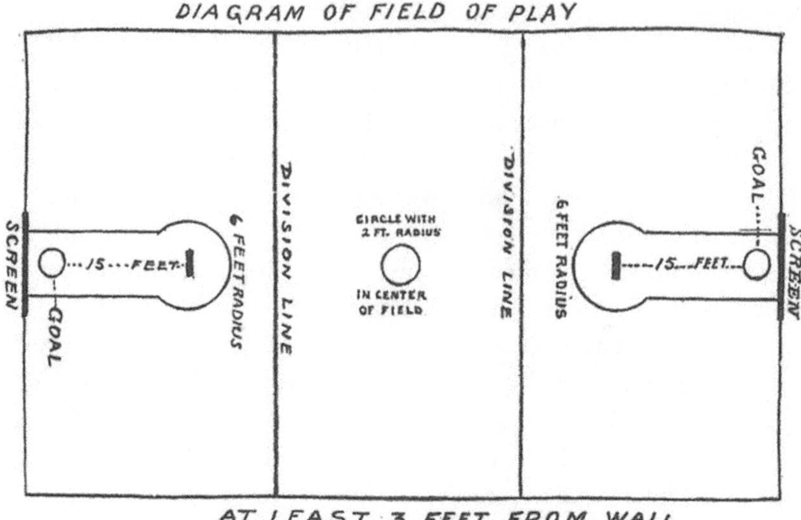

Three sections marked for a 1901 women's basketball court

the match occurred, it would have been the first intercollegiate contest for women in any sport.[27] Instead, that historic game was played on April 4, 1896, between the basketball teams of Stanford University and the University of California at Berkeley. With seven hundred fans in attendance at the game in San Francisco, Stanford prevailed by a 2–1 score.[28] These events remained anomalies, as resistance to competitive play between women continued well into the next century.[29] (Two days later, the Modern Olympic Games were launched in Athens, but they didn't yet include women's sports.)

Other women's sports were also being introduced across America, although mostly on all-women's campuses. These included tennis in 1874, bowling in 1875, track and field in 1882, softball in 1887, golf in 1889, and volleyball in 1895.[30] The University of Texas (UT) bucked its region's conservative trend and hosted its first intramural women's basketball game in the basement of the old Main building in Austin on January 13, 1900, a contest that consisted of "four rudimentary 10-minute quarters" and ended in a 3–2 score. The newly formed team later competed against high school teams and the Austin YMCA.[31]

If the archived stories and pictures from Trinity's first campus are indications of student life, however, few of these intramural and intercollegiate activities found their way to the women of Tehuacana. Even with the shift toward more competitive athletics for men (and some women), Trinity administrators joined their university peers and persisted in their reluctance to include women in these new opportunities, a prohibition that persisted for almost a century. The only competition considered appropriate for Trinity women was in the classroom. Even in that venue, officials felt compelled to assure parents that such competition would not threaten traditional gender roles, as noted in the 1901 catalog summary:[32]

> The university's long list of students furnishes many names of women who have successfully competed with men in scholastic studies and in whom such competition has developed no sign of masculinity. Our women have become more womanly and our men more manly under the system. The natural education of the sexes can be accomplished only in mixed schools, where, under prudent and wholesome restrictions, men and women meet and stimulate each other in the class room.

On the international stage, amateur sportswomen could claim a small victory, when the second Modern Olympic Games in 1900 allowed women to enter golf and tennis competitions. This development wasn't welcomed by the International Olympic Committee chair, who believed that the public spectacle of women competing in athletics was "undignified."[33] Once that door cracked open, more women's sports were gradually added in the ensuing decades.

Meanwhile, Trinity administrators were facing the realization that the school could not prosper in the secluded town of Tehuacana, which lacked railroad connections and the amenities of a thriving commercial center. Although they had just completed construction of an iconic limestone building in 1892—referred to by locals as the "Pride of Limestone County"—enrollment was declining. Multiple attempts to create a substantial endowment were hampered by two economic recessions since the school's founding. And the fact that faculty morale was reaching a low point did not go unnoticed by students. In a letter to his parents, one student wrote, "Tehuacana is a dead town. Even the teachers seem like they are half asleep all the time."[34]

Faced with the options of closing or relocating, the Cumberland

The Trinity graduating class of 1899

Presbyterian Synod of Texas voted to move the university to a more accessible and prosperous setting. After seeking bids from various towns in North Texas, the university accepted an offer from Waxahachie, the county seat of Ellis County. The growing town of five thousand inhabitants was located sixty miles north of the current campus, and officials agreed to provide funding for a new building and promised continuing patronage. While Tehuacana residents had mixed emotions about the exit, Trinity students expressed excitement about the impending move. An editorial in the *Trinitonian* affirmed that Trinity would "soon be the leading denominational educational institution in the state.... Arouse ye, Cumberland Presbyterians! Let's boom this thing right now!"[35]

Before accepting the offer, Trinity asked Waxahachie to close its saloons and prohibit the sale of alcohol in any venue, and town boosters succeeded in scheduling a referendum to make the entire county dry. To the satisfaction of the university and synod officials, the vote passed by a large margin.[36]

This relocation also set the stage for Trinity's increasing endorsement of intercollegiate athletics and signaled the onset of efforts by female students to join in sports-related activities.

CHAPTER 2

A Small Step Forward

1902–42

The boys seem to be the only persons in the University who have an opportunity for athletics.

—*TRINITONIAN*, OCTOBER 1902

Enormous social changes and worldwide disruptions surrounded Trinity in the four decades spent in Waxahachie, including one "war to end all wars," the liberating Roaring Twenties, a paralyzing economic depression, and the rumblings of a second world war. These seismic events contributed to an unstable era for women, taking them to new heights before shuttling them back to the sidelines.

Some historic breakthroughs—the ratification of voting rights in 1920 and the introduction of the Equal Rights Amendment in 1923—provided the illusion that steady progress was being made for women. Female students on Trinity's second campus also found new outlets for social activities and recreation, but they were still limited to refined endeavors that required restrictive dress. Then a decade-long parade of false starts during the 1920s reversed the trajectory for amateur sportswomen. Even the growing men's intercollegiate sports scene experienced setbacks in response to perceived overreach for the sake of winning.

The Great Depression that began in 1929 persisted throughout the 1930s, forcing American women back into domesticity and female athletes away from competition. It also compelled Trinity officials to figure out how to escape their own financial difficulties.

A Waxahachie postcard

Settling into Waxahachie, 1902–20

Since the citizens of the much larger town of Waxahachie had an affinity for winning sports teams, Trinity students and administrators found a more supportive environment for men's intercollegiate athletics. In addition, the national momentum that began in the late 1800s accelerated in the first years of the new century, as sports were being promoted as an integral part of developing manhood.[1] In 1902, the same year of the campus relocation, Trinity joined the Southern Intercollegiate Athletic Association, fielding men's teams in football, basketball, and track, and later adding baseball and tennis.[2] A new national organization was founded in 1906 as a response to concerns about safety in football expressed by President Teddy Roosevelt. The new regulatory body was initially called the Intercollegiate Athletic Association, but it became better known by the name it adopted in 1910: the National Collegiate Athletic Association (NCAA).[3]

Not much had changed for the women. A 1902 *Trinitonian* article, "Woman's Place in the World," ambitiously traced the "mystery of woman and her place in the world" from ancient times when she was "considered far below man and little above the lower animals" to the present when "the higher a nation stands in civilization, the higher a woman stands in society." The writer (gender unknown) is explicit about a woman's domestic role in society:

> The primary place for a woman to do her work is in the home. No matter how high a woman's station in life or how great are her resources, it is an honor to her to be a housekeeper. Her character may be judged by the home she keeps. A disorderly home is a badge of idleness and carelessness, but refinement and self-respect are marked by the neat and tidy keeping of a home. A neat and attractive house is the best way to teach the boys and girls carefulness and neatness through life. As a wife, she should make the home the most delightful and attractive place on earth for her husband; this is the place where he should spend his leisure hours instead of the gambling halls or other places of wickedness. The greatest blessing bestowed upon man is his wife.
>
> In late years, attempts have been made to take women out of the home and permit her to hold public office, to plead before the courts of justice, and to go to the polls and cast her vote in all elections. Wishing to deprive her of no privileges that adds to her pleasure, nor to place her inferior to man, the writer is inclined to the belief that she should be left in the home where she has been filling her place so creditably.[4]

Most male leaders of the era agreed with the gender roles advanced by the *Trinitonian* writer. One was educator Luther Halsey Gulick Jr., who applied Darwin's evolutionary theories to athletic activities in a 1906 article for the *American Physical Education Review*. Gulick opined that since men had evolved as hunters, runners, and fighters, they were physically conditioned to handle stress and endure pain. Men who could strike the hardest, run the fastest, and throw most accurately were more likely to survive, and their male descendants also developed a love of exercise and athletic competition.

Although his role as cofounder of the Camp Fire Girls program in 1910 portrayed him as an advocate for females, Gulick viewed their evolutionary roles differently. "It was not the woman who could run, or strike, or throw best who survived," he wrote. Instead, he believed their domestic destiny was to care for the home, weave the cloth, make the baskets, till the soil, care for domestic animals, rear the children, and prepare the food. He also had a narrow view of athletics for college-age women. "Strenuous training associated with team sports tends to be injurious to both body and mind. Public competition emphasizes qualities that are on the whole unnecessary and undesirable."[5]

Trinity officials were well aware of the benefits college sports could bring to their new campus in terms of enrollment and financial support. University president Leonidas Kirkes boasted in 1904 that Trinity's football success placed it second only to UT in athletic achievement. In carefully crafted language, Kirkes endorsed Trinity's increasing commitment to intercollegiate athletics: "While it is not the desire of the management of the University to give undue prominence to activity in athletics, it is their feeling that intelligent direction of this feature of college life can be made to serve a good purpose."[6]

The president's words soon translated into concrete action, when the university established its first athletic committee in 1906. The governing group would oversee all sports on campus and included the president, three faculty members, and athletic team managers. Officials also proposed adding a "physical director" to organize activities in the exercise rooms "as soon as the resources of the institution will permit."[7] Those resources must have been limited; four years would pass before a male employee was hired to oversee indoor and outdoor recreational activities for men and women. In announcing the delayed appointment, the committee said, "We feel that the health of students will be promoted by systematic physical culture under his direction." Finally in 1911, the board of trustees approved the addition of physical education to Trinity's curriculum, requiring all freshman and sophomore students to take an exercise class and mandating annual physical examinations for all incoming students.[8]

Reinforcing this broadening view was Trinity's first policy statement about the addition of physical education and athletics to its curriculum:

A Trinity women's volleyball team in 1928

> The institution believes in a strong physical manhood and womanhood and will allow nothing to hinder the development of pure college athletics. This institution believes that careful attention should be given to the physical man and woman as well as the intellectual. There is yearly an increasing number of ambitious and competent young ladies availing themselves of the opportunities of higher culture offered by the various colleges of the country which are opening their doors to them. And there is no sufficient reason why they should not enjoy the same advantages in this respect that are enjoyed by the young men. It is the belief of the faculty, that, under careful restrictions, athletic sports may be fostered by the institution without disadvantage to the student body.[9]

These evolving views were further revealed to faculty and students when the *Trinity Bulletin* reprinted an article by A. C. Scott, "The Importance of Physical Education." Scott, a chief surgeon with the Santa Fe Railroad, applauded the shifting attitudes in favor of physical fitness, while faulting the country's educational system for its emphasis on forcing children "to sit still and be good." He argued there was no more justification for neglect of the body than for neglect of the mind. "An educated mind without a healthy body to support it and its bidding is an anomaly and almost useless, so far as pleasure, effective service, and satisfaction in life are concerned," he wrote.

Scott also emphasized the importance of exercise for women, particularly in the region of the country that included Trinity. "Our southern people, especially, are slow to appreciate the necessity of work and physical development for girls—a relic of the days of slavery when most of our dear grandmothers had one or more slaves always ready and willing to respond to their every wish," he said. "But thanks to the awful struggle [the Civil War], we are now waking up to the fact that work means development of body, and development means health and happiness."

Scott added a few words of caution, however, about competitive sports, warning that games such as football and baseball "should not be considered sufficient substitutes for the work of the gymnasium." He felt that the overriding desire to win might compel college athletes to exert themselves beyond a reasonable limit, leading to permanent injuries. Making the case for "regular, systematic, sensible exercise" to achieve the desired balance between the development of mind and body, he instead suggested:

> Every college and university should have a good gymnasium in charge of a competent physical director, and almost every student should be required to do gymnasium work every day. If, for any reason, the regular gymnasium student cannot get the use of the gymnasium every day, he should be required to play tennis or outdoor basket-ball, or finally not walk less than two miles. A boy or girl who cannot train up to do this needs a physician or should be on a farm or ranch and not in a college.[10]

Almost two decades would pass before residents of the Waxahachie campus could employ Scott's advice in an indoor gymnasium. Fortuitously, the absence of a campus baseball field played a pivotal role in the adoption of a nickname that follows Trinity athletes to the present day. In 1916, when the major league Detroit Tigers held their spring training in Waxahachie at the town's municipal diamond, city leaders and Trinity players eagerly engaged with the big-leaguers during their visit. The city expressed its appreciation by renaming the facility Tiger Field, and Trinity players began referring to themselves as the Tigers, replacing the monikers of the Presbyterians or the Trinitonians bestowed on them by local media.[11]

Although men's sports teams were flourishing, administrators continued to limit recreation for female students to physical education classes and intramural sports. In the first year on the new grounds, some vented their frustration after being barred from the basement exercise rooms in the administration building. One wrote to the *Trinitonian*, "We girls are getting tired of such partiality. We would enjoy a few swings on the horizontal bars ourselves."[12] In response, the university opened an exercise room for women and furnished it with similar equipment.

Female students still had to travel to use the facility, since women were not allowed to live on campus. This was a common situation around the state. In fact, it took an act of (Texas) Congress to build a dormitory for women at UT's main campus in Austin.

When UT officials requested funds from the legislature for the building in 1903, many lawmakers in the all-male body objected to the expense and questioned the need. About half felt that women required more supervision and should continue to stay with local families. The house speaker's tie-breaking vote was needed to approve the expenditure.[13]

Trinity females got their own residence hall in 1912, a building that included elaborate indoor exercise facilities. But it wasn't until 1919 that Trinity hired full-time, professionally trained female physical education directors to teach gymnastic classes and oversee the nascent intramural program.

Inaccessible facilities weren't the only obstacles for sports-minded women. Even when they could join a team, they typically found themselves playing only against fellow students under different rules and in more restrictive attire. For example, a 1902 student article announced, "The young ladies of Trinity have organized two basket-ball teams which will soon be practicing. They have already ordered costumes and are preparing for good work."[14] But any games were certainly conducted under Senda Berenson's modified rules, and there is no evidence that they competed against other schools. However, archives at UT chronicle that school's first women's intercollegiate basketball game in 1907, where

Grace Haynes, basketball player and cheerleader.

the Longhorns lost 19–18 to their Southwestern University neighbors from Georgetown.[15]

Also, in an era of long skirts and concealed limbs, female competitors were expected to don restrictive "costumes" that ensured no flesh was exposed except the hands and face. Some featured corsets that historians said made them "prisoners of their tight and complicated clothing." Basketball uniforms consisted of long middy blouses and bloomers, which prompted observers to refer to female teams as Bloomer Girls.[16]

The desire for modesty sometimes overshadowed safety. According to one male swimming instructor, the dead weight caused by the women's bulky swimsuits could slow a swimmer or even pull her under the water. His proof? He tried to swim in one of the costumes and quickly grasped the increased risk of drowning.[17]

On some occasions, players had to be resourceful with their "costumes." Grace Haynes (1911) recalls falling during one basketball game and ripping her bloomers from seam to seam. During the ensuing time-out, Haynes borrowed a safety pin from a spectator, pinned it to her belt, pulled the blouse over the torn clothing, and reentered the game. In what some may consider a double standard, her attire as a cheerleader at men's intercollegiate games was somewhat less restrictive; her dress was cut shorter and her arms exposed, but the rest of her body was discreetly covered.[18]

Rules for this impractical active wear were loosened, so to speak, over the years. But the mandates continued to underscore the prevailing belief that a female athlete's appearance was more important than her performance.[19]

Found Freedoms, then Back to the Sidelines

The 1920s dawned with great promise for Americans; a world war and flu pandemic were behind them and optimism was ahead. Women now had the right to vote and seemed on the cusp of attaining other freedoms in society and the workplace.

Male college athletes observed the construction of massive arenas on their campuses, many dubbed Memorial Stadium to honor students lost in the war. According to one historian, this building boom ushered in football as the center of campus life after 1918. Welch Suggs cited not only large schools but also "tiny colleges," such as Centre College in Kentucky and University of the South in Sewanee, Tennessee, who sponsored dominant barnstorming football teams. (These two small colleges would become conference opponents for Trinity in a less competitive conference seventy years later.) Suggs deemed this "the age of the first generation of college athletes as folk heroes."[20]

As popular as the men's programs were becoming, concerns about the perils of competition began to percolate. Even the Trinity board of trustees lamented that "athletics constitute a real problem in college life." After several successful football campaigns, it seemed Tiger coaches were resorting to questionable recruiting tactics to maintain their dominance. Expressing their concerns about the "growing tendency on the part of athletics in the violations of the rules and regulations of the conference, the subsidizing of players, and the incurring of increased expenses," trustees replaced the athletic leadership in 1930. Of course, no similar response was needed for a nonexistent women's program.[21]

A 1929 Carnegie Foundation report, "Bulletin 23," indicated these tactics were becoming common across the male intercollegiate landscape.

The authors provided what one historian called "the first systematic critique of college athletics and its relationship to educational goals." The report focused mostly on the amount of money being showered on big-time men's programs and also criticized the "fictitious exaggeration of the importance of athletics, especially football." This public report led to a temporary deemphasis on football.[22]

Meanwhile, the more modern role of women in twentieth-century society finally began to make small steps forward, most visibly in the 1920 passage of voting rights for American women that effectively retired the first feminist wave that had started in Seneca Falls in 1848. The Nineteenth Amendment also ushered in the Roaring Twenties, characterized by automobiles, motion pictures, bootleg alcohol, and liberalized sexual values. The first attempt to pass an Equal Rights Amendment, however, was rejected by Congress in 1923; it would be almost fifty years before it came up again for approval.

This newfound equality didn't immediately translate into opportunities for female athletes who wanted to engage in competitive sports.

In 1917, Blanch Trilling established the Athletic Conference of American College Women at the University of Wisconsin in Madison. Physical education staff and students from twenty-two schools across the Midwest gathered to share their goals and concerns and then fanned out as national spokeswomen for the women's sports movement. The conference's participatory philosophy sparked interest in intramural sports and helped launch WAA chapters across the country. Pioneering educator Anna Hiss started a chapter at UT in 1919, and Trinity women followed with their own affiliate in 1927. A national survey revealed that 75 percent of educational institutions had WAA chapters by 1937.[23]

Sports historian Elaine Gerber described the expectant atmosphere of this period: "Opposition to high level competition has been dissipated. Under the control and sponsorship of women physical educators, regional and national tournaments are now sponsored in seven sports. Colleges are developing varsity teams with full schedules, some with rigorous training and long hours of practices. Scholarships will soon be sanctioned for women athletes." Gerber noted, however, that female physical educators were ill-equipped to cope in this new world. Not only did the novel concepts contradict their own formal training, but many also lacked the technical skills to coach and officiate women's teams.

These difficulties further calcified their opposition to intercollegiate competition and high-level skill development.

Controversial events across the Atlantic didn't help. After international officials rejected women's running events for the 1920 Olympic Games, a rival track and field competition was staged at the 1922 Women's World Games. But the Paris event's success was fleeting and instead instigated a renewed backlash. One response was the formation of the National Amateur Athletic Federation, which focused on regaining control over American amateur sports. Soon after its founding, it added a women's division (NAAF/WD) that would reaffirm the noncompetitive model for women's sports. Recruited to lead the cause was Lou Henry Hoover, whose role as president of the Girl Scouts of America made her a natural fit. (Her husband, Herbert, would soon be elected US president.)[24]

The foundational opinions of the new division were captured by member Ethel Perrin, who wrote: "Under prolonged and intense physical strain, a girl goes to pieces nervously. A boy may be physically so weak that he hasn't the strength to smash a creampuff but he still has the 'will' to play. A girl is the opposite." At one of its first conferences, NAAF/WD members rejected the men's win-at-all-costs philosophy, since it didn't align with their views that citizenship and character formed the foundation of women's athletics. Gerber writes that members "came to the belief that women's sports should be 'play for play's sake,' that competition which involved travel and the winning of championships be minimized, and that all international competition be condemned."[25]

The debates culminated in the development of new guidelines that formalized these beliefs and stalled prospects for competitive girls' and women's sports for almost half a century.[26] Introducing the concept of "every girl in a sport and a sport for every girl," the creed provided a bulwark against the competition model and was endorsed by most sponsors of girls' and women's sports—except, curiously, the influential Amateur Athletic Union (AAU). Specifically, the platform's fifteen points aimed to

1. Promote physical activities for all members of a social group, not for an elite group selected for their physical skills.
2. Protect athletes from exploitation (e.g., to please spectators or commercialization).

3. Stress enjoyment of sport and sportsmanship rather than individual accomplishment and winning.
4. Restrict recognition to awards that are symbolical and not of great monetary value.
5. Discourage sensational publicity and emphasize institutional recognition to the sport and not individual competitors.
6. Put well-trained and qualified women in charge of athletic activities.
7. Work toward having well-trained and qualified women placed in administrative and leadership roles in athletics.
8. Secure medical exams and medical monitoring basic for participation in athletics.
9. Provide sanitary and adequate facilities for women athletes.
10. Work for adequate time in programs to accommodate abilities and needs of different age groups.
11. Promote a "reasonable and sane" attitude toward certain "physiological conditions" that may occasion temporary unfitness for participation in sports.
12. Avoid the sacrifice of an individual's health for the sake of athletic competition.
13. Promote adoption of appropriate costumes for various activities.
14. Eliminate gate receipts.
15. Eliminate types and systems of competition that put the emphasis upon individual accomplishment rather than the enjoyment of the sport and the development of sportsmanship among the many.[27]

Another international event later in the decade further sabotaged arguments in favor of female competition. Track and field events were finally opened to women at the 1928 Olympic Games, but American physical educators joined forces to lodge a formal protest against US representation. According to Gerber, "The usual arguments against the

Waxahachie campus. Drane Hall in the center, and administration building on the right

sacrifice of the many for the few, the exploitation of girls and women, and the possibility of overstrain, were offered as reasons for their disapproval." The outcome of the 800-meter (half-mile) event seemed to vindicate the protesters. When several female contestants appeared to faint at the end of the two-lap race, some observers blamed a basic lack of conditioning or coaching. But others used the fiasco to further their premise that women couldn't compete in prolonged physical activities. The naysayers prevailed, and the event wouldn't be reinstated for women until the 1960 Olympics.[28]

On a positive note, female physical education students in Texas could pursue a more modern degree that taught more than recreation. In 1921, Texas Woman's University expanded the major to prepare women for a profession based on the sciences, adding biology, physiology, kinesiology, and motor learning to the classroom requirements.[29] This development would be a major factor in a generational shift in the coming decades.

At Trinity, qualified women began arriving to assume the role of physical education director and oversee the school's exercise and intramural programs. The *Mirage* heralded 1924 as the "first year that Trinity has had regular work in physical education for women with a full-time instructor." The reporters also listed handicaps confronted by director M. Estelle Angier, such as access to limited equipment in the basement of Drane Hall, and "the most erratic weather which has practically prohibited any outdoor work."

The Trinity Tramps were formed in 1926 as the "girls' athletic club of Trinity." The group's stated goal was to "encourage women's athletics, and try to make well-rounded sportsmanlike women." Meetings took place in "the form of hikes, with an occasional social function." Trinity faculty approved their activities, as long as members didn't take overnight trips or carry firearms.[30] (During the Depression, the organization changed its name to reflect a common sight in the era: the Hobo Hikers.)[31]

One of Trinity's longest-serving physical education directors—and the administrator with the highest credentials—was Sue Rainey. She earned her undergraduate degree from Vanderbilt University's Peabody Teachers College and a master's degree from Columbia University; and she completed additional graduate work at the University of Southern California. The well-respected faculty member also sponsored the Pep Squad and other women's social organizations between 1924 and 1942.[32]

Increasing female faculty representation, however, still couldn't offset persistent inequalities on the Waxahachie campus in the 1920s. A peek into Trinity's 1927 school catalog provides a stark comparison between the physical education approaches for male and female students. Male instruction focused on bodybuilding to prepare athletes for the punishment of physical contact, emphasizing first aid for injuries over coaching techniques. Probably most revealing was that male students could substitute time spent playing intercollegiate athletics for missed class work. For athletes involved in multiple sports, this significantly reduced classroom obligations.

Women's courses were broader in scope and included classes in "elementary rhythm and folk dances," outdoor sports "suited to the ability of students," and "the theory, practice and coaching of athletic sports."[33] In fact, two pages in the 1928 *Mirage* are dedicated to the interclass competition between female students in several sports, including basketball, playground baseball, and volleyball, all under the watchful eye of Miss Rainey.[34]

As noted earlier, despite the evolving science, many in this generation of female educators were still allied with their male colleagues in the cause to protect women from the perceived stress and dangers of intercollegiate competition. For example, while the NAAF/WD's 1923 guidelines didn't call for an outright ban on competition, they established a strict framework under which women's sports should take place. As a result, several compromises were introduced as substitutes for the higher-stress intercollegiate alternative. One early "interclass" team approach featured intramural contests between classes, such as sophomore teams playing other sophomore teams from their school. Contests between each class champion were also held, such as those noted in the *Mirage*. This might be followed by an extramural event pitting interclass champions from one school against class peers at other colleges. After her school participated with the University of California at Berkeley in a 1917 interclass/interschool event, a Stanford instructor enthusiastically endorsed this approach, suggesting that stress levels were lessened since each of the four (class) teams from a school would share in overall wins or losses and no one team was responsible for the "nervous strain of the responsibility for winning."[35]

Another method that was used was the "telegraphic" extramural meet, where students participated in a sport on their own campuses according to agreed-upon conditions. Results were sent via telegraph wire to a designated official, who later announced the results. These worked best in individual sports like archery, bowling, or riflery. This strategy not only saved travel funds; it also shielded the contestants from any unwelcome emotions that might arise in face-to-face competition.[36]

Few of these remote meets were well received, since students and faculty preferred in-person contact with their peers from other institutions. These desires led to the introduction of "Play Days" between schools. This movement, which began in 1926 and reached its peak in 1936, featured a more formal approach to extramural events that still skirted interschool competition. Women from different colleges met on one campus, were placed on mixed teams with students from other schools, and competed in a variety of recreational activities. Play Days provided an alternative to intercollegiate conferences that had begun to emerge, such as the Triangle Conference of California schools: Mills College, Stanford, and University of California at Berkeley.

Historian Elaine Gerber described one of the earliest known Play Days in 1926:[37]

> An enthusiastic group of girls gathered on the University of California campus. These girls were given tags upon which their names were written and were assigned to color squads. These squads met on the field, where time was given for choosing a name, yell, and captain. The first two events were ones in which all members of the squads took part. These were shuttle relay and pass ball relay. The next events were ones in which selected members of squads participated, while the other members watched and cheered. These were net ball, hockey, tennis, and swimming. A blue ribbon for first place, a red ribbon for second, was given to the squad winning these events, as well as promptness for squad formation at the bugle sound which was given between each event.

While the goal of these interschool activities was to provide recreational team sports for the health and enjoyment of female athletes, Trinity women still faced restrictions not applied to males. Even as they organized intramural competition in basketball, volleyball, softball, and tennis, the female students remained subject to a strict dress code, mandatory church attendance, and prohibition from going into town without chaperones. As a result, any athletic contests had to be conducted on campus, either between classmates or with local amateur teams. Also, while basketball was one of the most popular early games, the women had to play it outdoors until their gymnasium was built in 1928, and they were still restricted by the modified rules.[38]

Facilities built during this period were designed to mitigate the perceived risks to female athletes. While it is unclear what amenities Trinity students found in their new gym, the 1931 construction of a new women's facility in Austin illustrated the continued focus on the recreational strategy. UT physical education director Anna Hiss assisted in the building design that called for undersized basketball courts to discourage spectators. In addition, the baskets were installed directly on the wall to prevent her women from playing out of control.[39]

Toward the end of the decade, Trinity women were finding more seats at the university table; they could serve on the student athletic council and participate in the selection and scheduling of intramural activities through the WAA chapter, which sponsored volleyball, (playground) baseball, and tennis.[40]

A Regression with a Depression

As they were entering the 1930s, American women finally found more liberated role models, including Amelia Earhart, who piloted a plane across the Atlantic Ocean in 1928; Gertrude Ederle, the first woman to swim the English Channel in 1926; and Texan Mildred "Babe" Didrikson, a multitalented athlete who earned two gold medals in track and field at the 1932 Berlin Olympics and later won ten professional golf championships.[41]

Unfortunately, the modest gains for women in the 1920s were severely offset by the impact of the Great Depression. According to historians, the market crash of 1929 had negative effects beyond the economy; it also stalled the social progress women had made since the Seneca Falls Convention of 1848. Fewer women were able to work, attend college, or live away from home, sending them back into domesticity and dependence—albeit in a less-restrictive version than that of the Victorian era.[42]

For those sports-minded women who could still attend college, Play Days were morphing into a slightly more competitive Sports Day format. This approach allowed female students to form teams representing their own school rather than competing on mixed teams. Still, many colleges entered squads of players who had not practiced together, and who often did not know in advance which sport they would participate in. Sometimes results were announced days later—or not at all—and games were usually officiated by students rather than more experienced referees. Event organizers, like Trinity's Sue Rainey, closely monitored the games to ensure that they did not devolve into controversial varsity competitions.[43]

It's difficult to ascertain the state of Trinity women's sports going into the 1930s, as documentation of participation by female students in extramural events is sparse. Even UT, Trinity's larger cousin to the south, offered no records for its women's club sports since they didn't want to endorse "serious" athletes. UT's Anna Hiss did include a "posture contest" in her portfolio of women's activities, an event that endured into the 1960s and foreshadowed a similar effort at Trinity.[44]

One Trinity report does mention female students joining in campus field days, featuring intramural contests for males and females. These events were usually held in conjunction with Founders Day, an annual celebration of the day when church officials selected Trinity's first site in Tehuacana. According to the *Mirage*, field days "formed a valuable part of the social and recreational life of the institution." Apparently, the women's games attracted large crowds, and the contestants displayed "exceptional skills" in their team sports. Interestingly, the *Mirage* account noted that in the volleyball contests, "the girls' games showed less individuality and more teamwork than did the boys' contests."[45]

Yet despite these positive developments, Trinity women were no closer to participating in intercollegiate athletics than they were at the turn of the century. Opposition to their entry into competitive athletics continued unabated. Athletic directors, administrators, and physical education instructors—both men and women—were reluctant to incorporate women into intercollegiate athletic structures. And the wider population considered serious female competitors as odd. Women's athletic contests were sideshows rather than main events.[46]

A rare bright spot during the Depression was the federally sponsored construction of recreational facilities across the country, including playing fields for the increasingly popular sport of softball. Thus the Works Progress Administration supported emerging physical education programs for girls and women.[47]

During the Depression, however, any prospects of professional sports for women were rebuffed at every turn, including one edict from baseball commissioner Judge Kenesaw Mountain Landis. After seventeen-year-old female pitcher Virne Beatrice "Jackie" Mitchell struck out major league stars Babe Ruth and Lou Gehrig in a 1931 exhibition game, Landis banned women from professional baseball.[48] But a decade later, World War II caused a player gap, which resulted in a women's professional baseball league. In fact, many of the teenagers who honed their skills on the WPA-built diamonds competed in that league.[49]

Little else is recorded about the plight or progress of female collegiate athletes in the 1930s, most likely because of their reduced social status during the Depression. Because of the historically high unemployment rate for American men, women previously in the workforce were encouraged to go back to their homes. Decades of stagnation passed before a second feminist movement and new opportunities emerged for women's sports.

The status of gender roles during the forty-year Waxahachie era can be seen in student publications: a scripted play and two illuminating illustrations.

Miriam L. Clark (1911) wrote a two-act play for the *Trinity University Bulletin* portraying how Trinity men belittled women's athletic skills and showing the futility of trying to change those male attitudes. *A Strike* opens as a group of college women study in a dormitory room after playing in a basketball game earlier in the day. Their conversation drifts to the perceived slight from the few male fans, who failed to support the women athletes as vociferously as the female students did the men's teams. They decide on a "strike against helping the boys with their projects," but their enthusiasm seems to wane by the second act. Just one week later, they accept the men's excuses, decide to go "back to old times," and pull up the dormitory window shade to listen to a group of men serenading them from below.[50]

Two drawings in the *Mirage* further personified the prevailing views of male and female athletics all too common on college campuses. The male football player is portrayed with an aggressive facial expression and his foot on his opponent's head; the female, overweight and out of condition, is portrayed from the rear, submissively hunched over a dormitory washboard scrubbing her clothes. True to the well-worn phrase, a picture is indeed worth a thousand words.

It is a mistake, however, to attribute this exclusionary attitude solely to males; opposition also came from women. National women's groups advocated the limited and closely monitored intramural and extramural programs that reinforced these cultural norms. These influential attitudes from both male and female leaders greatly hindered the progress of women fighting for equal opportunity in competitive sports. Intercollegiate athletics remained an exclusive male win-at-all-costs enterprise, while women's sports continued to emphasize recreation, enjoyment, and camaraderie.[51]

On an ominous fiduciary note, football continued to drag down Trinity's feeble finances, with the program running a $10,000 annual deficit in its

The Freshman's debut on the athletic field.

Two sketches capture the era's sentiments about the role of men and women in "athletics."

final year on the Waxahachie campus. This was just one factor in the school's next existential fiscal crisis, prompting three years of merger negotiations with fellow Presbyterian institution Austin College, with the goal of settling on a neutral site. When the city leaders of Sherman, Texas, balked at losing their local college, the potential partner backed off and Trinity began exploring other relocation options.[52]

Not only did Trinity's own future look grim at the end of the difficult decade; other educational administrators were also appraising the post-Depression period while shifting their focus to the specter of a second world war. This impending international crisis vaulted women back into the spotlight.

CHAPTER 3

Wartime Holding Patterns

1942–51

We have no gymnasium, no useable tennis courts,
no swimming pool, and no athletic fields.
—PRESIDENT MONROE EVERETT
TO TRINITY TRUSTEES, MAY 18, 1943

Trinity's agreement to relocate to its third city coincided with America's entry into World War II. The conflict diverted the country's focus to supporting the massive war effort while upholding the economy, a shift that filtered down to curriculum on college campuses.

In a repeat of the Roaring Twenties, a woman's status in American society was elevated as millions flooded into the workforce to fill positions vacated by males drafted into military service. Some women also joined the military, but many more entered factories to take on—and excel in—these critical manufacturing tasks. Their newfound self-confidence not only led to the heroine status personified by Rosie the Riveter but also planted seeds of self-esteem and activism for future equal rights movements. Some women believed their success in the workforce earned them the right to take their talents to athletic fields, finding opportunities in company and industrial leagues, and even in major league baseball stadiums. There were still few school-sponsored options for women's sports, but hints of more progressive administration began to appear, including the rare appointment of a female to lead a Trinity men's team.

Regrettably, advances were again reversed once peace was declared, and Trinity's time on its Woodlawn campus concluded with another

An aerial view of the Woodlawn campus in the 1940s. None of the buildings exist today.

period of regression for women, who were dismissed from the factories and fields and expected to retreat to homemaker roles.

The Move to San Antonio

After Trinity officials recovered from the collapse of merger talks with Austin College, their fortunes improved with an invitation to relocate from Waxahachie to San Antonio, a teeming metropolis of three hundred thousand residents. Trinity accepted the offer from the city's chamber of commerce on December 8, 1941, the day after the Japanese attack on Pearl Harbor drew the country into the second world war.

The South Texas municipality provided Trinity a solid foundation that enabled it to survive and thrive well into its second century.[1] The chamber's efforts were spearheaded by James H. Calvert and C. W. Miller, local retail executives for Sears Roebuck and Joske Brothers, respectively.[2] While the business leaders were looking for a strong Protestant institution to complement the city's three Catholic universities, it seems that sports also played a role in their agreement to subsidize the move. One city historian said chamber members yearned "with unutterable longing for a great university with a mighty football team," hoping Trinity could fill the year-old Alamo Stadium and compete for "pigskin glory."[3]

In its third move in seventy-three years, Trinity merged with the University of San Antonio, a small Methodist institution also in financial straits, and moved to the Woodlawn campus west of the city center. Classes began in September 1942 under national emergency conditions that affected activities and curriculum at Trinity—and every other American college campus.

Sports were deemphasized, as instruction for male students shifted to support of defense initiatives. Trinity organized a Texas Defense Guard platoon and hosted a Naval Reserve training program, and science department faculty offered classes in lifesaving, first aid, and safety. One popular course was based on physical combat tactics used by military commandos. Trinity men were required to work out regularly in activities such as boxing, wrestling, rope climbing, and tumbling. Since varsity competition was curtailed, options for male students were limited to a few intramural sports.

In contrast to the men's military regimen, Trinity women could still participate in traditional intramural sports such as archery, softball, tennis, badminton, soccer, speedball, field hockey, and tumbling. In 1942, the university hired Virginia B. Elliot, a graduate of Louisiana State University with bachelor's and master's degrees, to oversee the growing intramural program on the new campus. Described as "an outstanding director of recreation and pageantry," Elliot instituted "social and recreational games, folk games and rhythms" to round out the physical fitness program, adding ice skating, horseshoes, swimming, and horseback riding.[4]

Elliot also incorporated elements of military preparedness into her physical education classes, offering first aid instruction and inviting a special guest to teach combat tactics to her students. Dale Morrison, the commandant of Trinity's Texas Defense Guard unit and the school's director of physical education, considered his classroom visit a success. The *Trinitonian* reported that, after Morrison's lecture, "the Trinity girls were even practicing commando tactics in the halls and on the campus, leading to the belief that Lady Marines are in the making at T.U."[5]

However, Trinity's Woodlawn campus had little to offer in resources or equipment for recreation, as President Monroe Everett noted in his 1943 update to trustees.[6] Although conditions improved after 1945, they continued to be substandard and had to be augmented by off-campus facilities.

One Step Backward and Two Steps Forward

As the war intensified, old mindsets lingered while new opportunities emerged for female athletic competition. The first development was the renaming of the primary governing body for women's college sports from the Women's Athletic Association to the Women's Recreation Association (WRA). The word choice appears intentional, as noted in purpose summaries of the two organizations. The mission statement of the former WAA read "To foster good citizenship and to provide recognition for athletic ability; to foster college spirit by developing intramural and interclass athletics for all women, and to promote high physical efficiency among women." The updated 1940 WRA constitution, however, stated that its purpose was "to provide recreational and social activities for all women; to foster good citizenship; to foster school spirit; to inspire good sportsmanship and love for playing the game."[7]

The reference to "love for playing the game" stands in sharp contrast to "high physical efficiency." The logical conclusion? While the groups shared some common goals, the WRA appeared intent on emphasizing recreational and social activities over intercollegiate competition. To what extent this philosophical shift affected campus attitudes is uncertain, but it seemed to reflect the determination of leaders in the national women's organizations to maintain opposition to the win-at-all-costs approach dominating men's athletics.

A more positive milestone was the 1941 establishment of the National Collegiate Golf tournament, the first national championship for college women in any sport. Gladys Palmer, a physical education director at Ohio State University, petitioned the two major governing groups to sponsor the event. After being rejected by both groups, Palmer forged ahead and hosted thirty college women in an event that garnered praise from several women's organizations.

Finally, the All-American Girls Professional Baseball League became a popular wartime distraction. The league, which was featured in the 1992 movie *A League of Their Own*, was founded by Chicago Cubs owner and chewing gum mogul Philip K. Wrigley. Their games helped fill otherwise empty professional stadiums and provided a welcome respite from the somber war news. More than six hundred women participated in the modified game, which featured aspects of both softball and baseball. The women were recruited for their athletic prowess and "all-American or girl-next-door look," and their deportment vacillated between the heat of competition on the diamond to requisite charm-school classes held off the field.

While teams were based mostly in the Midwest, one star player hailed from San Antonio. Alva Jo Fischer, a youth softball prodigy and Brackenridge High School graduate, pitched the Rockford Peaches to the 1945 league championships. Her teammates with the Peaches and Muskegon Lassies called her Tex, a nickname that followed her back home to city league competition, where she would play with a future Trinity tennis star in the early 1960s.[8]

The league continued to draw fans after the war concluded, but the experiment ended in 1954, partly a victim of decentralization and over-expansion. To put a fine point on the brief endeavor, Major League Baseball banned women's contracts in 1952.[9]

Alva Jo Fischer in 1945 as a member of the AAGPBL champion Rockford Peaches.

Trinity reinstituted men's intercollegiate athletics after the war ended in 1945, emphasizing football, basketball, baseball, and tennis. In fact, while the game occurred almost five years after their invitation, chamber of commerce members must have been delighted to see fifteen thousand fans filling Alamo Stadium for the school's first postwar football contest on September 20, 1947. The Tigers lost 39–0 to a legendary Hardin-Simmons University team led by future Trinity coach Warren Woodson.

Since the city didn't host a large state university, local fans joined business and community leaders in hopes that Trinity would field competitive programs and join the prestigious Southwest Conference. That sentiment wasn't shared by all campus residents. When the university announced its intention to join the other large football programs in the conference, a rare student demonstration ensued, as women crawled out of their dorm windows to join fellow students in a march around the Woodlawn neighborhood. (This may have been a harbinger for future sport-related campus protests.) Those aspirations were never fulfilled, but Trinity administrators continued to promote sports as a path to national fame, financial support, and increasing enrollment.[10]

A 1951 WRA tennis team leaves the Woodlawn campus for a match.

While the school catalog listed only five women's sports as varsity (volleyball, basketball, softball, golf, and [field] hockey), tennis surely deserved the designation as well.[11] According to the *Mirage*, in 1949, thirty women signed up for a spring tennis tournament program, and the five top seeded players competed against other schools. The Trinity team was composed of Nancy Chadwell, Polly Knolk, Janet Fajkus, Jane Mills, and Carol Ekloft.[12]

In this period, writers often applied the term *varsity* interchangeably with *extramural* or *intercollegiate*. None implied official sponsorship, dedicated coaches, or athletic budgets for women until the 1970s. Also, this 1949 tennis article was the sole reference to a female intercollegiate squad in any sport at Trinity that year and for years to come.

A Hint of Better Days Ahead

Although cultural opposition to women's intercollegiate athletics continued to bedevil female athletes as the 1950s approached, some positive developments at Trinity suggested a brighter future.[13]

June Byrd's unprecedented appointment as men's tennis coach was a significant step forward for women in leadership at Trinity. Two years after being hired into the department of health and physical education in 1948, Byrd was selected to lead the men's tennis program and guided the team until 1954.

Also in 1948, Trinity women renewed their organizational commitment to the national WRA, formerly the WAA. With Byrd as their sponsor, the WRA chapter conducted intramural contests in softball, basketball, volleyball, and tennis. Group leaders reported the activities were "met with enthusiasm," and expressed gratitude that the participants displayed "sportsmanship, competition, and sheer eagerness to learn."[14] The next year the chapter added tumbling, square dancing, and field hockey and sponsored a campus picnic to present individual performance awards and introduce new officers.[15]

In addition to intramurals and social events, Trinity's WRA introduced extramural activities in the form of the modified Sports Days where a female student could participate on a team with players from her own school. However, the acceptance of this innovative approach didn't immediately extend to the more controversial concept of varsity teams in the era, since that would require the selection and training of an elite group of women athletes.[16]

The *Trinitonian* covered a Women's Sports Day in spring 1949, but since the story described mixed teams, it was probably conducted under the older Play Day rules. The event was hosted by Southwest Texas State Teachers College (later Southwest Texas State University and now Texas State University) in San Marcos and included participants from Trinity, UT, Baylor University, Mary Hardin-Baylor College, Texas Lutheran College, and Howard Payne College. In the morning, women accumulated points while playing on generic teams composed of "representatives from other schools." The teams squared off in basketball, softball, volleyball, tennis, badminton, archery, and table tennis. In the afternoon, individuals competed in swimming and track and field events.[17]

The hosts finished first in the institutional competition, followed by Trinity and Baylor. The *Trinitonian* reported that individual participants from Trinity did exceptionally well. Sophomore Polly Knolk accumulated the second-highest total in individual points that day. She won the Red Cross rescue jump and the racing breaststroke in swimming and teamed with Maurine DeArman for second in the back crawl. Other

Coach June Byrd measures the net height with members of the 1951 men's tennis team.

competitors on Trinity's nine-member team earned points by placing in form swimming, high jump, basketball throw for distance, and game relays. Point winners included Jane Mills, Doreen Naylor, Edwina Johnson, and Janet Fajkus.[18]

Curiously, Polly Knolk was the only Trinity student identified by first name in the article. The other female participants were referenced with "Miss" in front of their surname, as in "Miss DeArman." Only a search through online archives of the *Mirage* and *Trinitonian* helped identify the first names of Polly's teammates. In stark contrast, male athletes were not referred to this way (e.g., Mr. Smith had two doubles and a single). Clearly the lexicon embodied the persistent cultural attitudes toward women.

Shirley Rushing: From Mississippi to Texas

As our story moves into the 1950s, a brief side trip with a young Shirley (Moser) Rushing provides a glimpse into the many challenges for female athletes of the era.

Rushing's own athletic journey began in Iuka, Mississippi, where the sports-minded teen was relegated to playing basketball, since it was the only sport offered at her high school in the late 1940s. She recalls her team traveling with the boys' squad to perform in a "warm-up" contest at each location. Although teams in the area typically commuted on a school bus, a local fan who was a Greyhound bus driver ferried the Iuka teams to road games in his more luxurious vehicle.

Rushing continued her education in 1952 at Northeast Mississippi Junior College, chosen primarily because of its proximity to her childhood home. This time she was forced to board a more rustic school bus to attend classes forty miles away. She wasn't aware of any women's athletic teams at the two-year college until a friend told her about some partial-scholarship spots on the basketball team. The road-weary student saw her chance; if she could make the team (she did), she could live on campus and avoid the eighty-mile daily round trip. While the dorms for women on the Booneville campus weren't as nice as the men's, Rushing fondly recalls the large four-person rooms and shared showers.

Career options for women in the postwar 1950s were limited mostly to teacher, nurse, or secretary, so Rushing studied business for a secretarial track during the week and traveled on weekends with the basketball squads to play junior colleges around the state. Remembering the many opportunities for competition, Rushing says, "Mississippi was ahead of the game."

Her 1954 move to Mississippi Southern University (now the University of Southern Mississippi) to finish her studies came with one surprise: it didn't have a basketball team. "We wouldn't have needed a coach. We would have just gotten on the floor," she said. Despite begging, the women couldn't find anyone on the faculty who would sponsor them. Instead of a varsity experience, Rushing participated in one of the early mixed-team Play Days that served as a recreational alternative to intercollegiate competition.

Before sitting down with an academic advisor to decide her major,

Shirley (Moser) Rushing geared up for junior college basketball, c. 1953

Rushing received some unsolicited career advice. Her sister, who was working as a secretary, bluntly said, "You don't want to do this." That counsel prompted the junior to make a decision that would have long-term ramifications for hundreds of future Trinity athletes and students; she shifted her studies to physical education, a subject she thought she would enjoy because she "liked sports."

Rushing remained in Hattiesburg after graduation, earning a fellowship to study for a master's in health, recreation, and physical education while running the intramural program and teaching classes. After earning her graduate degree in 1957, she was pleasantly surprised when a large private university in Waco, Texas, hired her fresh out of college. It was a timely move for the twenty-two-year-old, since she joined a Baylor University staff that had just hired Olga Fallen, a pioneer in the

Spotlight on Choosing a Major

When Olga Fallen decreed that every female physical education class at Baylor would field a basketball team, Shirley Rushing was assigned to coach the class that included Jody Conradt, a talented player who had averaged forty points per game for her high school team in Goldthwaite, Texas. But rules prohibited women from joining a team unless they majored in physical education. Conradt, who had played only for male coaches, didn't envision a future for females in the coaching profession and was pursuing another field of study. Once Fallen saw Conradt's skills, she pressured her to switch until she relented, changed her major, and joined Rushing's team. Rushing considered herself lucky to pick Conradt's class and said the skilled player made her job easy. "I told everybody I had only one offense: get the ball to Jody."

Olga Fallen, Baylor University

Conradt's impact on women's sports went far beyond that Baylor class team: she completed a thirty-eight-year Hall of Fame collegiate coaching career in 2007. Most of her time was at the University of Texas in Austin, where she led the vaunted basketball program to national prominence and a championship.

It just goes to show that a leader's persistence can change the course of college sports.

progressive age of women's athletics. (Trinity coach Libby Johnson and Tiger athlete Glada Munt also studied with her.)

At Baylor, Rushing had up-close experience with the transition to Sports Days. Her department hosted the Baylor Olympics, inviting other universities to campus to compete in "every sport imaginable," Rushing said. Individuals amassing the most points received awards, with trophies going to the school with the highest cumulative point total at the end of the day. It must have been a huge undertaking; Rushing said that after hosting the competition for two years, "Olga invited another school to host it the next year but got no takers."

Rushing moved on to San Antonio in 1960, but Fallen would play a critical role in the formation of Trinity women's tennis a few years later.[19]

A cartoon captures the crumbling facade of the Woodlawn administration building.

One Last Move

After less than a decade, Trinity's Woodlawn campus was bursting at the seams. Just two years after moving to San Antonio, Trinity's board of trustees was discussing the need for a modern campus that would foster an environment of learning, adaptation, and growth, but the aging structures and small footprint restricted the vision. A *Mirage* retrospective called the conditions on the Woodlawn campus "cramped and uncomfortable," pointing to the growing number of student veterans who required more dormitory space. The temporary solutions were (appropriately) installing surplus military barrack buildings for housing, as well as makeshift Quonset huts that accommodated classrooms, the library, and an office for veterans' services. After researching the long-term possibilities for funding and space to expand, the administration came to the realization that the cost of renovating the old structures—including the deteriorating administration building—would be cost-prohibitive.[20]

In 1944, trustees decided to build a new campus and considered several locations north of the city center.[21] They selected an abandoned quarry site, and by 1952, enough buildings had been completed on the Skyline campus to welcome Trinity students, faculty, and staff.

CHAPTER 4

Progression and Regression

1952–69

Obviously if there's no gym, there's no team sports.

—SHIRLEY RUSHING

The 1952 move to the Skyline campus—so named for its spectacular views of a growing downtown San Antonio—marked the beginning of the modern era in Trinity's long history. But the timing of its fourth relocation paralleled the postwar period of regression for women in US society. The story of Shirley Rushing's educational journey underscores the challenges she and her fellow females faced as the doors that had opened to women during World War II slammed shut when deployed soldiers returned. Once again, men dominated the workforce and women were expected to retreat to a destiny of domesticity.

Women resisted, however, slowly melding their voices into a chorus demanding equal rights. Rushing's arrival at Trinity in 1960 marked the beginning of what one historian calls the "Two Sixties," describing the first few years of postwar optimism and progress in attaining civil rights for minorities, followed by a contentious backlash in the decade's second half that devolved into violent antiwar protests.[1]

In San Antonio, Trinity's campus shook with new construction, men's athletic programs were revived, and for women, social activities were sponsored that provided less risky paths to recreation. Women athletes yearning for official intercollegiate competition continued to be disappointed, but the most determined plowed their own paths.

Aerial view of the campus in the late 1950s
The Slab *(far left)*, the Alamo Stadium parking lot *(far right)*

When the university commemorated its hundredth anniversary in 1969, it marked the end of a century on the sidelines for Trinity women, as campuswide and countrywide changes again opened the doors to participation. This time, there was no going back.

A New Campus on an Old Quarry

Trinity's move from the 60-acre Woodlawn campus to its new 107-acre home was conducted in a matter of days and attracted national attention. A caravan of vans, trailers, and trucks ferried books, furniture, and classroom equipment five miles east to the site perched on the edge of a former limestone quarry. One yearbook reporter described the rugged, barren terrain of the two-tier layout, writing that "the brow of a craggy hill forecasts a sheer drop to the lower campus."[2] The school's neighbors—Brackenridge Park, the San Antonio Zoo, Alamo Stadium, and the Japanese Sunken Gardens—had sprouted from the same abandoned site.[3] Trinity's distinctive red-brick footprint took form under the guidance of renowned architect O'Neil Ford, who implemented the innovative lift-slab method to lower costs and speed construction. Today the campus is regarded as one of the most attractive and functional small undergraduate settings in the country.[4]

Greeting the fifty-one moving vans on May 13, 1952, was a sparse development of four buildings, only two of which were ready for occupancy. The only thing that could be considered an athletic facility was a rectangular block of concrete. Affectionally nicknamed the Slab by

Physical education class on the Slab, used for recreation, school dances, and drama

campus residents, the 118-by-142-foot foundation functioned as a makeshift outdoor gymnasium for physical education classes and intramural contests in tennis, badminton, basketball, and volleyball. It also hosted an occasional extramural tennis or basketball contest and a variety of social events. Until Trinity constructed its own facilities, the university relied on nearby high schools, churches, or public venues for practices or games.[5]

Records about athletic programs for Trinity women during the 1950s are sporadic and lack specifics. Rare publication coverage featured random extramural teams competing in short seasons with local clubs and colleges, and chaperoned by part-time sponsors who didn't act as official coaches. Some women participated in the increasingly popular Sports Days during the decade, but most social and recreational activities came from the campus WRA chapter, which emphasized "wholesome recreation" and offered "every Trinity woman interested in sports an opportunity to become a member and improve her muscular coordination, leadership ability, and sportsmanship." At the end of each academic year, the WRA celebrated intramural accomplishments by awarding trophies to clubs accruing the highest number of points and honoring the top three individual point winners with WRA letters.[6]

In 1955, the still ambiguous term *varsity* reentered the lexicon, and tennis reclaimed its place as Trinity's most popular sport for women. The year after June Byrd left her men's coaching position (a year in

A WRA "letter."

which Trinity did not field a men's team), the university bulletin again listed a WRA varsity tennis program sponsored by women's dormitory counselor Helen Windham. Team members Ruth Naylor, Marilyn Montgomery, Esther Leigh, and Susan Homey were featured in a *Mirage* piece that proclaimed that Trinity "had never fielded a girl's tennis aggregation before," but despite the lack of experience "promised to represent the Cliffside school favorably in every competitive event they entered."[7] In its second year, the players welcomed new sponsor and physical education instructor Ruth M. Cady, who guided the teams in 1956 and 1957. The fledgling varsity team lasted only three seasons, and any published references to women's varsity, intercollegiate, or extramural tennis disappeared for almost a decade.[8]

Joan Griffiths, who sponsored the WRA riflery and fencing teams, said her goal was to teach life skills and felt that shooting could "certainly be classified as an activity for both male and female students." A 1958 *Trinitonian* story portrays a Monday afternoon practice in Myrtle McFarlin dormitory basement, where team members fired at targets set fifty feet away. Griffiths instructed women "in the general knowledge of .22 caliber rifles, ammunition, proper and safe handling of the weapons, range procedures and class firing." The reporter added that "heavy emphasis is placed on the prone position which is a standard position for women rifle-men." Some of their extramural contests were conducted as telegraphic dual meets.[9]

The WRA also sponsored social events to boost camaraderie and build relationships. One example in 1954 prompted the front-page *Trinitonian* headline, "W.R.A. Sponsors 'Miss Posture' Contest" (a competition introduced in the 1930s by Anna Hiss at UT). At another WRA meeting in McFarlin Lounge, Windham invited members to

The 1956 WRA tennis team *(left to right)*, Kay Barnes, Ruth Naylor, Marilyn Montgomery, and Susan Homey. Naylor models the Trinity letter she designed for the players' blazers.

participate in a "guaranteed weight-reduction game of touch football" and in less energetic activities such as a bridge tournament, pool lessons, and a talent show.[10]

As the decade progressed, the WRA's influence waned on campuses across the country. One positive factor was the growth of intercollegiate and intramural athletic programs, which compelled schools to centralize the administration of women's sports. Also, both academic and recreational activities were increasingly coeducational, and providing separate buildings for men and women was no longer feasible. Finally, an increased reliance on funding from student fees through student councils prompted the consolidation of control to one office serving an entire student body.

The last reference to Trinity's WRA chapter appears in the 1959 *Mirage*. In 1960, oversight of women's sports at Trinity shifted to a Women's Athletic Council and soon thereafter to a Women's Board of Social Clubs.[11] Intramural sports for men and women weren't fully reintroduced until a few years later, when the school finally had facilities to host games.[12]

Meanwhile, little progress was made in the quest for international participation. With the 1956 Olympics looming, US committees were attempting to attract female talent to offset the dominating medal count won in previous games by women from the Soviet Union. Their efforts were stymied by the country's educational leaders, who still advocated for a "distinctly feminine" curriculum for their female students. This view was succinctly captured in a 1955 poll that asked (mostly male) superintendents if their schools should encourage girls' track and gymnastics to improve American odds in international competition. Ninety-seven percent rejected the notion. "Let the Russians continue to develop their women into Amazons," one answered, "but let us continue to develop femininity and charm in our women." Remarked another: "Our primary objective should be to turn out homemakers, not athletes."[13] Even Anna Hiss, UT's longtime female physical education director, promoted sports that weren't unfeminine or dangerous. She especially encouraged those activities that reflected "modesty and dignity," such as tennis, golf, archery, swimming, and interpretive dance.[14]

Despite these hurdles, US viewers of the first televised Olympic Games in 1960 took pride in watching female African American athlete Wilma Rudolph win three track and field gold medals in Rome. Perhaps, against the odds, the race against Russia was finally poised at the starting blocks.

The Tale of the "Two Sixties"

Rushing started her long Trinity career in 1960, on the cusp of a tumultuous decade that has been carved into the collective American conscience. In *The Sixties: Years of Hope, Days of Rage*, historian Todd Gitlin outlines the early forward momentum in immigration, civil rights, voting rights, and investment in the Great Society. This optimistic period seemed to promise unfettered progress and culminated with President Lyndon Johnson's signing of the 1964 Civil Rights Act, legislation that elevated the status of minorities and fueled a second wave of feminist activism.[15]

The movement also resurrected the long-dormant debate for an Equal

Rights Amendment (ERA), which was originally proposed to Congress in 1923. The revived effort had encountered a roadblock from a presidential commission established by John F. Kennedy. After a two-year study, members concluded in 1963 that no amendment was necessary, since they determined the Constitution already embodied equality for women. Their report recommended that complaints instead be resolved by the federal courts. By 1969, no such judicial interpretation seemed forthcoming, and efforts to pass the ERA began anew.[16]

As with previous reform movements, the optimism of the early 1960s devolved as the progressive movement splintered into fractious sects, while a conservative silent majority fueled a backlash over cultural issues such as pluralism, race, government spending, and crime. According to sociologist Robert Putnam, this reversal was marked by Vietnam War protests, urban unrest, the rise of the Black Panthers, and the "law and order" counterattack. He writes: "Almost all historians agree that a major historical turning point took place between roughly 1968 and 1974—a 'revolution,' a 'renaissance,' a 'fracture,' a 'shock wave,' a point after which 'everything changed,' creating a 'new America.'"[17]

This swing between progression and regression followed Rushing's first decade in Trinity's physical education department. After three years of teaching (and coaching class teams) in Waco, her career path would crystalize after she learned about an opportunity at Trinity. She applied for the job and took a campus tour after her interview. While she was captivated by the landscaped grounds and the scenic overlook of the tennis courts, swimming pool, and city skyline, she failed to register two oddities before she reported to work that fall: she was the only woman in her small department, and Trinity didn't have a gymnasium.

"The first time I met with the president, he asked if I had seen the blueprints for the gym they were going to build when they got the money," Rushing said. When she saw that the blueprints were "yellow and cut out of newspaper," she realized they had been sitting on a shelf for years, and she adjusted her expectations accordingly. In her first three years at Trinity, Rushing taught classes at the nearby Trinity Baptist Church gymnasium, on the multifunctional Slab on lower campus, or—if her class was scheduled before the men's tennis team began practice at 2 p.m.—on the four varsity courts.

The acceptable wardrobe for female professionals presented another

Shirley Rushing, in appropriate upper-campus dress, on the tennis courts with department colleagues Gene Norris, Jess MacLeay, and Houston Wheeler (1963)

challenge for the young professor. "On upper campus, women did not wear slacks," Rushing said. So, she reported to her Northrup Hall office wearing the obligatory dress, hose, and heels, and toting a suitcase of clothes for the day's activities because there were no locker rooms then. She had to pack a swimsuit, leotards for modern dance, and shorts and a shirt for her classes. "A lot of my first three years were spent just changing clothes from one place to another," she said, pointing out that she quickly became an expert on the location of all the women's restrooms on campus.[18]

The facility issues that led to Rushing's inconvenient routine were resolved during the campus building boom of the 1960s. The previous decade's successful fundraising spurred new academic structures, the

The Olympic swimming pool, completed in 1958

Murchison tower, the Parker chapel, a dining hall, and recreational facilities. The Olympic-sized outdoor pool was one of the first amenities, built in 1958 into the quarry ledge separating the campus's upper and lower levels. Students nicknamed the facility the Byrd Bath to honor David Byrd, the 1960 graduate who donated the funds for the pool. The pool joined the outdoor Slab and four tennis courts as the only outlets for recreation or competition.[19]

Additional lower-campus construction accommodated the increasing demands for intramurals, physical education classes, and men's intercollegiate sports. The centerpiece was the indoor athletic center named after Earl C. Sams, a philanthropist and cofounder of retailer J.C. Penney. The 1963 addition was considered by *Trinitonian* reporters as "a long walk from upper campus." Although the facility hosted both male and female students, the designers didn't foresee female intercollegiate participation, and it showed. Men's football, baseball, and basketball varsity players could change in locker rooms separated from

The Earl C. Sams Center, dedicated in 1963

the public side and had access to dedicated conditioning and therapy services that were inaccessible to women. These disparities became more apparent as women's teams forming in the late 1960s shared lockers and changing rooms with female physical education students and intramural participants.[20]

The Sams Center featured two gyms (one air-conditioned), a weight room, a rifle range, handball and squash courts, and an eight-lane bowling alley. While Rushing must have been delighted to move into an office in the center with her physical education department colleagues, she also certainly appreciated the ballroom, which provided a perfect venue to lead dance classes during her long Trinity career.[21]

Early outdoor construction was limited to a baseball stadium and the E. M. Stevens field and track. Beginning in 1967, the football team used the field for practice but played their varsity home games at nearby Alamo Stadium until 1972.

While opportunities for female athletes to compete against other schools remained scarce in the 1960s, Trinity's exploding intramural program did offer its women a foundation for more participation and skill building.[22] The small program was initially led by baseball coach and physical education staff member Houston Wheeler, who directed

The E. M. Stevens field. The track and practice field were completed in 1967; stadium seating was added in 1972.

men's intramurals on a part-time basis. Rushing's status as the department's lone woman meant she was assigned sponsorship of women's sports programs, in addition to supervising Trinity cheerleaders and majorettes. She also played a critical role in organizing, mentoring, and securing financial support for the unofficial women's tennis program, all in addition to a full load of classroom teaching assignments.

Both professors tapped into the exercise science class created by department chair Jess MacLeay for their recruits, since MacLeay required his students to participate in physical activities outside the classroom. However, those first years of the intramural program were "skimpy," according to Rushing.[23] Still, female students could compete in intramural volleyball, basketball, tennis, swimming, track, table tennis, and paddleball.

The intramural program's growth accelerated after 1967, partly due to MacLeay's increased emphasis on recreation as an integral part of student life and partly due to more athletic facilities. But the most consequential cause was hiring alumnus Jim Potter as intramural director. After just three years developing relationships and applying innovative

Intramural director Jim Potter in 1968.

approaches, he had more than 70 percent of the student population engaged in intramurals.[24] Potter guided the popular program from 1967 to 2000.

Aside from intramurals, tennis and bowling provided the most opportunities for female competition early in the decade, mainly due to their popularity and coed appeal. They were also considered appropriate for women since they did not threaten harm through physical contact with opponents.

Bowling benefited from extensive city league competition that occasionally extended into the collegiate ranks. Before the Sams Center bowling alley opened in 1963, little is recorded about female participation, other than a few *Trinitonian* ads and pictures. A photograph in the 1965 *Mirage* indicates Pat Luke as the lone female in the leadership ranks of a local intercollegiate league.

Tennis vaulted to popularity as a professional, recreational, and intercollegiate sport after World War II. It also became the most visible women's sport of the era, thanks to the new technology of television that began to proliferate in postwar American households. Coverage

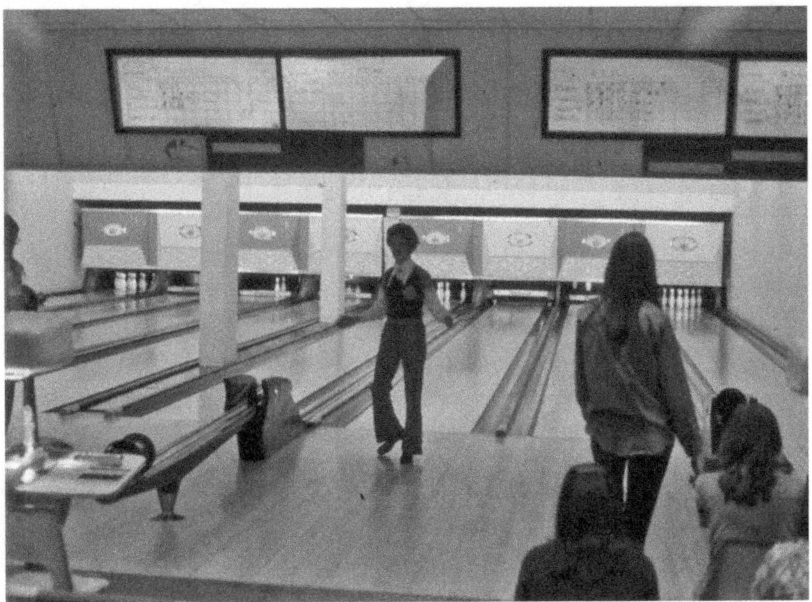

Eight bowling lanes in the Sams Center basement

of tournaments like Wimbledon and the US Open made household names of players Maureen Connolly, Doris Hart, Althea Gibson, and later, Billie Jean King and Rosie Casals. These women became female role models to schoolgirls eager to compete at the college level, including many who were considering Trinity in the 1960s because of the renowned men's program. Three tennis players who were motivated by these athletes and helped advance their sport at Trinity were Sally Goldschmeding, who was the first player to represent Trinity in a tournament (1965), and Emilie Burrer and Becky Vest, who brought home the school's first national tennis titles in 1968 and 1969.

By the end of the decade, other sports gained traction, and female students sought ways to improve their skills. Some of the best recruits for this next big leap—from Sports Days to extramurals—came from within Potter's staff and from standouts in the intramural contests. To fulfill their desire for more challenging competition, Potter partnered with departmental colleague Bob Strauss and tapped into his minuscule budget to sponsor women's extramural teams in volleyball and basketball. The two professors supervised practice sessions, scheduled games with local clubs or colleges, and accompanied players (sometimes with Rushing) to contests.

It helped that other schools were resurrecting their programs after decades of inactivity. UT, which hosted its first women's intercollegiate basketball contest in 1907, restarted competition in basketball and volleyball in 1966 with a paltry budget of $700.[25] That wouldn't have surprised Potter, who recalls digging into student activity fees to find $600 that he had to spread between two sports.

Lack of an official budget wasn't the only factor weighing down these early extramural efforts. The female players typically lacked access to expert instruction (sponsors weren't expected to coach), uniforms were rarely provided, and equipment was either hard to come by or provided by athletes themselves. Also, without travel funding, Potter could only schedule games with the few nearby schools that fielded teams. For most of the next decade, opponents included San Antonio College, Incarnate Word College, Our Lady of the Lake University, St. Mary's University, and Texas Lutheran College in Seguin.[26]

Extramural basketball games between Trinity and other local schools were first mentioned in 1965, with most teams composed of select all-star intramural players. Tennis player Emilie Burrer recalls participating in these "looser and less established" sports later in the decade, including a trip in Rushing's gray Buick Skylark sedan to a basketball game against Baylor.[27]

The first appearance of women's extramural volleyball occurred not long after the dedication of the Sams Center, when an all-star volleyball team from Trinity hosted a December 1963 match against San Antonio College on the new floor. According to the *Trinitonian*, the "girls" were chosen by sponsor Shirley Rushing "because of their high scoring averages during the intramural volleyball season." No results were recorded.[28] Later in the decade, the sport's increasing popularity in high schools, churches, and town clubs prompted local colleges and universities to establish their own volleyball teams. A brief blurb in 1968 reports that a "newly formed" extramural team was preparing for a fourteen-team regional tournament at Incarnate Word after playing a warmup match with San Antonio College.[29] The next year, the record shows the Tigers beating Incarnate Word to win the San Antonio extramural championship, finishing second to Southwest Texas State in

Gals Begin Intramurals

A common 1963 headline. Male students were always referred to as men in student publications.

the district tournament, and posting a season record of 7–2. That 1969 roster listed Rushing and Potter as coaches and included Blanche Barboza, Julia Gonzales, Estella Vela, Wendy Winborn, Mimi Mead, and Kathy Polansky.[30]

Little else was documented about these early contests in student publications. When a rare game story was published, prejudicial language persisted, with student reporters referring to female athletes as *girls*, while male athletes were called *men*. A review of intramural coverage in the decade's *Mirage* and *Trinitonian* issues shows that virtually all stories or photographs were of male participants. One *Trinitonian* page from 1963 illustrates the disparity: While the headline for one story makes no reference to gender, it focuses on the men's program and features quotes from men's intramural director, Houston Wheeler. Adjacent to the large article is a shorter one with a smaller headline, referring to female intramural participants as *gals*.

However, in the same issue, sports editor Chuck Henry came to the ladies' defense when he wrote: "Intramurals are not for men only. Miss Shirley Moser [Rushing] is in charge of the women's program and they will also be active throughout the year in various sports."[31] And in 1968, sports editor Mark Horstmeyer wrote

> As surely as the earth is round, there is a women's intramural program going on right here at Trinity U. Behind closed doors of the auxiliary gym every Tuesday come the shouts and cries of co-eds mixing it up in volleyball or basketball or soon to come badminton. Excitement is high and attendance low. Participation is enthusiastic, and attendance is still low. Competition is keen, yet attendance is still low. What Trinity students are allowing to slip through their fingers is the opportunity to view athletic combat of the highest skill and daring.[32]

One reason for the low attendance could have been that the women's games were typically held on the Sams Center auxiliary court instead

Spotlight on Women's Sports Organizations

The proliferation of governance organizations in the second half of the century created state and national guidelines for women's physical education and addressed the escalating interest in sports. Groups emerged, merged, morphed, and splintered—until the behemoth NCAA took over in 1981. A list of women's national and regional associations from the twentieth century looks like an explosion of alphabet soup—the AAAPE, AAHPERD, ACACW, AIAW, CAIW, CISW, CWA, DGWS, NAAF, NJCESCW, NSWA, TAIAW, TCIAW, WAA, and WRA. The history of these developments is a subject better explained by sports historians in other publications. For most schools in the state, the primary driver of women's intercollegiate sports in the late 1960s was the Texas Commission for Intercollegiate Athletics for Women (TCIAW). After Title IX, national oversight shifted to the Association of Intercollegiate Athletics for Women (AIAW), which was founded in 1971.

As a point of comparison, oversight of men's collegiate athletics fell mainly to three national organizations. The National Association of Intercollegiate Athletics (NAIA) was created in 1937 to sponsor men's sports for 250 mostly small schools, and the National Junior College Athletic Association began a year later and currently serves more than 400 member schools. Today, the 116-year-old NCAA, with 1,200 member institutions (more than 440 in Division III), rules the landscape for men's and women's intercollegiate sports.

of the main gymnasium. The secondary gym had less than three feet of cushion outside the boundaries of the basketball court. Also, absent any seating, student spectators had to stand or sit on the floor against the wall.

For female athletes, positive tweaks to policy language showed that decision makers were bowing to the reality of their desire for increased competition. After the regressive wording change prompted by the WAA-to-WRA conversion in 1940, purpose statements switched back to endorsing "desirable forms of extramural competition" like Sports Days and Play Days and approving "supervised" intercollegiate activities. But the philosophical doors finally propped open in the 1960s with the aid of progressive policies allowing varsity programs for the "highly skilled." Now state-level championships could be sponsored for tennis, badminton, basketball, volleyball, track and field, golf, and bowling. In fact, the 1966 formation of a governance group to oversee limited national championships came two years after a meeting convened specifically to address the NAAF/WD platform that had hampered women's intercollegiate sports since 1923.[33]

Empowered by the decade's social movements, aspiring female athletes began exerting pressure on these sports organizations. The fate of the Women's National Golf Tournament suggests one early inflection point. When it was in danger of folding in 1956, a joint committee of association leaders and students convened to discuss adopting the event.[34] This successful collaboration sparked a cascade of changes between 1957 and 1981; it extended the golf event for ten years, which enabled it to continue as the only national intercollegiate championship for women. It also stimulated further debates about hosting national championships in other sports.[35]

Paving Their Own Competitive Paths

Despite the expansion in sports governance, schools around the country still offered few official outlets for female athletes. That didn't stop the most determined to find their paths to competition, however. Some cobbled a team together, found other like-minded women to play against, and solicited sponsorship from wealthy sports enthusiasts or corporations. Often, a factory, bank, or soft drink company might sponsor a women's team to improve employee welfare by providing recreation while also burnishing their brand image in the community.

Not all physical education leaders had fond feelings for these amateur leagues. Many "abhorred" their existence, since most were run by men for economic profit and emphasized intense competition. One female educator repeated the still pervasive motivation to protect their students' femininity: "I don't think the world needs [more] highly aggressive, competitive, tough-minded women." Another potential factor in this mostly middle-class perspective was that many teams were composed of working class, rural, or African American women playing games that were considered "unladylike and unnatural for women."[36] A fact not widely publicized was that the United States populated their few women's Olympic teams from these unofficial squads.[37]

The backstory of a future Trinity tennis champion and coach provides insight into these leagues and their value for sports-minded girls. In the early 1960s, while Trinity was beefing up its offerings for mostly men's athletics, a young Emilie Burrer found few organized sports in her local secondary schools. Like many of her tomboy peers, she played games with neighborhood boys, including stickball.[38] She honed her skills by salvaging a discarded broom from a neighbor's trash can and cutting off the straw head. She used the makeshift bat to practice hitting pea gravel plucked from the unpaved side street by her house. When the boys saw her talent, Burrer was typically one of the first players chosen for a pickup game.

On summer evenings, Burrer's father took his family to San Pedro Park to watch the female Pepsi-Cola softball team play in city league games. The team was sponsored by soft drink magnate Jodie McCarley and featured talented local pitcher Alva Jo Fischer. A San Antonio youth sports prodigy, Fischer played five years in the wartime women's All-American Girls Professional Baseball League and is a familiar name to thousands of players who have competed on the softball fields named for her in northeast San Antonio.[39]

Believing that his daughter was just as skilled as Fischer and her Pepsi teammates, Burrer's father asked coach McCarley if Emilie could try out for the team. First, the twelve-year-old displayed her defensive talents in the Koger Stokes infield. Then she stepped up to the plate and was shocked at how easy batting could be. After years of perfecting her skills with a broomstick and small rocks, she recalls that the softball "looked like a stinkin' watermelon."

Burrer participated in other sports leagues, often as the youngest player, and sometimes accompanied them on international trips. One of the nicknames she inherited from her older teammates was Tiger, a nod to her tenacious play and a foreshadowing of her future at Trinity. But Burrer had never played tennis. That changed when a course credit requirement forced the fifteen-year-old to settle on joining the Jefferson High School tennis team, since it was the only girls' varsity program at her school. Her athletic ability easily transferred, as she quickly rose to the number one spot on the team and won the 1965 4A state singles championship her senior year.[40]

Burrer's singles crown was the first title for any San Antonio player in any sport since fellow Mustang Butch Newman dominated boys' singles in 1960 and 1961. Because of what one sportswriter called her

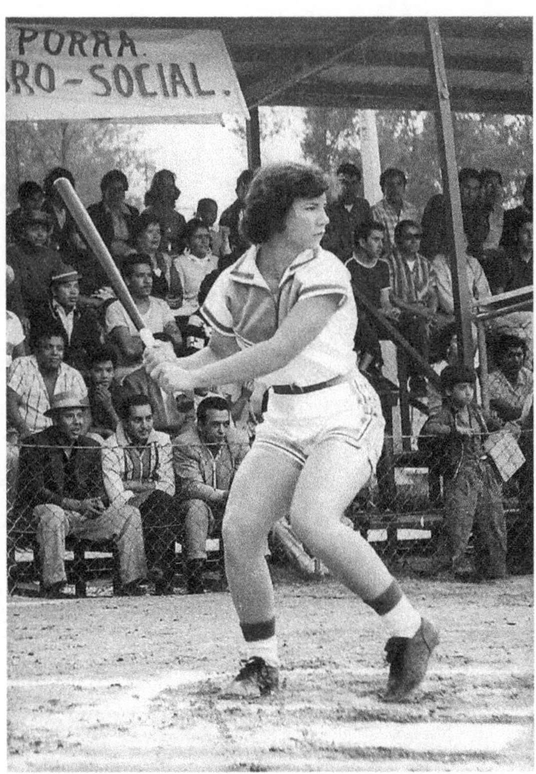

A teenaged Emilie Burrer bats for the Pepsi Cola softball team at an exhibition game in Mexico City, c. 1961.

"astonishingly short career," Burrer's preferred college, Arizona State University, rejected her request for a tennis scholarship, so she played her first two years of intercollegiate competition at Lubbock Christian College (LCC).[41] After her freshmen year, she was selected for the prestigious Junior Wightman Cup under Trinity alumnus Marilyn Montgomery. She played from 1966 to 1968, accepted the program's 1968 Player of the Year award, and served as team captain in 1969. She also represented the United States in the 1967 Pan American Games before enrolling at Trinity with an academic scholarship.

While at LCC, Burrer's brief encounter with a legendary program in another sport almost derailed her budding tennis career. Burrer was coaching a church league girls' basketball team to earn extra money. When she learned that Wayland Baptist University was holding tryouts,

The logo for Wayland Baptist University's legendary Flying Queens basketball team.

she encouraged her teenage players to attend. They agreed but only on the condition that their coach accompany them.

At the time, the more physical sport of basketball hadn't enjoyed the same broad acceptance as tennis, and few colleges were fielding female teams. One exception was the college in Plainview, Texas, which hosted the spectacularly successful Flying Queens. With the support of local businessman and alumnus Claude Hutcherson, the team toured the country on his private planes and became one of the most successful women's teams—of any sport—in the 1950s and 1960s. (Originally called the Harvest Queens because Harvest Queen Mill provided team uniforms, the team changed the name to the Flying Queens to honor Hutcherson.) Between 1954 and 1958 the Queens compiled a 131-game winning streak and won four AAU championships against mostly non-collegiate amateur squads.[42]

Burrer joined her players in the intensive Saturday evaluation and impressed Queens coach Harley Redin. Two days later, Redin offered Burrer a basketball scholarship since her time at the two-year LCC was ending. Although she loved the sport, she had already committed to an academic aid package from Trinity to finish her studies and play tennis on the side. Not only was she eager to return home to her recently widowed mother, Burrer wanted to take advantage of the school's academic reputation.[43]

One of Burrer's dormitory neighbors had experienced her own moment of amateur sports fame in a national magazine. Lubbock Christian track team member Janis Rinehart was one of Burrer's "wall mates" in Katy Rogers Hall and had appeared two years earlier on the cover of *Sports Illustrated.*[44] The 1964 cover story, "Flamin' Mamie's Bouffant Belles," highlighted the Texas Track Club's success in toeing the fine line between athleticism and femininity.

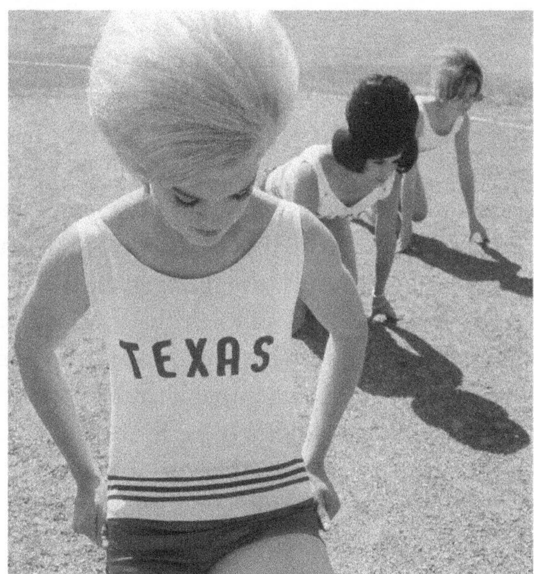

The Bouffant Belles, 1964 *Sports Illustrated,* marking the first time a US women's track team graced the cover. Janis Rinehart is the blonde in the foreground.

The girls' team was founded in 1961 by Margaret "Mamie" Ellison to give her own track-happy daughter opportunities to compete, and the red-haired secretary from Abilene traveled to area AAU meets to scout other speedy prospects. She was invested in the team's success in meets around the country, but she was also intent on challenging the masculine image of women athletes by emphasizing their attractiveness.

Gil Rogin, the editor who penned the cover story, quoted the flamboyant sponsor on her approach. "Every year we have a good-looking team and good-looking uniforms," Ellison said. "I prefer pretty girls. I insist they wear makeup. We all go to the beauty shop before each meet, so we can get beautiful and get our minds off the meet." Echoing this prevailing view, another coach praised his own female track team as neat and feminine, saying there was "not a dog in the bunch."

So why the hair-themed nickname? In addition to extolling her team's "uncommon beauty," "dazzling uniforms," and "elaborate makeup," Ellison also promoted their "majestic hairdos." Whether a bouffant, beehive, or flip style, these became their trademark—but not just for the glamour factor. The runners also said the styles, held in place by Aqua Net hairspray, kept the wind from blowing hair in their face during a race. While the Belles paid some expenses out of pocket or through fundraisers, Ellison and local business sponsors also helped fund the team. But Ellison's job stopped there. She said she didn't take on the role of coaching because she claimed they would listen to and have more confidence in a man. She added, "[A]nd a woman likes to show off for a man."[45]

Rogin wrapped up his feature by suggesting the Texas Track Club proved "you can be beautiful and still run the 100 in 10.9." In retrospect, the article fit neatly into what some called the "beautification bandwagon" trend of the times, when publications focused on female athletes' attractiveness instead of their performance.[46] Some female runners voiced their displeasure with the story, equating it to the magazine's annual male-targeted swimsuit issue. More than half a century later, Rogin admitted to *Runner's World* that his article was more about beauty regimen than running skills. "It was all just a stunt. It wasn't a track story," Rogin said in 2017.[47]

Another athlete concerned about remaining attractive while running was Katherine Switzer, the first official female entrant in the Boston Marathon. She signed her 1967 application using the initials "K. W. Switzer" so she would be accepted in the male-only competition. She donned bulky sweats to disguise her female figure but made sure to apply makeup and lipstick before leaving for the race. It was a habit she admitted she wasn't willing to break, even on that historic day.[48]

This emphasis on femininity, whether favored or forced, fed into what one sports psychologist labels "apologetic" behavior. According to Jan Felshin, this is how some women deal with participating in the male-centric sphere of sports. She suggests that the desire to protect their identity extends beyond outward appearance (like wearing jewelry or makeup) to rationalizing "the socially acceptable aspects of sports while minimizing the perceived violation of social norms." Felshin cites the example of a fiercely competitive basketball player who feels compelled to wear a pink hair ribbon on the court: "Both actions, in effect, proclaimed to her audience 'I may be playing basketball, but it's still important for me to be a normal woman.'"[49] In contrast, as former Trinity tennis player and sports sociologist Nancy Spencer notes, few male athletes experience pressure to prove their own masculinity.[50]

A National Movement Surges

Some significant national developments merit mention before closing the chapter on the 1960s.

The first was Betty Friedan's controversial *Feminine Mystique*, published in 1963. Historians consider the bestseller to be the literary starting gun for second-wave feminism, which challenged the paradigm of the women's domestic role over the next two decades.[51] Friedan, a summa cum laude graduate of Smith College, was raising children in a suburban home when she began to question the postwar notion that women's role was to seek fulfillment as wives and mothers. "The problem lay buried, unspoken, for many years in the minds of American women," she wrote. "In the fifteen years after World War II, this mystique of feminine fulfillment became the cherished and self-perpetuating core of contemporary American culture." In retrospect, one historian observed, "It was a strange stirring, a sense of dissatisfaction, a yearning that women suffered in the middle of the twentieth century." H. W. Brands noted that Friedan was "afraid to ask even of herself the silent question 'Is this all?'" The book's runaway success moved Friedan to the frontlines of the women's rights struggle.[52]

Indeed, Friedan spearheaded the decade's second influential development: the formation of the National Organization for Women in 1966. The twenty-eight founding members convened in Friedan's Washington, D.C., hotel room after a conference to discuss the perceived lack of enforcement of the Civil Rights Act passed two years earlier. Friedan scribbled the acronym NOW on a hotel napkin, and the name stuck. In 1968 the group issued a Bill of Rights addressing a number of complaints, including equality in education for women. According to historian Elaine Gerber, NOW wanted to bring women off the sidelines and into the mainstream of society's institutions: "Its members pointed out the obvious as a problem: that women as a group lacked voice (and equal opportunities) in arenas of power like business, politics, education, religion, and the media."[53] NOW's actions and influence with lawmakers foreshadowed the debates over Title IX in 1972.

Finally, at least two governance organizations were adjusting their philosophies, shifts that may have been assisted by advancing science. A groundbreaking report from the American Medical Association in 1964 not only dispelled myths about the danger of sports for women but also implored them to become more active.[54] Four years later, the Division for Girls and Women's Sports reversed its stance on national championships. In its revised mission statement, it explained:

> Members of DGWS believe that creation of national championships will give talented young women something more to strive for and will give them greater incentive for continuing to develop their athletic skills. The championships and the naming of national annual champions in the different sports should motivate less talented girls to learn sport skills and to enjoy them on their own. In other words, sports activity will become more desirable as an endeavor for women.[55]

Leona Hollbrook, president of the National Association of Physical Education for College Women, echoed the organization's own evolving goals in the pre–Title IX era:

> We women in physical education and in sports leadership have a number of special opportunities to contribute to some unusual and excellent aspects of education. The structured games provide a course of action, a challenge to skill, a propriety in rules and behavior, and a natural setting for active participation and social interchange.... Sports well taught and well pursued is an activity of a classic nature and an admirable expression for human quality.[56]

In the five years after the DGWS declaration, national intercollegiate championships began for women's gymnastics, track and field, swimming, badminton, volleyball, and basketball.

As its first century concluded and the countdown to the 1970s began, Trinity was poised to welcome a new kind of student: one who was competitive on the field and in the classroom. But work was yet to be done—and legislation yet to be passed—to provide female students the same opportunities as their male counterparts.

At the national level, any hopes for a less chaotic political environment were dashed in the first spring semester of 1970, when college campuses erupted in protest over the expansion of the Vietnam War into Cambodia. In one demonstration, four students were killed and nine were wounded by National Guard troops at Kent State University on May 4. It seems the unrest would continue into the new decade.

CHAPTER 5

The Unique Status of Women's Tennis

1965–73

GALS GET JOB DONE
—HEADLINE FOR *SAN ANTONIO LIGHT* ARTICLE ABOUT BURRER AND VEST WINNING TENNIS CHAMPIONSHIPS

Tennis was one physical activity that didn't challenge the conventional notion of proper femininity. The sport had blossomed from the start of the century and well into the golden age of women's sports in the 1920s. But, along with other female endeavors, progress had been stymied by external factors for almost four decades.[1]

Then, straddling the years between the tumultuous late 1960s and progressive post–Title IX period, the Trinity women's program experienced a slow but steady resurgence. Many talented and persistent women not only met—but exceeded—the successes of their famous male counterparts. Under the guidance of a young physical education sponsor, this era featured many milestones for the program, including its first intercollegiate representative, first national titles, first budget, first (part-time) coach, first athletic scholarships, and first dedicated coach—in that order.

Progress on an Unofficial Scale

Once the 1908 photograph of a female team "ready to serve" faded into the archives, few references were made about Trinity females in the sport, save the notable 1950 appointment of June Byrd to lead the men's

John Newman makes the first serve in the dedication of the men's tennis courts in 1959.

tennis team on the Woodlawn campus and a brief period of extramural play under the WRA varsity banner in the mid-1950s. Byrd left in 1954 but remained in San Antonio the rest of her life and didn't seem to lose her attachment to Trinity sports; her 2012 obituary requested that memorial donations be sent to the school's women's athletic programs.[2]

Her departure opened the door for major changes to men's tennis when Trinity hired athletic director and head football coach W. A. McElreath, who had been an assistant at Tulane University. He soon persuaded former college star and Texas native Clarence Mabry to take over and upgrade the men's program, which had become dormant in 1955 after Byrd's exit.[3]

Mabry delivered. By the 1960s, Trinity was receiving the national recognition it craved, but not for its academic standing. Instead, media coverage fixated on the accomplishments of the male Tiger netters, many of whom advanced into the professional ranks, including Chuck McKinley, Frank Froehling, and Rod Susman. These on-court successes vaulted the school into the upper echelon of American colleges and universities, attracted standing-room-only crowds to its matches, and earned it the nickname Tennis Tech from local sportswriters.[4]

Marilyn Montgomery

During these glory days for men's tennis, no official Trinity's women's team existed (i.e., no budget, coach, or planned activities), and little mention was made of female players in campus publications or local news media. Although Mabry's vision didn't encompass women's tennis, the reputation he built lured many talented women to the campus, some hoping to learn from the celebrity coach but unaware the school didn't field a women's varsity team.

Two Trinity students, Marilyn Montgomery and Karen Hantze, stand out for their independent rankings and accomplishments around the turn of the decade.

Montgomery was born in Beeville, Texas, but raised in San Antonio, where she picked up tennis her senior year at Brackenridge High School. She played three years on Trinity's WRA squad, the first one to be labeled varsity in the course catalog. After graduating in 1957 with a math degree, she continued to play in tournaments and win more state and national rankings before pursuing an education career.[5] Later in the decade, her role as coach of the Junior Wightman Cup team played a key role in attracting one of Trinity's first female collegiate champions.[6]

The second star was Karen Hantze, who was ranked second in the

From left, Billie Jean Moffitt and Trinity student Karen Hantze defeated Margaret Smith and Jan Lehane in the 1961 Ladies' Wimbledon final, the youngest team ever to win the doubles title.

nation by the United States Lawn Tennis Association (USLTA) when she enrolled as a freshman in January 1961. The summer after her only semester at Trinity, the eighteen-year-old San Diego native won the 1961 Wimbledon doubles championship with seventeen-year-old Billie Jean Moffitt, whom she knew from California youth tennis. They advanced as an unseeded team to the title match and became the youngest double champions in the tournament's history. Just months later, Hantze married Rod Susman, a member of Trinity's undefeated men's team from the previous season. Suitably, the bride was given away at the October ceremony in San Antonio by Susman's coach Clarence Mabry, and Marilyn Montgomery served as a bridesmaid.[7]

During their second Wimbledon run in 1962, she and Moffitt defended their doubles crown, and the newlywed captured the prestigious women's singles title. The duo added a US Open title in 1964 before Hantze Susman took a break to raise a family.[8] Moffitt married in 1965 and pursued her own illustrious career as Billie Jean King, winning twenty Wimbledon titles, among many other accomplishments. Margaret Smith, their opponent in that first Wimbledon doubles crown, married Barry Court in 1967 and had her own successful playing career.

In 1962, Karen Hantze Susman and Marilyn Montgomery were honored at an alumni banquet for bringing "widespread recognition to San Antonio and Trinity University." Notably, they never officially represented the school on an intercollegiate team.

In the early 1960s, tennis was typically one of the few acceptable sports for high school girls, primarily due to its elite status, feminine attire, and noncontact nature. One of those young veterans was Sally Goldschmeding, whose 1964 arrival at Trinity marked the shaky starting point for official intercollegiate representation.

While the Dallas-area native was attracted to the pristine Skyline campus, she was also eager to try out for a women's tennis team. As a varsity player at Highland Park High School, Goldschmeding was aware of the reputation of the men's team and closely followed the Wimbledon singles titles won by Hantze Susman in 1962 and Trinity senior Chuck McKinley in 1963. Based on this, Goldschmeding simply assumed Trinity had an established program, but she had little success locating tryouts. Finally, after multiple calls to the Sams Center, the tenacious student was steered to Shirley Rushing, who was consumed by classroom and intramural responsibilities and advised the freshman to call back in the spring when tournaments were scheduled.

Only at that moment did Goldschmeding realize Trinity did not have a women's team or coach. She later discovered the school also didn't welcome her on the courts; the few times she and her friends tried to play on one of the four upper-campus courts, they were told the facility was reserved for the men.

The next semester, the student found a collegiate tournament at Mary Hardin-Baylor College in Belton, Texas, but players couldn't enter unless they were sponsored by their school.[9] Goldschmeding asked if she could say she represented Trinity. Rushing recalls, "I thought about it for about five or ten seconds, and I said yes." Later she questioned her quick response, wondering if she should have asked for permission, but she didn't know who to ask. "Nobody had anything to do with women's tennis," Rushing said.[10]

Since Goldschmeding didn't have access to a vehicle, the school didn't offer transportation, and no planes or trains connected Belton to San Antonio, she took a passenger bus to the tournament. In order to arrive in time for Friday morning matches, she had to start the 150-mile bus trip early Thursday morning. Further complicating her plans were strict campus regulations prohibiting female students from leaving campus before 7 a.m. To avoid alerting the house mother, she instructed her taxi driver to come up the circular driveway to Susanna Hall at 6:45 a.m. but refrain from blowing his horn. Fortunately, the driver complied, the outside door wasn't alarmed, and she arrived at the bus station on time. Once on the road, however, she was shocked to discover that the driver didn't use the main highway and made frequent stops to pick up and discharge passengers. The passengers arrived at their destination eight hours later—a bus depot located at the Belton Dairy Queen.

Despite the all-day adventure, the trip was a success, with Goldschmeding finishing second in singles and qualifying for a tournament in Amarillo. Because of her bus experience, she decided not to participate.[11]

After a year-long gap, another opportunity arose when Rushing was approached by former Baylor colleague Olga Fallen at an association meeting. Fallen told Rushing that the Texas group was organizing into regions and would sponsor a state tennis tournament the following spring. Knowing the reputation of the Trinity men's program, she expected that Trinity had good female players and told Rushing, "You *will* bring a team."[12]

It seems few people ignored this larger-than-life personality, so Rushing returned to campus to seek out players to fulfill Fallen's request. She recruited intramural doubles champions Betty King and Judy Arndt as well as physical education majors Dorothy Dowling and Barbara Knoll. After King and Arndt finished second in doubles at that first regional competition, they thought they had lost their chance to advance to state, but a phone call a few days later changed their fate. Fallen told Rushing the winning team was unable to attend and asked if the Trinity duo could go in their place. Since one of them had a car, the Chi Beta sisters accepted. They made the 700-mile round trip to Odessa and returned with "one-and-a-half-foot blue and silver trophies" for winning the 1966 state doubles title.[13]

The next spring, the *Trinitonian* reported: "Something new is happening this afternoon in the Trinity sports world. For the first time [*sic*] under organized play, a women's varsity tennis team has taken to the courts." It seems Rushing had found enough interested women to build a team around talented senior Mary McLean. While the 1967 squad wasn't the first and still had no coach or budget, it did enter a few tournaments and come closer to resembling an official team, including a group picture in the March 17 *Trinitonian*.[14]

Because Trinity still prohibited women from using the campus courts, Rushing hosted a home match on the McFarlin courts at the city's San Pedro Park. Dubbed "tennis debutants" by the *Trinitonian*, the players won their first matches against San Antonio College and Southwest Texas. Leading the Tigers were McLean, Goldschmeding, Ginger Parker, and Betty Meadows in singles; and Melissa Parsons, Barbara Knoll, Sara Smith, and Alleice Toldan in doubles. At the district tournament, McLean won the singles title while Parker and Parsons finished second in doubles. Although all three earned spots in the state tournament, McLean attended the event by herself.[15]

Thanks to Rushing's initiative, the nascent program finally began to draw some attention on campus. For the first time, the Trinity University *Course of Study Bulletin* included women's tennis in the list of recognized student organizations in 1967–68, describing the team as "providing outstanding women tennis players an opportunity to compete in intercollegiate competition."[16] Unfortunately, terms like "organized play," "intercollegiate," and "varsity tennis" didn't translate into official status or funds. Trinity's female players could be better described as Rushing's Recruits. As the program slowly grew, Rushing's duties expanded—she handled all the administrative tasks of scheduling practices and tournaments—but the women still did not have an official coach, and their budget was limited to whatever Rushing could wrangle from student activity fees and departmental funds. Her requests for support were often greeted with derision—or even laughter—from the men in charge.

Spotlight on Mary McLean

Although she played youth tennis in Fort Worth and attended summer camps hosted by Coach Mabry, Mary McLean's primary reason for attending Trinity wasn't its sports offerings. She studied physical education, became a cheerleader, worked on Jim Potter's intramural staff, joined the Chi Beta sorority, and was named Winter Lancerette her senior year. Tennis was not among her activities until Rushing recruited her to the ad hoc team. "She created that experience for us because we didn't even know about it," McLean remembers.

After graduating in 1967, McLean was instrumental in the first of many intergenerational handoffs between Trinity women's sports standouts over the next few decades. In one of her first jobs, she established a tennis team at local Roosevelt High School, where she mentored future Trinity multi-sports star and Title IX pioneer Glada Munt.

McLean's short-lived education career ended in Corpus Christi, Texas, and she competed briefly on the professional tennis tour, where she won about $200. "I wasn't that good," she recalls. "But I enjoyed playing." She met her husband, Ralph Wilson, at a New York tennis club, and from there the couple's influence on tennis and sports overall extended far and wide. Their efforts included starting a tennis league in Austria for older players and hosting an annual sports day for underserved girls in and around Buffalo, New York. McLean continues to play in senior leagues and is restoring the 1967 blue and white Camaro convertible she bought with one of her first paychecks.

Mary McLean, c. 1967.

Though no tournaments were held on Trinity campus, Rushing was the director for the few events held in San Antonio, where she often encountered a lack of coordination between association leaders and coaches. One terse exchange captured her irritation in working with a group that functioned with part-time leadership and inadequate funding. Rushing began her letter: "I would like to nominate this organization to receive the disorganization award for the year.... I would like to suggest that you take a year off from your teaching duties and try to straighten things out." A handwritten reply from association director Kitty Magee included an apology to Rushing and a request that she host the state tennis tournament the following year. She complied.[17]

Rushing had to improvise to keep the tournament functioning smoothly, including stretching scant departmental budgets to meet players' needs. In another letter to Magee, Rushing described her frustration with the conditions she faced as host and ended with a modest proposal:

> Although each school is supposed to furnish balls for its own participants, I have furnished three dozen each year the past two years. Some schools bring the wrong balls—some don't bring enough. I prefer that each school furnish six balls or money be provided for the hosting school to buy all the balls. I had one sponsor who insisted that her player have more rest between matches. This girl played three matches on Saturday. On Friday, two teams and two singles played five matches without complaints. It means that some people don't understand that once you go into the loser's bracket you must play more matches, and a time schedule must be met. Perhaps the answer might be to send the players and leave the sponsors at home.[18]

Two Future Champions Arrive

The focus of John Corbitt's September 1967 "Behind the Scorecard" column was transfer students Emilie Burrer and Becky Vest. The *Trinitonian* sports editor introduced the two tennis players as "complete with the kind of talent Coach Clarence Mabry likes to work with." (It was an odd statement, considering Mabry only officially supported Trinity's male players.) The local media was equally impressed, and headlines about Trinity's women athletes began to follow. Sports editor Karl O'Quinn, of the *Express-News*, who had chronicled Burrer's youth

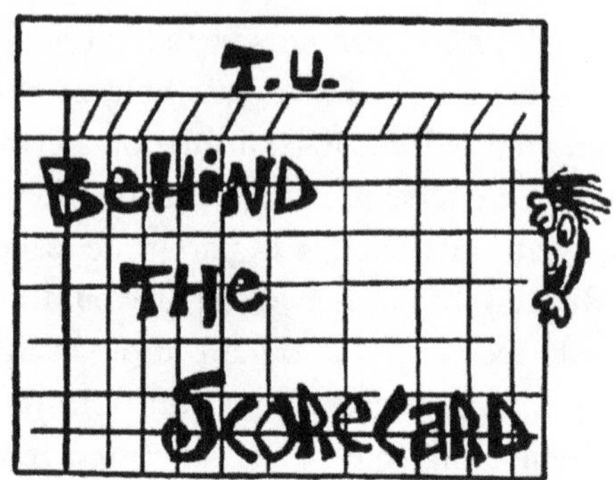

A column head from 1967.

sports accomplishments, applauded her return to San Antonio. Referring to Vest as "another newly enrolled Tiger kitten," he predicted the two would be among the favorites to win that year's intercollegiate championships.[19]

Vest, whose parents were tennis professionals in Mississippi, had been playing since age eight. In 1966, her many regional victories earned her a number-one ranking in the South, and she accepted a tennis scholarship to Odessa Junior College, where she played one year.[20]

Burrer and Vest met while attending tryouts on the Skyline campus for a US Junior Wightman Cup team captained by Trinity graduate Marilyn Montgomery. During their visit, they met other influential coaches and sponsors who would impact their Trinity futures, including men's coach Clarence Mabry and local tennis supporter John McFarlin.

Like their predecessors, both women were attracted to Trinity by the reputation of Mabry's program. Vest, who transferred with financial assistance from McFarlin, said, "I knew it would be good for my tennis to come here." Burrer recalled Mabry's influence on her own decision to finish her studies at Trinity. After meeting him during a summer tour, she said his tip on cross-court service returns greatly improved her game. "It takes someone who knows what he's doing to find the little things. Anyone can find the big faults," the future coach said.

Another influence for Burrer might have been an earlier encounter with Rushing, who gave the LCC student a ride home from a tournament in Waco. Rushing was not aware of Burrer's tennis reputation but said "by the time we got back to San Antonio, I knew she would be a good student at Trinity."[21]

In fact, at Trinity, Rushing became Burrer's faculty advisor and dance instructor. The junior told a *Trinitonian* reporter she would focus her last two years on physical education. "I'd like to teach P.E.... if I can get through Modern Dance," she said.[22] She lived up to Rushing's academic expectations, passed the dance class, and ensured that tennis didn't impede her education. One summer, Burrer was traveling on an amateur tennis circuit and sent a letter to Rushing with an unusual request: send anatomy books. "The people on the tour here all read cheap novels," Burrer wrote, "and I really need some books that are interesting."[23]

Few players remained from the unofficial team Rushing had sponsored the previous year, leaving the two transfers with scant support. Despite the lack of uniforms, shoes, or tennis balls, Burrer said, "All I wanted to do was play tennis. And I was going to do it regardless. It didn't matter to me if the university funded us or not."

The help that Burrer and Vest hoped to receive from Mabry never materialized. The men's coach had invited them to work out with his team on the varsity courts, but one afternoon he met them at the gate and politely asked them not to come back. Mabry didn't cite a reason, but some suspect that Vest and Burrer were beating some of his male players in challenge matches. Since the varsity courts were the only ones on campus and the McFarlin tennis complex was being renovated, the women had to improvise. Vest continued to hit with the men after practice, but she rarely got to volley with her teammate. Burrer's daily commute from home, heavy classroom load, and work obligations forced her to squeeze in half an hour of practice time in a Sams Center racquetball court during her lunch break.[24] Again, credit goes to Rushing. "Fortunately, [she] was there to put the pieces together so that we had some matches and tournaments in which to participate," Burrer said. "But for the most part, we were on our own."[25]

Undeterred by the circumstances, Burrer and Vest lived up to their billing by winning the team crown at the May 1968 USLTA Collegiate Women's tournament and garnering the school's first championship headlines. This was the first year a team championship was awarded since the USLTA began hosting women's tournaments in 1958, with the title determined by points players earned in the singles and doubles competitions.[26]

In what must have felt like sweet revenge, Burrer won the singles

Emilie Burrer and Becky Vest, c. 1968

championship and partnered with Vest to capture the doubles title against players from the school that had rejected her two years earlier. In a close match with an Arizona State University player, Burrer won in split sets after fighting off three match points in the final frame. The doubles win was a less stressful straight-set victory over an Arizona State duo.[27] Records from the tournament list Rushing as the team coach, since the terms *sponsor* and *coach* were used interchangeably in those early days.

Winning a national title, however, failed to generate excitement on the Trinity campus. The same day the women captured the titles at Carleton College in Northfield, Minnesota, Trinity was hosting the NCAA men's tennis championships on the newly constructed lower courts. It wasn't until a public address announcement was made about the Burrer-Vest title that many campus residents even knew Trinity had women's tennis players, much less that they were representing the school at the national level. Yearbook coverage was equally inadequate; the 1968 *Mirage* included a brief and inaccurate reference that read, "The unofficial women's team of Emilie Burrer and Becky Vest captured the women's singles and doubles titles and team championship in the Ladies NCAA [*sic*]." The NCAA wouldn't sponsor any women's championships for

EXPRESS-NEWS

Sports

Saturday, Jan. 18, 1969 ★★ Page 1-D

KARL O'QUINN'S

Morning Line

A Unique Problem

An O'Quinn newspaper column, 1969.

another thirteen years, but writers were correct about the team being unofficial.[28]

The local press paid attention. The lead sentence in a *San Antonio Light* recap read, "San Antonian Emilie Burrer gave Trinity University what its men could not—national tennis titles."[29] Under the headline "A Unique Problem" *Express-News* sports editor O'Quinn later suggested, "The Trinity people have a problem." After describing Burrer's and Vest's accomplishments, he wrote, "What's the problem? Well, you see, Trinity doesn't have a girls' tennis team."

According to O'Quinn, Clarence Mabry didn't know the women were playing in the national tournament until the first day's results appeared in the newspapers. "I did know they were going," the men's coach insisted, "but I forgot exactly when the tournament was being held." O'Quinn said other Trinity administrators he contacted showed even less awareness of the women's achievements: "None of them even knew the girls were to play in the tournament. The announcement made over the public-address system, between matches of the men's NCAA tournament on the Trinity courts, that the girls had given the University in the Sun its first national net title came as somewhat of a surprise, to put it mildly."

O'Quinn concluded with an accurate description of the school's meager support for women's tennis and a dose of sarcasm:

> Now that Trinity has this national championship girls' team—plus a couple of other players of state and regional prominence—what is it going to do with them?... High-quality tennis players need high-quality opposition to practice with, and the boy's team is off limits to them for practice purposes.... Trinity loves them for the national prominence they've brought the school—as long as they don't want to practice with the boys or play other schools' girls.[30]

As the 1969 season approached, women's tennis was gaining in popularity and colleges were recruiting top players and providing more robust regular season competition. Trinity, however, continued to rely almost exclusively on Burrer and Vest to defend the title while still in their unofficial roles. A *Trinitonian* reporter said the pair was aiming for another crown but added, "A great deal of self-discipline is required since the Trinity women's team does not play a regular schedule."

Burrer feared a repeat team title would be difficult since schools were now entering four players, making the competition for total points even more challenging. Rushing also understood the need for extra players, but her still skimpy budget wasn't enough to cover the additional travel expenses. When reminded that her own department didn't provide funds for women's athletics, Rushing approached Trinity business manager Derwood Hawthorne, who found the money. With Hawthorne's help, sophomores Debby Darby and Susie Shulte joined their teammates at the 1969 USLTA championships, held again at Carleton College. Burrer defended her singles title by again vanquishing an Arizona State player, this time in straight sets (6–2, 6–4). In the doubles final, rain forced Burrer and Vest to face their UCLA opponents indoors on a hardwood floor, where they captured their second doubles crown with a 6–3, 6–2 victory.[31] The addition of points earned by Darby and Shulte proved to be the deciding factor, giving the Tigers a one-point edge over Arizona State for its second team championship. Burrer remains one of only two women in Trinity history to win four individual national titles.[32]

This time Burrer was the subject of positive headlines in both campus and local publications. A summer *Trinitonian* story reported on the team's second title: "[S]hining accounts were entered into Tiger tennis history this summer as Trinity graduate Emilie Burrer racked up opponents, points and trophies."[33] A *San Antonio Light* columnist praised hometown hero Burrer, writing, "[P]erhaps the most satisfying reward is the realization that the neighborhood in which you grew up thinks you're great and isn't a bit surprised at your success."[34]

By the time Burrer graduated in 1969, her titles with Vest had elevated Trinity's women's program to national prominence and helped launch her own professional playing and collegiate coaching careers. Burrer moved into an interim coaching position at Arizona State, which now seemed willing to accept her credentials. She led the female Sun Devils to the 1970 national championship title, the same crown denied the school by Trinity the previous two years. After one year, she moved to Lubbock to marry Rudy Foster and established a tennis team at Texas Tech University. She returned to Trinity in 1978 to join former advisor Shirley Rushing on the physical education staff and head the women's Division I program. She also competed briefly in the professional ranks and played in 1974 for the Houston E-Z Riders (coached by Clarence Mabry) in the first year of the new World Team Tennis league.

Vest left Trinity after the second USLTA title, playing in the US Open in 1970 and the French Open and Wimbledon in 1971. She joined the new Virginia Slims professional tour and won a 1972 tournament in Mexico. She continued to play and coach the rest of her career and also worked on projects that introduced special needs children to the game. She was inducted into the Mississippi Sports Hall of Fame in 1998, where she was later joined by her mother, in 1979, and her sister, in 2002. Vest continues to teach at a club in Mandeville, Louisiana.[35]

Burrer also left an impression on lower-ranked teammates who weren't skilled enough to play at the elite level. Betty Meadows (1970) recalled the program's disorganized nature in her time at Trinity, but she was grateful that Rushing found them area tournaments to compete in. A self-proclaimed "mediocre" player from San Antonio, the education major still gleaned many life lessons from her playing days, including how to win well, how to lose well, and how to compete. Playing in the shadow of future champions, she accepted that she would never be a number one seed. "We're not all going to be Emilie Burrer, and that's fine," she said. "But I can learn from them. And to be around an Emilie, who was so gracious with her time and her technique, showed me how to be a gracious number one in anything." Ten years after her 1970 graduation, Meadows entered the Presbyterian seminary in Austin and retired in 2018 after pastoring in several churches and serving as an executive with the denomination's national organization.[36]

Another impression left by the duo was their unusually bold vision to play at the highest level of competition. Historians would consider Burrer and Vest to be role models for a more modern philosophy that rejected the prevailing image of women as weak, fragile, and incapable of coping with stress. Jan Felshin chronicled this emerging feminist construct of the 1960s, suggesting that it encouraged women to be more assertive about developing skills and engaging in competitive athletics, and it also built self-esteem.[37]

On the larger stage, women's tennis was moving away from all-amateur (nonpaid) status, thanks in part to the efforts of Karen Hantze Susman's former doubles partner. Billie Jean King joined other activists in luring sponsors and establishing a professional circuit for women. The first tournament on the Virginia Slims Circuit was held in September 1970 at the Houston Racquet Club. Just a few years later, King founded the Women's Tennis Association as the first international governing body to oversee the profession.[38]

With her two titlists gone, Rushing entered the new decade continuing to shoulder responsibility as team sponsor for competition in the nascent TCIAW. New arrivals, like Sarah Scott from Arkansas, came to Trinity to win a tennis championship after hearing the Burrer-Vest stories from school recruiters. But like their predecessors, they were surprised to discover the female players had no coach and Mabry was inaccessible to them. According to Scott, if it weren't for Rushing taking them "under her wing," the players would have had no access to courts, organized practices, balls, or tournaments.[39] In that 1969–70 season, senior Debbie Darby played with Scott, Nancy Spencer, Mary Dunn, and JoAnn Board, and they finished fifteenth in the USLTA national championships in Las Cruces, New Mexico.[40]

Resentment over lack of support began to build, perhaps sparked by uneven media coverage. After the players won an away match, they saw headlines about their accomplishments in other newspapers but came home to little local recognition. One fall day in 1971, Scott and Spencer

Sarah Scott

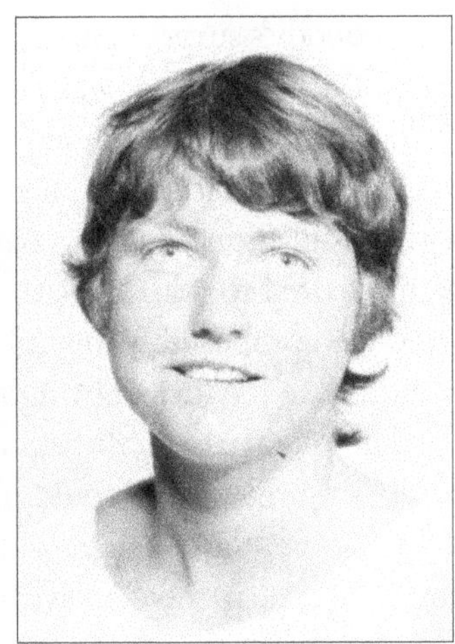
Nancy Spencer

vented their frustrations to Rushing, saying they deserved more, including recognition as an official team with a coach and budget. Scott remembers telling their sponsor, "We're not doing this again."[41]

While Rushing was sympathetic, she advised the players to take their issues to the athletic council, which was composed of faculty and administrators who had oversight of all university athletics. Rushing said she would set up the appointment but that Scott and Spencer would have to make their case before the group. "You have a better case than I do, because Trinity is paying me and you are paying Trinity," she remembers telling them.[42]

With their sponsor in attendance, the women presented their argument, articulating the situation and proposing the remedy. Council members asked Mabry, who was also in the room, if he was ever asked about women's tennis at Trinity in his travels. He responded, "Yes, all the time," adding that he told people that he thought the women had a tennis club.[43]

The meeting was a success. "We left with official recognition and a budget," Rushing said, calling it a "red-letter day." The council agreed to confer official status to women's tennis, with the stipulation that physical education faculty members be appointed to oversee all women's athletic teams and accompany them on road trips. Under this directive, department chair Jess MacLeay offered Rushing the choice of volleyball or tennis. To nobody's surprise, Rushing opted for tennis. She still has fond memories of that day. "That was one of the biggest things that happened when I was involved with women's athletics. Sarah and Nancy deserved a lot of credit," she said, downplaying her own contribution.

But they still didn't have a coach. After the meeting, Rushing recalls being invited to a lunch with a Trinity administrator and a tennis supporter, who proposed hiring a local tennis pro to coach the women. Mabry didn't like the idea of bringing in an outsider, so he appointed his assistant John Newman to the job in spring 1972, promising the women that their part-time coach would meet with them after the men's practice. While some players regretted not having the full-time attention of a coach that also traveled with them, they appreciated Newman's teaching efforts.[44]

Even with a designated coach, Rushing wasn't relieved of her sponsor duties. "I was doing everything I was doing before," she said. She continued to perform the tasks usually assigned to a full-time coach, such as scheduling home and away matches, registering the team for tournaments, hosting tournaments on the Trinity campus, driving players to road matches, making reservations for overnight trips, keeping records, and submitting reimbursements related to food, entry fees, gas (at six cents a mile), and other expenses. Since Newman didn't usually accompany the team to road contests, Rushing also often made the critical ranking assignments that determined which Trinity player would be across the net from the opponent's seeded players. She was never given compensation time from her teaching load or extra salary for these duties.[45]

The now official team fared well the next two years but failed to reclaim a national title. In the 1971 season, Spencer and Scott represented Trinity in the TCIAW district finals and returned to that year's USLTA national tournament in Las Cruces. Although they struggled in the high altitude and failed to advance to the championship round, they have fond memories of driving to New Mexico in Spencer's 1964 Plymouth Fury with a push-button transmission.[46]

After graduation, Scott applied the motor lab skills she learned under physical education instructor Bob Strauss to design youth sports training programs and later founded a sustainable children's clothing company, Cotton Tots. Spencer continued to play on tour before earning a doctorate in kinesiology and returning to her home state of Ohio as a professor at Bowling Green State University.

With Newman scheduling formal instruction, the 1971–72 team improved, posting an undefeated record in the regular season. Susan Mapes and Nancee Weigel won the district doubles crown on the Trinity courts, and Jana Hooton was runner-up in singles. Weigel, Mapes, Hooton, and Dru Duggins—all freshmen—represented Trinity at the 1972 USLTA nationals in Auburn, Alabama, where Weigel and Mapes won consolation doubles, and the team surprised their skeptics with a tie for fifth in the nation. Other team members included Scott, Karen Brumbaugh, Donna Letteri, Glada Munt, Brenda Richards, Bonny Sandy, and Pam Steinmetz.[47]

Although the new AIAW didn't yet allow scholarships or recruiting for female athletes, Trinity's tennis program continued to attract talented prospects with its national reputation and mild climate that allowed players to practice and play throughout the year.[48]

Finally, in 1972 Mabry's men captured their first NCAA team title after finishing second the previous two seasons. It seemed both the men's and women's tennis programs were on the verge of national dominance as they entered the 1972–73 season.[49]

The Miracle of 1973

According to Rushing, "the world turned upside down" in fall 1972. Mary Hamm, one of her new advisees, appeared one day in the tennis sponsor's office and talked casually about hitting balls with her freshman roommate, Donna. Rushing later learned that Hamm was a highly regarded player from Mount Pulaski, Illinois, and her practice partner was Donna Stockton of Port Washington, New York. Also, Val Franta, an Ohio transplant, had enrolled at Trinity that fall. In January 1972 the trio was joined by standout JoAnne Russell from Naples, Florida. This freshman foursome quickly claimed the top seeds on Newman's team and altered the trajectory of women's tennis at Trinity for years to come.

Since none was actively recruited, the reasons behind this alignment of tennis stars were varied. Stockton followed in the footsteps of older brother Dick, a Trinity All-American and 1972 NCAA singles champion. Hamm learned about the school from her junior coach Cliff Buchholz, another former Tiger tennis All-American. Russell transferred to the warm Texas climate after one cold semester at Mary Baldwin College in Virginia. And Franta had been lured to San Antonio by an "outrageous suggestion" from Nancy Spencer, who knew Franta from youth competitions in Ohio. The summer after her own 1971 Trinity graduation, Spencer traveled to tournaments with Franta and convinced the younger player to move south to finish high school and enroll at Trinity, which the young lefty did.[50]

Imagine coach Newman's delight to find his four walk-on freshmen were accomplished junior players, each with a regional or national ranking.[51] So equal was the talent that Newman and Rushing were rotating the number one singles player each match. Returning players like Susan Mapes, Glada Munt, and Pam and Jana Steinmetz continued to play but mostly in doubles competition.[52]

Russell recalls that the team's first intercollegiate match at Schreiner College featured a memorable finale "under the lights." Darkness was falling in Kerrville while she and doubles partner Hamm played the last match of the day, and organizers came up with a plan for the unilluminated courts. "All the cars were parked around the court so everyone could turn on their lights so we could finish the match," Russell said, remembering that the light was good until someone hit a lob. "It was pretty tough playing a shot when the ball came back down out of the darkness." She felt she and Hamm won the match because they had better night vision than their opponents.[53]

That Schreiner match was one of very few Rushing was able to schedule, and most of the action that first semester was against fellow players in practice. An unexpected invitation to a Dallas tournament helped them break out of the rut—and open their sponsor's eyes. After driving them to Dallas and observing them for first time, Rushing realized the program had reached a new level.

Early the next semester, the women were invited to a tournament in Arizona. Since it included top-ranked teams, Rushing knew the event could provide critical experience and help her players get more appropriate seeding for nationals that summer, but she again had to scramble for funding. Knowing that the sparse travel funds had already been earmarked for the national championships and that she wouldn't get help from her own department, she approached the men's athletic director. Although he refused the request, he gave Rushing permission to approach Trinity's business manager but suggested it wouldn't make a difference. Undeterred, the sponsor made her now familiar trek to Derwood Hawthorne's office with a creative budget approach. He agreed, and the women participated in both tournaments.[54]

The foursome put the money to good use at the February event, capturing the team title in both divisions against nationally ranked teams.[55] After that tournament, the team compiled an 11–0 record in dual matches, including two victories over UT Austin.[56]

San Antonio Light reporter Johnny Janes soon jumped on the enthusiasm bandwagon, writing an April feature, "Another Title in the Works?" in which he predicted the Trinity women could reclaim a national crown. Janes felt the only difference between the school's two programs was that men received athletic scholarships. In a question that was answered by the AIAW that summer, he asked, "How's about that, you female libbers?" Newman told Janes that, although the school couldn't offer scholarships to the women, they could offer "excellent facilities," "good weather," and "good coaching that will help the girls to improve their games." While the coach thought his women had a good chance to win, he refrained from forecasting an outright victory but added a prescient prediction: "If they win this year, then Trinity is going to dominate women's collegiate tennis for a long time, because this group is so young."[57]

The national championships, cohosted by the USLTA and AIAW and featuring forty-seven teams in Auburn, Alabama, provided the backdrop for what Rushing refers to as the "miracle of 1973." With Newman staying in San Antonio, she accompanied the team and watched them suffer difficult losses early in the week-long, double-elimination tournament. On Wednesday, after she witnessed Russell's return of service sail out of bounds on the ninth tie-break point against her Southern Methodist University opponent, she thought they were out of it.[58] The disappointed sponsor returned to the hotel, convinced the team had been mathematically eliminated. Then Stockton and Franta came into her room and laid out a scenario—albeit unlikely—of how they had a chance to claim the team title. In their estimation, seven matches had to go their way; five were in Trinity's control and the other two required losses by UCLA to other teams.

The players' predication came to pass. After trailing the UCLA squad

1973 USLTA national champions *(left to right)* Val Franta, JoAnne Russell, sponsor Shirley Rushing, Donna Stockton, and Mary Hamm

by four points that evening, the Trinity women rallied the next two days, with Stockton and Hamm winning critical semifinal matches to seal the team championship on Friday. "That was by far the most exciting and nail-biting day I've ever spent with Trinity tennis," Rushing said.[59] In what the local newspaper pegged as "an unbelievable comeback," the Tigers were victors in their five remaining matches—three of them in dramatic split-set style—and UCLA dropped both its contests.[60] A student reporter used another analogy to sum up the "comeback of the season." In the *Trinitonian* article reporting the event, sportswriter Kevin O'Keeffe wrote, "The girls were so strong in their effort that if they had been with Custer, he probably would have won the Little Big Horn Deal."[61]

This championship also gave Trinity the distinction of being the first school to win three women's national intercollegiate team titles at that time (1968, 1969, and 1973), and the first to field men's and women's champions in consecutive years.[62] But it also signaled the pivot to an entirely different path for a women's team at Trinity.

A common topic of conversation that season was Title IX, which had passed the previous summer. Players and coaches wondered aloud whether women were going to get scholarships and—if so—when? Many thought the legislation would be implemented gradually, especially in light of the pushback from men's athletic departments. But the issue was resolved much more quickly than expected when the AIAW reversed its original position and approved athletic scholarships for women in the summer of 1973. This decision addressed the Title IX requirement that men and women participating in the same sport must have equal benefits. For Trinity, where men's tennis was the only athletic scholarship sport, this meant that the women tennis players were now eligible.[63] Rushing, fully aware of the scholarship debate and recent AIAW decision, returned to San Antonio—national trophy in hand—and immediately set up an appointment with President Duncan Wimpress.

In the meeting, she told Wimpress the four new national champions had chosen to come to Trinity on their own and were paying their own tuition and room and board. While updating the president about the AIAW decision, she explained that Title IX compliance would be easier for Trinity, since—thanks to the board's 1971 decision—the school offered only eight scholarships in one men's sport (tennis). Most other schools were having to match scholarship funds for up to ten programs. Rushing also reminded the president that the rule meant that Hamm, Russell, Stockton, and Franta would be matched up against scholarship players the next season, suggesting that the right thing to do was to award them full athletic scholarships. After confirming with Hawthorne that Trinity had the funds, Wimpress gave Rushing permission to call the four players and their parents to tell them they would be on full athletic scholarships for the remaining three years. Rushing had one more request: would Trinity refund the deposits that they had already paid for the fall semester? Wimpress's answer was yes.[64]

Around the same time the Tigers were wrapping up their national title, the founding of the World Tennis Association by Billie Jean King meant their prospects beyond college would be brighter. The game kept gaining in popularity, according to a *Trinitonian* writer who reported that the "tennis bug, currently ravaging the exercise-starved American public," was going viral.[65]

Newman led the female Tigers to an injury-plagued second-place finish in the 1974 tournament behind perennial contender Arizona State

University before claiming Trinity's fourth USTA national championship in 1975.[66] Not only did his women's teams win two titles in four years, but they also notched a perfect 29–0 dual match record. Newman left in 1975 to become a tennis pro in Phoenix, Arizona, but returned to college coaching and ended his long career near his former campus, overseeing the University of the Incarnate Word scholarship program for twenty-three years.[67]

With Newman moving on, Marilyn Montgomery Rindfuss was hired as the team's first full-time coach. The 1957 graduate was one of Trinity's first players on the WRA teams and was considered a pioneer on the women's circuit. She retired her racquet in 1964 to earn a master's degree at Louisiana State University and returned home to teach mathematics at San Antonio College. She stayed involved in the game as captain of the US Junior Wightman Cup team between 1961 and 1968, where she mentored a college-aged Emilie Burrer.[68]

The hiring gave Rushing a break after a decade of almost single-handedly propping up the program; she could return to her "day job" as a physical education instructor and advisor. Rindfuss led her team, featuring scholarship recruits Stephanie Tolleson and Sandy Stap, to another USTA championship in 1976.[69] After that title, Rindfuss stayed only two more years before returning to teaching mathematics. She was inducted into the Texas Tennis Hall of Fame in 1991, continued a teaching and consulting career, and died of cancer in 2006.[70]

As a postscript to this era, all championship teams (1968, 1969, 1973, 1975, and 1976) were inducted into the Athletics Hall of Fame. Missing from the 2005 ceremony was left-hander Val Franta, who died at age thirty of an undiagnosed heart condition.[71]

Former four-time champion Emilie Burrer Foster took over to lead the Division I women to perennially high rankings in the next twelve years. Her 1978 appointment was welcomed by Bill O'Bryant in his *San Antonio Light* tennis column: "Trinity is lucky to have her on their staff and the tennis community will profit by her presence. And let it be known, sports fans, comments of this nature, coming from me, are few and far between." O'Bryant, who was the head pro at the McFarlin Tennis Center, ended his column with, "Best of luck, Tigerettes."[72]

Since 1970, Foster had been transforming the Texas Tech tennis program from a club sport with no budget to the third-ranked women's

Coach Emilie Burrer Foster.

team in the state.[73] Despite her success in Lubbock, she was pleased with the opportunity to return to San Antonio and its calmer climate. "We would watch New Mexico drift by during practice," she joked of the perpetually dusty and windy days in West Texas.[74] Foster brought the same combination of passion and discipline she displayed as a student and player to her coaching position. While she credited physical education department chair Jess MacLeay for nudging her into teaching instead of research, her long career eventually included both roles.[75]

The new Trinity coach became famous for her motivational office plaques, such as "No Guts, No Green Stamps," as well as pithy quotes, including: "We have an obligation at Trinity to prepare people for the field, whether it is in English, economics, or tennis. When they are prepared, we put on their little boots, pat them on the back, wish them good luck and kick them out of the nest."[76]

Foster amassed an impressive Trinity resume: a record of 259–94, two second-place and three third-place finishes at the NCAA Division I championships, 1983 Division I Coach of the Year, and USTA Education Merit Award. She and the team were also frequently recognized for their involvement in the community.

Foster's decision to take a leave of absence from Trinity in 1990 was driven by the school's shift away from scholarship tennis. As competition from large universities intensified, Trinity's Division I teams had trouble keeping up, and it became clear that President Ron Calgaard's support for the pay-for-play approach was waning. The Tennis Tech era ended in October 1990 when the board of trustees voted to move both teams into Division III.[77]

In her post-coaching career, Foster earned an international reputation for consulting work in analyzing sports movement. She was inducted into the Women's College Tennis Hall of Fame in 2000 and elected the following year to Trinity's Athletics Hall of Fame. Foster's nomination complimented her as an exemplary role model for the women whose lives she touched as a player and coach. Fiercely competitive as a player, she transformed that energy into coaching, not solely to win games but to teach skills, mold character, and promote teamwork over individual performance.[78]

In more personal terms, former All-American Louise Allen had a different tribute for her coach: "We are important to her as individuals, not just talent to be manipulated."[79]

In 2020, Foster retired from her thirty-year biomechanics consulting career to return to Trinity once again, this time as a volunteer assistant to former player and then head coach Gretchen Rush Magers.[80]

During Trinity's tennis heyday, many talented female athletes enrolled with the vision of cracking into the Tiger varsity squad. Those who didn't make the cut often experimented with—and excelled in—the other sports offered to aspiring athletes of the 1970s. Pam Steinmetz, a sophomore transfer from Saint Louis, said she arrived in 1971 as a competitive tennis player hoping to make the team and graduated three years later as a four-sport varsity athlete. While she played varsity tennis that first year, she said, "I found my true happy place in Trinity team sports."[81]

THREE DECADES

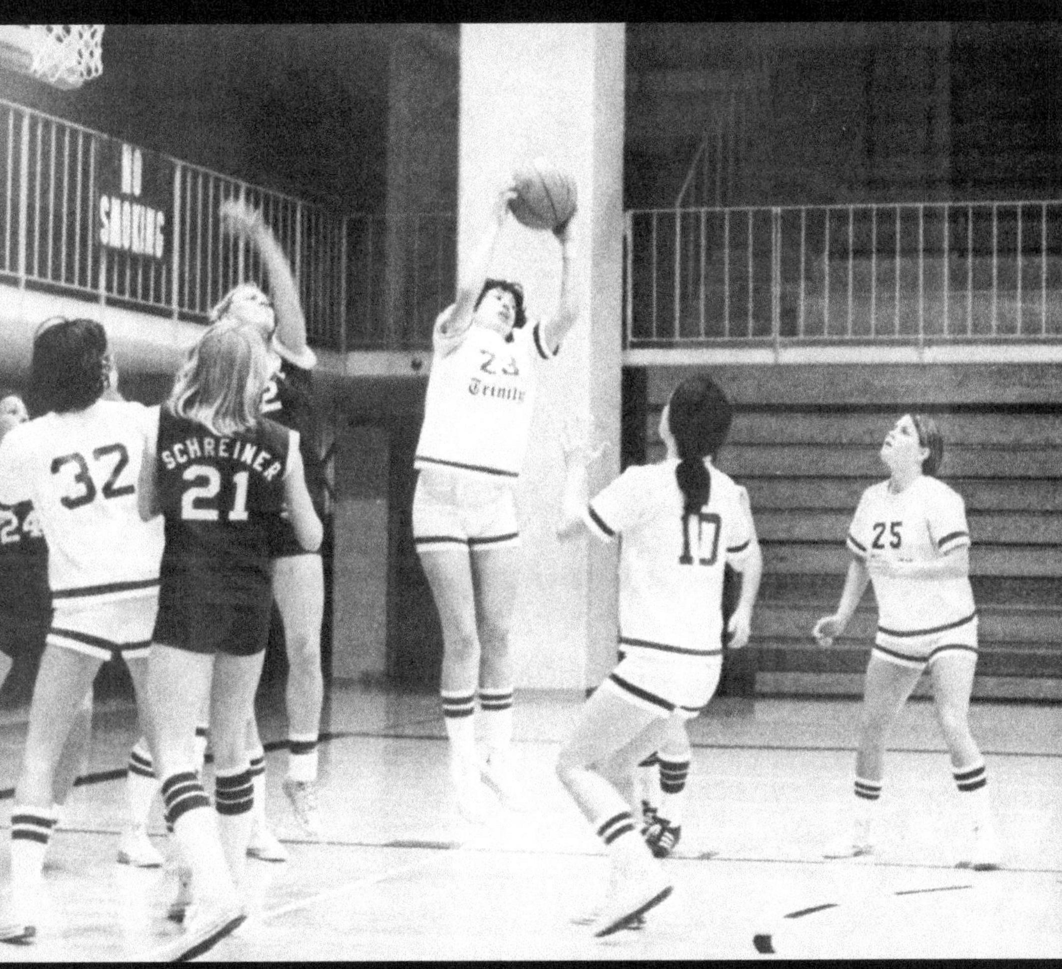

OF PROMISE AND PROGRESS

Marchers at the Women's Strike for Equality in New York City, August 26, 1970

CHAPTER 6

Building a Bridge to Equality

1970–72

> For the most part, prior to Title IX and the women's movement of the 1970s, society dictated, and women accepted their roles as caretakers, sex objects, and/or decorative objects.
>
> —DONNA LOPIANO[1]

In the brief span between Trinity's 1969 centennial celebration and the momentous 1972 passage of Title IX, an avalanche of cultural and legislative change cleared a path for American women in education, athletics, and the workforce. The expanding call for women's rights engaged Americans of all genders, whether in political, media, academic, or private spaces. But the activists in this second wave of feminism had to share the stage with other social movements, including protests for civil rights and against US involvement in the Vietnam War.

The 1970 Kent State shootings characterized the turbulence of the era at many colleges, but Trinity seemed to be an exception. In fact, campus residents in the early 1970s seemed less concerned about a foreign war than a controversial scholarship decision at home.[2] But for the university's female athletes, glimmers of hope appeared on the horizon. While two male physical education professors were propping up informal teams to compete with other schools, a young Libby Johnson migrated from West Texas to hone her teaching skills for a future in San Antonio.

Taking to the Streets and Arenas

On August 26, 1970, an estimated hundred thousand marchers in New York City participated in the Women's Strike for Equality, protesting inequality and war while celebrating the fiftieth anniversary of the constitutional amendment that codified voting rights for women. One writer described the participants: "In miniskirts and bell-bottoms and sheath dresses, flowered and paisley, they hooked arms and raised clenched fists and carried signs. They marched for equal rights and equal pay, for lesbian and gay rights, and for an end to the war in Vietnam."[3]

Supporters of this newly named women's liberation movement felt that the fundamental lack of equality—particularly in areas such as education—sabotaged the future for women who desired more choices for careers, parenting, sports, and other rights historically afforded to men. The dismissive news coverage, however, exemplified the male-dominated media perspective of the era. On the evening of the women's march, anchor Howard K. Smith opened his ABC news broadcast by repeating a remark attributed to then vice president Spiro Agnew: "Three things have been difficult to tame: the ocean, fools, and women. We may soon be able to tame the ocean, but fools and women will take a little longer."[4]

Why were women taking to the streets? They could point to many rights still denied females in the early 1970s, such as access to contraception, jury service, and the ability to make claims against sexual harassment. But this statement from women's sports trailblazer Donna Lopiano offers a succinct overview of women's social status at the time:

> Few remember that in 1972 boys were enrolled in wood shop and auto repair and girls in sewing and home economics. In colleges and universities there were admission quotas preventing women from accessing graduate professional school programs that led to the highest paying jobs such as in science, engineering, law, medicine and architecture. Women were relegated to the professional schools leading to "caretaking" professions with the lowest salaries: teacher, librarian, social worker, and nurse. There were few women in the front lines of the military, police, or fire departments. Women were secretaries, and men were managers. If a woman wanted a credit card, her husband, brother, or father had to sign the application, even if he was unemployed.[5]

Louise Raggio, an attorney who helped pass a Texas law that gave women the right to start a business or own property without their husband's permission, wrote that prior to the law, women in Texas had the same rights as "infants, idiots and felons."[6]

A US Department of Justice report acknowledged the educational gap of college degree holders in 1970 (8 percent of women versus 14 percent of men) and also raised the possibility of a different kind of discrimination: "Although men benefited from a majority of the opportunities offered, they were prevented from taking classes in fields stereotypically associated with women, such as home economics and nursing."[7] It appears few men were willing to take to the streets to protest this injustice.

The women's movement reignited the battle for the ERA, which had first been proposed in 1923 but hadn't gotten very far. In 1971, success seemed at hand when the amendment finally passed Congress and was sent to state legislatures for ratification. Although contentious statehouse debates slowed (and eventually stopped) the amendment's approval, the momentum from its passage sparked a raft of less sweeping but still effective legislation and court rulings that benefited women—including one called Title IX.[8]

Although Texas wasn't exactly regarded as a center of feminist activity, it wasn't immune to the fever of the moment. Little is recorded of women clogging San Antonio streets in 1970, but a local newspaper published a provocative preview of an upcoming women's conference in Houston: "The days when the Young Women's Christian Association was just a place to play volleyball or learn needlepoint are long gone.... When 2,500 delegates representing 7 million women attend the twenty-fifth national YWCA convention Monday, the subject will not be the old-fashioned sewing basket but the modern problem of women's rights." To the writer's point, some of the topics scheduled for discussion were relaxation of abortion laws, an enlightened approach to marijuana, and empowerment of African Americans and other minorities. Said YWCA president Helen J. Calytor, "This convention dare not do business as usual."[9]

The national demonstrations seemed to have little effect on Trinity's campus, which—like its host city—was geographically and culturally distant from the centers of social activism. This calmer approach was endorsed from the top; in his last public address before stepping down from nineteen years as university president, James Laurie urged the 1970 graduating class to seek social and political change through nonviolent means. Most heeded his call. Although one student government leader sardonically referred to Trinity as a "hotbed of political rest," there was a sprinkling of small rallies from 1970 to 1972. A few hundred students, faculty, and administrators held an informal candlelit memorial service after the Kent State shootings; students joined local citizens in challenging nearby freeway construction (soon to be US Highway 281); and Murchison residents gathered to oppose the conversion of their all-male residence hall into a coed dorm (succeeding, briefly).[10]

The national argument for women's rights extended to female athletes, who still had few opportunities to play official interscholastic or intercollegiate sports, much less national championships to strive for. Part of the problem was the unlevel playing field girls had to negotiate in their formative athletic years. Even in the few sports offered to girls and women, officials felt that their versions should be adjusted to protect the fragile participants. Popular sports like basketball were subjected to a variety of restrictions and regulations that further complicated the transition for many high school athletes entering the college game.

The notable exception to these modifications was the feminine sport of tennis, where Trinity had parlayed the national reputation of a successful men's program into attracting skilled female players. But they too participated without formal coaching, athletic scholarships, or a budget in this span.

For other female athletes at Trinity, competition was found mainly in the friendly arenas of intramural play, with little chance to increase their skills or compete against other schools. Although the extramural programs Jim Potter and Bob Strauss created in the mid-1960s attracted several women from the intramural ranks, they received little administrative support and found scarce prospects for local competition. Their meager budget was enough to pay for meals and gas to ferry the female players forty-five miles up Interstate 35 to play one away game at Southwest Texas State in San Marcos.[11]

As in the early years, volleyball team slots continued to be filled by intramural standouts. Players participated in mostly informal practices

The 1970–71 extramural volleyball team. Linda Sue King *(holding the ball)* and Rindy Lobdell *(top left)*; other players not identified

and played a limited schedule with other collegiate intramural all-star squads or city league teams. One welcome development was the introduction of city championships, as indicated by a local newspaper story that mentions Trinity hosting its second straight "San Antonio extramural volleyball championships" in 1970, with the Tigers finishing third out of six teams. Notably, that year's winner was St. Mary's University, which defeated Incarnate Word College for the title and was led by future Trinity coach Libby Johnson.[12]

Three members on the 1971 extramural volleyball roster—Pam Steinmetz, Nancee Weigel, and Glada Munt—also played on the varsity tennis squad and were recognized as intramural volleyball all-stars. Any potential conflict between the programs wasn't addressed until 1976, when female varsity athletes were finally prohibited from intramural participation in their specialty sport.[13]

In the 1971–72 academic year, Potter expressed high hopes for his extramural basketball team, as eighteen students tried out for the squad, including five veterans from the previous year's intramural all-star team:

Brenda Richards, Cheryl Hardin, Karen Brumbaugh, Rindy Lobdell, and Gina Swift.[14] In addition to finishing second in that season's city league, they played in invitational tournaments that featured competition against UT, Baylor University, and the University of Houston.[15] A note in a St. Mary's University student publication indicates that the Tigers defeated Johnson's Rattler team to win that year's city basketball crown.[16]

Simon-Pure Upends Tiger Athletics

As their female counterparts dipped their toes into extramural sports and debates about gender equity swirled around them, Trinity's male varsity athletes soon learned they weren't exempt from disruption. After decades of unfettered access to athletic scholarships, coaches, facilities, trainers, and budgets, their elite status was challenged in 1971.

A philosophical shift was prompted by the 1970 hiring of Duncan Wimpress, who replaced James Laurie to become Trinity's fifteenth president. Wimpress had served six years as president at Monmouth College, a Presbyterian institution in Illinois.[17] One of his first actions was opening the books to the university's finances, which surprised many people. "At that point the budget was not widely shared with anybody," recalls biology professor Robert Blystone.[18] This act of transparency exposed the disproportionate share athletics represented in the overall budget. Of the 7 percent slice, most sports-related expenses were earmarked for a hundred football scholarships. More troubling was the fact the athletic budget was running at a $414,200 deficit, with football alone responsible for $230,226 of the loss.[19]

Wimpress solicited input on the issue and heard from many faculty and student leaders that too much was being spent on intercollegiate sports at a time when budgets were tight and important academic projects were unfunded. Considering the fragile national economy and the school's escalating operating expenses, they believed that failing to address the situation would force the school to raise tuition at a time when inflation was already squeezing many family budgets.[20]

The original target of Wimpress's investigation was football. But after months of research into other conferences and teams, the scope was expanded to the other men's sports—except tennis.[21] The findings resulted in the athletic council drafting a proposal to abolish athletic

Duncan Wimpress, Trinity's fifteenth president.

scholarships for football, baseball, basketball, and golf. Wimpress agreed to present the recommendation to the board of trustees at their 1971 annual meeting that fall.[22]

While the issue was being deliberated, one *Trinitonian* writer weighed in by suggesting several solutions, including the basic points of what she called the simon-pure system. In what appears to be the first mention of the unusual term plucked from the script of a 1718 London play, Mona Charles explained, "Another alternative is the 'Simon Pure' policy. No athletic scholarships are given. All students are admitted to Trinity as other students, on a purely academic level. If, after he has enrolled, a student decides he would like to play football, he may join the team."[23] From that moment forward, *simon-pure* began appearing in student conversations and publications to describe this new approach to men's athletics. According to other student reporters, who cited the "uncertain origin" of the nickname, the term was adopted by many at Trinity.[24]

As expected, at its October 13 meeting the board of trustees voted to stop awarding men's athletic scholarships and exit the Division I Southland Conference. Players already receiving scholarships would continue to receive the aid until their graduation.[25]Also as expected, there was a significant exception. Keeping Trinity's famed Tennis Tech Division I scholarship status remained possible through the NCAA's one-sport exception for its nonscholarship members. In the absence of any official varsity sports for women, the decision had no impact on female athletes.

Wimpress later claimed that the board was prepared to "eliminate sports altogether" had he not proposed his compromise. He also told the

Trinitonian that "hundreds of schools" had been operating in this mode for years, but sports editor Claudia White noted at the time of his comments that only two other Texas schools (Austin College and McMurry College) had adopted what she called this "un-Texas policy."[26]

Finally, students found a cause worthy enough to roust them from their dormitory couches and participate in campus protests. The board's unanimous vote sparked emotional reactions from many students. On October 23, playing in front of three thousand fans in Alamo Stadium at the first home game since the decision, Tiger football players visibly registered their dissent by affixing a large X in black tape over the T logo on their helmets, signifying a double-cross. Head coach Gene Offield, who led the 1971 squad to an exemplary 8–2 record, rallied behind his players. "They've been abandoned, and I support them," he told the *Mirage*.[27] The next spring Offield explained his reasons for resigning after two years: "When they cut out those athletic scholarships I was no longer interested in Trinity. I won't be back period."[28]

Considering their desire for a winning college team that would put San Antonio on the map, members of the local community shared the coach's outrage. In an unusual move, the *Mirage* editor ceded an entire page of the 1972 yearbook to *San Antonio Express-News* sportswriter Barry Robinson, who summarized the controversy under the headline "The Great Ripoff."[29] Alumni director and former varsity baseball player John Burleson remembered that the media got caught up in the issue "in the wrong way," with local sportswriters accusing Trinity of denying the city the presence of premier intercollegiate athletic programs.[30] Burleson later said this "lousy press" resulted in Wimpress "getting calls from drunks in the middle of the night."[31]

Four months after the fateful decision, local philanthropist E. M. Stevens announced a donation that would allow Trinity to build a stadium around the existing track and football practice field, giving the next year's (nonscholarship) team a permanent home. The move also helped Trinity's finances by eliminating rental expenses for nearby Alamo Stadium and adding income from concessions.[32] After viewing the new facility, a *Trinitonian* reviewer was less than enthusiastic about the design, writing that "the stadium is architecturally mediocre when compared to the architectural excellence of the surrounding buildings and the rest of Trinity's campus."[33] In the first game played at the new

"X" marks the scholarship double-cross in 1971.

E. M. Stevens Stadium, the tradition of tepid attendance continued, with one national sportswriter noting that the new stadium's seating capacity of 4,800 would rarely be "strained," writing, "Fewer than a thousand fans turned out for Saturday night's [Trinity] game, while a few miles away 8,000 braved a drizzle to watch a high school contest."[34]

Leaving the Southland Conference, which Trinity helped form in 1963, also required a new competitive mindset.[35] Wimpress predicted that a conference of nonscholarship peers could be in Trinity's future and shopped the idea over the next few years. Baseball coach Houston Wheeler also dreamed of the day they would find a "conference of Simon Pure schools."[36] *Trinitonian* sportswriter Kevin O'Keeffe noted that despite the success of the new independent football team, "there is no championship to win, and for any athlete this is quite a letdown."[37]

O'Keeffe's preview of the 1973 spring sports season approached the topic this way:

> Trinity President Duncan Wimpress announces the new Simon Pure Pre-Med program. Hailing the idea as a "bold new concept in education,"

E. M. Stevens attends first campus game held in his football stadium, September 9, 1972. Escorting him are cheerleaders Rindy Lobdell *(left)* and Carolyn White.

A popular question raised in the 1975 *Mirage*

> Wimpress says the class will be offered with no books and no teachers. Athletic Director Warren Woodson announces 55 Simon Pure [football] recruits, but is dismayed when 37 of them are girls. Trinity's baseball team begins the year with five straight losses and Coach Houston Wheeler blames Simon Pure for this poor start. "Well it's hard to win with no gloves or bats."[38]

Debates continued into the mid-1970s, when scholarship athletes moved on and a new generation of students arrived. Reporter Claudia White summed up the slow but steady transition. "Cries of abandonment and frustration have died down since autumn of 1971," she wrote. "Hurt pride, hard facts and sporadic arguments creep to the surface occasionally, but Simon Pure has settled into Trinity's Athletic department and he's here to stay."[39]

When the NCAA added the nonscholarship Division III in 1973, Wimpress cited trends showing this version of intercollegiate competition was growing fast, and he was right.[40] Two years later he helped birth a new coed nonscholarship conference.

On the bright side, the abandonment of athletic scholarships provided a boost to the university's academic reputation. Phi Beta Kappa sent a team in 1972 to evaluate Trinity's academic progress, including the quality of faculty and student body, library facilities, and financial resources. The chair of the visitation team told Wimpress that the university's stance on intercollegiate athletics had considerable influence on the committee's decision to grant the charter. This selection made Trinity only the fifth Texas institution to be awarded a prestigious Phi Beta Kappa chapter.[41]

The Libby Legacy Begins

Born on October 10, 1941, Elizabeth "Libby" Johnson lived with her parents, Arnold and Pearl, and her brother Donald in their tiny hometown of Hamlin, Texas, where she developed traits early in life that served her well into adulthood.[42]

At Hamlin High, she excelled at almost everything she attempted. She was a member of the National Honor Society and student council vice president. She also served on the newspaper and yearbook staffs. A talented musician, she was band president, a drum major, and an award-winning French horn player. She was in the senior play, crowned High School Queen, and lettered two years in tennis. In addition, Johnson was an officer in the Future Homemakers Association of Hamlin and an active member of the Junior Girls Auxiliary at the First Baptist Church. When asked about her future, the senior expressed interest in either a music career or working at computer giant IBM. Sadly, Pearl Johnson died in the middle of her daughter's junior year, so she didn't see her graduate with her nineteen classmates.[43]

Johnson moved forty miles northwest to continue her education at McMurry College. Her energy and work ethic followed her to the Abilene campus, where she averaged an eighteen-hour course load while holding down two part-time jobs.[44] Her interest shifted to physical education, as she played varsity tennis and helped organize women's intramurals, one of the few athletic outlets at the time for college women. She spent her summers as a counselor at Camp Arrowhead in Hunt, Texas, where she taught swimming, canoeing, horseback riding, archery, and tennis. She later coached some of those campers at Trinity.

Johnson earned a bachelor's degree in science in 1963 and taught at the Stamford Independent School District and Reichter Catholic High School in Waco before enrolling at Baylor University for graduate work. She still played tennis and once subbed for an ill Baylor varsity player in

McMurry College women's tennis team, 1962.
Libby Johnson *(first row, far right)*

a doubles match at a 1966 district tournament.[45] Johnson graduated with a master's degree in physical education in 1967 and accepted a position at St. Mary's University in San Antonio, where she became its first full-time female physical education instructor.[46]

Johnson taught classes; established women's extramural teams in basketball, volleyball, and tennis; created curricula; and procured certification for a women's physical education major at the school. Her busy schedule was documented by student reporters in 1969, including one who wrote, "If any department at St. Mary's University could be said to have a monopoly on energy or on being felt for the sheer force of enthusiasm, the Physical Education Department would have a good claim on nominating Miss Elizabeth Johnson."[47]

Johnson's St. Mary's experiences between 1967 and 1972 mirror the challenges of her fellow coaches in those pre–Title IX days. She dealt with a stingy budget, fought for practice space, created schedules from scratch, and recruited through primitive means—flyers, student newspaper ads, and word of mouth. Her early female basketball teams occasionally faced superior opponents with players from established programs (e.g., Southwest Texas State). But most of their extramural games were against local colleges, including Trinity, where the coaches on the opposite bench were her future departmental colleagues Jim Potter, Bob Strauss, and Shirley Rushing. Due to the dearth of high school programs for girls, most of Johnson's players were either newcomers to basketball or had played the odd half-court version that was common at the time. Their shorter stature and raw shooting skills resulted in the inexperienced team averaging only eighteen points a game her first season.

It was Johnson's role as men's golf coach that caught the eye of local media. Athletic director Ed Messbarger had to field a team to satisfy a five-sport conference requirement and put Johnson in charge. In a 1969 column headlined "Miss Coach," *San Antonio Express-News* sportswriter Karl O'Quinn featured the unlikely appointment, writing, "A coach usually achieves optimum results when the players look up to him, but such is not the case with the St. Mary's golf coach. In the first place, coach is a her and not a him, and in the second place, she stands only five feet, five inches, and has to look up to all her players." In her "thick West Texas twang," Johnson told O'Quinn that she took her title lightly and her responsibilities seriously. "I'm really just a supervisor," she said. "I don't do much coaching." She added that players rarely called women "coach." They were addressed as Miss or Mrs. And that was true; her Trinity students usually called her Miss Johnson or Miss J.[48]

This gender confusion extended to correspondence, the primary communication of the time. Letters intended for the St. Mary's men's golf coach were addressed to "Mr. Libby Johnson." Even signing her name as Miss Johnson on university letterhead didn't work. In one case, the host coach of an invitational tournament who had been exchanging letters with Johnson was afraid he had mistakenly invited a women's golf team. Imagine his relief when Johnson arrived at Sam Houston State University with a male entourage. After her Rattlers won a match, Johnson quipped, "None of the other coaches like to lose, naturally, not to anybody, but they sure don't want to lose to a woman."[49]

In a 1970 application for a promotion to associate professor, Johnson noted her accomplishments in St. Mary's nascent physical education program, pointing out that her recruiting had created one of the biggest women's programs in the state even though it had been around less than two years. In the application, Johnson stated that she planned to start work that summer on a doctoral program; it seems she never found the time to pursue that advanced degree. The application was successful, however. A handwritten note on the archival copy says, "Promotion granted, June 1, 1970."[50]

Johnson's exemplary teaching, coaching, and administrative skills did not go unnoticed among other local officials, who had multiple opportunities to observe her in the early extramural contests. In fact, according to a former player, she turned down an offer to coach Division I basketball at the recently established University of Texas at San Antonio, expressing her preference for women who played without the incentives of scholarships.[51] When Trinity's health and physical education department decided in 1972 to hire a second female member to join Rushing, the staff didn't bother to form a search committee. "As soon as we were able to add another faculty member, there was no question as to who we wanted," said Rushing, who had been in the department since 1960. Johnson accepted the offer, excited to move to a modern campus where she could play a leading role in building intramural and extramural programs for women.[52]

St. Mary's president John W. Langlinais wrote Johnson a letter thanking her for all she had done at the school and particularly for how she'd developed their women's physical education department.[53]

Despite the persistent challenges, Johnson's career-building years were shaping up to be positive ones for female athletes. In addition to the existing Ladies Professional Golf Association, the creation of the Virginia Slims Circuit for tennis meant there were now two avenues for women to earn money in sports. Also, the AAU finally allowed women to participate in more sanctioned events, including the 1972 Boston Marathon. Eight women entered the twenty-six-mile race and all finished, including female winner Nina Kuscsik.[54] Billie Jean King was continuing to claim Grand Slam tennis titles and was recognized in 1972 as the first female Sportsperson of the Year by *Sports Illustrated.* Progress for women's collegiate athletic programs was inching forward, including access to slightly bigger budgets, more dedicated resources and coaching, increased opportunities for intercollegiate competition, and improved high school feeder programs. And the budgetary decisions that eliminated men's athletic scholarships at Trinity had set the stage for a new era of athletes playing for the love of the game.

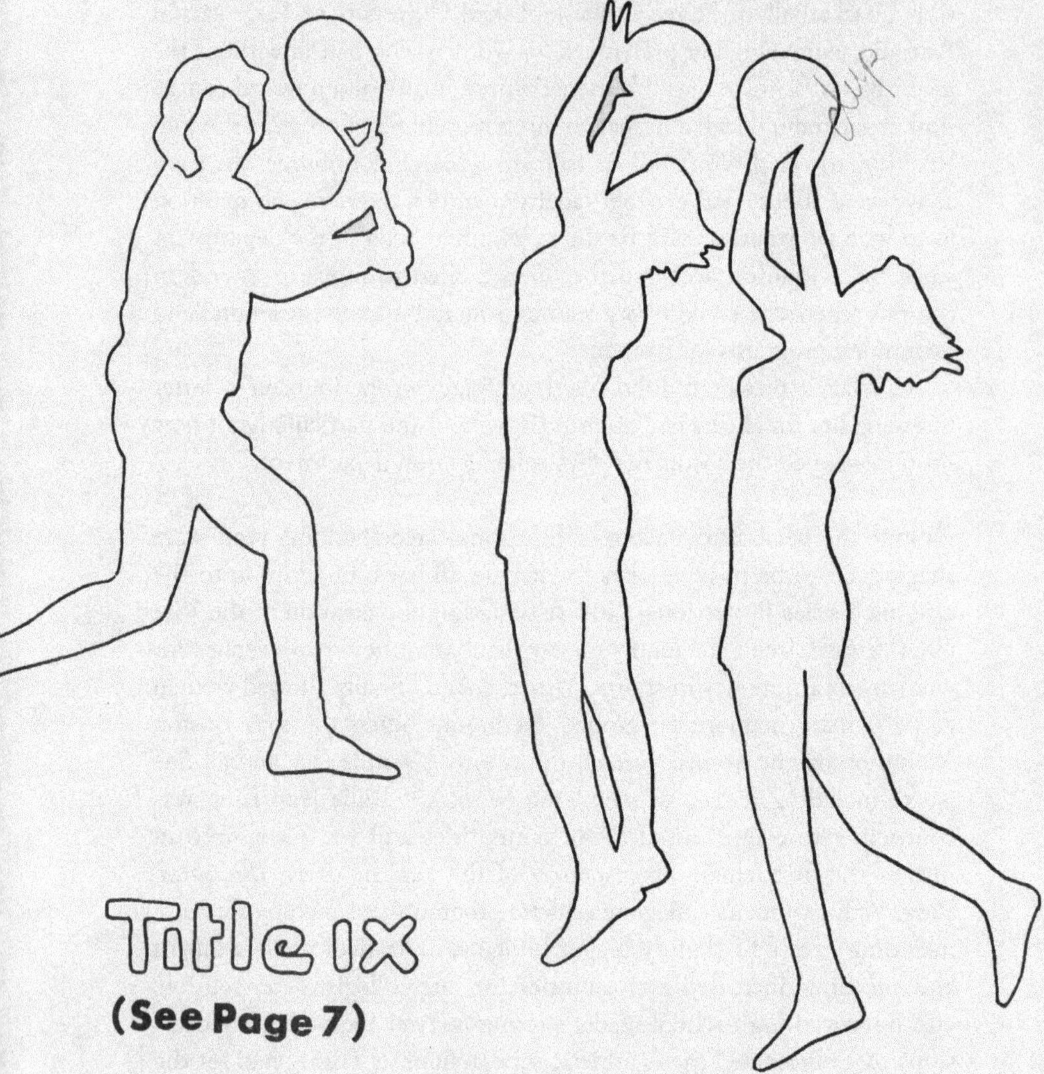

1975 *Trinitonian* issue evaluated Title IX.

CHAPTER 7

Signing and Defining Title IX

1972–75

> No person in the United States shall, on the basis of sex, be excluded from participation, be denied benefits, be subject to discrimination under any educational program or activity receiving federal financial assistance.
>
> —TITLE IX OF THE EDUCATION AMENDMENT ACT

In the early 1970s, Trinity was resolving its men's athletic scholarship issues, and Libby Johnson was advancing her career at St. Mary's University. Little did these actors know the doors to education and sports for women were about to burst open, thanks to the transformative dialogue and ensuing action that led to Title IX of the Education Amendment Act. Defining and implementing the provisions of the new legislation was a long and often painful process, however. The law passed in 1972, but Congress didn't define the specific regulations until 1975, and they were not enforceable until 1978. Legal challenges continued into the next decades.[1]

In the months leading up to the legislative debates, a study by a doctoral candidate and women's sports pioneer astutely captured the status of female athletes in Texas and the obstacles to success for coaches like Johnson. Discussions between leaders of state and national women's governance organizations revealed sharp disagreements, not just over the well-worn concerns about the dangers of competition but on new issues, such as athletic scholarships for female students.

The State of Women's Sports

On the eve of Title IX, women's sports leaders celebrated a major milestone with the 1971 formation of the Association for Intercollegiate Athletics for Women. The member-based body resulted from a reorganization of the Commission for Intercollegiate Athletics for Women, and its full-time staff was tasked with providing a bulwark against the perceived threats of encroachment from the NCAA.[2] In the eight years after it began operating, the organization grew from 278 charter institutions to almost 1,000 members. By 1980, it would oversee an increase of intercollegiate participation from 30,000 women in 1972 (vs. 170,000 men) to 125,000.[3] Each year the AIAW expanded offerings for regional and national championships for member schools, providing teams a path to advance beyond their own state championships.

AIAW leadership boasted of being both founded and led by women and stated that its mission was to "lead and conduct" competitive nonscholarship intercollegiate programs focused on education rather than athletic performance. In that spirit, the AIAW denied membership to schools that awarded athletic scholarships or financial assistance to women, especially if athletic talent was the criteria for selection. Female athletes could receive academic scholarships as long as they were competing with the general student population for positions on sports teams.

An interesting snapshot published in *Sports Illustrated* explained the massive gender gap in sports scholarships. The 1973 study showed that major colleges awarded an average of 120 football scholarships to male players, while only about 50 athletic scholarships were given to women across all schools. The eye-opening upshot? One large university offered twice as many scholarships in one sport as the total offered to collegiate sportswomen nationwide.[4]

The purity of the AIAW's nonscholarship vision proved difficult to sustain.[5] Some schools found crafty ways around the prohibition, including a small college in an oil-rich West Texas town. Odessa College, where Trinity tennis doubles champion Becky Vest attended her freshman year, didn't offer a four-year educational track but did host powerful women's programs that brought national recognition. The Wrangler tennis team boasted several top-three finishes in the USLTA collegiate championships, including a doubles title in 1970, and their golf counterparts captured their own national crown in 1969.

Odessa's secrets to the women's success? A supportive administration, well-compensated coaches, and a variety of funding sources from the community for supposedly academic subsidies. A 1971 feature in the *Odessa American* paints a picture of the tension between the state governing body and the college's women's programs. The controversy began with a letter from a TCIAW district commissioner to tennis coach Virginia Brown saying the state organization had learned "through rumor" that Odessa College was giving financial assistance to women on its tennis and golf teams based on athletic ability. Benefactors included the OC Wrangler Club.[6] In fact, this assistance possibly lured one Trinity freshman to transfer. Nancee Weigel, a top player on the first official Tiger team that finished fifth in the nation in 1972, met Brown while playing a match in Odessa. She left to play for Brown the following year.[7]

In this article, the reporter predicted a showdown between the school and the TCIAW, writing they were "carrying flags of a different allegiance." Brown responded by accusing other schools of "disguising" their own athletic scholarships.

A *San Antonio Express-News* column hints at a similar arrangement at Trinity. In 1969, Karl O'Quinn wrote that the school offered Emilie Burrer and Becky Vest neither a team nor the chance to practice on campus. In discussing how the two players ended up at Trinity, he confirmed Burrer's academic scholarship. But when he mentioned to men's coach Clarence Mabry that Vest's subsidy had come from a local tennis patron, O'Quinn said the news was "a surprise to Mabry."[8]

These stories illustrate a time when schools were fighting for recognition, and many of them—and their benefactors—were still uneducated about the rules defined by the newly formed women's organization.[9]

A flurry of lawsuits filed on behalf of high school girls provided another source of conflict in the early 1970s. The plaintiffs were prohibited from playing on boys' teams, even when they had no other options. Some of the responses echoed the "archaic thoughts" future Trinity coach Libby Johnson complained about throughout her career. One article paraphrased male baseball officials who claimed they were protecting girls from the hazards of the game. These arguments included that "baseball was 'a contact sport'; that boys would quit if girls were allowed; that girls' bones were weaker than boys'; that facial injuries could ruin a girl's looks and therefore prospects in life; and, most outlandishly, that girls struck in the chest by a ball might later develop breast cancer."[10] A comment from a Connecticut judge in a 1971 ruling provided another stark reminder of obstacles yet to overcome: "Athletic competition builds character in our boys. We do not need that kind of character in our girls."[11]

Some schools reacted by proactively providing exceptions for girls, a move that helped future Trinity standout Jill Harenberg. An accomplished youth circuit tennis player, Harenberg observed fellow New Mexico athlete Nancy Lopez make a case to play golf on her high school's all-boys team. Not only did Lopez prevail, but she became one of the nation's premier female professional golfers. Inspired by that victory, Harenberg joined the boys' tennis team at her high school in Santa Fe. When the school established a girls' team the next year, she joined it and went on to win three state girls' singles championships.[12]

Physical education pioneer Emilie Burrer Foster paints a vivid picture of Texas women's collegiate sports in the early 1970s. When the four-time national tennis champion arrived at Texas Tech University, her assignment was to teach physical education and establish a tennis program at the large Southwest Conference school. But resources in 1970 were minuscule—a sadly familiar story. "Our total budget was $640. That was for rackets, and strings, and travel, and no [extra] salary, of course," she said. This matches the findings from other sources that collegiate women's programs received only 1 to 2 percent of overall athletic budgets across the country at the time. Also reminiscent of her playing days at Trinity, Foster recalls the challenges of finding practice courts: "We couldn't use the men's courts, so we practiced on the intramural courts from 5:30 to 7:30 at night."[13]

A more academic analysis is found in a doctoral dissertation by Carla Lowry. A star basketball player from Mississippi, Lowry was an AAU All-American and member of the legendary Wayland Baptist Flying Queens that had a 131-game winning streak and won two national titles. She also played on the US gold medal team at the 1959 Pan American

Carla Lowry.

Games and captained a US cultural exchange team that toured Russia in 1961.[14]

Lowry's dissertation on women's athletic leadership and training was approved by Texas Woman's University in Denton in May 1972, the same month Title IX passed the US House of Representatives. The purpose of her report was to "discern scale values of leadership functions, sources of power, and sources of group attraction as determined by the players, coaches, and/or administrators involved in women's intercollegiate team sport groups—volleyball and basketball teams—in the state of Texas."[15]

From studies conducted across Texas in spring 1971, Lowry found that 52 percent of the 120 institutions surveyed offered intercollegiate athletics for women, engaging a total of 2,384 athletes. Note that her report uses the modifier *intercollegiate*, a label that was still used interchangeably with *extramural* and *interschool* to represent competition between colleges and universities.

Here are a few highlights of the sixty-two institutions that hosted women's sports:

- Volleyball, basketball, and tennis were the most frequent activities offered, followed by badminton, track and field, bowling, gymnastics, golf, and swimming.

- 79 percent had an athletic director or coordinator for women's intercollegiate athletic programs. Half were governed by a joint men's and women's physical education department, and fewer than 18 percent were run by women only.
- 78 percent (138) of the 170 coaches involved were female, but only 40 percent were financially compensated for their additional responsibilities.
- 68 percent allowed female students to participate simultaneously in two sports.
- Only 26 percent offered designated team physicians or athletic trainers typically provided to the men's teams.

Lowry suggested that the ability to attract athletes was partially dependent on girls' sports experiences in society and secondary schools. She also recommended, "Programs should not only make available 'expert' coaches but should also strive to place persons in coaching whom players can identify with, will like, and will admire."[16] While this isn't revolutionary thinking today, many of Lowry's peers were expected to teach and coach a variety of sports. Glada Munt recalls that she had to be "a generalist, and a specialist of none" early in her Southwestern University career. That trend continued for years at many colleges.[17]

In a small-world example of an intergenerational handoff, much of Lowry's long career was spent at Southwestern, where she was hired in 1984 as one of the nation's few female athletic directors, in charge of men and women. One of her coaches—and a member of the search committee that selected Lowry—was Munt, a 1974 Trinity graduate and multisport athlete in the early days of Title IX. Munt filled the athletic director slot in 1995 after Lowry became Southwestern's associate dean of students.[18] Lowry retired in 2001, and her illustrious career was recognized through multiple awards and Hall of Fame inductions, including three in Texas. In 2019, four years after her death, Southwestern dedicated its fitness center in her name.[19]

Passing Title IX

Under the conditions described by Foster, Lowry, Munt, and others, the stage was set for Congress to begin addressing educational inequities for women. One specific goal of Title IX was to remedy a glaring omission in the Civil Rights Act, for while the 1964 law prohibited discrimination for race, color, and national origin, it neglected to include sex as a protected class. Some considered the effort to be a fast-track fix for specific educational issues, as the broader Equal Rights Amendment was slowly working its way through state legislatures for ratification.[20]

Edith Green, chair of the House Special Subcommittee on Education, used her position to schedule hearings in 1970 to investigate obstacles to educational opportunities for women.[21] The Department of Education calls this investigation "the first ever devoted to this topic and is considered the first legislative step toward the enactment of Title IX."[22] Green, an Oregon Democrat, was one of eleven female members of Congress (out of 535) at the time. Ten were in the House of Representatives, and one was in the Senate.

After the committee hearings, Green created a proposal for Title IX and presented it to the House on April 6, 1971. The next winter, Indiana Democrat Birch Bayh introduced the legislation to the Senate. In his speech on February 28, 1972, Bayh credited his deceased first wife for inspiration, since she had been denied admission to the University of Virginia, the college of her choice, in 1951. He declared, "One of the great failings of the American educational system is the continuation of corrosive and unjustified discrimination against women. It is clear to me that sex discrimination reaches into all facets of education—admissions, scholarship programs, faculty hiring and promotion, professional staffing and pay scales. Because education provides access to jobs and financial security, discrimination here is doubly destructive to women." Bayh, who was also a chief senate architect of the ERA, suggested that Title IX would guarantee that women would "enjoy the educational opportunity every American deserves."[23]

Appearing next on the scene was Rep. Patsy Mink of Hawaii, who helped author the final legislation. Mink had her own reasons to support the change. She had been turned down by multiple medical schools because of her gender, so she applied to the University of Chicago law school. Ironically, in a misinterpretation of Hawaii as a US territory, she was accepted under the "foreign" student quota. Even with a law degree, the large legal firms she applied to wouldn't hire her. It may have been because of her gender, her interracial marriage, or the fact she was a mother who they felt wouldn't be able to work enough billable hours.[24] She opened her own private firm and later ran for political office, joining the House in 1964 as the first female representative of color.

Mink, Green, and Bayh finalized the legislation, which was passed in the Senate on March 1, approved in the House on May 11, and signed by President Richard Nixon on June 23, 1972.[25]

Undeniably, this was the moment that began the transformation of women's education and intercollegiate athletics. But no specifics accompanied the legislation, and the long process of defining regulations began in earnest. Also notable was the absence of any reference to sports. But that omission didn't prevent supporters of men's intercollegiate athletics from reframing the broad educational debate into one about sports. The apocalyptic claims of threats to their lucrative programs led to multiple attempts to derail the legislation over the next three years.[26]

Regardless of the immediate backlash, the significant moment wasn't lost on Emilie Burrer Foster, who said, "When Title IX came in, everything changed." Baylor's Nancy Goodloe agreed: "While Title IX was given many descriptions over the years, some good, some not so good, there is no question that it was the most significant piece of legislation to impact equity in athletics for girls and women in the twentieth century."[27]

The legislation's timing marked a career inflection point for Libby Johnson, who started her Trinity job as the ink was still drying on President Nixon's signature.

Solving the Scholarship Dilemma

After the legislation was signed, one issue that required almost immediate resolution was athletic scholarships for women, which had been prohibited by the AIAW. At its first member meeting in 1972, delegates adopted the scholarship ban, denying membership to schools that provided women financial assistance to play intercollegiate sports. Their intent was to prevent exploitation of female athletes and protect member schools from falling into the trap of commercialism common to men's sports. However, the combination of Title IX, legal challenges, and looming threats from the powerful NCAA forced a speedy response.

Their most consequential legal challenge came from the Kellmeyer discrimination lawsuit filed in January 1973, just seven months after the AIAW enacted its scholarship policy.[28] Fern Kellmeyer was the director of physical education at Marymount College, but the lawsuit was filed on behalf of a group of women from two Florida colleges. The complaint was against an extensive list of national and state defendants, including the AIAW. While the lawsuit wasn't a complete surprise to the organizations, it presented a unique perspective, since it was a discrimination claim made by women against women.[29] After unsuccessful mediation efforts, the defendants relented, the lawsuit was never litigated, and the AIAW agreed to modify its policy. The leadership forwarded a recommendation to members for reversing its position on athletic scholarships but placed limits on the number and size of scholarships in different sports and retained the organization's strict recruiting requirements. In an indication that the original ban may not have been widely supported, an AIAW news release proposing the changes claimed that 80 percent of its national membership agreed with the modification.[30]

Texas officials seemed split in their reaction. TCIAW District VII members received a letter from commissioner Judy Watson stating, "[S]cholarships are here whether we like it or not. The courts have taken the matter out of our hands and declared that if scholarships are available to male athletes, they must also be available to female athletes." She concluded, "Now the real 'fun' begins."[31] That summer, all TCIAW members received a missive from association president Sue Garrison calling for support of the national organization's proposal. "Now, more than ever, we need to consider our philosophy and our responsibility toward women's intercollegiate athletics," she wrote her Texas colleagues. "The current is becoming swifter, ladies. Shall we just ride with the tide or shall we pilot the boat?"[32]

According to her contemporaries, Libby Johnson abhorred recruiting and the idea of pay for play. Glada Munt remembers sitting in her Georgetown apartment arguing over the phone with her former Trinity coach about the issue. The Johnson acolyte had just started her career at Southwestern and was in favor of scholarships, while Johnson was "vehemently" opposed to the idea. After forty-five years in collegiate sports, Munt now believes the move was necessary. "You can't be giving all these males a free education to play sports and not do that for females," she said. But she also thinks the Division III approach of no athletic scholarships for males or females—which Trinity and Southwestern adopted in the early 1990s—offered the best-balanced solution.[33]

During the TCIAW debates, Johnson penned a letter to association colleagues urging them to keep their priorities in proper perspective. "With so many changes happening in women's athletics and all of us concerned over our own institutions and situations," Johnson wrote, "we should not lose sight of our major concern—the students."[34] That statement encapsulates the motivating force behind her entire career.

But Johnson couldn't turn the strong tide, as the national association yielded to the pressures and dropped its scholarship ban in 1973. An AIAW press release stated, "[T]imes are changing, and we must change with them." It also said, "The consciousness of women as to their rights and privileges has been raised, and the whole theory of protecting women from exploitation, of paternalist action 'for their own good,' has been a casualty of the student movement and the women's rights movement."[35]

The decision had a positive effect for the AIAW, broadening its reach and accelerating interest in women's intercollegiate athletics. One year after the policy reversal, AIAW membership grew from 278 charter members to 379, and the next year it jumped to 757.[36] One sports historian thought the ultimate effect of the Kellmeyer lawsuit was greater than even the Florida plaintiffs had intended, however, saying it paved the way for an NCAA takeover and "symbolized the beginning of the AIAW's loss of power and control over women's intercollegiate athletics under the impact of Title IX."[37]

Defining Title IX

These consequential policy decisions were being made in the absence of details written in the law itself. After it was signed, the Office for Civil Rights (part of what was then called the US Department of Health, Education, and Welfare, or HEW) was tasked with defining what specific regulations this antidiscrimination act should include. The overriding philosophy of this tedious assignment was reflected in HEW's declaration: "[I]n a knowledge-based society, equal opportunity in education is fundamental to equality in all other forms of human endeavor."[38]

It took another three years to define the regulations, and three more before they were enforced. This extended process frustrated many educational institutions and women's sports leaders, but Judith Lee Oliphant, a University of Kentucky law student, had a positive view: "The long delay between enactment of Title IX and publication of the final implementing regulations is evidence of the care with which HEW proceeded in attempting to formulate workable, reasonable standards."[39]

The Office for Civil Rights had no problems eliciting feedback, which flowed in from all corners of the educational and athletic landscape. When the agency drafted proposed regulations based on the input and posted them for public comment in June 1974, the response was overwhelming: almost ten thousand comments were submitted, and many raised issues of funding for athletics. It took more than six months to process them all.[40]

In the meantime, opponents turned up the heat and advanced proposals in Congress to blunt the law's effect on intercollegiate sports—or take them out altogether. Texas Republican senator John Tower introduced an NCAA-backed amendment in May 1974 to exempt money earned by (men's) revenue-producing intercollegiate sports from the legislation. The proposal inspired a full-court press from the AIAW and its advocates, who registered their dissent with members of the Senate Joint Conference Committee. It must have worked. Believing a blanket exemption for all men's sports went too far, the committee rejected Tower's proposal and instead approved the Javits Amendment (named after New York Republican senator Jacob Javits), altering the language so that Title IX included "reasonable provisions" concerning intercollegiate athletics. According to one historian, this successful protest "foiled the NCAA's first major attempt to block women's equality."[41] A separate attempt by North Carolina senator Jesse Helms to exclude athletics from the act was also rejected.[42]

An NCAA report found in Wimpress's papers provides an example of the group's attempt to mobilize its institutional members in opposing Title IX. Summarizing their feedback to HEW, the NCAA authors repeated the rationale that "men have been more interested in athletics generally, both as participants and as spectators." While the possible intent of the report was to compel Wimpress to join fellow NCAA members in calling for limits to the legislation, the authors failed to mention that the suppressed "interest" in women's sports might have been caused by the absence of opportunities.[43]

Public opinions proliferated in response to the proposed regulations. Darrell Royal, the legendary gridiron coach at UT, predicted that implementation of Title IX would eventually "be the death of intercollegiate athletics as we know it today."[44] In Waco, many of Nancy Goodloe's Baylor University colleagues actively protested the regulations. Although the school had been an early trendsetter for women's sports, Goodloe said the administration "opposed Title IX legislation ever since its passage in 1972 and had written many letters to Congressmen, athletic supporters, booster clubs, former students, and others in an effort to mount a strong opposition to the legislation."[45]

Even some female Texas leaders feared that the regulations might go too far. Sue Garrison, president of the renamed Texas Association of Intercollegiate Athletics for Women (TAIAW, formerly TCIAW), expressed her concerns in a 1974 letter to the women's athletics committee chair for the powerful Division I Southwest Conference. Garrison said the equal opportunity section of the HEW proposal was "entirely irrational, impractical and impossible." She added, "To 'equalize' by radical curtailment of men's athletics can only result in mediocrity for both programs, if not the demise of both." In light of HEW secretary Caspar Weinberger's request for feedback, Garrison said she would offer her assistance and expressed hope that the agency's new guidelines would be "clearer and fairer to all concerned." She concluded: "We want women's athletic programs to grow through careful planning and foresight. Many of the problems we are encountering at the present time are new to us. We need and solicit your help in working out solutions."[46]

One *Trinitonian* sports editor waded into the controversy, countering an apocalyptic statement made by an "official at a major university." Addressing the official's contention that the pressures of offering scholarships to women would ruin their sports programs, Danny Garcia suggested, "That's like guzzling all the booze at a party to protect the other guests from the evils of drink."[47]

After multiple lobbying strategies failed, NCAA commissioner Walter Byers asked member executives to make direct pleas to President Nixon. Calls to the White House that summer went unheeded, as Nixon had his own issues with the Watergate investigation and was forced to resign his office on August 8, 1974.

Amid the Office for Civil Rights definitions and congressional debates, the promise (and perceived threat) of Title IX dominated conversations

Title IX and sports on the Hill

It's been a long time coming, most places

1975 *Trinitonian* headline for an article about Title IX at Trinity

in physical education and athletic department offices across US campuses, including Trinity. Some athletes were oblivious to the moment's historic significance. Amy Brown, a freshman extramural basketball player the year Title IX was signed, overheard Trinity's physical education department staff discussing the legislation in what she called "empowering terms." She heard the comment, "'Now that we've got Title IX, the world's gonna' change.'" Brown's reaction? "I went out for a Coke. I was just glad we got to play."[48] Glada Munt, whose college career straddled the Title IX era, also claims that she and her teammates weren't aware of the inequities addressed by the legislation. "We just played and did the best we could," she remembers.[49]

When a *Trinitonian* writer broached the subject in January 1975, Title IX's impact on Trinity was still uncertain. The full-page report by sports editor Carolyn Kluttz still covered a lot of speculative ground about the issue. Kluttz, who succeeded Claudia White as the second consecutive female in that traditionally male position, solicited input from Trinity athletic director Pete Murphy, Libby Johnson, and other university administrators.

Her interviews reflected a mixture of confidence, confusion, and complacence. University attorney Luther Coulter said he was unaware of Title IX being a possible threat to Trinity. When asked about the amount of federal funds that the university received, vice president for fiscal affairs Derwood Hawthorne (a supporter of the early women's tennis program) admitted that he was unable to estimate the figure. Assistant dean of students Thurman Adkins thought if nobody filed a complaint and university funding remained relatively equal between the sexes and minorities, enforcement of Title IX would not be a problem.

A joint interview conducted with Murphy and Johnson elicited similar opinions. Murphy was "not at all disturbed about Title IX" and thought Trinity came close to complying with its mandates and was not in danger of losing federal funding. Although he was not able to provide a budget breakdown of how athletic funds were dispensed, Murphy assured Kluttz that "understanding people handling finances on the Hill [are] going to take care of things." Included in this group, he said, was President Wimpress, who agreed to use part of his budget to meet Title IX requirements.

Even so, Murphy acknowledged uncertainty regarding the interpretation of Title IX and whether the legislation was even in effect. Johnson informed him that the guidelines were already enforceable but mentioned the planned congressional hearings meant to clarify requirements in the areas of facilities, equipment, and budgets. "No one knows at this stage of the game what the ramifications of Title IX are," she admitted.

Despite these ambiguities, Johnson said Murphy had been accommodating to her volleyball, basketball, and softball teams, claiming, "We've always talked things out." Also, despite the documented disparities, she diplomatically added, "Men's and women's teams share athletic facilities at Trinity with little difficulty. Trinity's athletic policy has traditionally been one of providing whatever the student wants." Johnson considered Trinity to be "about three years ahead" of most universities in athletic trends.

Kluttz concluded that there was a consensus among Trinity administrators that "athletics are more secure and stable at Trinity than at many universities across the nation." Based on the evidence at the time, Kluttz's supposition appeared sound, but her analysis proved to be overly optimistic. Murphy, while indicating an openness to change, also vented his frustration with the perceived sense of urgency: "It's taken the NCAA years and years to build men's athletics to the level it is today, and now women want to get there overnight."[50]

Murphy's comment echoed the sentiments of many of his peers, who remained convinced the law would cripple their lucrative men's programs. While NCAA leaders and members' earlier lobbying attempts to block the legislation had failed, they hadn't given up. In fact, the same month Murphy was referencing the NCAA in the student newspaper, the sixty-nine-year-old organization was advancing new strategies. In preparation for its annual meeting in January 1975, NCAA executives forwarded a pilot recommendation to host championships for women. Only half of the group's membership even had women's programs, but the leaders felt the proposal would allow them to extend their authority over women's sports and counter the perceived threat of Title IX.

Members rejected the motion but approved further study with a promise to include input from all parties, including the AIAW. The promise was broken and divisions deepened when AIAW leaders learned a full report was published and circulating among NCAA members without AIAW's involvement. Considering that female representation was a core value of the AIAW, its leaders felt betrayed, and they accused the men's group of wielding its "monopolistic" power, a term that resurfaced in an antitrust lawsuit filed by the AIAW against the organization six years later.[51] A letter from AIAW president L. Leotus Morrison to her institutional members echoed her frustration: "It was difficult to interpret the NCAA announcement as anything but an attempt to take over the women's intercollegiate program."[52]

Morrison also wrote to the presidents of NAIA member institutions about the NCAA's intervention attempt. The NAIA was a competitor with the NCAA for oversight of men's intercollegiate sports, but most of its members were from smaller institutions.[53] Morrison called the NCAA proposal a surprise, since the AIAW was already hosting national championships for ten women's sports. She wrote, "It is understandable that our initial reaction would be one of betrayed disillusionment." After expressing her appreciation for the NAIA's support, she ended her letter stating the obvious: "No doubt the future will bring many changes in college athletic programs."[54]

The AIAW was also contemplating a contrary strategy. With the goal of emphasizing sports as a truly educational activity instead of a semiprofessional one, the AIAW established its own advisory panel whose recommendations could "take women's sports even further away from the men's model than they are now."[55]

The summer after Kluttz's *Trinitonian* article and the skirmish over the NCAA's controversial proposal, congressional debates about the specifics of Title IX began in earnest. Once the Office for Civil Rights reviewed the extensive feedback, their fine-tuned regulations were signed into law by President Gerald Ford on May 27, 1975, and submitted to Congress for a forty-five-day review period before going into effect. Strong pushback from supporters and opponents compelled the legislators to open their debates to the public.[56]

Since there were no female senators in 1975, defense of the regulations in the senate chamber was left to men. Dick Clark told his male colleagues that the barriers against women "desperately" needed to be torn down and that Congress did the right thing in passing the legislation in 1972. Acknowledging that women's sports received only 2 percent of the $300 million spent on athletic budgets in 1975 (an improvement over 1 percent in 1972), the Iowa Democrat endorsed the "reasonable provision" compromise, saying, "Title IX will not require equal spending, but it does require equal opportunities for men and women in athletics." In a nod to naysayers, Clark said, "No one wants to see [big-time college athletics] destroyed, nor can we reasonably expect that this will happen where Title IX is enforced. What will happen is that women, as well as men, will now be able to participate fully in athletics. No longer can women be consigned to inferior facilities, equipment, or scheduling options."[57]

Even after the debates, passage of the final regulations still wasn't a slam dunk, as efforts to exempt athletics from the legislation persisted. When one last-gasp attempt was rebuffed by a senate committee and returned to the House for a final vote, Patsy Mink was the only original sponsor around to defend the proposal; coauthor Edith Green had retired from her Oregon seat the previous December. Before the floor vote began, however, Mink was informed that her daughter had been in a serious automobile accident, and the Hawaii representative left the chamber before recording her vote. This resulted in a 212–211 victory for Title IX opponents. Once her sudden departure was explained, Mink's allies encouraged their colleagues to take a revote. Mink was in attendance for the second roll call, which included an additional thirty-seven votes to "recede and concur" with the Senate's proposal. The House's history archive reads, "Mink's daughter (and Title IX) survived."[58]

The final regulations reflected changes driven by public comments and congressional debates over the three-year period. When presenting the new directives, Secretary Weinberger remarked on the specific impact on athletics, saying, "We wanted to eliminate the very evident and obvious discrimination that has taken place against women in athletics and sports over the years, mostly unconsciously, I think, by the schools. At the same time, we did not want to disrupt the entire pattern of American college life, or indeed a large part of American life itself."[59]

Spotlight on Title IX Legacies

Appreciation for Patsy Mink's and Birch Bayh's contributions only deepened over the years. After Mink's death in 2002, Congress renamed Title IX as the Patsy Mink Equal Opportunity in Education Act. In 2014 President Barack Obama posthumously awarded her the Presidential Medal of Freedom. In presenting the nation's highest civilian honor to the congresswoman, Obama said, "Every girl in Little League, every woman playing college sports, and every parent, including Michelle and myself, who watches their daughter on a field or in the classroom, is forever grateful to the late Patsy Takemoto Mink. Patsy was a passionate advocate for opportunity and equality and realizing the full promise of the American Dream."

Hawaii representative Patsy Mink

When asked about the greatest satisfaction from his life of public service, Bayh said Title IX "had a more profound impact on more Americans than anything else [he] was able to do." Billie Jean King agreed. In her reaction to Bayh's death in 2019, she said, "You simply cannot look at the evolution of equality in our nation without acknowledging the contributions and the commitment Senator Bayh made to securing equal rights and opportunities for every American."

While the sports-specific rules have been updated over the past half century, the original ones can be found in some online sources. They explicitly include sports: "No person shall, on the basis of sex…be discriminated against in any interscholastic, intercollegiate, club or intramural athletics offered by recipient, and no recipient shall provide any such athletics separately on such basis." Specific mandates addressed scheduling, coaching, academic tutoring opportunities, and compensation. Change was also expected in the provision of locker rooms, medical and training services, housing and dining, equipment and supplies, travel and per diem allowances, and publicity.[60] Concerns expressed in lawsuits about females infringing on men's teams or contact sports being damaging to women were also addressed: "This section does not prohibit separation of students by sex within physical education classes or activities during participation in wrestling, boxing, rugby, ice hockey, football, basketball and other sports, the purpose or major activity of which involves bodily contact."[61]

The Department of Health, Education, and Welfare gave colleges and universities three years to meet the new standards, and enforcement was transferred to the Department of Education after that agency was established in 1980.[62]

Judith Lee Oliphant's 1975 *Kentucky Law Journal* article presented this optimistic conclusion: "In the long run, the required changes concerning financial support and better training, facilities, equipment, and publicity should, at a minimum, produce more women athletes and more careers for women in sports."[63] She was right about "the long run"; the debates didn't end in 1975, as critical challenges were litigated in the 1980s and continued well into the new millennium.

CHAPTER 8

From Intramural to Intercollegiate

1972–75

Back then Libby was teaching twelve hours a semester and coaching four sports. Do you think men's coaches were doing that?

—JULIE JENKINS, IN AN INTERVIEW, FEBRUARY 20, 2020

Mirroring the first three years of the signing and defining of Title IX was the beginning of Libby Johnson's tenure as Trinity's first official women's coach. The thirty-year-old was charged with operationalizing the still vague legislation signed a month before she reported to her Sams Center office. Her legendary will and work ethic were tested in the next eight years, but she was equipped with the energy to navigate the storms ahead and leave a lasting imprint on women's intercollegiate athletics.

The initial years after Title IX were ones of discovery and possibility, as Johnson expanded women's intramurals and formed intercollegiate programs out of the previously unorganized extramural teams. During this time a new women's sport emerged, and Trinity earned more national fame from tennis stars.

Ms. Invades Sports

In national conversations, the (re)appearance of the term *Ms.* provided an answer to two prickly questions arising out of the women's movement: What do you call a woman when her marital status is unknown?

"Miss" Libby Johnson

And why should a female be defined by her marital status anyway? The title *Ms.* had appeared randomly in literature for centuries and was even suggested as an option for business correspondence in the 1950s. But it was formally adopted in the early 1970s as the universal calling card for the feminist movement.

The word made an early appearance in the *Trinitonian.* Shirley Wells reviewed the country's first feminist magazine, *Ms.*, and noted a toning down of the raucous protests of the 1960s. "The radical women's liberationists have just about disappeared," she wrote, "but the struggle for women's equality still goes on, in a much more rational yet equally spirited way." Wells also called the $1.50 newsstand price "not cheap."[1]

Later, under the headline "Ms. Invades Sports," Claudia White wrote about her notable appointment as the *Trinitonian*'s first female sports editor by pairing the term with one that arose from the 1971 athletic scholarship discussions. "I suppose Trinity athletes thought the Simon Pure adoption was the final blow to their herculean endeavors. Well, here's another—me," she wrote. "I'm not the first female sports editor of a newspaper and I hope I'm not the last. The point is that I enjoy sports as much as the next guy (or girl) and hope my sports coverage is adequate. 'Nough said."[2] No longer would female staffers be relegated to the society pages.

Advances Bring Challenges

Female representation on Trinity's physical education staff doubled in 1972 when Libby Johnson joined departmental colleague Shirley Rushing. But it didn't lighten Johnson's load, as she inherited a virtually nonexistent varsity program, high expectations, and a full plate. For most of her time at Trinity, Johnson taught several classes and coached multiple teams—demands rarely imposed on her male colleagues. The frenetic pace left the new coach with little opportunity for rest and relaxation. When asked about details of Johnson's personal life, those who knew her best invariably responded, "Teaching, coaching, and mentoring Trinity student athletes."

In her first two years, Johnson became Jim Potter's right-hand person in women's intramural and extramural programs. At first, she directed women's intramural volleyball, paddleball singles, basketball, basketball free throws, and golf. Later, water basketball, tennis doubles, bowling, field hockey, softball, swim meets, and coed track and field were added to her responsibilities. Johnson and Potter also piloted a novel coed intramural program that was "strictly for fun" that included volleyball, paddleball, badminton, tennis, softball, golf, and innertube water polo. Creative rules ensured more balanced competition. For example, a right-handed man playing coed softball had to bat left-handed. This allowed female players to contribute more to the outcome. The coed program quickly grew in popularity and became a permanent part of Trinity intramurals.[3]

In 1973, Johnson was relieved of her intramural responsibilities so she could focus on developing a viable women's intercollegiate program, which one *Trinitonian* writer described as "a no-budget program" with basketball and volleyball seasons that "consisted of six to eight games, all of which were played in San Antonio." Under Johnson, participation went from fewer than ten to more than fifty female athletes in just two years. Softball was later added to her job description. All three of her sports had seasons that overlapped, forcing her to deal with scheduling challenges that often found her coaching one sport while conducting preseason practices in another. Also, since many players participated in more than one sport, Johnson often struggled to field full-strength teams for games when seasons conflicted. She must have been relieved that coed bowling, trap and skeet, and Division I women's tennis had their own coaches.[4]

The traveling squad for Johnson's first Trinity extramural event included volleyball players Glada Munt, Pam Steinmetz, Karen Luhks, Monica Flores, Rindy Lobdell, Ann Aycock, Jeanne Freeland, and Laurie Lee. The entrants in the October 1972 tournament at Sam Houston State reflected the competitive reality of the 1970s, as Trinity played among twenty-seven teams across the collegiate spectrum, ranging from other small private schools to much larger state universities. Although Trinity lost its two matches, Johnson felt her players "gained valuable experience."[5]

Media coverage, however, was less than enlightened, as this 1973 *Trinitonian* report on the women's final home volleyball match illustrates:

> Monday night the girls suited up again, and employed the spike so fatal to opponents, and fingernails, to snatch the final pair of home games this season from St. Mary's 15–3 and 15–8. But following the battle, the troops and their exalted coach Johnson reverted temporarily to the tears and soggy hugs of femininity, as Ann Aycock, Jeanne Freeland, Glada Munt and Pam Steinmetz were given silver cups recognizing four years of service above and beyond the call of duty.[6]

Her 1975 team gained inspiration from top-ranked player Beath Donahoe, who enrolled at Trinity after honing her skills with the US Volleyball Association. Donahoe's talent helped the team win the zone championship and qualify for the TAIAW state tournament, an accomplishment Johnson said "is just like the football team winning the conference if they were in a conference. This is the first time that Trinity has ever gone as far as state." After that successful season, Donahoe left

Trinity to try out for the national team but failed to make the squad that played in the 1976 Montreal Olympics.[7]

Basketball was next on Johnson's slate. She coached her first Trinity cager squad in the 1972–73 season, inheriting veterans Aycock, Lobdell, and Karen Brumbaugh. Joining them were Munt, Patty Hartley, Betsy Ascani, Amy Brown, Janet McMillan, and Lucy Bundy.[8] In the next two years, they played in several invitational tournaments and twice defended their city title.

In fact, in Johnson's first four seasons, all three of her teams won city titles and advanced to postseason play.[9]

A departmental reorganization in 1974 brought a quiet end to decades of hazy terminology—Play Days, Sports Days, extramurals—that marginalized women's collegiate competition. Following a consolidation trend on other campuses, Trinity moved oversight of women's varsity teams from the physical education department to the athletic department, joining men's teams under a new athletic director, Pete Murphy, who was also the head basketball coach. In another precedent-setting move the next fall, head football coach Gene Norris named Kara Christian (a.k.a. Fuzz) as the first female student manager of the football team.[10]

Buried at the bottom of an April *Trinitonian* story about the "new regime" was a comment that the women's varsity teams "had formerly been classified as extramural sports."[11] Finally, Trinity's female athletes had attained official intercollegiate status. While this might appear to be a simple change of terminology, the announcement underscored a significant shift in balance between men's and women's programs, thanks to governance from the AIAW and equity mandates imposed by Title IX. These shifts set the stage for what was to come.

Ninety miles north of the Skyline campus UT bucked the consolidation trend by appointing Donna Lopiano as women's athletic director in 1975.

Joining a Johnson Team

Johnson encountered a variety of challenges in her transitions from intramural to extramural to intercollegiate competition: recruiting limitations, lack of expertise, inadequate facilities and resources, and unbalanced competition. Amid obstacles she had little control over, Johnson was mentor to her young charges, instilling high expectations

Pam Steinmetz referees an intramural volleyball game, Sams Center auxiliary gym, early 1970s. Note limited space between the court sidelines and the walls.

of discipline and decorum while shielding them from the political whims of the day.

The quality and availability of campus facilities didn't match up with women athletes' increasing participation. Johnson's basketball and volleyball teams had access to the indoor courts at the ten-year-old Sams Center, but they often faced practice restrictions when the men's team was in town or the Division I tennis teams needed the main gymnasium on a rainy day. In those cases, the women were usually shuttled to an auxiliary gym. This cozy space had no seating and what one player called "dead boards" on the court slowed down a basketball in mid-dribble.

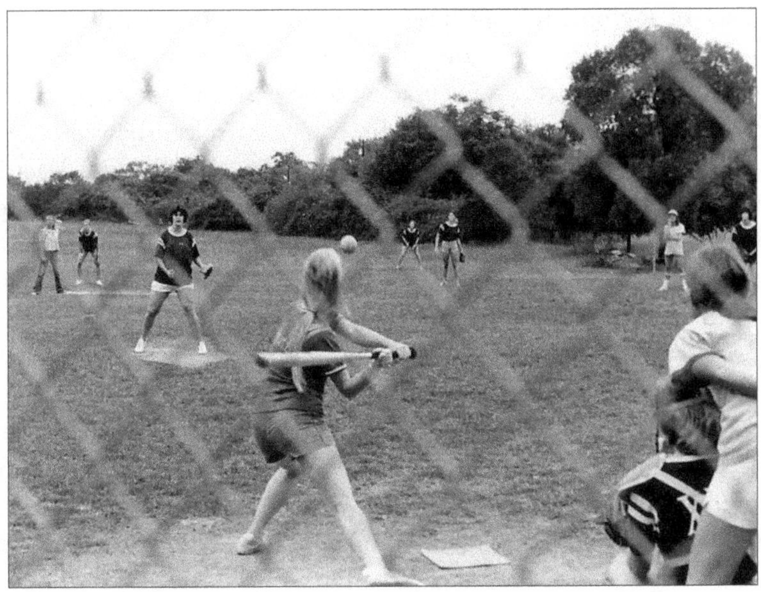

Catcher's view of softball field for intramural and varsity

Because of the lack of space between the court and the walls, chasing a ball past the sideline or baseline might result in a player colliding with the barrier directly under the basket.[12]

The sport that suffered the most was softball. In the first seventeen years of Trinity intercollegiate softball, players had no home diamond, and practices were relegated to an intramural field below High Rise (now Thomas) dorm. Described by first basewoman Alison Taylor as a "scruffy little grass patch," the field featured a backstop and little else. Johnson and her players brought their own portable bases and pitching rubber to transform the undeveloped lot into a makeshift practice diamond. The right fielder had to deal with the obstacle course of a sloping, uneven, and stone-laden surface bordered by bushes. Johnson considered the field "unsafe, even for practice."[13]

Lacking an official facility, home games were played at neutral sites in the area or at the opposing team's field. One common venue was Lambert Beach in nearby Brackenridge Park, which abutted a soggy landmark. Softball player Julie Roba remembers that a ball hit past the right fielder was an automatic home run, since it typically rolled into the San Antonio River.[14]

Lack of appropriate uniforms and equipment also created issues for female competitors. Since the school provided no practice clothing, players were on their own for practice attire—within reason. One raw recruit, who hadn't yet learned Johnson's team rules, showed up for her first basketball practice with multicolored socks. "Boy did I get in trouble for that," Jill Harenberg remembers. Many women of the 1970s appeared in ragged cut-off jean shorts, the fashionable casual wear of the day.[15]

Softball players weren't given protective caps or helmets and were expected to provide much of their own equipment. In place of softball cleats, they wore tennis shoes. Even when the school offered windbreakers for cooler game days, Alison Taylor recalled that the jackets were usually in extra-large men's sizes and emblazoned with "Trinity University Men's... something."[16] Unlike male players who had athletic staff to take care of their laundry, women were expected to clean their own uniforms. Since they had to scrounge up quarters for the coin machines in the dorms, it was a chore they didn't perform after every game. Apparently, jersey quality was also an issue; one basketball player recalled her two-tone uniform "discolored quickly" after she and her teammates jumped into a hotel pool to celebrate a road victory.[17]

The absence of proper attire and equipment—such as long pants or helmets—could contribute to injuries. Sliding into a base on the dirt infield in softball shorts often resulted in "strawberries," angry red scrapes on the players' legs. Some players recall getting hit in the head with a thrown ball while batting or running bases.[18]

Some of these deficiencies were simply the fate of trailblazers. The only shoes available to the earliest female runners were generic Keds tennis shoes, which track team founder Peggy Kokernot remembers being able to bend in half. Because distance runners log dozens of weekly training miles on asphalt or concrete surfaces, shoes without cushioning or arch supports resulted in more shin splints, tendonitis, fallen arches, and stress fractures. Only later did Brooks, Adidas, and Nike manufacture training shoes especially designed for women.

With these experiences, were the players jealous of their better-equipped tennis colleagues? Not necessarily. The small size of Trinity's community meant that many had friends and sorority sisters on the scholarship squad. Terri Hailey, who wore the same uniform in basketball and softball, was aware that "tennis had all the money" but recalls her elation when tennis coach Emilie Foster gave her a pair of Nike shoes imprinted with a Trinity logo. "I thought I was just about the coolest person around," Hailey said.[19]

Female players had little access to training resources, since the Sams Center had been designed before women's athletics existed. Sharing a locker room with other students may have been inconvenient for players, but lack of access to dedicated trainers and treatment facilities was a critical health issue for female athletes and became a perpetual agenda item at athletic council meetings.

At Trinity, one of the most popular members of the Sams Center staff was athletic trainer Levi "Knock" Knight, but he was strictly devoted to supporting the men's teams.[20] In the early part of the decade, student Sandy Champion assisted Johnson's players, mainly by treating injuries. Basketball and volleyball player Betsy Ascani recalls the casual approach common at the time for athletes injured during a game: "She [Champion] sat us on the bench, taped us up, and said, 'Get the hell back out there.'" Today, an athlete is immediately taken off the floor and treated with ice or other appropriate methods.[21]

In 1975, the athletic council finally secured funding for a part-time trainer. Johnson hired Barbara Jones, who tended to female players the next two years and became an informal "scorekeeper, engineer, organizer, and intermediary," according to the coach. Johnson appreciated Jones's positive approach and felt that she had the perfect personality for the job. "She genuinely and sincerely cares about people," Johnson said, "and that's more important than putting on a Band-Aid."[22]

In the absence of a dedicated training facility, Johnson's office doubled as a training room. Often a player would use the edge of the coach's desk to elevate an ankle that needed taping. Whether the treatment was given by a fellow teammate, Champion, or Jones, it was always under the watchful eye of Johnson, who ensured that they used proper techniques in treating and assessing each player's unique needs before the games. Another feature of the small office was a medicine cabinet, which housed boxes of bottles of vitamin C that Johnson liberally prescribed to players when they exhibited cold or flu symptoms.[23]

Still, women were not allowed to use the men's more sophisticated training and treatment facilities. Weight training, which wasn't yet a common practice for female athletes, was almost impossible since the first-floor room was reserved almost exclusively for male students. On the rare occasion when a female athlete was granted use of the whirlpool, she had to be accompanied by another female after the men cleared out of the locker room. Terri Hailey recalls Johnson chaperoning her to the men's locker room to treat a minor back sprain. After the shock of seeing a hot tub and TV, the student imagined Johnson thinking, "Oh, I probably shouldn't have brought you in here."[24]

Despite repeated recommendations from institutional self-studies and athletic council meetings to provide comparable resources, Johnson's office continued to function as the primary training room before and after games.

Fan support was lacking not just for the women but for most teams on campus. A *Trinitonian* article, "Athletes in Limbo," described cheerleaders trying to drum up enthusiasm at a home football game while fans folded programs into paper airplanes and floated them onto the E. M. Stevens field. In response, the frustrated yell leaders devised a cheer to meet the moment: "We know you're in the stands, we can hear you breathing." A letter to the editor lamented, "The varsity athletes on this campus deserve far better treatment," describing the spectators as "pathetic." The student concluded, "How difficult it must be to carry Trinity's banner so well and receive as little in the way of thanks!!"[25]

In contrast, tennis was soaring in popularity, and the men's and women's teams were at the top of their fame game. Many Division I home matches drew overflow crowds. Also, bowling was still in vogue, and the team could attract crowds of family and friends to its coed matches in the Sams Center basement.

But for other female athletes, the situation was just something they accepted. "I think we played so many times without a crowd, we knew exactly how to motivate ourselves," said Lynn Walker, who participated on multiple teams and learned to adapt when road games featured fans in the stands. "When there were people there, I didn't pay any attention."[26]

While athletic director Pete Murphy had a men's recruiting budget, the women had none. The blame went not to Trinity but to the governing

AIAW, whose regulations prohibited coaches from discussing sports with female prospects unless the student made the first contact. The insufficient high school pipeline also meant few women with extensive experience were enrolling. Although participation in girls' high school sports almost tripled between 1970 and 1974 (from 300,000 to more than a million), most schools still offered limited varsity options for girls. Teenagers who did show interest in athletics were often marginalized and ridiculed by their peers as tomboys or worse. In high school, if you wanted to play football or basketball, you were called a misfit. Mary Walters, a basketball player who attended a Catholic all-girls' school in Dallas, said that her teams didn't compete in a league "because the principal felt that athletics were not ladylike."[27]

Of course, an underlying issue for the women's program was the fact that many incoming freshmen had chosen Trinity for its academic standing rather than its athletic reputation. Those who had no sports experience preferred more casual recreational alternatives, such as intramurals.

Some of the most fertile recruiting hotspots were the intramural office and playing fields. When director Jim Potter saw talented females, he encouraged them to join the extramural teams he was cosponsoring with Bob Strauss. Partly due to Potter's prodding, intramural staff members Glada Munt and Jana and Pam Steinmetz abandoned their varsity tennis dreams to star on the early volleyball and basketball teams.[28]

Most other prospects had to be informed about team tryouts through the kind of informal tactics that Johnson perfected at St. Mary's. "I always joke about putting up signs encouraging girls to come out for the team, but really, that's the way we do it."[29] She also leaned on the *Trinitonian* for ads or other support. Female sports editor Claudia White tried a lighthearted approach in one weekly column. After mentioning upcoming tryouts for softball, she wrote, "Speaking from experience, the practices are fun, and the games are exciting. Besides, it's a good way to get a tan."[30]

Serendipity sometimes lent a hand. Jill Harenberg had earned a coveted spot on John Newman's Division I tennis team but was sidelined by an injury. So, she spent fall afternoons watching the women's varsity basketball practices. Johnson noticed Harenberg in the stands one day, and—knowing nothing about her skills—asked if she wanted to try out for the team. The freshman agreed and made the team as a starter. She recalls going home to New Mexico for the holidays and telling her family she wanted to shelve her ten-year tennis career to participate in other team sports at Trinity. Her parents overcame their initial surprise and supported their daughter's eventual forays—with Johnson's nudging—into varsity basketball, volleyball, softball, and track for the rest of her outstanding college career.[31]

The paucity of feeder programs and experienced prospects compelled Johnson to ask players like Harenberg to join her other teams, what some considered a "natural progression" in the early days when few athletes specialized in one sport.

Once Johnson found her players, she prepared them for more rigorous intercollegiate competition by focusing on building endurance and strength, stressing the importance of team cooperation, and teaching the fundamentals of each sport. Rindy Lobdell, who played on Potter's basketball squad, recognized an immediate change of pace under the new coach. Although Potter had run some drills for his extramural players, Johnson brought practice to another level. When Johnson assigned sprint drills—so-called suicides—to increase their endurance for the full-court game, Lobdell recalls thinking, "Uh-oh, I'm in trouble now."[32]

Most who attended tryouts made the team, since there were few prospects, and Johnson became adept at creating a functional team with those who showed up. The few players who had high school experience often had to make major adjustments at the collegiate level. For example, girls' slow-pitch players had to adapt to fast-pitch softball game in college. And in Texas high schools, where many of Johnson's players attended, girls' basketball still featured the six-player half-court game instead of the five-player style standard for collegiate squads. In 1958, the Office for Civil Rights considered banning the girls' six-on-six high school game, but it took thirty-seven years for the archaic practice to end across the country.[33]

Since many of her basketball players arrived without shooting skills, she centered her strategy on defense and relied on the players to "freelance" on offense. She admitted that the approach meant they needed "a lot of experience to keep from just killing themselves out there without a patterned offense to run."[34]

Some new recruits soon learned that Johnson lacked technical knowledge in their sport. This was common in the early days of women's athletics, when physical education majors were schooled in basic techniques. But once they moved into the field, they found themselves in Johnson's position, often assigned oversight of multiple teams and learning on the fly how to coach sports outside their skill set. Ironically, Johnson's only previous playing experience was in tennis, which already had its own program at Trinity.

Many of the first extramural athletes found ways to sharpen skills on their own. When Pam Steinmetz returned for her second season on Johnson's volleyball squad as a significantly improved player, the coach asked if she had been practicing over the summer. No, Steinmetz confessed, she had just used her time on the bench the previous season observing teammate Lynn Walker's passing technique.[35] Terri Hailey explained how Johnson capitalized on the talents of the players who showed up to a tryout. When the freshman arrived at the dusty field to learn about the fast-pitch team, she quickly realized they had only one returning pitcher. Johnson repeatedly asked if anyone else had pitching experience, and Hailey reluctantly admitted she'd pitched once in fifth grade. After Hailey threw a few rusty pitches, the coach handed her a pitching instruction book and said, "Here you go. You're our backup pitcher."[36]

To her players, Johnson's gifts for teaching and coaching made up for any lack of knowledge, and many considered her a "master motivator." Jill Harenberg credited Johnson for recognizing her players' strengths and applying her sharp analytical skills in games. "She could look at other teams and see where their weaknesses were, and direct us to attack them that way," said Harenberg, who coached high school sports early in her own career. "I think that's the sign of a good coach."[37]

The AIAW's 1973 athletic scholarship decision exacerbated the already disparate skill levels between teams. Johnson's multiple city championships proved that her teams could win against local opponents like Incarnate Word, Our Lady of the Lake, or St. Mary's. But the school's status as an independent in TAIAW District IV pitted them against larger schools, including Baylor, UT, Southwest Texas State, and Texas Lutheran. Since many of these colleges took advantage of the scholarship option, Johnson's squads often faced more physically intimidating and talented opponents. But the Tigers refused to cower. "We had enough confidence on the teams that I played on that we were not outmatched," Harenberg said.[38]

A *Trinitonian* summary of the Tigers' lopsided loss in the 1974 home basketball opener highlighted the size mismatch, describing the opponents from Waco as "six-foot plus amazons."[39] But the Baylor *Lariat*'s account of the same January contest noted that four Tiger players missed the game due to illness, a fact unaddressed in Trinity's story. Another *Lariat* article provides a stark example of how some coaches chose to mitigate their competitive advantage. Bearette coach Olga Fallen (former colleague of Johnson and Rushing) had benched her 6'4" forward for the contest because Trinity's height "wasn't exceptional."[40] It's hard to fathom a men's basketball coach making the same gameday adjustment. Finally, a glance at a 1978 tournament roster portends the inevitability of the Tigers' first-round loss to a dominant Baylor team in the state championships. Of the seventeen Bearettes registered in the TAIAW program, five were listed at more than six feet tall, while the tallest of the eight players on Trinity's roster was Val Stein at 5'11". (Baylor defeated the still formidable Wayland Baptist Flying Queens for that year's state title.)[41]

Johnson was painfully aware of her team's shortcomings. Once, when asked what she wanted most for the upcoming basketball season, the coach replied, "All I want for Christmas is a six-footer."[42] Santa delivered in 1975, with 6'0" Betsy Chenault, from Checotah, Oklahoma. She and her schoolmate, star guard Kathy Stidham, joined the Tigers. Complementing the two talented freshmen were veterans Jill Harenberg, Patti McBee, and Ann Burbridge. The scrappy squad posted its first winning record (16–11), scored a significant upset, won the TAIAW Zone title, and qualified for the state tournament.[43]

Johnson's players learned they couldn't count on their coach for sympathy. When an injured Lynn Walker needed help walking off the court after another loss to Baylor, Johnson told her, "You walked in here, and you're walking out."

The players did appreciate the coach's humor when preparing to play superior teams. Hailey remembers Johnson's pitching advice before facing Texas A&M, which was ranked number one in the country at the time: "Well, throw the ball and get out of the way."[44]

1975–76 freshmen Betsy Chenault and Kathy Stidham

The bright side to this uneven competition was that athletes got to play in the most impressive facilities in the state in match-ups that soon became a rarity. "We probably didn't appreciate it as much then," said basketball player Sue Bachman, who now considers it a privilege to have played at large institutions like Baylor or UT. Walker was often in awe of away-game venues and remembers the moment she "froze" the first time she entered the intimidating Gregory Gym on UT's Austin campus.[45]

Tangible issues aside, many memories of Johnson are tied to her intangibles, like the power of her outspoken personality and positive approach in her role as mentor.

Players could sometimes sense their coach's stress when sending them up against teams with athletic scholarships, superior facilities, and strong administrative and fan support. Johnson often endured needling from other coaches about her small squads. At one road game Hailey remembers the opposing coach joking about Johnson's "little geniuses," suggesting they should be studying instead. Johnson smiled and shrugged off the lighthearted comments, but Hailey thinks she

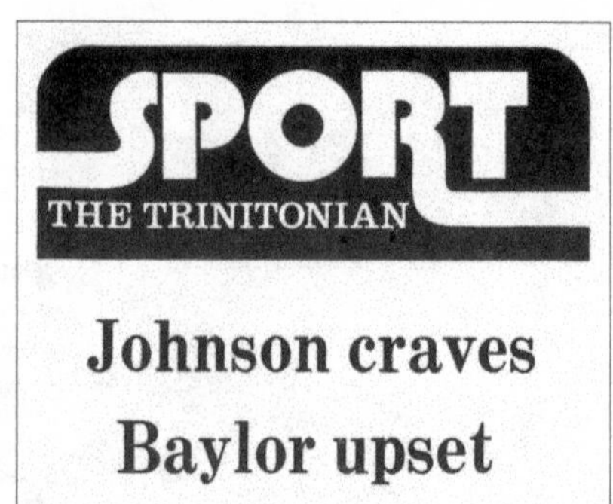
SPORT
THE TRINITONIAN
Johnson craves
Baylor upset

Johnson's 1978 wish was never granted.

was trying to not show that she was upset or hurt. That didn't mean the competitive coach didn't want to defeat her former colleagues, as indicated by the *Trinitonian* headline: "Johnson Craves Baylor Upset."[46]

Despite the rivalry on the courts and fields, Johnson partnered with her peers at other schools in the organizations overseeing women's collegiate sports, dedicating her time and expertise at both the district and state levels of the TCIAW.[47] Her colleagues were familiar with her outspoken demeanor but never questioned her intent. At one state meeting in Jasper, Texas, Johnson became frustrated when asked to vote on an issue before she could consult with fellow district members. She reacted with a passionate speech from the floor criticizing the leadership's actions. Later, she apologized for the tone of her comments in a letter to TCIAW president Sue Garrison but added that she couldn't apologize for her "intent" and pledged to represent her district in a "quieter" manner at the Athletic Institute.[48] Garrison's response indicated her high regard for Johnson's candor: "You are sincere in your efforts to represent all of the institutions in your district, and I respect and admire your zeal in speaking for their preferences and beliefs. Your concerns are my concerns, Libby, and I hope you know that."[49] Apparently Garrison assisted the Trinity coach on other matters. A 1972 note from Johnson to the director ended with thanks for a letter that Garrison sent to Wimpress. While the content of the correspondence isn't clear, Johnson wrote, "It has already helped a great deal."[50]

Team discipline and decorum were other hallmarks of Johnson's coaching style. She expected her players to prepare physically and mentally for games and to arrive at practices and games enthusiastically and on time. Once, a volleyball player missed the team bus to a game, so she drove herself to the nearby Incarnate Word gym and joined her teammates on the bench. Before the match began, Johnson ordered her to return to Trinity. After the incident, members of that team became renowned for their punctuality.[51] Monica Flores, another of Johnson's early players, said that they were expected to arrive at games looking professional and encouraged to play with integrity, determination, and honesty.[52]

The self-control that Johnson asked of her players she also expected of herself. While some described Johnson as "competitive but composed on the bench," the coach's competitive streak sometimes got the best of her. In one hotly contested basketball game on a visitor's court, Johnson felt the referees were favoring the home team. After a call she considered egregious, she shouted, "We're getting screwed!" Afterward she apologized to the team for her unprofessional behavior and pledged no repeat performances. Players appreciated her sincerity in acknowledging the lapse in decorum.[53]

Despite the infrequent outbursts, the coach never took her anger out on players and rarely singled out an individual for poor—or positive—performances in public. One player said, "The only time Johnson would get upset at [us] was if we were not playing up to our potential." Another noted, "She could be intense and tough, but you always knew that she was on your side." Even when asked by a student reporter to comment on an outstanding individual performance, Johnson typically commended the player for her contributions to the team's success rather than setting her apart from her teammates.[54]

When praise was called for, however, Johnson occasionally complied. Mary Walters, a product of the Texas high school "half-court" basketball format, was disappointed being a backup her freshman year after she'd been a defensive starter in high school. After her boyfriend taught her shooting skills the next summer, however, she returned to campus with new offensive skills. "Miss Johnson actually stopped practice and told me how amazing that was," she remembers. In her junior year, Walters became a starter on the Tiger team.[55]

Another conversation revealed the coach's openness to players' opinions. At a home basketball game, Glada Munt complained about not getting as much playing time as she wanted, despite Johnson naming her captain of the 1973–74 team. When Johnson said she needed to be a

Mary Walters shoots at a road game.

strong team leader, the senior responded, "It's kind of hard to lead from the bench." From then on, she got to play more."[56]

Like most coaches, Johnson experimented with a variety of motivation techniques. In one locker room speech, while her team was preparing for a high-profile tournament game against a rival, the coach said, "Okay, girls. Here's how it works. When we win, we'll go to this really nice seafood place on the water in Austin. If we lose, we'll go to Dairy Queen." After the Tigers upset their opponent, they dined on seafood and played the song "We Are the Champions" on the ride home. Johnson's positive approach was especially appreciated in the shadow of poor seasons or tough defeats. After losing one hard-fought basketball game, she told the *Trinitonian*, "Tonight was by far the best effort we've had all season. We ran a totally different offense the second half than we did the first, and they never adjusted to that change." Tongue in cheek, sports editor Dave Pasley commented, "Johnson must get a salary for being optimistic."[57]

But the coach didn't want her players to get too cocky. In one of

Spotlight on Glada Munt

Glada Munt wasn't just a pioneer in women's sports at Trinity; for more than half a century she played an outsized role in Texas athletics. When she followed her sister to enroll at Trinity in 1970, the only non-intramural opportunities for women were an unofficial tennis team and two budding extramural squads. Tennis was an easy choice since Munt had been coached in high school by former Trinity player Mary McLean. She also joined Potter's intramural staff, officiating games, which supported her Whataburger habit. When Potter and Bob Strauss established new teams, however, she retired her racquet and joined basketball and volleyball extramural squads under Potter and Libby Johnson.

Munt graduated in 1974 with a dual major. ("Biology and premed for my parents, and PE for me," she explains.) Johnson and Shirley Rushing encouraged her to continue her education and helped her find a job at Baylor University, where they had earned their graduate degrees. Munt said that Rushing's small gesture "was a springboard for [her] whole career." In addition to her studies, Munt was head coach for the Baylor tennis team and assisted the volleyball and basketball programs. She earned her master's degree and took a job at Southwestern University in Georgetown, Texas, where she taught kinesiology and led the women's varsity programs, often finding herself across the court from her former mentor.

Glada Munt performs her intramural officiating duties.

Not long after Munt earned her doctorate from the University of North Texas in 1992, she replaced women's sports pioneer Carla Lowry as one of the few female athletic directors in the country. One of her first tasks was to transition to Division III and join Trinity in the Southern Collegiate Athletic Conference. In addition to her many other career contributions, the SCAC commissioner especially commended Munt for her powerful voice in support of women's representation in the conference. After forty-five years at Southwestern, Munt retired in 2020.

her last games playing for Johnson in 1980, Terri Hailey scored more than forty points and grabbed more than twenty rebounds against a lesser opponent. Instead of congratulating her, Johnson expressed disappointment that the player Hailey was defending scored ten points.[58]

Another role Johnson took seriously was academic mentor. She encouraged her players to maintain high academic standards—not simply to achieve a certain grade average but also to prepare for future careers. With Rushing's help, she kept close tabs on their academic progress and, when necessary, gave advice and support. One student who floundered in her first semester admitted she might have flunked out of Trinity without Johnson's timely intervention. "I was having a really good time," basketball player Sue Bachman recalls. "I was good kid. I wasn't drinking, I wasn't doing drugs, but I was staying up until all hours of the night." A week before finals, Johnson heard about the freshman's poor grade report, so she told her, "You're coming home with me, and you're going to live with me until finals are over. And you are going to study. And you are going to pass." Bachman followed her coach's lead, passed her finals, and practiced her newfound academic discipline and time management skills the rest of her college career.[59]

Most memories shared by former players were of Johnson's role as coach and advisor, but Pam Steinmetz also remembers her teaching prowess. The physical education major took many classes from Johnson and admired the professor's field of knowledge and ability to set goals for her students. When later composing her own postgraduate paper on education, Steinmetz's report about "good teaching" was simply titled "Miss Johnson."[60]

Johnson had a notoriously dry wit. As a new Southwestern coach, Glada Munt was already dealing with a slim squad at a basketball tournament in Kingsville when several more of her players had to drop out. When Johnson saw only three Southwestern players on the floor, she remarked, "I could have sworn I taught you to play with five."[61]

She also had a propensity for assigning nicknames. Freshman Lynn Walker, who wasn't aware that Lamar University was five hours east of San Antonio, showed up for her first volleyball road trip without a suitcase. "You really are a rookie, aren't you?" quipped the coach. Even though Walker evolved into one the best female athletes on campus,

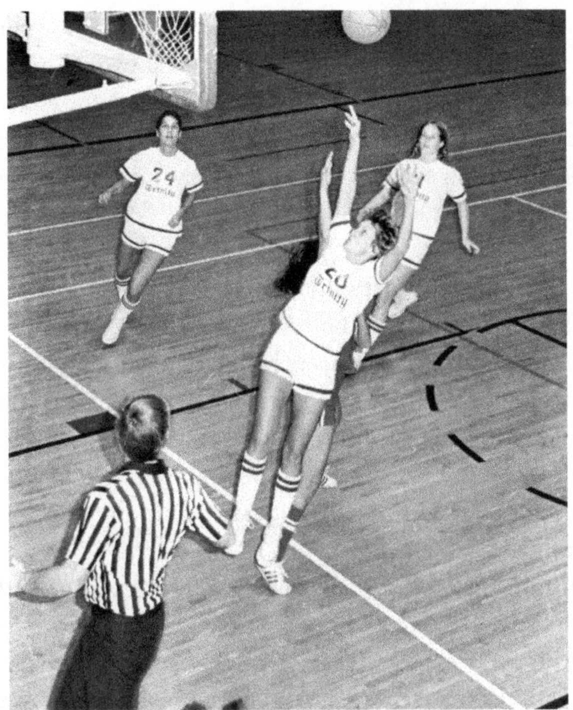

Sue Bachman (20) blocks out for rebound; Myra Tucker (24) and Trudy Fucik (11) get in position.

the Rookie nickname stuck. When Pam Steinmetz got mad, her cheeks puffed out like Winnie the Pooh. Once Johnson nicknamed her Pooh, no one in Sams Center ever called her by her first name again. Her sister Jana was dubbed JanJan.

Johnson's beloved blue van was nicknamed Fluver. The 1969 Ford Econoline often served as team transportation, with John Denver songs providing the soundtrack to road games. She loaned the van to Pam Steinmetz and Glada Munt to run errands, and in return, they washed it and filled it with gas. "Libby's surprise and appreciation was priceless," Steinmetz recounts.[62]

Even though Johnson had no children of her own, players called her Mama Libby behind her back but never to her face. Had she known, she might have embraced the nickname, since she never received motherly advice as a young adult herself. She proved adept at balancing her roles as disciplinarian and teacher with those of mentor and friend, and her open-door policy attracted students to her small office. Since there wasn't room for a sofa, the young women would shove aside the softball scorebooks and settle in between the large bookcases for conversations, both lighthearted and serious. Some players considered the office a safe haven to seek advice on sensitive issues, and several recall receiving life-altering guidance from the coach.

Perhaps one of Johnson's most impressive feats was her ability to shield her young charges from the turbulent politics of the Title IX era. Her cool demeanor in front of her players belied her subliminal frustrations from the daily battles for equitable treatment. Whether it was her subtle deception or their own youthful ignorance, the majority of her players look back fondly on the halcyon days of being on a varsity team. When asked if they felt cheated by the inequities, a common response was "We were just happy to be playing."

Three alumni most attuned to their coach's dexterity in handling conflicts were those who later worked in their own athletic departments. Glada Munt notes, "We really just weren't that aware of the discrepancy in resources."[63] Trinity grad Mary Walters, who worked at the University of Dallas in a variety of roles, including athletic director, agrees: "You don't have awareness at that age of what other people are doing for you." But looking back, Walters recognizes what Johnson did: "She fought for us."[64] Teresa Machu, a 1984 graduate who played for Johnson her freshman year, admitted that all she ever wanted to do was play. In her own long coaching career, however, Machu faced many of the same obstacles and found herself applying Johnson's tactics while fighting for a batting cage or equal time in the gym.[65]

Most of all, Johnson's players remember her as "a deep thinker, with a strong character and a strong conviction." She let everyone play not just to their strengths but with their hearts.[66]

Two unlikely victories during the 1975–76 academic year stand out. The first was an early basketball upset that jumpstarted a memorable season. In a home game on December 9, the Tigers upended a UT team in what was perhaps the pinnacle of collegiate play for the coach and many of her players. The *Trinitonian* had pegged the team as an underdog against the Longhorns, giving the Tigers "a snowball's chance of

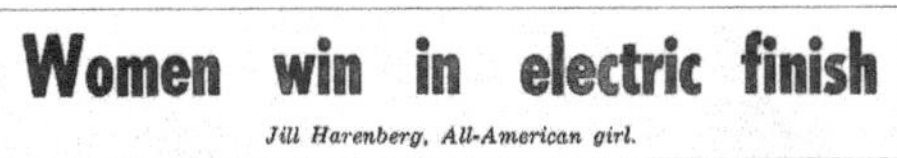
Women win in electric finish

Jill Harenberg, All-American girl.

***Trinitonian* covering UT basketball**

winning in hell." The women proved them wrong. Sports editor Danny Garcia described the nail-biter:[67]

> Trinity's diehard crew of cardiac kids, the women's varsity basketball team, beat Texas 67–66 in an exciting game that had simply the most incredible wind-up in the history of basketball—men's, women's, or children's. "This is the greatest victory Trinity has had in anything," Coach Libby Johnson bubbled excitedly about the dramatic performance of her cage marvels, Patti McBee, Jill Harenberg, freshman wonder Betsy Chenault and the rest of her gang. Coach Johnson's gritty bunch trailed on the wrong side of the scoreboard, 66–60, with just 33 seconds left in the Tuesday night thriller at Sams Center before pulling it out with an effort that has witnesses still shaking their heads.

Garcia recounts defensive plays, rebounds, and points scored in great detail right up to the exciting finish when Jill Harenberg was fouled. He concludes, "With 0:17 left she sank the bonus point and then stole the opponent's final pass with 0:4 remaining as the incredulous crowd flooded the bench in joyful pandemonium."[68]

Reflecting on the victory decades later, Harenberg merely remarked, "That was pretty exciting."

The women's team went on to post the school's first winning season and qualified for the state tournament. Not surprisingly, it didn't make it into the 1975 yearbook. The *Mirage*'s sparse coverage consisted of four photos topped by the headlines "Women Add Beauty to the Sport" and "Women Cagers Show Their Style." Although the men's team had a losing season, editors dedicated five pages to them.[69]

In another upset, Johnson's 1976 softball team defeated Southwest Texas State, a school she rarely had success against. The Bobcats coach called Johnson for a challenge game, probably expecting the uneven matchup to boost her scholarship team's record. To her consternation, the Tigers scored six runs in the first inning, pounded twelve hits, turned two infield double plays, and trounced their rivals 8–3. Key to the victory were the contributions of Ann Burbridge, Julie Roba, Jill Harenberg,

Starting pitcher Ann Burbridge *(left)* with top hitter and first baseman Alison Taylor

Patti McBee, and first basewoman Alison Taylor, who batted in three runs. The ecstatic Johnson described the win as "the greatest victory [they] have ever had—softball wise." That team also beat Texas Tech, won the city championship, and qualified for the 1976 state playoffs.[70]

Track and Field Takes Off

The running program actually had its origins in South Hall. Peggy Kokernot and I lived in the two-story building perched on the edge of the upper-campus quarry wall. Our spectacular balcony view of downtown and the track below our cliff inspired us both to start running.

Then, one autumn day in 1974, Shirley Rushing observed Kokernot running around the hilly campus and approached her with a pitch: petition for a women's track team. Aside from the intramural Turkey Trot, Trinity offered no official competition for female distance runners. Kokernot liked the idea. She solicited input, created a proposal, and

South Hall balconies offered an expansive view of downtown and Trinity's running track.

petitioned the athletic council, who approved her proposal. Athletic director Pete Murphy agreed to set up a program if the team could attract enough runners and recruit a coach. Kokernot and freshman Sue Davis won support from men's track coach Rick Davis.

I met Peggy at that fall's Turkey Trot race, and we both also ran with a noontime group of Trinity professors, so I was excited to join them in knocking on women's dormitory doors in search of teammates. Although both my brothers were accomplished runners at my Houston high school, I had never participated in organized sports.[71]

Practices began the next spring with Kokernot, Davis, Linda Keuchel, Dianne Youngblood, and me. We dealt with many of the same challenges as our peers in other women's sports at Trinity: lack of equipment and uniforms, minimal direction from the coach, few schools to compete with, and little budget.

The hard work paid off that first season as four of us advanced to

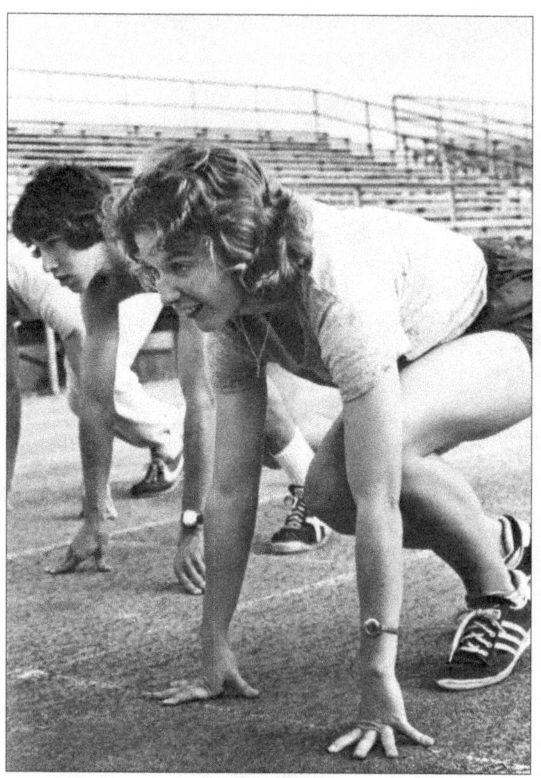

Betsy Gerhardt lines up against the men.

the 1975 TAIAW state championships in March. At the meet in San Marcos, Kokernot qualified for nationals with a fourth-place finish in the 880-yard dash (2:22.3), and Sue Davis finished third in the long jump. Keuchel and I joined them in the mile relay, finishing eleventh.

Davis's performance at the state meet prompted two proposals that took her away from the Tiger team after just one year. The first was a track scholarship offer from UT coach Jack Daniels. The second was an offer from Flamin' Mamie Ellison, who was still coaching the female squad she had established in 1961, but they no longer called themselves the Bouffant Belles, and beauty salon visits were not required any more.[72]

With Davis's departure and Kokernot's graduation, I tried to keep the program alive in its second season. Not only had we lost two stars, but our meager squad trained under three coaches. John Holland had been recruited from a local YMCA to fill in for Delbert Rowland, who

Spotlight on Peggy Kokernot

In addition to being the track team's "founding mother," Peggy Kokernot was a drama major, a budding playwright, and a renowned animal rights advocate. (A *Trinitonian* story about her is headlined "Stray Dog Finds Home at Trinity.") She began running to provide long-distance emotional support for her mother, who picked up the sport to deal with life changes back home in Houston. Kokernot learned to like the exercise, even venturing to the oval below her dorm balcony to wind down after late nights of studying.

As a sophomore, she finished eighteenth in the 1972 male-only Turkey Trot, prompting the *Trinitonian*'s Kevin O'Keeffe to write, "The blond-haired flash silenced numerous Trinity Hill male chauvinists with her high finish among the 35 entrants." It's possible that her showing is what inspired Jim Potter and Libby Johnson to add a women's division to the annual intramural event in 1973. Because Kokernot spent that fall semester studying overseas, she didn't participate in the inaugural women's Turkey Trot. But she won it her senior year.

Peggy Kokernot, 1975

Despite her national qualifying time at her only state meet, lack of official funding prevented Kokernot from making the trip. "I was a poor college student," she said. "And going all the way to Eugene, Oregon, just wasn't in my mindset." After graduation, Kokernot had more successes in track, including more running victories and an Olympic trials appearance. She had a moment on the national stage of the feminist movement and continued to be an activist. She pursued a broadcasting career before moving to Ohio, where she lives with her husband and rescue dogs and cats. She no longer runs marathons, but she continues to follow a healthy lifestyle.

According to Rushing, Kokernot was an outstanding student who wasn't just passing through: "She left her mark in San Antonio." More than four decades after her graduation, she was the catalyst for the project that resulted in this book.

was sidelined with illness and had replaced coach Rick Davis after he moved into an administrative position. Lynn Walker joined the team, and she and I qualified for the 1976 state meet in the long jump and mile run, respectively. In 1977, I stepped aside for other commitments, including sports editor of the *Trinitonian* and *Mirage* and assistant to sports information director Gary Gossett. The newly married Lynn Walker Luna led that squad and was named Outstanding Field Performer for her accomplishments at the first TIAA meet held in San Antonio.

Trinity almost had a women's cross country competitor in those early years. I had made arrangements to join the Southwest Texas State team at an intercollegiate meet, but it was cancelled due to a rare Texas ice storm. It would be another fifteen years before women had a cross country program.[73]

After Johnson's fast-paced first years, it seemed that women's intercollegiate athletics were a permanent fixture on US campuses. The AIAW was doing well: membership kept increasing, more championships were being offered, sponsorships were being procured, All-Americans were being named, and the first national broadcast of a women's intercollegiate basketball game was aired in 1975 between Immaculata College and the University of Maryland.

One momentous event that helped shift cultural attitudes toward women athletes was the 1973 Battle of the Sexes tennis exhibition, when Billie Jean King defeated Bobby Riggs in the nationally televised match at the Houston Astrodome. Trinity women were well represented at the event: former player and 1971 graduate Nancy Spencer volunteered to be a lineswoman at the match, and Munt and the Steinmetz sisters got permission to skip class and drove to the competition in the Steinmetz's Buick Biscayne (nicknamed the Tank) to support King.[74]

At Trinity, the women's athletic budget increased each year with the support of athletic director Pete Murphy and business manager Derwood Hawthorne, and the new intercollegiate sports of basketball, softball, volleyball, and track and field expanded opportunities for female athletes.

In a 1975 interview, Johnson called the elevation of her Trinity teams to intercollegiate status "an important accomplishment for women" while noting that it marked the beginning rather than the end of women's quest for recognition.[75]

CHAPTER 9

New Hurdles Emerge

1976–80

> It's the biggest crock of farce when people say that women are going to sexually damage themselves by playing sports. I think the answer to these attitudes is education and awareness.
>
> —LIBBY JOHNSON, IN *TRINITONIAN*, APRIL 1976

As the momentum of the women's movement began to falter in the face of increasing opposition, Johnson's Trinity career stagnated. Unexpected changes in university administrative leadership and chronic fiscal difficulties lowered campus morale and contributed to an atmosphere of uncertainty. Rising academic pressures on incoming students reduced the time women could devote to extracurricular activities, and student body support of women's intercollegiate athletics remained tepid. In the decade's closing years, Johnson sensed that she was losing the battle.

Also, on the national stage, two major events were unfolding that shaped the future of women's rights.

Dueling Conventions in Houston

Outside the walls of Libby Johnson's Sams Center office in 1976, America was recovering from the depths of a sixteen-month recession, one that featured record unemployment, high interest rates, double-digit inflation, and a quadrupling of oil prices that resulted in epic lines at gasoline stations.[1] Citizens were still reeling from the resignation of Richard Nixon, his subsequent pardon from successor Gerald Ford, and the elevation of Georgia peanut farmer Jimmy Carter to the office of President of the United States.

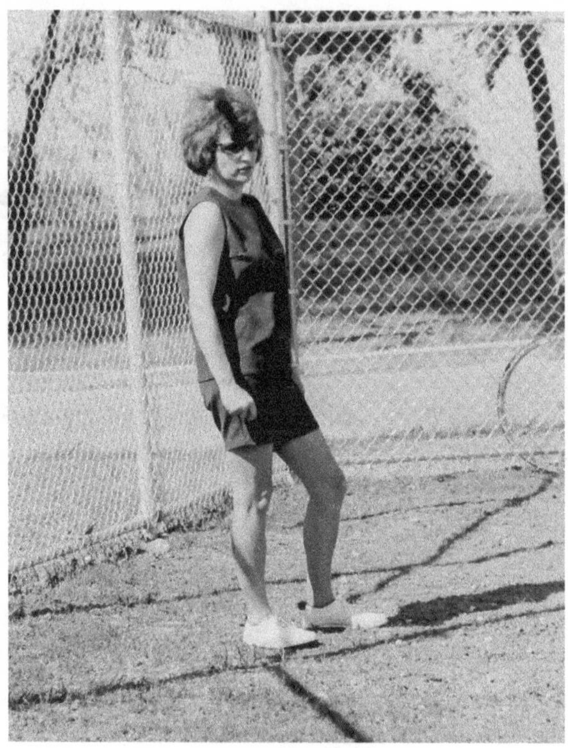

Libby Johnson at a softball backstop

In the arena of women's rights, debates escalated, opposition mobilized, and solidarity splintered. The Equal Rights Amendment, which passed Congress in 1971 and was rapidly ratified by many states, hit a roadblock in the form of a conservative firebrand who perceived a threat to the "older norms of womanhood." Phyllis Schlafly, whose previous cause was sounding the alarm about communism, brought a discipline and organization to this new front in the culture wars. According to historian Daniel T. Rodgers, it was a natural transition. "The Cold War issues that had been the entry point for many moral conservatives remained acute and quickly ignited. Desire to take back the nation to an old-stock European and Christian past ran hard below the surface. [T]hey mobilized along all these fronts." The group's hyperbolic response to the feminist movement relied on "runaway scenarios" that included women on the front lines of the military, alimony abolished, and "unisex bathrooms roamed by whoever happened to walk in." Schlafly's

STOP ERA campaign provided a powerful counterpoint to the feminist movement and stalled the ratification process with only three states still needed to approve the amendment.[2]

Another event that raised the temperature of the dialogue was the Supreme Court's decision to declare abortion legal across the country. The 1973 *Roe v. Wade* ruling was hailed by women's rights activists, but it sparked a Christian conservative backlash, led by pastor Jerry Falwell's Moral Majority organization. Their persistence eventually succeeded, when a more conservative court overturned the ruling in 2022, sending the decision back to voters in each state.

The first National Women's Conference was held in Houston in 1977. Proposed by former president Gerald Ford and funded by Congress, the event attracted 1,400 delegates and 20,000 attendees to discuss women's rights and commemorate the International Year of the Woman. The Declaration of American Women that was created for the event summarized its significance and purpose: "For the first time in the more than 200 years of our democracy, we are gathering in a National Women's Conference charged under Federal law to assess the status of women in our country, to measure the progress we have made, to identify the barriers that prevent us from participating fully and equally in all aspects of national life, and to make recommendations to the President and in the Congress for means by which such barriers can be removed."

En route to the conference, *Ms.* magazine editor Gloria Steinem stopped in San Antonio to share her views on the ERA and other issues. *Trinitonian* editor Uma Pemmaraju covered the event for the November 18 issue, which also featured a preview of the conference and printed the full declaration. After mentioning that Schlafly's Pro Family, Pro Life Coalition was hosting a counter-programming event at the Astrodome south of downtown Houston, Pemmaraju ended her story with a wish for the two efforts to come together to "clear the air and hopefully unite individuals on this spotlighted women's weekend."[3]

Conference organizers had arranged a seven-week, fifteen-state torch relay from Seneca Falls, New York—the birthplace of the women's suffrage movement—to the opening ceremony in Houston. More than three thousand runners had volunteered to cover most of the 2,610 miles, but they struggled to recruit runners for one sixteen-mile stretch in Alabama because of a local boycott led by Schlafly. The relay committee

Front row of marchers escorting the relay torch to the opening of the 1977 National Women's Conference. Left to right, Billie Jean King, Susan B. Anthony, Bella Abzug, Sylvia Ortiz, Trinity's Peggy Kokernot, Michelle Cearcy, and Betty Friedan

asked Peggy Kokernot if she would fly to Alabama to carry the torch on that problematic leg. She had continued competitive running after her 1975 graduation from Trinity, gradually working up to marathons. So she agreed, and the relay continued uninterrupted. She was one of three volunteers selected to accompany the flame on its final mile to the convention's center stage, where former first ladies Betty Ford and Lady Bird Johnson joined current first lady Rosalynn Carter in accepting the torch on behalf of the conference.[4]

A *Time* magazine photographer at the event snapped a picture of Kokernot, which graced the cover of the December 5, 1977, issue. She is also prominently featured in another photograph hoisting the torch while marching with women's rights luminaries Betty Friedan, Bella Abzug, Billie Jean King, and others.

Kokernot credits the event as having ignited a spark in her mother, who was at the event and experiencing "culture shock" after a divorce and thirty years out of the workforce. She said that it "brought out a new, stronger woman who was ready to take on the world, or at least the world in her back yard."[5] The annual Women's Conference continues to this day.

Glimmers of Hope

Most indicators appeared positive for Johnson going into Trinity's 1976–77 academic year, including the establishment of a coed conference, a reduced workload, and increasing acceptance of women's athletics as an integral component of Trinity's overall mission. The athletic council was becoming more unified in its support of the women's programs. The committee, which was the recommending body for Trinity athletics, comprised six faculty, three administrative employees, and one student. It had previously recommended Johnson's promotion to associate professor and appointment as assistant athletic director in charge of women's athletics. In its April 1976 meeting, members acknowledged increased interest in competitive women's sports, recording in their minutes, "There seems to be no question that the latter [women's sports] is here to stay." Eventually Johnson's workload was alleviated when the school hired Susan Howle in 1977 to oversee volleyball and women's track. Addressing another relevant agenda item, the group declared the women's athletic budget "inadequate" and called for substantial increases for travel and equipment, as well as enhancing training and locker room facilities.[6]

Also, in a milestone unrelated to sports, Trinity's 1977 graduates heard from the first female commencement speaker in the school's 108-year history. Elizabeth Luce Moore, the first woman to preside over the policy body of a large university system (State University of New York) spoke to the 576 bachelor's and master's candidates on May 14.[7]

As female students improved their performance, the mismatch in skill sets between intercollegiate and intramural-only athletes became apparent, forcing a revision to the intramural program's eligibility guidelines. The language, which had certainly been crafted in the men's-only scholarship era, required an athlete who lettered in an intercollegiate sport to sit out one season before participating in that same intramural sport. The rationale was that varsity athletes learned from school-compensated coaches and benefited from regular team practices. Johnson, who had earlier been responsible for women's intramurals, expressed her concern that the better-conditioned athletes would discourage other students from participating. She pinpointed a loophole in the rulebook: since players on her teams received no physical felt T's for varsity participation like the men, they hadn't officially lettered, making them eligible for intramurals based on the literal interpretation.

Evidence of this escalating issue could be found in the names of

For much of the 1970s, only women on the trap and skeet or track and field teams received official varsity letters. Left is Carla Brundage's, and right is Betsy Gerhardt's.

intercollegiate players who also appeared in women's intramural results. The summary of the 1973 intramural volleyball finals listed five players in the championship match who had just completed the varsity season under Johnson. Winners of the women's basketball free-throw contest were invariably members of the intercollegiate squad; Jill Harenberg set a new intramural record by hitting forty-four out of fifty shots in the 1976 competition, and her varsity teammates Betsy Chenault and Kathy Stidham helped their Thomas Tiggers capture the team title.[8]

The issue came to a head when three varsity basketball players helped their Chi Beta sorority win the 1976 intramural title. With Johnson's endorsement, the student-led intramural staff changed the rules and benched the players. Two accepted the ruling, but a third disagreed with the prospect of sitting out for a full year. Jim Potter, who was tasked with enforcing the new rule, admitted that the program was at a crossroads, saying, "I'm not sure we did the best thing, but we did something." The decision did allow varsity players to play coed intramurals in their sport.[9]

A coed conference was one of the most positive developments of Johnson's tenure. In the 1976–77 academic year, Wimpress fulfilled a promise made after the 1971 athletic scholarship decision, spearheading the

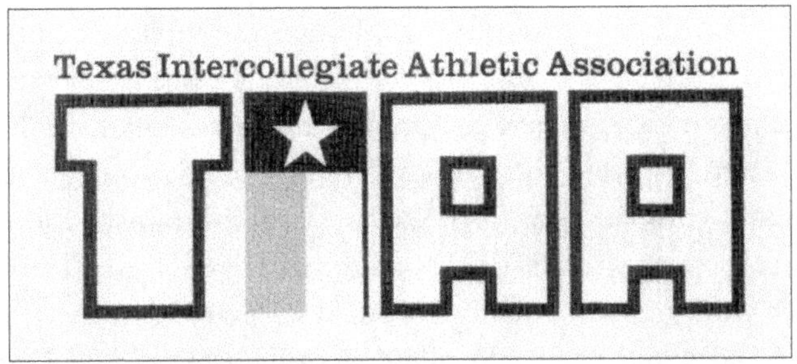

The 1977 *Mirage* introduces the TIAA.

formation of the five-member Texas Intercollegiate Athletic Association (TIAA). The move was made possible by a 1973 reorganization of the NCAA, which created the nonscholarship Division III. Although the term had faded from the scene, it seems the simon-pure conference had finally arrived. According to the *Trinitonian*, "Trinity Athletics have finally found a home. Or, better yet, Duncan Wimpress has built one."[10]

The timing seemed to coincide with a trend at other colleges that were rethinking the value of athletic scholarships. In a two-page feature the previous spring, before TIAA's official announcement, the *Trinitonian*'s Danny Garcia and Jim Woodruff wrote a detailed review of the school's scholarship decision five years earlier. Under the headline "Trinity Athletics—Ahead of Our Time?" alumni director John Burleson reported that a national petition advocating for nonscholarship sports had support from more than two hundred college presidents and coaches. Athletic director Pete Murphy agreed that the decision to drop athletic scholarships put Trinity "about four years ahead of many schools."[11]

The constitution for the new coeducational conference included an exemption to the scholarship ban for one sport at each school, matching the NCAA's own loophole. Wimpress's hand in crafting the language ensured the continuation of Trinity's successful Division I men's and women's scholarship tennis programs, although no other TIAA charter members took advantage of this exception at the beginning. In fact, several of the schools were still in the process of phasing out their own scholarship programs.

Wimpress envisioned a conference in which student-athletes "play for the enjoyment of the game and are neither paid nor 'owned' by the institution." He was also intrigued by the idea that the coed organization might "break new ground in contemporary intercollegiate athletics." Indeed, until 1971, Trinity men's teams had been participating in conferences that did not have programs for women's athletics. Thanks to Wimpress and his peers, the new conference provided a major platform for women to compete against other nonscholarship institutions.[12]

The first forward-looking TIAA members were Johnson's alma mater McMurry College, Austin College, Sul Ross State University, Tarleton State University, and Trinity. While the conference promised savings in travel costs Trinity teams had previously incurred as an independent, it still covered a lot of ground. "The conference members all sit within the borders of Texas, but as some may have heard Texas really is a big place," wrote *Trinitonian* sports editor Dave Pasley. "T.U. athletic squads will have an opportunity to see most of it as they travel from the banks of the Red River in Sherman to the ragged western frontier of Alpine."[13]

A subsequent amendment to conference rules removed an important equality provision. The progressive constitution originally specified that when men and women played basketball games on the same night, the teams would swap their schedules so each had equal opportunity to play in the more popular prime-time slot. In 1978, prompted by disparities in spectators and gate receipts between the teams, TIAA administrators amended the language to specify that women always play first and men second.[14]

Terri Hailey, who competed in the conference all four years of her Trinity career, thought participating in the TIAA was good for Trinity teams. "Because there is so much focus on academics here," she said, "there is no way that we could have survived if we hadn't gotten into a conference like this."[15]

To help the organization get up and running, Trinity offered its facilities for all of the first conference championships, and sports information director Gary Gossett was tasked with handling all related public relations. In that first year, men had championships for basketball, track, golf, and tennis; women had volleyball, basketball, track, golf, and tennis. The other schools balked at Trinity's proposal to enter its nonscholarship junior varsity tennis teams in the conference competition, however. Johnson's players took immediate advantage, defeating McMurry and Tarleton State to win the TIAA's first volleyball title. Eventually the TIAA provided competition in eleven sports for both men and women.[16]

1977 ***Trinitonian*** **asks Who pays for students to play?**

Minutes from a 1976 athletic council meeting suggest that the athletic budget suffered a 60-percent decrease from 1972, and more funds were being funneled to the women's programs.[17] In Pasley's full-page feature about how Trinity funded athletics, Pete Murphy said his proposed 1977–78 budget followed Title IX financial guidelines "as much or more than anyone in the state." Although the 58-percent increase in that year's women's budget demonstrated Murphy's continued commitment to women's intercollegiate athletics, a later self-study revealed that it fell short of full compliance with Title IX mandates when men and women fielded teams in the same sport.[18]

The highest budget item was for football expenses, but this did not present a compliance issue since women had no equivalent sport. The main culprit seemed to be travel and per diem budgets for other men's sports, which generally exceeded the budgets allotted for women. Murphy noted that the per-mile bus transportation expense had increased from 68 cents to 98 cents in the previous few years.[19] But the athletic department's primary justification for the gender inequities centered on the different travel needs of male and female teams. The women played most of their games in the San Antonio area, while men had to travel longer distances for their contests. In addition, the men's basketball team was permitted one out-of-state game that added to their funding requirements. No such opportunities were offered to the women's teams.[20]

Spotlight on Gymnastics

The brief and controversial life of the gymnastics program illustrates the fractured approach to the management and oversight of women's intercollegiate programs. While Libby Johnson was growing her three varsity teams, track was barely hanging on with part-time coaches, and tennis was doing its own scholarship thing, gymnastics appeared out of the blue with the arrival of Elaine Hodges in 1976.

Hodges, a Kansas state champion, had changed her college plans when her coaches moved to San Antonio to manage a large gymnastics center. Talented and tiny (5'2", 100 pounds), Hodges enrolled at Trinity, continuing her daily four-hour practices and attending collegiate meets under the direction of Jan and Tom Heineke. Although she had to compete individually (an official collegiate team required three members), she represented Trinity well, winning both state and regional championships and qualifying for the 1976 AIAW national meet in Boone, North Carolina.

Hodges's disappointing thirty-second-place finish at nationals wasn't what created controversy, however. It was how the next year's "team" would be funded. While the athletic council approved the funds for Hodges to travel to the 1976 national championships (just one year after national track qualifier Peggy Kokernot wasn't granted the same financial support), council members and coaches were surprised to see a pricey proposal for gymnastics in the 1976–77 budget discussions. Athletic director Pete Murphy requested $5,827 for the sport out of a total varsity budget of $308,401.

Gymnast Elaine Hodges

The suggestion apparently came from President Wimpress, and it sparked heated debate, since Trinity had no official gymnastics team or even any other students showing interest in the program. According to council member Shirley Rushing, "Wimpress's decision to start gymnastics was signed, sealed, and delivered without telling Libby Johnson, the women's coach." Wimpress later said he talked to Hodges's coaches about a team but didn't recall the specific budget request. Allegedly this wasn't the first time miscommunication between the parties had occurred.

Murphy's request became moot when the program died a natural death a month later. Hodges told the *Trinitonian* she "had enough" of the sport after seven years of grueling daily practices and competition. She quit, and her coaches retreated to their private gym. Hodges remained at Trinity, where she excelled in intramurals, joined the Gamma Chi Delta sorority, made the honor roll, and was elected to Phi Beta Kappa her senior year.

When the men's and women's basketball teams traveled together to road games, the disparities were difficult to ignore. Women were housed four players to a room, while two men could share a double. Also, the school paid for two daily meals for men but one for the women.[21]

The budget process was an enigma to some athletic council participants. Murphy presented the budget to the council after conferring with his coaches, but members had no authority to make changes. After one council member read the faculty handbook's description of the council's responsibilities on budget matters, he concluded, "We have a little blurb that tells us what to do and it tells us not to do anything." Instead, the power to determine how much money was available and how it was to be spent resided with the athletic director, who defended the budget, and the vice president for fiscal affairs, who decided what was appropriate. Budget requests then went to the university president and the board of trustees for final approval.[22]

Although Johnson was omitted from some of the budget discussions, she continued to see increasing financial support for her programs. In fact, excluding tennis, the budget for women's athletics had risen from $100 to $35,000 in six years.[23] Johnson was more concerned about attitudes toward women, however, than she was about budget disparities. She told a *Trinitonian* reporter, "We are just asking for a share on an equal basis if we have a women's team." Asked to assess the funding at

Trinity in 1976, she said, "I think at this stage, realistically, the women's teams are about where they should be."[24]

After the 1975 Division I women's tennis team returned with its fourth national championship—its first title playing as a scholarship squad—Wimpress awarded them two more athletic scholarships, making its allotment of eight equal with the men's team. Interestingly, funding for tennis scholarships did not appear in the tennis or athletic budgets. When a student reporter asked about the source of tennis's tuition subsidies, athletic director Pete Murphy shrugged his shoulders and said, "I don't know where it comes from."[25]

Signs of Stagnation

Certainly, much progress had been made in Johnson's first four years. But considering the deficiencies outlined in the 1976 accreditation self-study, she must have felt like her Trinity career was just a continuation of her work at St. Mary's, as she still found herself mired in a society where myths persisted about a female's inability to handle the emotional and physical demands of competitive sports. As a coach and now as assistant athletic director for women's sports, Johnson encountered these tensions daily and found herself still challenging what she called "archaic thoughts."[26]

Trinitonian sports editor Danny Garcia summarized the state of play for women's sports in a 1976 feature. Referring to a popular comedian at the time, Garcia wrote, "Women are the Rodney Dangerfield of sports. They don't get no respect. Generally speaking, they also don't get no money, they don't get no equipment, and they don't get good facilities. They also don't get good press coverage, adequate coaching staffs and good high school programs in which to cultivate their basic athletic skills."

Johnson also still carried a heavy workload. According to Terri Hailey, even after Howle was hired in 1977, Johnson was still coaching multiple sports, teaching twelve hours, and serving as assistant athletic director—all while making less money than a high school coach.[27] Another familiar female joined the athletic staff in 1978, when former national tennis champion and 1969 graduate Emilie Burrer Foster returned to take over for Marilyn Montgomery Rindfuss. But as coach of the scholarship women's tennis team, she couldn't alleviate the burdens on Johnson's time.

A look at Women's Sports

"Brother, can you spare a dime?"

1976 *Trinitonian* status report

Wimpress's actions in the first semester of the 1976–77 academic year provided both high and low points for Johnson's vision. His promise of an athletic conference was fulfilled that fall, and then—in the first sign of institutional instability in Johnson's tenure—he was gone, abruptly resigning not long after Johnson's teams began play in the new conference. In December, Dean Bruce Thomas came out of retirement to fill the gap while a committee searched for a replacement. This was Thomas's second stint as interim president; he had also succeeded Monroe Everett from 1950 to 1951. Since his immediate focus was on major academic and fiscal issues and morale building, he maintained a holding pattern on athletic policy issues. As a result, much of the momentum for women's athletics stalled.[28]

The ensuing turnover of campus leadership foreshadowed significant shifts in the institution's mission. Over time, these changes proved to be beneficial to Trinity. But they created uncertainty and anxiety in the moment, as all campus programs were scrutinized to assure compatibility with the interim leadership's priorities. In this context, most of the athletic staff and team members harbored doubts about long-term institutional support of their programs. Johnson was especially concerned that the women's teams were vulnerable because of their modest size and low visibility.

Another looming obstacle to her vision was the escalating threat of an NCAA takeover of women's intercollegiate athletics. During her years at Trinity, she watched the AIAW grudgingly modify some of its policies, including support of athletic scholarships, to counter perceived encroachment by the NCAA. For females dedicated to the educational model of sport, as opposed to the men's commercial model, the AIAW's addition of sponsorships and television contracts in the late 1970s must have felt like a betrayal. Having devoted her career to opposing a win-at-all-costs philosophy, Johnson and many of her peers became discouraged as they scanned the changing landscape. Even their low-key recruiting approach seemed to be in jeopardy. Rumors spread about younger coaches who violated AIAW rules by using NCAA-type tactics. This included part-time male coaches who came from "a different background of athletic regulations" and weren't aware of the rules. AIAW leaders dreaded these exact situations and didn't want a full-time staff dedicated to enforcement as the men did.[29]

The *Trinitonian*'s coverage of women's sports varied widely in the 1970s, depending on the sports editor's priorities, the number of reporters, and the availability of game results from the sports information staff. Another limitation was the size of each issue, which rarely ran longer than twelve or sixteen pages. In September 1978 the student newspaper expanded its page count and reporting staff.[30]

The *Mirage* was even less consistent. Tight budgets during the decade resulted in meager (or no) funding for the annual publication, and a counter-establishment posture by some student editors didn't help. The 1973 and 1974 editions veered so far from tradition they could hardly be called yearbooks. The 1978 volume boasted more than three hundred pages, but the following year featured a paltry twenty-seven-page capsule of the senior class—and little else. Because the book had to be finalized in late winter to give printers time to complete it before graduation, most winter and spring sports weren't included.

However, sometimes the *Trinitonian* dedicated a full page to thoroughly researched issues of the day, such as Title IX, or presented athletes' perspectives. One 1977 survey asked the question "[H]ow do the men regard women athletes?" and printed three replies that illustrate the range of support and level of competition female athletes experienced.

Ann Close, a sophomore halfback on the newly organized women's club soccer squad, had this to say: "At Trinity, women athletes get a tremendous amount of respect, much more than almost any other school I've seen." She admits that it was a struggle, "fighting a history of male-dominated and male-populated sports," but claims that once the male students saw they were serious, many offered to work with them. She also cedes "anatomical differences" but maintains that the women are "no less aggressive."

Val Stein was a senior forward on Johnson's intercollegiate basketball team and played volleyball and junior varsity tennis as well. She expressed a less positive view. "The men's basketball team has no regard

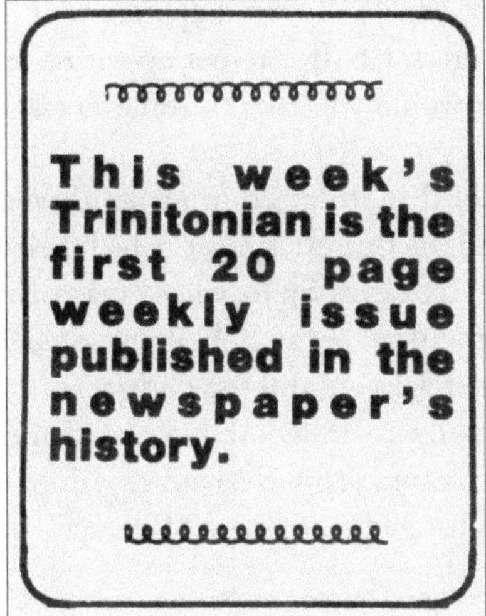

This week's Trinitonian is the first 20 page weekly issue published in the newspaper's history.

1978 sidebar heralds a historic moment for the *Trinitonian*.

for the women's program. Some of the guys think that a few of the girls are okay athletes, but for the most part, they don't think much of us. I think that we are doing better in our competition than the men do in theirs. Last year we went to the finals of the TIAA tournament. The men stress more endurance, while we work mainly on technique and offensive drills. Also, we work more as a team than the men."

Carrie Fleming, a scholarship varsity tennis player, had her own perspective as a member of the 1976 Division I national champion team:

> We have no trouble with recognition or respect—national champions don't have those problems. I think that we get as much recognition as the guys, as far as being athletes. It used to be looked down on for a woman to be athletic, but now I think that having a sport is an asset. It adds an extra dimension to your life. The men's and women's tennis teams all know each other and respect each other as athletes. While we might train a bit differently, we're all working toward the same thing—becoming a better player.[31]

While appreciative of publicity, some female athletes objected to terminology used in *Trinitonian* reporting, such as *Tigerettes*, *Jockettes*, *Fems*, or *Girls*. In 1978, volleyball player Suzy Gray wrote in a letter to the editor: "We are not a drill team or a pep squad. . . . We are an athletic team representing Trinity University. The Trinity mascot is the

Tiger, not the Tigerette. In future articles, I would appreciate it if you would refer to all TU teams as Tigers. P.S. If you met up with a female tiger while in a deep, dark jungle, would you take the time to call her a tigerette?"[32]

Trinity was not the only school that struggled to name its women's teams in the early days. Baylor had the Bearettes, UCLA had their Bruinettes, and regional rival Southwest Texas State, whose mascot is the bobcat, used to refer to their women's teams as Bobkittens. Stephen F. Austin's counterpart to the Lumberjacks are still the Ladyjacks.

Acceptance of female athletes by their fellow male students was evolving. In a 1978 *Trinitonian* column, John Neyland explains why a Trinity women's basketball game changed his opinion of women's sports:

> The argument is that women are as good as men are even in athletics. Male chauvinists, as women refer to them, don't agree. They contend that men can do anything women can do, only they can do it better. This weekend, however, the women's basketball team proved they do some things as well as the men—win. They won all four games they played en route to capturing this weekend's basketball tournament, which they hosted. The teams they beat weren't slouches either. This reporter, somewhat a male chauvinist himself, responded with both curiosity and disdain when the editor assigned him to cover the tournament's action. I figured I would sit in the stands, either laughing or crying at the errors that I thought were part of women's basketball. Surprisingly, I couldn't find enough errors to laugh or to cry.
>
> Oh, I smiled a lot—mainly at my own ignorant expectations. I couldn't help comparing the women to the men, and of course, there were some very conspicuous differences. Physically, the women were not as good as the men. They weren't as quick, or as fast, and they couldn't jump as high. What they lacked in physical prowess, however, they made up for with hustle, intensity, intelligent play, and teamwork. . . .
>
> As far as this observer is concerned, there is no argument concerning athletic abilities between men and women. In a matchup between two quality teams, one men's and one women's, the men would win without exception. But this argument is invalid. A true fan goes to a contest because he loves the sport. He doesn't care so much about who wins, but

> instead wishes for a hard-fought, well-played game. The women's game provides this. . . . On paper, the women's game may not be impressive. On the court, however, it is.[33]

Neyland's words were typed not long after the Olympics finally introduced women's basketball. Although it probably had little effect on Trinity's nonscholarship athletes, the 1976 Montreal games opened a new door for the most talented collegiate players. The timing was impeccable since US schools had moved away from the half-court game. American women could finally compete against international teams who had been playing the full-court version for decades.[34]

In my last semester, I was a co–sports editor for the *Trinitonian* (with my husband-to-be, Dave Pasley) and wrote about my own experience as an active member of one of the most obscure organizations on campus: women's sports. In one of those columns, I reflected on the early days of track and field:

> My sophomore year, I had the golden opportunity of being one-fourth of a group who attempted to breathe life into a women's track program. We operated on a non-existent budget—all of our money was taken from the men's funds. Although we probably lost a lot of friends that way, when two of the girls qualified for the national meet, we felt that our efforts had paid off. After that year, we were guaranteed funds that were comparable to men's track and field allocations. That experience taught me one thing about athletic philosophy—the school will provide opportunity if students can point out the need.[35]

External coverage for Trinity's women's teams appeared poised for improvement with the 1976 hiring of experienced journalist Gary Gossett as sports information director in the public relations office. Gossett was a familiar figure in San Antonio sports journalism for his television and newspaper work and had attended Trinity in the 1950s. He promised to supply local media with information about all Trinity intercollegiate sports, male and female.[36]

After the initial flush of enthusiasm, Gossett's publicity efforts didn't seem to match his promises. The (non-tennis) female athletes and coaches felt the local newspapers didn't give their teams fair coverage in the sports section. "They were treating us like an intramural team or a team from the YMCA," Johnson said. "I mean, we're an intercollegiate team that competes on a same level as the men in sports like basketball." Channeling her familiar wit, Johnson said, "I called them up and threatened that we were going to play a game topless. That got the media's attention. We would never have done it, but it sure served to get them thinking."[37] The strategy briefly worked, as both the *San Antonio Light* and the *Express-News* gave her teams better coverage with personal interviews and detailed game statistics.

However, the 1979 women's softball team qualified for the national tournament but received no media recognition. An internal report conducted that year by Professor John Moore on the status of Trinity's women's intercollegiate activities included a summary statement about Gossett: "Women's coaches have been extremely critical of the public relations officer assigned to cover women's athletics by the University. The coaches maintain that little time or effort is invested covering women's athletics by the official."[38]

In 1980, public relations director Jim Harford said Trinity's redefined liberal arts emphasis meant that athletics needed to fit in as part of the liberal arts education and thus must be promoted as such. "Our emphasis should shift from filling bleachers to promoting programs which students can participate in and which offer athletic competition," he said. When asked to take on assignments in addition to athletics, Gossett balked at the idea and quit. At first, new university president Ron Calgaard wasn't going to hire a replacement for Gossett, but he changed direction after Harford and Pete Murphy submitted a proposal for a part-time position.[39]

Not only did this lack of publicity mean that it was left up to *Trinitonian* staffers to record women's sports statistics, but there were few official photographs documenting women's varsity teams. This issue resurfaced in 2005 when Terri Hailey was inducted into Trinity's Athletics Hall of Fame. The staff scrambled to find a photo of her playing in the late 1970s and soon realized there was nothing to show from her college career. "So, basically, they took a picture of when I played slow-pitch softball and then just put a Trinity uniform on that picture," she said.[40]

A Turning Point for Johnson

In addition to the regular skirmishes that chipped away at Johnson's optimism, several major developments spurred the coach to alter her career plans. First, she had to bid farewell to two of her most versatile and talented athletes in 1978. Patti McBee and Jill Harenberg, who played all four years under Johnson in multiple sports, led the Tigers to many of their victories, including the 1975 upset over the UT basketball team. The loss of her star players at the end of what she called her "most successful season in seventeen years of coaching" marked a pivot point in Johnson's career. However, women's collegiate sports were gaining legitimacy at the national level. From 1974 to 1978, athletic scholarships awarded to women increased from 60 to 500, the number of varsity sports available to collegiate women doubled, and budgets for their programs swelled from 2 percent to 16 percent of the overall departmental pie. Despite doomsday predictions, men's sports remained stable, with some increasing their own overall expenditures.[41]

The next landmark date for Title IX was July 21, 1978, when the regulations finalized in 1975 became enforceable. While Title IX Day passed with little fanfare, concerns persisted. One national opinion writer, reflecting on the significant progress made in women's sports, said the NCAA was still predicting "destruction to college sports worse than any disaster movie."[42] In one of the few syndicated stories to run in the *Trinitonian*, a College Press Service writer claimed that lack of awareness and absence of government enforcement made it hard to fulfill the law's intent. Attempts by the Department of Health, Education, and Welfare to toughen its rules for "substantially equal per-capita expenditures" resulted in more apocalyptic predictions from male athletic directors. According to the author, attendees at the 1979 NCAA annual convention rededicated themselves to opposing the act, maintaining that Congress never intended Title IX to be applied to intercollegiate athletics.[43] Less than three years had passed since the NCAA lost its lawsuit against HEW challenging the regulations' validity.[44]

By the 1978–79 academic year, most men's and women's intercollegiate sports programs had consolidated under a single structure (usually led by a male athletic director), putting pressure on university executives to standardize under one governance organization. But there was still no

Spotlight on Patti McBee and Jill Harenberg

It's difficult not to think about Johnson's graduating stars as a matched pairing. Even a local sportswriter referred to Jill Harenberg as Patti McBee's "regular partner in scoring madness."

Patti McBee was a local high school graduate whose quiet demeanor and average size didn't immediately intimidate the scholarship players she confronted on a court or diamond. However, her tenacity would confound many opponents who were picked off base by a timely softball throw or surprised to have a basketball pass intercepted. Even her teammates risked the sting of McBee's glare when they ran the wrong play.

The quiet floor leader consistently led the basketball team with double-digit outings and set a scoring record of thirty-two points against conference champion Tarleton State her junior year. After four decades, many of McBee's basketball stats still rank high at Trinity: she is tied for fourth in field goals made against Texas Wesleyan, second in total season points, and fourth in career points. She remained in San Antonio following her 1978 graduation and died in 1989 at the age of thirty-two.

After her ankle injury paused her tennis career, Jill Harenberg joined the basketball team. Without any prior experience in organized team sports, she became a top scorer on that year's city championship team. Then she got into softball and volleyball as well. The fact that she was named captain or co-captain of every team she participated on illustrates the respect she earned from her coach and fellow players.

Johnson felt that Harenberg could have been an All-American had she competed at a larger school. In fact, coach Jody Conradt suggested to Harenberg that she transfer to her team at the University of Texas at Arlington. Luckily for Johnson, Harenberg said the idea "was in one ear and out the other," and she stayed at Trinity. (Conradt moved to UT-Austin the following year.)

While highlights of Harenberg's career show why she was named to multiple all-conference teams in basketball and volleyball, some observers feel that her basketball statistics would have been better had she not shared the floor with McBee. While Harenberg consistently scored in double figures, she twice finished second in team scoring. Once, she set a single-game record of twenty-nine points, only to see it eclipsed days later by McBee's thirty-two points.

In softball, pitcher Terri Hailey called Harenberg the best catcher she'd ever seen. Harenberg also helped the track team at the 1977 TIAA championships, winning the 440-yard dash.

Her Trinity legacy continued beyond her 1978 graduation: she coached future Trinity standout athlete Teresa Machu when she was at Alamo

Partners in "scoring madness" Patti McBee and Jill Harenberg with coach Libby Johnson *(center)*

Heights High School. Machu remembers Harenberg as "extremely competitive, and knowledgeable, and very caring of her athletes." After a brief education career, Harenberg married, moved to Colorado, and raised two children while working in administration in the energy and health care industries. She remains active in year-round outdoor activities in the mountains. In 2022, Harenberg was inducted into the Trinity Athletics Hall of Fame.

viable alternative to the national championships offered by the AIAW. In fact, for two consecutive years NCAA members had rejected leadership recommendations to host national championships for women in Division II and III, but the votes were getting closer each time. A splinter group emerged for women's intercollegiate athletics that was more in sync with the NCAA's commercial model. According to one sports historian, the purpose of the newly formed Council of Collegiate Women Athletic Administrators was "to lead women into the NCAA structure." And the AIAW suffered a "severe blow" when its longtime ally, the NAIA, announced that it was establishing its own competitive women's programs; the news was shared just three days before the Title IX implementation deadline.

While the AIAW's membership was peaking at almost a thousand institutions, finances were weak, and its philosophy was under attack. In one historian's words, "It soon became clear that the AIAW was facing a multidimensional dilemma: adhere to the educational model but fail financially and risk legal challenges, or abandon it for monetary security and legal protections."[45] The duel between the AIAW and deep-pocketed NCAA was nearing a climax.

At Trinity, another warning sign was the midseason disbanding of the 1979 volleyball team. Just two years earlier, in an effort to reduce Johnson's demanding workload, Susan Howle became the fourth female member of the physical education staff (in addition to Johnson, Rushing, and Marilyn Montgomery Rindfuss). Howle, a San Antonio native and recent graduate of UCLA's doctoral program in public health and nutrition, was hired to teach exercise physiology, set up a laboratory component, and coach Trinity's women's volleyball and track teams. While accustomed to classroom settings, Howle had never coached a team before.[46]

After leading successful volleyball campaigns (25–10 and 27–16) in her first two years, Howle struggled when few prospects tried out for her 1979 team. Those who showed up had trouble balancing their academic work with team obligations. In that fateful season, the coach was unable to hold effective practices and complained about the lack of academic allies for her cause, since some faculty still considered female athletes a novel phenomenon. Earlier squads had been big enough to fill in the gaps lost to conflicts, but that year's small turnout left too many holes.[47]

Howle maintained a positive attitude, but the challenges proved too great to overcome. After starting the season with a dismal 1–6 match record, the team decided to shut down after a "soul-searching" meeting.[48] The morning after the meeting, Howle notified Johnson, who had already been warned about the possible outcome. When Johnson informed Murphy, the athletic director, he said the announcement was premature and ill-conceived, and thought that he and Johnson should have been involved in the team meeting before the decision was finalized. While Murphy and Johnson were optimistic that they could have a team in place the next season (they did), they realized that the episode raised serious questions about the stability of women's intercollegiate athletics at Trinity.[49] According to one of Johnson's basketball players, the frustrated coach felt that the event signaled not only the lack of faculty and administrative support but also a shift in student attitudes. "Nobody would back us," Terri Hailey stated. "I think that really discouraged her, the fact that that could happen."[50]

Howle left coaching in 1981 and went on to attain a medical degree and set up a practice in emergency medicine in San Antonio.

The most transformational event affecting Johnson's outlook was probably the arrival of Ronald K. Calgaard, who came from the University of Kansas to become Trinity's sixteenth president. The hiring announcement, which ended Bruce Thomas's three-year interim tenure, failed to mitigate Johnson's growing pessimism about the uncertain future of the women's programs. Although Calgaard's official term didn't start until June 1979, he made weekly visits to campus the preceding November to familiarize himself with all phases of campus life. By the time his family took up residence on Oakmont Court, the president had broadcast his intention to implement institutional changes on an accelerated scale. As Douglas Brackenridge wrote in *Trinity University: A Tale of Three Cities*, "Ronald K. Calgaard hit the Trinity campus with the intensity of a Kansas tornado."[51] One trustee, attending his first board meeting when the hiring decision was finalized, said, "I realized immediately that he would be a real change-agent for the university. He brought a tremendous amount of passion to the job, earned the full support of the board, and convinced us all that Trinity needs to build the highest-caliber faculty and bolster its sense of community, to be the very best we could be."[52]

Calgaard's dynamic presence and passion both intimidated and energized campus staff and residents. To reach his goals of academic excellence and national recognition, he was determined to transform Trinity into a premier undergraduate liberal arts university with select professional and graduate offerings. During an inflationary period when many institutions sought to increase enrollment and decrease tuition, Trinity decreased enrollment, increased tuition, and became more selective in its admissions standards. Calgaard planned to recruit faculty with degrees from nationally regarded educational institutions to challenge a new generation of Trinity students. He proposed to accomplish this feat within the next decade.[53]

One of his first official acts was to commission a self-study to be completed before he arrived. The report was to include a follow-up to the prior analysis of the women's intercollegiate athletic program and Title IX compliance, which he assigned to chair of education John Moore. He was a natural fit, since in 1977, his department merged with Pete Murphy's.[54] He consulted with Murphy, Johnson, and members of the health and physical education department before submitting his final report on August 7, 1979. The analysis confirmed that problems outlined in the 1976 accreditation self-study—in regards to facilities, budgets, salaries, and publicity—had not been fully remedied. Moore recommended "a more equitable travel budget for women's athletics" and pointed out that male athletes had access to paid tutors, but AIAW prohibited them for women. He also added that the provision for equitable facilities had not been met, listing the women's dressing room area and the softball field as areas of concern.[55] The dissatisfaction with the sports information director was also cited.

Moore complimented Johnson for navigating the deficiencies and wrote that she was "extremely effective in shaping the women's athletic enterprise at Trinity University." He concluded, however, with these words: "The University, by and large, has been successful in satisfying the provisions of Title IX. Two or three rather minor problems exist at this writing, but the University is in a position to resolve these problems almost immediately."[56]

No response from Johnson was recorded, but her subsequent words and actions indicate that what Moore described as "minor problems" she considered significant issues. Five months after the report's release, Johnson announced her intention to retire at the end of the 1979–80 academic year.[57]

In her formal resignation letter, Johnson told the administration she needed to take a personal break at her home in nearby Boerne before deciding on her next career move. After acknowledging that she would miss interacting with students, she wrote, "I think I made the right decision."[58] She offered a more nuanced view in the *Trinitonian*, describing what she saw as a change in atmosphere at Trinity. She said that in 1972, the university was "very, very, interested in the students, and the faculty and the students were a family." But in more recent years, she sensed an erosion of support at the institutional level. She speculated that the shifts in administrative leadership and student attitudes compelled her players to prioritize classroom obligations over practices and out-of-town games. She also encountered fewer quality recruits for her nonscholarship teams, especially in light of the increasing number of schools offering athletic scholarships to women. "It is difficult to get good athletes to pay tuition to play sports," she said.[59]

Johnson feared for the future of the intercollegiate athletic programs she had labored to build and shape in the previous eight years. "I think it is crumbling," she told a *Trinitonian* reporter. "Numerous programs are being cut."[60]

Given the time, energy, and effort Johnson had devoted to her work, and the close relationships she had established with her players, the situation was more than she could bear. Rushing summed it up succinctly: "Libby simply burned out."[61]

Johnson was treasured as the heartbeat of the women's varsity programs, so her decision created a shockwave on campus, especially among those who shared her passion for women's athletics. Ann Cannon, a former student sports trainer, declared, "Miss J. *is* women's athletics. Without her it cannot function."[62] When physical education department chair Jess MacLeay called athletic council member Gerald Smetzer to inform him of Johnson's resignation, he said, "We have lost Libby." Smetzer was shocked, thinking MacLeay meant she had died. Though relieved to learn she was still alive, he was sad she was leaving.[63]

Johnson wasn't the only one concerned about the future of athletics in the new administration. Under the auspices of a student senate subcommittee, twenty students met with Calgaard in January 1980 to express apprehension about the changes and the impact of Johnson's impending departure. The most important question was whether Johnson's position would be filled. Calgaard said it would and had set aside funds in the next year's budget for that purpose, adding that he didn't believe the department could maintain its programs otherwise. While affirming his endorsement of women's sports, he qualified his remarks, saying, "It is foolish to offer a sport when there is no interest. A successful program engages the interest of the students and campus community and gives the university visibility. You don't start with money and say, 'Here, build a program.' You start with the program and provide the money as the program grows."[64]

Most students left their meeting with Calgaard hopeful about the future of women's athletics. Nevertheless, some voiced a need for continued vigilance, and female athletes feared the new president would not fund what he perceived to be an unstable program.[65] An unsigned *Trinitonian* editorial offered this advice: "If the female athletes of Trinity are truly concerned with the future of their sports, they would be wise to request the formation of a student committee that would have a significant part in the search and choosing for a new director for women's sports." The editorial also warned, "If the new director falls too far short of Johnson's energy, enthusiasm and leadership, women's athletics will surely suffocate and it's certain that a dying program will not be first in line for future funding."[66]

In her final fall semester, Johnson's softball players gifted the cherished coach with the school's first non-tennis state title when they defeated Incarnate Word in a best-of-three format to win the Texas nonscholarship division. At the annual all-sports banquet the following April, Johnson was recognized for her herculean efforts to build and sustain the women's programs during a turbulent decade. It would be ten years before another female held the title of assistant athletic director at Trinity.[67]

The momentum Johnson generated for women's intercollegiate athletics at Trinity continued long after her departure. She legitimized the presence of female athletes on campus and laid the foundation for successful women's teams today. Beyond those cultural achievements, she found personal satisfaction in helping raw recruits become accomplished athletes and inculcating values that shaped their adult lives. While winning was important, her goal was to teach, support, inspire, and nurture the women under her charge.

"She always had a door open, and she was a counselor and an encourager," said Amy Brown, one of Johnson's first varsity players. "She had a great deal of wisdom that didn't relate to the game that we were playing."[68] Student trainer Barbara Jones expressed deep appreciation for Johnson and credited her with Trinity's first intercollegiate successes. Describing Johnson's relationship to the women's athletic program, Jones remarked, "It's practically her whole life."[69]

Following her retirement in 1980, Johnson remained in the San

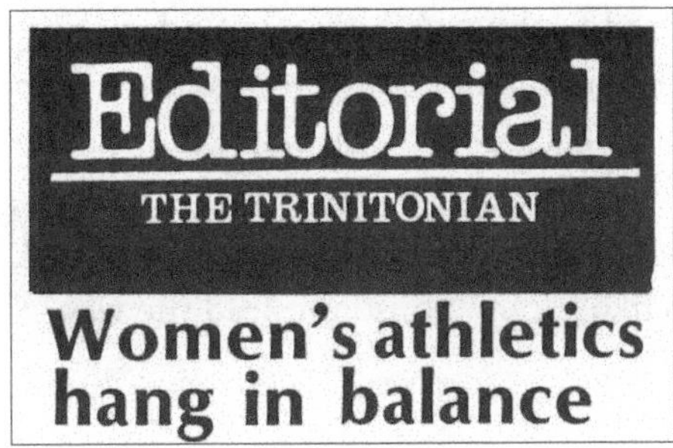
Editorial
THE TRINITONIAN
Women's athletics hang in balance

Unsigned *Trinitonian* editorial after Libby Johnson's resignation announcement.

Antonio area and occasionally ventured to campus to watch women's basketball or volleyball games, entering discretely and slipping away without interacting with players or spectators. However, she stayed in touch with some of her former players, attending games with parents and writing letters of recommendation. Terri Hailey remembers Johnson offering to meet her parents when they made their annual trek south from Missouri to watch their daughter play. On another occasion, Johnson asked Hailey to call her parents. If she didn't? "I'm going to hear it from your mother!" Johnson warned.[70]

Elizabeth "Libby" Johnson died of a heart attack at her home in Boerne on June 13, 1991, at age forty-nine while she was preparing for a hike with a friend. Johnson's mother had died at exactly the same age. The beloved coach was interred in the Boerne Cemetery, and her brief obituary requested that memorials be sent to the Wildlife Animal Refuge in Boerne.[71]

Johnson lived long enough to see the ultimate fruits of her labor. She died not long after the announcement that her former teams would begin competing in the NCAA Division III Southern Collegiate Athletic Conference under the nonscholarship education-focused model she had advocated for throughout her career. Glada Munt, one of Johnson's first athletes and long-time administrator at Southwestern University, reflected on Johnson's vision. "She wanted athletes who were there because they wanted to be there and not because they had to," she said. "She would have fit great within Division III."[72]

The university acknowledged Johnson's contributions by inducting her into Trinity's Athletics Hall of Fame in 2011, honoring her as "the instigator and inspiration of women's athletics on the Trinity campus."

Perhaps the most fitting tribute to Johnson's influence and inspiration is found in the words of 1984 Trinity graduate Teresa Machu, who played briefly for Johnson and later became a coach herself. Speaking for her female colleagues who found themselves fighting for budgets, assistant coaches, equal time in the gym, or batting cages, she said, "Thank goodness we had women like Libby Johnson to lead the way."[73]

CHAPTER 10

Transition Woes

1980–85

Make no mistake, we are committed to maintain athletic programs at Trinity.

—RONALD K. CALGAARD, 1982

When President Calgaard settled into his Northrup Hall office for the 1979–80 academic year, his focus was squarely on transforming Trinity into a highly regarded undergraduate liberal arts institution. While he and his administration repeatedly stated their support for athletic programs, players and coaches felt that promises were made but not fulfilled.

The increasingly popular game of soccer replaced track and field on the women's varsity menu. Traditionally tepid fan support swung from enthusiastic to apathetic. In addition, several concerns spilled over from the previous decade—the gap left by Johnson's departure, a carousel of part-time coaches, inadequate outdoor athletic facilities, and abandonment of the TIAA conference.

Also, the nightmare became reality: in 1981, oversight of most women's intercollegiate sports was forcibly wrested from a wobbly AIAW and moved to the male-dominated NCAA.

A Retreat to Norms

As the decade dawned, the nation welcomed economic stability and a new president. In the first few years, feminists celebrated some tangible successes—the appointment of Sandra Day O'Connor as the first female

President Ronald K. Calgaard, 1984

justice on the Supreme Court and Geraldine Ferraro as the first woman to become a major party nominee for vice president. In other legislative victories, the Pregnancy Discrimination Act prohibited companies from refusing to hire or fire women because they were pregnant; birth control became available to unmarried women; the Equal Credit Opportunity Act meant that women didn't need their husbands to cosign financial documents; all fifty states were allowing women to serve on juries; military service academies and Ivy League colleges began opening up to female students; and in 1980, the Equal Employment Opportunity Commission determined that sexual harassment was a form of sexual discrimination.[1]

But the path ahead became more complicated. The backlash initiated by conservatives such as Phyllis Schlafly and pastor Jerry Falwell had begun. The momentum of the women's movement was interrupted by the 1980 presidential election of Ronald Reagan. The former California governor and movie actor was elected on a New Right Republican platform that omitted support for the ERA for the first time in 40 years. That same national election unseated Democrat Birch Bayh, the two-term Indiana senator, ERA supporter, and Title IX coauthor.[2] He was defeated by Moral Majority candidate (and future Republican vice president) Dan Quayle.

Some historians consider Reagan's rise to be a reaction to the cultural strides made by women, African Americans, and other historically underrepresented groups.[3] Activist Ann Snitow described the 1980s for feminists as years of "frustration, retrenchment, defeat, and sorrow."[4]

As the June 1982 ratification deadline for the ERA loomed, *Trinitonian* assistant editor Jacqueline Pontello expressed her opinion:

> Over half the populace of this nation, i.e., the 51 percent who are of the female gender, still has no legal assurance of being accorded the rights guaranteed to all citizens in the Constitution, since women remain unmentioned in the definition of "citizen" contained in that document—two centuries after Americans revolted against a denial of God-given rights. The social fabric of our nation has changed in ways the framers of that Constitution never envisioned. Democracy, like people, must change with the times. To reaffirm our commitment to the stirring ideals of freedom they advanced, we must refine this nation, this great experiment of ours. I'd like to be able to utter the last words of the Pledge of Allegiance—"with liberty and justice for all"—without wondering when that line will apply to me.[5]

Even though the ratification clock ran out that summer, the topic still inspired debate. Students on campus in 1986 were able to witness a conversation about the failed amendment between two opposing voices at Laurie Auditorium. The Atherton Lecture in Politics and Public Affairs featured Schlafly and Sarah Weddington, the Texas attorney who argued in favor of the landmark 1973 *Roe vs. Wade* abortion case before the Supreme Court. According to a report in *Trinity Magazine*, Weddington acknowledged the lack of momentum for the national ERA but said the need for women's rights remained, especially in education and employment opportunities. Schlafly's rebuttal was that the ERA would have mandated taxpayer funding of abortions, given homosexuals the right to obtain marriage licenses, and threatened the tax-exempt status of religious schools.[6]

Nancy Goodloe summed up the effects of the conservative backlash on women's sports this way:

> The progress in civil rights/Title IX implementation and interpretation seemed to come to a halt in 1980 when Ronald Reagan was elected President of the United States. He was swept into office on a wave of a conservative social agenda that featured a backlash from the women's rights and feminism movements of the past 20 years.... Reagan made two decisions that effectively put a hiatus on the rapid growth of Title IX programs during the decade of the eighties. Opportunities for women in athletics slowed during Reagan's term of office, and many viewed the decade of the eighties as the dark days for women's athletics in this country.[7]

Opposition from men's athletic leadership continued to hinder progress. Oklahoma State University golf coach Ann Pitts told a *Golfweek* reporter, "Title IX was not very popular because [the men] felt like it was going to take away from what they had. I think that sentiment stayed clear through the '80s."[8] In fact, a series of votes by NCAA members altered the landscape of women's collegiate sports forever and prove Pitts's point.

After three years of perceived neglect under an interim administration, intercollegiate sports were being shaped by Trinity's new president, who was integrating athletics into his broader mission. Calgaard's long-term agenda included requiring incoming students to live on campus, building new residence halls to accommodate the mandate, and securing funds to expand and improve campus athletic and recreational facilities.

Committed to implementing Title IX standards and nonscholarship athletics, Calgaard envisioned Trinity's participation in a sports conference composed of peer institutions that shared his academic values. He agreed that athletics were an integral part of the college experience. His formula also matched that of the AIAW philosophy of students playing for the love of the game, balancing high-performing academics with equally competitive athletic performances.

At first, however, his initiatives on top of changes in national intercollegiate athletics created an upheaval for Trinity and its stakeholders, and it was almost a decade before Calgaard's athletic vision came to pass.

A Win for the Commercial Model

The decade opened with a collegiate controversy that seemed to validate the AIAW's complaints about the men's commercial model, including the fear that female athletes could be exploited for financial gain. An extensive NCAA investigation, which merited a cover story in *Newsweek*, found that several large athletic programs were altering academic transcripts and manipulating grades for their male scholarship athletes. "In the pursuit of victory, the vast majority of fans, alumni, even coaches and administrators, have accepted the notion that a winner may have to cheat to win," the authors claimed.[9]

A 1980 *Trinitonian* article referencing the *Newsweek* coverage set out to uncover whether any similar misdeeds were occurring on Trinity's campus. When sports editor Dorian Martin interviewed varsity players and coaches about the controversy, most not only denied any altering of grades but also pointed to the attention coaches gave to academics. Several reaffirmed that their recruiters always emphasized both the academic side and the sports side of Trinity. The respondents also pointed to the many allowances professors made so student-athletes could travel to road contests.

Athletic director and coach Pete Murphy told Martin that Trinity put student interests ahead of winning. In an accompanying opinion column, Martin supported the Trinity academic model, commenting that athletic scholarships put an extraordinary burden on players and coaches: "Due to pressure from the coach who must win in order to preserve his own job, in too many cases the athlete has totally concentrated on his sport, not his studies." She concluded, "Athletics used to be secondary to education on America's university campuses. For the sake of all involved, the 'winning at all costs' attitudes should be changed—or all will lose."[10]

This national controversy didn't impede the NCAA's push toward a hostile takeover of women's athletics, which the female-led AIAW had been valiantly fending off for almost a decade. Since its inception in 1971, the AIAW sought to protect its oversight of women's intercollegiate

TU athletes not affected by major grade scandal

Trinitonian **story addresses national sports scandal.**

athletics from being taken over by the powerful men's organization. Developed by women and led by women, the vision of the AIAW was "to foster broad programs of women's intercollegiate athletics" that prioritized academics. In other words, the AIAW student-athlete was expected to be a student first and an athlete second.[11]

NCAA leaders had shown little interest in women's intercollegiate athletics until Title IX. However, once they failed to convince Congress to alter the final regulations in their favor, their gaze shifted to the expansion of women's sports and the increased potential for financial and political gain. Although the leadership was determined to exert power over women's intercollegiate athletics, it took their membership longer to come around. After years of rebuffing their leaders' proposals to host women's national championships, the dam finally broke at the organization's annual convention in 1980, when members approved five women's championships each for Division II and Division III programs.[12] At the time of the debates, the AIAW was offering forty-two national championships in nineteen different sports.

In January 1981, the future of women's intercollegiate athletics hung in the balance. At the NCAA's seventy-fifth annual convention in Miami, a vote to rescind the previous DII and DIII decisions failed, and the proposal to add Division I championships for women passed. Thus, all twenty-nine divisional and open championships, for nine sports in all three divisions, would begin in the 1981–82 academic year.

Perks offered to participating schools put the final nail in the AIAW's coffin. The NCAA would pay all expenses for teams competing in national championships, charge no additional membership fees for member schools to add women's programs, and create identical financial aid, recruitment, and eligibility rules for men and women.[13] Additional provisions mandated minimum female representation on decision-making panels and guaranteed more television coverage.

The time was ripe for this transformation, especially considering that most universities had already consolidated their men's and women's athletics operations after Title IX, similar to Trinity's actions in 1974. The decisions by the two major men's organizations to place all women's and men's sports under one umbrella made life easier for college administrators.[14]

The NCAA vote's impact was immediate: between 1981 and 1982 the AIAW, which relied almost solely on membership dues, lost more than 200 of its 961 members—including 120 of its larger institutions—and the accompanying income. In another setback, NBC and ESPN pulled out of their AIAW television contracts because of conflicts with NCAA agreements. The obituary of the AIAW—whose $1 million budget couldn't stand up to the NCAA's $20 million—had been written.[15]

After only a decade of operation, the AIAW closed shop on June 30, 1982. The sole remaining stone for their metaphorical sling in confronting Goliath was the courts. On October 9, 1981, the AIAW filed an injunction and antitrust suit against the NCAA, claiming that it used its monopoly power to take over women's intercollegiate sports and asking the courts to prevent the NCAA from holding the championships. They lost those battles—and ultimately the war—in judicial decisions in 1982 and 1984.[16]

Not everyone in women's programs mourned the end result. Many recognized the benefits of using the NCAA's clout to get more exposure and resources. According to Nancy Goodloe, while coaches appreciated the work the AIAW had done to advance women's sports, "they were ready to move on to bigger and better things for their athletic programs."[17]

In 1982 UT coach Jody Conradt had a choice of which national basketball tournament to enter—AIAW or NCAA. She wanted to participate in the first NCAA championship because it would have provided the "best competition." But women's athletic director (and former AIAW president) Donna Lopiano overruled her coach, and the Longhorns went to the final AIAW tournament in Philadelphia, where they finished second to Rutgers.

The star of the inaugural NCAA championship was a scrappy 5'4" guard named Kim Mulkey, who led her Louisiana Tech teammates to a title over Cheney State. Mulkey would be hired at Baylor in 2000 and coach the Bears to three national NCAA titles.[18] Conradt also prospered

UT athletic director Donna Lopiano and Longhorn head basketball coach Jody Conradt, c. 1977

in the NCAA, leading her UT team to a 1986 national title and logging thirty-eight years in her Hall of Fame career.

The January 1982 AIAW convention in Spokane, Washington, was the organization's last. After receiving the presidential gavel from Donna Lopiano, Merrily D. Baker closed the session with emotional remarks, telling delegates they could take pride in the group's accomplishments and asking them to "consider students as students above all else and construct athletic programs and models of governance so that their time to develop as thinking and feeling human beings is not deformed by the demands of athletic pursuits."[19]

In her own summary of the AIAW's legacy, Goodloe borrows from Suzanne Willey's 1996 doctoral thesis, which concluded that the vision of an educational model was still very much alive. Willey, an Indiana University administrator, credits the AIAW with three critical roles in the history of women's athletics: it filled a governance void for women; built a competitive network through state, regional, and national structures; and provided a place for women to develop and model leadership skills.[20]

The female voices amplified by the AIAW were muted as athletic departments consolidated. By 1984, more than 86 percent of women's programs were reporting to male athletic directors, and 38 percent had no female administrative representation.[21] The result? Men did much of the hiring and decision making, contributing to a substantial decline in the number of female coaches across the college spectrum.

Back to Independence

President Calgaard's actions in the early 1980s weren't surprising to those paying attention on Trinity Hill. Ever since the 1971 men's athletic scholarship decision, rumors had swirled about the possible demise of football, and the apprehension about Trinity's place in a conference for men and women was still palpable.

From the outset, Calgaard had expressed his dissatisfaction with the TIAA. Even though the conference schools were more geographically accessible, he disparaged their lower entrance requirements as he was trying to elevate academic standards for Trinity students. "It's almost as big a disadvantage to compete with schools of lower academic standards as it is to play schools that offer athletic scholarships," Calgaard told *Trinitonian* writer and varsity tennis player John Benson. "There are no natural rivalries, no real relationships between the schools."[22]

As an example of the shallow criteria for NCAA athletes, the organization touted Proposition 48 in 1983 as its "most strident move" in setting academic standards. The rule required that in order to compete in intercollegiate sports, incoming freshman must have a high school GPA of at least 2.0 and a minimum combined SAT score of 700. These benchmarks were well below those Calgaard envisioned.[23]

The negative rhetoric coming from the administration prompted a variety of student reactions. In the same column he used to summarize Calgaard's concerns about the TIAA, Benson disclosed an audacious proposal from a student senator (and former *Trinitonian* sportswriter) to eliminate most Trinity sports except men's basketball. Almost a hundred students—mostly football and baseball players—convened to discuss the proposal. After an extensive analysis of the debate, Benson predicted: "With pros and cons of almost equal balance for any possible action, a decision may be reduced to a choice of the lesser of the evils. Yet, structural changes in Trinity athletics in the coming decade are probable." The article ended with the observation that although Calgaard claimed the issue wasn't a major concern, a national basketball magazine sat conspicuously on his desk.[24]

Around the same time the AIAW was dissolving, Calgaard made the inevitable announcement that Trinity was withdrawing from the TIAA in the 1982–83 academic year. This was the nonscholarship conference his predecessor had a hand in forming just six years earlier and made Trinity the first founding institution to depart the group. The article announcing the decision quoted new athletic director Bob Hockey, who suggested the move would "broaden the scope" of Trinity athletics, creating more interest and promoting more participation. Men's football coach Gene Norris welcomed the change, since it would offer his team more variety than the TIAA-mandated home-and-home games that monopolized his schedule. But the athletic director also acknowledged some potential downsides: "It may be a bit tougher in the women's sports, but we are not phasing out any sports."[25]

After the decision to exit the conference, Calgaard reiterated his support for intercollegiate athletics. "We believe that for Trinity to maintain an athletic program that would generate enthusiasm, we must compete with schools that are roughly comparable to Trinity," he told attendees of a varsity sports banquet.[26] His early attempts to create a compatible conference with other private institutions failed, however, placing both men's and women's teams back in the difficult independent territory.[27]

Student opinions varied on the TIAA decision. Football captain Tom Fleaner applauded it: "With this move we will be playing more schools of our academic caliber, hence improving our reputation through this association. It seems that our ideals are now in line. Trinity athletes play for the pure nature of the sport, for what it means to be a member of an intercollegiate team representing one's school. We are proud of what we do and that we represent Trinity."[28]

In contrast, women's varsity basketball player and *Trinitonian* editor-in-chief Dorian Martin provided a gloomier analysis. Citing the loss of publicity from conference championships and the increase in travel costs of competing as an independent, she predicted that the withdrawal from TIAA would cause "the extinction of Trinity varsity athletics." She concluded, "As it has now been done, the only options left to the athletes are prayer and sweat to keep the varsity athletics program existent."[29]

Editor-in-chief (and varsity basketball player) Dorian Martin breaks in new typesetting technology for the *Trinitonian*.

In 1982, Calgaard also withdrew the school's membership from the NAIA, which Trinity was required to join in 1976 with its fellow TIAA members. In his letter to the organization's director, Calgaard said leaving the TIAA was the primary reason for canceling Trinity's NAIA membership, but he also stated his preference for the NCAA separating scholarship and nonscholarship divisions (which allowed Trinity to maintain its Division I tennis programs). And he added, "More of its championship competitions are funded by the association."

Tennis again remained unaffected, as Calgaard elected to retain the athletic scholarship-supported men's and women's NCAA Division I teams. The number of membership organizations Trinity had to manage was whittled down from four (NCAA, AIAW, NAIA, and TIAA) to one (NCAA). Despite the diminishing alliances, Calgaard did not abandon the philosophy of prioritizing academics over athletics.[30] The net effect for all other men's and women's sports—with two coed exceptions—was banishment to the independent ranks that would force them into competition against mostly superior teams for the rest of the decade.

The two unaffected coed sports that provided competitive opportunities for Trinity women but didn't fall under the same national umbrella were bowling and trap and skeet. Operating instead under the Association of College Unions International, the programs attracted a few female participants and earned their own headlines in the 1970s and early 1980s.

Julie Roba, who also played Trinity junior varsity tennis and varsity softball, opened the door for a women's bowling squad in 1976. The sport was still riding a wave of postwar popularity, and the presence of city league teams—and then the inclusion of an eight-lane bowling alley in the Sams Center basement—provided prospects for collegiate competition. The early years featured only male bowlers, but a partnership between Roba and sponsor Dick Yerley culminated in the first all-women's team in 1977. By 1980, the performances of Roba, Trish Pillsbury, and Robin McCarthy helped the team qualify for its first national tournament in Milwaukee, Wisconsin.

Trap and skeet rivaled the tennis program in bringing national recognition to Trinity in the 1970s and early 1980s. Col. Tom Hanzel brought his military expertise to an elective shooting sports class that became one of the most popular on campus. Out of that class sprang a collegiate team that was mostly male until it was infiltrated by talented women, including Carla Brundage (1980). The high school tennis standout parlayed her strong hand-eye coordination into skeet successes. She earned All-America honors each year of her four-year career while helping the team capture multiple national titles. Hanzel left in 1985, and the team was eventually demoted to a club sport.

The sudden loss of traditional national, state, and regional conference affiliations affected most of the athletic programs. Many of the coaches were part-time or interim hires and had difficulty recruiting athletes, securing opponents, planning schedules, and attracting students to athletic events.

Even with all the changes and despite poor season records, participants exhibited remarkable resiliency and still enjoyed their athletic experiences. Coaches praised players for their competitive spirit and willingness to advance their skills, and most athletes began to view academics and athletics as complementary rather than competing aspects of campus life.

Another column by Dorian Martin documented adjustments students were making to the new reality. After reporting that the football

Col. Tom Hanzel observes Carla Brundage's shooting form.

team was "embarrassed" by a 42–0 shutout loss to McMurray, the sports editor pointed to "deeper reasons" for the lopsided contest:

> Since the Trinity athlete is not being "paid" by scholarships for his services, only the athletes who are truly dedicated and who truly love their game will be participating. And since the academic requirements are so stringent, the athlete must be able to juggle his studies with practice or games, or, finally, must choose whether to participate in collegiate athletics at all. So, in all of Trinity's sports, except tennis and perhaps trap and skeet, should little be expected? Will Trinity often be in the losing column? Perhaps, but because of their dedication and true love for the sport through all circumstances, the athletes' spirit will always come through. And in many cases, that is enough to win.[31]

Certainly, any perceived priority of a winning athletic program over academic success would have undermined the new president's vision, and at first there was no threat to that vision. But this painful shift seemed necessary to nudge Trinity into the balanced Division III philosophy of playing primarily for the love of the game.

A Coaching Cavalcade

Calgaard's initial administrative actions had a profound effect on those guiding the women's programs. First, he eliminated Johnson's position of assistant athletic director in charge of women's athletics and hired Bob Hockey in 1981. The native Australian served as department chair of health and physical education and replaced Pete Murphy as athletic director. Hockey earned a doctorate of education with a concentration in physical fitness and health from the University of Toledo.[32]

For women athletes and Trinity administrators, the decade dawned with the realization that the two people who had carried most of the weight of coaching for the 1970s—Johnson and Howle—were gone. While Calgaard assured students that he would replace Johnson, the promise proved difficult to fulfill. The major exception, as usual, was with the women's tennis program, which Emilie Foster expertly guided in Division I scholarship competition the entire decade.[33]

A parade of part-time coaches—some pulled from local high school ranks—led the other women's teams in the 1980s before stability set in. This coaching carousel featured three coaches each in volleyball and soccer, four in basketball, and six in softball.

Rushing drafted former Trinity athlete Lynn Walker Luna to provide a stopgap solution as the search committee evaluated long-term prospects for Johnson's replacement. The Johnson mentee and exceptional three-sport athlete had just stepped down from three years of coaching at a local high school when Rushing broke the news about Johnson's resignation and asked if she would coach the women's teams and teach classes. Luna, who was pregnant at the time, admitted she was "overwhelmed" by the offer and didn't think she could do it at first. Replace Libby Johnson? After some negotiation, Luna agreed to coaching duties only.

Luna had the challenge of resuscitating the volleyball program the year after the team disbanded under Howle, but she was fortunate to be greeted by a freshman contingent with extensive high school experience. "I inherited a great team, and I just ran it like Libby ran it, because I didn't know anything else," she said. When it came to basketball, Luna had limitations, having no experience in coaching. She asked for ideas, admitting she didn't know much about the game.[34] Luna also enlisted

Spotlight on Lynn Walker Luna

Lynn Walker noticed the architectural features of Trinity while on a church retreat and told her parents she wanted to go to the college "with the red brick in San Antonio." Her El Paso high school had a robust girls' sports program, and Walker participated all four years in volleyball, basketball, and track. But sports weren't on her mind when she applied to Trinity. "I had no idea they had any athletics," she said.

Almost immediately after arriving, the freshman noticed flyers advertising volleyball tryouts. She attended her first practice in jeans, a Trinity T-shirt, and sandals, but she made the team.

In 1976, the senior married former Tiger football star Hector Luna, captained the volleyball team, and helped the threadbare track team field a squad for the spring TIAA meet. Her talent and positive leadership led to numerous awards and accolades from teammates and coaches. In addition to multiple all-conference honors, Luna was named most valuable player in both volleyball and track by her teammates. Johnson called Luna "the finest all-round player" she'd ever coached.

After Luna accepted Shirley Rushing's offer to return to Trinity, she juggled coaching duties in volleyball, basketball, and track before heading home to raise a family and support her church as both a volunteer and paid staff member.

Lynn Walker Luna holds her Outstanding Senior Female Athlete award from 1977.

spouse Hector Luna to informally assist from the bench that year.[35] And senior Terri Hailey certainly helped the young coach with a 21.1 point average while also collecting eleven rebounds a game. Sports editor Dorian Martin noted that Hailey's top conference rankings came in spite of being double- and triple-teamed in most games.[36]

When the team qualified for a postseason slated over spring break, many players said they'd rather ski or go to Mexico than play in a tournament in Lubbock. After a tie vote, Luna deferred to the team's lone senior. "Are you kidding me?" Hailey responded. "This is the end of my career. Of course, I want to go." Hailey later reflected on the coach deferring to a team vote: "Can you imagine that happening now?"[37] That team's final 11–16 record under Luna was the last season a women's Tiger cager team won more than six games for more than a decade.

As her pregnancy advanced, Luna found herself again leaning on her unofficial assistant, asking her husband to accompany the women's track and field team on the bus to the 1981 conference meet. The team consisted mostly of intramural standouts recruited by athletic director Pete Murphy and intramural director Jim Potter. It was Luna's final official role at Trinity, and that was the school's last women's varsity meet for a decade.[38]

Luna's replacement for volleyball and basketball was Carol Higy, a graduate of Malone College in Canton, Ohio, with a master's degree in outdoor education from the University of Akron. Her qualifications included eight years of teaching basketball from junior high level up to college, as well as directing summer basketball camps. While volleyball was not her specialty, she brought the same passion and effort to both sports. In addition to head-coaching duties, Higy assisted with softball, taught swimming classes, and participated in coed intramurals.[39]

Higy's coaching philosophy was more compatible with Trinity's Division III status than the scholarship program at Akron. In 1981, Higy introduced her volleyball players to more intense practice and drills, and they got off to a fast start in the final year of TIAA play, leading the team to a 20–16 record and the school's first invitation to a postseason tournament. This was the last championship hosted by the AIAW before it ceased operations in 1982.[40] In the next three years, Higy's volleyballers posted impressive records (23–11, 30–15, and 27–17), led by players Teresa Machu, Irene Hickox, Sue Lewis, Leslie Maines, and Rozie McCabe.[41]

Carol Higy chooses game ball with the opposing coach.

Higy's basketball squad struggled in the 1981–82 season, but one game attracted a larger-than-usual crowd and stood out in an otherwise forgettable season. The final game against Incarnate Word College was scheduled as a warm-up to a professional matchup between the NBA San Antonio Spurs and Golden State Warriors at the city's HemisFair Arena. Tickets for both contests cost a whopping $6.[42]

Some of the outstanding players on the Higy basketball teams were Kim Callicoate, Tracy Discepolo, and Machu, who led the team in scoring two of her four years and was the fourth Trinity player to surpass 1,000 career points. After four years leading the volleyball and basketball programs, Higy left in 1985 to do graduate work and earned a doctorate in education administration. In 2008, she served as associate dean and associate professor in the education department of the University of North Carolina at Pembroke. She died in 2017 at age sixty-two.

Unfortunately for softball, the 1980s were disappointing: they had mostly losing seasons, went through six coaches, and still had no field for practice or home games. The initial vacancy Johnson left in 1980 was filled by volunteer coach Gerald Smetzer. The mathematics professor was a sports enthusiast and had served on the athletic council for several years. He started his first season with no set schedule, picking up games by calling around to other athletic directors in the area. But he had good fortune in talented freshman Machu, who played both infield and outfield positions (and also partnered with her coach in intramural racquetball). In that first year Machu notched an impressive .483 batting average when facing Division I and II scholarship pitchers. Against peer Division III teams, she hit at a .656 clip, slugged four home runs, and was a perfect 13-for-13 in stolen base attempts.[43] For her efforts, the TAIAW recognized her as the state's Division III Player of the Year.[44] In her junior year, her batting average was second in the nation.

Smetzer's team delivered a second state Division III championship and a regional title, earning a May trip to Michigan to participate in the 1981 AIAW national tournament. The Tigers were eliminated in two close games (1–0 and 8–7) against previous national champions.[45]

In 1982, when Smetzer decided to refocus his energy on the classroom, Hockey assigned Duane Henry to the team. Henry, a varsity basketball player and 1975 Trinity graduate, was also assisting Murphy's men's basketball team and had never coached softball before. Also, in that first year of independent status, nearby Incarnate Word disbanded its program, which left Our Lady of the Lake University as the state's only other Division III program. In his second season, the 9–11 squad was bolstered again by Machu, whose .450 batting average placed her fourth in the division and helped elevate the team average to a second place .373 mark.

Despite the difficult seasons, two of Henry's players were recognized for their off-field excellence. Jamie Edney, a business major with a 3.75 GPA, had a team-leading .475 batting average. Catcher Nancy Walker, a biology major with a 3.79 GPA, had a .395 batting average. They were both named College Division Academic All-Americans, the only students from Texas to receive the honor. No other school in the nation placed more than one student athlete on the 1983 list.[46]

Due to the untimely death of Pete Murphy in 1984, Henry had to fill the men's basketball vacancy, stepping down from his softball role.

Exceptional softball player Deann Viebranz was recommended for the position by fellow University of Akron graduate Carol Higy. The players' first qualified coach lasted only one season, as Viebranz abruptly resigned after posting an 8–8 mark.

The athletic council promoted women's soccer to varsity in 1980. After toiling three years as a club team volunteer coach, David Groth enthusiastically formed his first official intercollegiate team, which included Suzanne Anderson. The nine-year youth soccer veteran had so many high school awards from multiple sports that her mother had to deploy a station wagon to drag home trophies from awards banquets.[47] The move to varsity didn't just improve team spirit; it also provided funds for uniforms and road trips, amenities Groth appreciated before leaving in 1986. Anderson later became the women's assistant coach and then head coach while in a Trinity graduate program.

Julie Jenkins's hiring as head volleyball coach set the stage for stability in the Trinity coaching ranks—at least in the sport of volleyball. Leadership for basketball, softball, and soccer continued to turn over in the unsettled decade.

Few major changes were made to the facilities and fields used by the Trinity women in the 1980s. The only improvement was the 1983 conversion of Trinity's northeast corner into a landscaped park with a crushed limestone trail to offer a secure on-campus setting for student joggers and, later, for varsity runners.[48] The softball team continued to compete on fields where adherence to regulation distances was dubious. At one off-campus home softball game, a usually reliable Tiger pitcher walked the first four batters, forcing in a run. Though she continued bouncing pitches in front of the plate, Smetzer kept her in the game until she finally retired the side. When the visitors took the field, their pitcher complained that the mound was too far back from home plate. After taking measurements, the umpire agreed and relocated the mound. Realizing why his pitcher was having problems, Smetzer argued vociferously that the game should be restarted, but the umpire denied his request. Accustomed to dealing with challenges, the Tigers recovered and went on to win the game.[49]

Female athletes in other sports at Trinity also faced the same challenges they had in previous years—they had to practice around men's

1980s home softball game held at a local public park field.

team schedules, share locker rooms with fellow female students, and have chaperones to use the resources in the Sams Center.

Trinity was not the only school with substandard women's facilities. The 1981 basketball playoffs, held at Lubbock Christian College, were conducted on a temporary surface laid over a large airplane hangar. The slick wood reportedly looked like it came from a bowling alley, and the court dropped off sharply behind the basket. Players attempting layups needed to use extreme caution to keep from falling to the concrete below. No spare basketballs were available, so when game balls bounced off the edge, play was delayed for up to five minutes while players retrieved them. On top of all that, "it was freezing in there," Terri Hailey recalls.[50]

Being a coach at Trinity in the 1980s required flexibility, especially after exiting the TIAA conference. Head volleyball coach Carol Higy had a bizarre week in 1983 when Trinity was scheduled to play Texas A&I University and the University of Texas at San Antonio at a tri-match in Kingsville. The UTSA team never showed, so Trinity played A&I twice, winning the first match but losing the second. Three days later, Schreiner College arrived unannounced on campus to play a match on a scheduled off day for Trinity. As the host coach, Higy rounded up her players but was unable to secure an official because of the match's impromptu nature. Unfazed, she served as referee and coach. Trinity won the match, and Higy received no complaints about her officiating.[51]

Spotlight on Terri Hailey

Like Lynn Walker Luna, Terri Hailey went to Trinity for the school's academic reputation and was unaware of opportunities for intercollegiate sports. The native of Joplin, Missouri, saw a flyer advertising softball tryouts in the barren field by her dorm and ended up on the 1977 team. After softball season ended, Libby Johnson suggested that Hailey try basketball. It was wise advice. She set multiple records that remain at the top of Trinity women's basketball statistics. But concerns about getting behind in the classroom compelled her to turn down a request from Johnson to play volleyball and a request from coach Gene Norris to play golf. She played on a Johnson varsity squad every semester of her college career.

In 2005, Hailey was inducted into the Trinity Athletics Hall of Fame. She still leads all female basketball players in career field goals made, total points, and points per game; and she comes in second overall in career rebounds, free throws made, and rebounds per game. She earned multiple all-state, all-region, and conference honors; and she was runner-up for AIAW's 1981 Division III basketball player of the year. In softball, Hailey became one of the team's most reliable pitching aces and was named 1979 TAIAW Division III Player of the Year.

Even after Hailey's 1981 graduation with a double major in history and health and physical education, the player-coach relationship lasted another decade. Johnson provided career guidance and hiring references, and Hailey continued to seek advice from her mentor and friend as she pursued a law enforcement career. She stood in for her coach when Johnson was inducted posthumously to the Trinity Athletics Hall of Fame in 2011.

Terri Hailey (34) set several basketball records at Trinity, in addition to other Hall of Fame accomplishments.

Teammates on the soccer squad found themselves facing much more experienced competition. One Saturday, since the team didn't have funds for overnight accommodations, they left campus at 6 a.m. to arrive in College Station in time for a morning match against Texas A&M University. The Tigers were at an even greater disadvantage against the physical Aggie squad, as several offensive starters stayed behind in San Antonio with academic commitments, forcing teammates who normally play defense to compete in unfamiliar attack positions. Also, with more alternates on the bench, the A&M coach could continually substitute fresh players against the tiring Trinity team. Finally, sheer intimidation played a role. "Walking on the field against an A&M or UT was scary as heck," player Suzanne Anderson remembers.[52] After the 8–0 thrashing, Trinity players theorized that the Aggies must have been told "fighting hard is the only way to get the ball, and that winning isn't everything, it's the only thing."[53]

Sometimes the talent imbalance worked in their favor. In one softball game, the Tigers' pitches were so slow that UCLA's batters couldn't hit the ball, and Trinity only lost by three runs.[54] Even perpetually sunny multisport athlete Teresa Machu expressed her frustration in playing bigger schools with players on scholarships. "I wonder sometimes why we were even out there," she told the *Trinitonian*.[55]

The Rise and Fall of School Spirit

Basketball star Tracy Discepolo set out on a heroic effort to increase fan support for men's and women's teams. "Tiger Fever" was announced in 1983 and even attracted a photo opportunity with the San Antonio mayor. According to Discepolo, the new group's president, the effort had some early success: "It increased the attendance at the games and got everyone more enthusiastic and involved. Not only that—it encouraged the players as well."[56] The positive vibe wasn't universal; Discepolo's own coach, Carol Higy, expressed mixed feelings: "Tiger Fever's great, but it hasn't come into the girl's stage yet."[57]

A full-page 1984 *Mirage* story, "Fever Breaks: Apathy Reigns," recounted its brief history: "It hit like an epidemic in 1983. It seemed that the campus would never be the same. Everywhere one turned, tiger paws and spirit posters appeared.... Dorm reps were elected, the group got funded by the university, and participation climbed. The club advertised

(left) San Antonio mayor Henry Cisneros with unidentified Tiger Fever supporters, 1985. *(right)* Tracy Discepolo tips off.

sports events and postgame parties, sold concessions and souvenirs, and held a spirit contest at the Tigerfest football game."[58]

Unfortunately, the interest that attracted more than a hundred students to the Tuesday evening meetings waned after football season, and the bulk of the work was left to a few steadfast volunteers. A vote to disband was taken in January 1985 by the remaining members.[59] Regardless of the demise of her pet project, Discepolo finished that junior season as one of the Trinity's most productive scorers, usually contributing double-digit offensive performances.

The same 1985 *Mirage* story that reported on the success and demise of Tiger Fever presented a mostly optimistic take on the status of men's and women's varsity athletics. The varsity overview noted 285 schools competing in the NCAA's nonscholarship division, giving Tiger athletes the opportunity to "travel more than most other Division III schools." What the authors failed to note was the reason: no other Texas schools had joined this new division, requiring a long-distance solution to find more equitable competition as an independent. Other improvements listed were better coverage in the student newspaper, teams receiving new uniforms every second or third season, and the enthusiasm of the cheerleaders. The one concern the article reported was "the lack of adequate outdoor facilities."[60]

Trinitonian sports editor Tim Lawless gave his own assessment of the sports landscape in his last Tigerbeat column, which also heralded improved coverage, thanks to the sports staff's doubling that year to four reporters. He felt that Trinity's athletics programs were "on the whole, very good," and suggested that they did "well against schools of the same academic caliber." However, he bemoaned the mismatched competition. He concluded, "It's a tribute to our players' enthusiasm and our coaching staff that we end up doing as well as we do."[61]

Female distance runners celebrated a milestone at the 1984 Olympics. The first women's marathon was held, and American Joan Benoit Samuelson won the gold medal. My old running mate Peggy Kokernot qualified for the Olympic trials but failed to make the final team. I had the privilege to run with the eight-pound torch as part of a team that carried the flame from Golden, Colorado, to Mountain Home, Idaho, on its journey to Los Angeles. And I was able to keep the torch as a memento.

CHAPTER 11

Hope on the Horizon

1985–90

> With the exception of tennis, which was Division I, athletics at Trinity at that time were really struggling. None of our programs had winning records, volleyball included. We were not a member of a conference. We were independent, and that concerned me.
>
> —JULIE JENKINS IN 2017 AT THE DEDICATION OF CALGAARD GYM

After women's collegiate championships were appropriated by the NCAA and NAIA, and the AIAW dissolved after losing its antitrust lawsuit, the national conversation about women's sports cooled off. Whether it died down naturally or was silenced is a matter of opinion. Either way, women's sports in general—and at Trinity specifically—were in a state of stagnation.

However, the promises Ron Calgaard made to volleyball coaching prospect Julie Jenkins in her 1985 job interview made her a believer. While she doesn't recall having the chance to speak much in the interview, Jenkins vividly remembers Calgaard sharing his educational vision: "He assured me that athletics were important to Trinity, and he planned to make improvements."[1] To address her hesitation about teams competing as independents, Calgaard promised her they would soon be in a conference.

Not in "Good Condition"

A sports summary in the spring 1986 issue of *Trinity Magazine* listed five varsity sports available to female students—volleyball, basketball,

Julie Jenkins at a volleyball timeout

soccer, tennis, trap and skeet, and junior varsity tennis. (Oddly, it omitted softball.) The article mentioned that 250 students were participating in intercollegiate sports "for the sheer enjoyment of participation, competition and self-fulfillment," adding that Trinity's academics-first philosophy was exhibited through practices and game schedules that minimized the athletes' time away from the classroom.[2]

Jenkins recalls that Trinity women's athletics at the time were not in "good condition." Most coaches were part time, and the same challenges that vexed Libby Johnson remained. Because women's teams still shared practice spaces and schedules with the men's teams, the women's coaches were often forced to schedule early practices that conflicted with classes so they could be off the court in time for the men's sessions. Treatment resources continued for the men's teams but were still inaccessible to

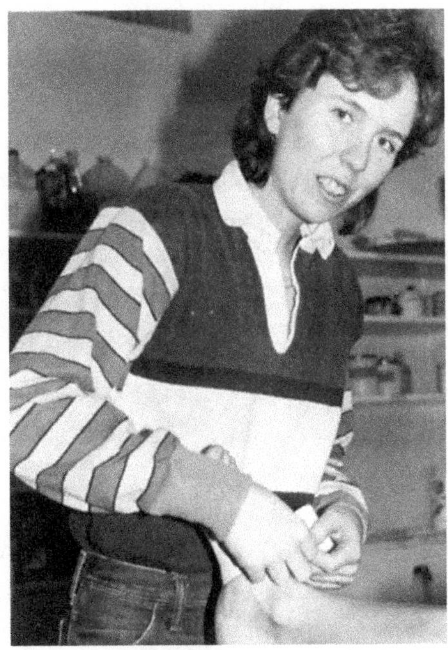

Roz McCabe as a trainer in 1985.

women. After all these years, female athletes were still using physical education offices to change into their uniforms.

One solution to the treatment dilemma was to put player Roz McCabe on call. The physical education major and varsity athlete attended to her teammates as an unofficial trainer, taping ankles, treating injuries, and ensuring that ice was always ready on the sidelines. "I'm at the game anyway, and it doesn't take a lot of time," she said. McCabe must have been at a lot of games, since by her 1986 graduation she had received ten varsity letters, four each in softball and volleyball, and two in basketball.[3]

Publicizing all of the school's athletic programs was the responsibility of one person, the sports information director, so it was impossible to cover every event, especially those that overlapped. Students had to keep game statistics, resulting in few records archived for athletes of the 1980s. Attendance was usually sparse, including home games. Since softball still played home games off campus, they got even less publicity.

Team successes were also elusive. But like their predecessors in the 1970s, coaches accepted the reality. Julie Jenkins kept her faith in Calgaard's promises. However, she added, "I was so happy to be here, I don't think I was even thinking about it."[4]

Student opinions on the state of athletics ranged from dire predictions to optimism for the future. In the absence of a conference and any visible administrative (or fan) support, reporters floated an assortment of opinions and potential solutions for male and female varsity athletes.

Trinitonian sportswriter Grant McFarland asked, "With an increased emphasis on academics, can the student-athlete continue to exist at Trinity?" He wrote about apathy forcing athletes to labor in obscurity and quoted a football player complaining about an "appalling lack of support" from the administration. McFarland concluded, "As the school changes, student athletes will try to maintain the tenuous hold they have on their place in the Trinity community."[5]

Sports editor Charles Kuffner tried to explain why so few men supported professional women's sports, suggesting that the emphasis on individual athletes rather than team sports hampered men's overall interest. (What he neglected to mention in his 1987 piece was that few professional women's team sports existed at the time.) Kuffner wrote that women's tennis and golf competition offered "no standings, no traditional rivalries, no home-field advantages, none of the things that team-sport fans live and die on." However, he did attack the myth of women not playing as hard, and he encouraged his fellow students to support the women's teams by going to their games, adding, "They're fun to watch." And, perhaps in an attempt to assuage his female readers, Kuffner's trivia question that week was about a women's collegiate basketball player.[6]

The anguish over the scholarship decision still simmered sixteen years later. In a *San Antonio Express-News* article, a former Trinity baseball player said, "As good as the school is academically, it's sad to see the athletic program where it is now."[7] Kuffner picked up on one idea from the article: creation of an alumni-endowed scholarship fund to return Trinity to its past level of prominence. But after he discussed the concept with Trinity coaches, he conceded defeat. First, moving from Division III to Division II scholarship status would be cost prohibitive, since it would require Trinity to fund scholarships for ten teams, including the women. Also, Division II would provide even fewer Texas rivals than Division III did. Finally, changing divisions would mean dropping the popular Division I tennis program for men and women. "I don't think I'll hold my breath," Kuffner wrote.[8]

Other students echoed the resignation to the stagnant status of (non-tennis) intercollegiate sports. In an editorial cautioning Trinity students to balance their time in pursuit of a liberal arts education, the author suggested that they should wander down to the "quiet gymnasium or empty stands" to watch athletic events, adding that while the Division III teams lost more games than they won, there was still value "attending the competition."[9]

Although Tiger teams were becoming accustomed to their independent status, some administrators provided hope that change would come. An extensive 1987 interview with James Vinson referred to an educational report that listed the top priorities regarding athletics. Vinson, who joined the administration as vice president of academic affairs in 1983—the year after Trinity exited the TIAA—called the scheduling issue presented by competing in Division III "a serious problem which is no one's fault," explaining that the situation was due to having "no natural competitors" on par with TU close by. Vinson was optimistic about the trend of NCAA Division I schools switching to Division III, and he reiterated the administration's support and hopes for a future conference: "I am enormously supportive of a vigorous, nonscholarship, intercollegiate athletic program because I know the richness of activity that that can bring to campus."[10]

After Vinson resigned to take a job as president of the University of Evansville, former mathematics and science division dean Ed Roy filled the position until a permanent replacement was found. In a 1988 story previewing the agenda for an upcoming board of trustees meeting, Roy said the board's subcommittee on athletics had decided to continue Trinity's "first-rate" tennis program by maintaining the NCAA Division I scholarship status. But his answer to a question about Trinity's prospects for entering a new conference for other sports was less specific; Roy said the committee was "very excited about the prospect for conference play."[11]

One theme was repeated in the lackluster game coverage of both men's and women's teams in the 1980s: next year will be better. To underscore the troubling trend, a page in the 1986 April Fool's edition of the *Trinitonian* displayed spoofs of game recaps. The summary of a fictitious woman's game against a fake opponent was penned by fabricated author Lou Sinagan. It read: "The Trinity Tigers lost this

Trinity falls just short

by Lou Sinagan
Sports Writer

The Trinity Tigers lost this weekend to Central Southeastern Texas State but it didn't really matter, they put forth a "good effort." This weekend's loss leaves the Tigers with a record of 0-21 on the season.

This weekend's loss won't be viewed as a major setback because

by Lou Sinagan
Sports Writer

The Trinity Tigers lost this weekend to San Antonio College but it didn't really matter, they put forth a "good effort." This weekend's loss leaves the Tigers with a record of 0-13 on the season.

This weekend's loss won't be viewed as a major setback because the members of the team still

***Trinitonian* April Fool's issue satirizing lackluster team performances of the 1980s**

weekend to Central Southeastern Texas State but it didn't really matter, they put forth a 'good effort.' This weekend's loss leaves the Tigers with a record of 0–21 on the season. This weekend's loss won't be viewed as a major setback because the members of the team still maintain a positive mental attitude.... Coach Andrews added, 'I'm really pleased with their performance, even though they lost.'"

The same recap was given for a male team's loss in another undisclosed sport. To make coverage easy for future sportswriters, the page included a helpful fill-in-the-blank template for covering Tiger games.[12]

Title IX Rebounds, ERA Stalls

On the judicial and legislative front, two major events in the 1980s helped shape what we think of today as Title IX. The first was a setback caused by the Supreme Court's 7–2 decision in *Grove City College v. Bell* in February 1984. The case pitted the small Pennsylvania liberal arts school (affiliated with the Presbyterian Church) against secretary of education Terrel Bell. During the arguments, one historian described President Reagan's small-government administration as "tepid" in its defense of the legislation.[13] The ruling dealt a substantial blow to Title IX by narrowing its scope to apply only to those educational programs that receive federal funding, and not to all activities offered by a school.[14] This interpretation allowed most college athletic departments to escape the law's provisions, and the Reagan administration responded by quickly closing nearly two dozen investigations of Title

IX noncompliance across the country, mostly in college athletic departments.[15] Within months of the decision, the House of Representatives passed a bill intended to ensure that Title IX's equity provisions be broadly enforced, but the bill bogged down in the Senate for three years over concerns about its potential to expand abortion, a nonstarter for Reagan's conservative coalition.

Supporters finally found enough votes to close the Title IX loophole, passing the Civil Rights Restoration Act of 1987. The prescriptive bill, sometimes referred to as the Grove City Bill, was introduced in the Senate by Massachusetts Democrat Edward Kennedy. The concerns about how the bill would impact abortion surfaced once again, but amendments were added to quiet the opposition. As a result, the legislation overwhelmingly passed the Senate in January 1988 and the House in March, both with strong bipartisan support.[16] Reagan vetoed the bill, but enough votes were mustered to comfortably override the veto, and any doubts about the reach and scope of Title IX in college athletics were effectively put to rest.[17] Thus, in a four-year span, Title IX had not only firmly reestablished the broad scope Congress had originally intended; it had also inspired other civil remedies the legislative body may not have contemplated.[18]

However, another 1988 court ruling closed the door on any hopes for the AIAW to get relief from its lawsuit against the NCAA, when the US Court of Appeals for the District of Columbia upheld a lower court ruling against the AIAW. In a twenty-six-page opinion, the three justices (including civil rights advocate and future Supreme Court justice Ruth Bader Ginsberg) said the AIAW failed to prove that the NCAA "provided irresistible economic inducements," after hearing some schools testify they had moved to the NCAA for a better-quality product.[19]

Slowing the Revolving Door

In 1985, a "changing of the shin guard" for Trinity's department of health and physical education was summarized in the *Trinitonian*. After four years, Bob Hockey stepped down from his dual roles as department chair and athletic director to teach health care classes and coordinate the Sams Center fitness lab. Football coach Gene Norris replaced Hockey

It's just a fact of life, Trinity just won't be competitive if they stay with part-time coaches.

-Hal Gatlin

This quote sums up part-time problems of the 1980s.

as athletic director, Rushing became department chair, and Jim Potter continued to serve as intramural director. In this new arrangement, Norris reported to the academic vice president, and Rushing reported to the dean of behavioral sciences. In her typical understated style, Rushing's response to the change was "I can see absolutely no problems with it whatsoever." She would serve as chair until her 1995 retirement.[20]

For women's varsity programs, the revolving door of coaches continued, and demands persisted for a staff laden with teaching and coaching duties. In one example, when Carol Higy left Trinity to pursue graduate work in 1985, her basketball duties were picked up by Harold Gatlin, a coach and teacher at local MacArthur High School, who left his "day job" to commute to Trinity. Gatlin led the team through three difficult seasons, which included the victory that finally ended a forty-four-game losing streak.[21] An April 1988 *Trinitonian* story announcing Gatlin's resignation quoted the part-time coach saying, "I've enjoyed my time here and leave with no bad feelings." His frustration about the lack of support was evident later in the story though when he questioned Trinity's ability to be competitive under the status quo.

Still operating in independent status with a limited budget, the administration couldn't offer hope for immediate relief. "It's got to be someone who has a job and can get off early at 3:30 to come over and run practices and coordinate the program," Norris said of Gatlin's likely replacement. "At this moment that's the way it has to be." He admitted that if Trinity joined a conference, they'd "have to make changes in all sports."

The job ended up going to former player Teresa Machu, who was already assistant volleyball coach and head softball coach at the time.

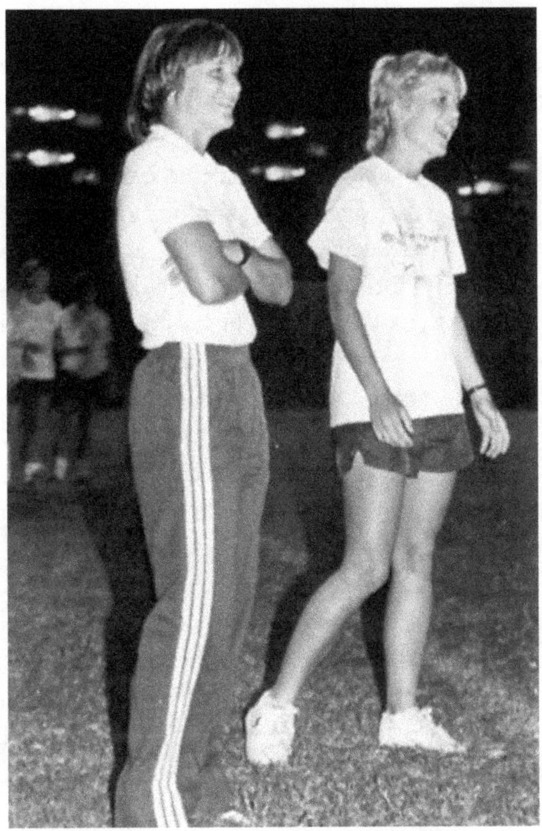

Head soccer coach Susan Glenn *(left)* assisted by Suzanne Anderson, 1986

She had returned to Trinity in 1987 after earning a master's degree, stepping into the softball vacancy left by Duane Henry's departure. Her multiple coaching assignments forced her to juggle practices and games in the three overlapping seasons.[22]

The women's soccer team lost the only coach it had ever known in club or varsity play when David Groth left in 1985. His final season highlight was seeing goalkeeper Becky Copeland named as Trinity's first female soccer All-American.[23] His replacement was part-timer Susan Glenn, another MacArthur High School teacher who made the daily commute to lead afternoon practices. She benefited from the assistance of former Trinity athletes Suzanne Anderson and Val Stein. When Glenn left the next year to pursue a doctorate, Anderson was promoted to head coach, and would lead the squad into the next decade while balancing her own graduate studies in educational psychology.

Julie Jenkins's arrival in 1985 was a welcome contrast to the revolving door, providing almost four decades of stability to the volleyball program.

Jenkins was an early beneficiary of Title IX. A 1977 high school graduate, the upstate New York native remembers her older sisters having little opportunity in sports. "I was so lucky I didn't even know it," she said. "Not only did we have everything, but I played boys sports too." She competed—and starred as the number one player—on the boys' tennis team. This was a feature of Title IX when schools didn't offer a girls' option. Jenkins parlayed that success into a tennis scholarship to William and Mary and then to an interim position at Virginia Commonwealth University.

In search of a permanent position, the twenty-five-year-old was impressed by the hospitality she received during her candidate interview: "They make you feel like you are part of the whole school, not just the department down here in athletics." But what really convinced her was Calgaard's long-range plan to support Division III intercollegiate athletics. Jenkins already knew she wanted to work with nonscholarship students because, as she told the *Trinitonian*, "the athletes you have out there are the ones that truly want to play."[24]

Like her predecessors, Jenkins was assigned multiple responsibilities. In addition to her primary role as head volleyball coach, she taught physical education activity courses, coached softball, and led the men's and women's junior varsity tennis programs. In her one year coaching softball, Jenkins saw Jill Doderer bat .310 and earn 1986 Academic All-America honors. When a 1987 schedule change limited junior varsity tennis to spring, the season no longer conflicted with her fall volleyball schedule, which gave the new coach some breathing room. She was also active in coed intramural basketball.[25]

In those first five years, when Trinity was still competing against scholarship schools, her teams consistently lost. Jenkins struggled to find recruiting time with the heavy workload, and recruiting was difficult due to competition with the ever-expanding athletic scholarships offered to female athletes. When Jenkins told athletic director Norris she couldn't succeed as both a professor and a coach, Norris carved out more time so Jenkins could make recruiting phone calls at night and travel to observe prospects.[26]

Staking a Claim on South Campus

When it came to improving on-campus facilities, Calgaard was quietly implementing his plan. His administration scouted out several options before acquiring six acres of property from homeowners on the south side of campus, and he secured the funding for new extramural and intramural fields. One site initially considered for the outdoor facilities was the campus's northeast corner, where a landscaped walking trail had been developed for students in 1983. However, that area had previously served as a garbage dump, according to the *Trinitonian*, which quoted an administrator who said, "Nobody knows how deep the garbage goes."[27]

When the property south of campus was ultimately selected, many neighbors were less than enthusiastic about the displacement of thirty homes, prompting a parody in the *Trinitonian* April Fool's issue: "University President Ron Calgaard ordered the napalming of Monte Vista Historical district last week in response to continuing complaints from Monte Vista Hysterical Association members about Trinity's proposed intramural complex." In a nod to Trinity's country club image, the piece reported that the destruction of Trinity Baptist Church would "make way for the new university stables and polo field."[28] In real life, a settlement was reached with the neighborhood group, the city's historic review board approved the plans, and the project moved forward. It included new outdoor extramural and intramural fields and a complete renovation of the Sams Center.[29]

Another facility-related controversy in 1987 cast doubt on the future of Trinity sports. In order to build a new dorm next to the football field, Trinity removed the upper portion of the stands at E. M. Stevens Stadium and donated them to an area school district. "They didn't want the new dorm looking out onto the back of a stadium," Norris told the *Trinitonian*. Although the seating capacity went from 6,200 to 3,500, the football coach suggested that it wouldn't have any impact on his team's performance. However, a small area newspaper incorrectly tied the stands' donation to the suspension of football at Trinity, and the story was repeated by a San Antonio television reporter. Norris vehemently

Monte Vista house makes way for South Campus fields.

denied the rumor and blamed it for a decline in football recruits that season, which resulted in a smaller-than-normal squad.[30]

The new dorm, according to a piece in the *Mirage*, was "the absolute farthest from any other important building on either upper or lower campus." It also displaced the women's varsity softball team, which now had to find off-campus fields for practices as well as its home games.[31] However, once Prassel Hall was completed, Trinity was able to house 1,900 students and move closer to Calgaard's goal of a residential university.[32]

The stadium bleacher donation inspired this 1988 April Fool's Day satire: "Calgaard Says Future Fuzzy for TU Tennis," which claimed that the president sold the metal supports holding up the tennis stadium's roof and felt that students should focus on their homework instead of attending sporting events. Though said in jest, the fiction had a kernel of truth when it intimated that the president would get rid of tennis by 1990.[33]

One program that wouldn't reap the benefits of Calgaard's facility plan was men's and women's bowling. The primary reason the program was dissolved in 1982 was the condition of the lanes in the Sams Center alley. They had fallen into disrepair, making them unfit for intercollegiate competition. As Trinity was drawing up plans and soliciting funds for a new gymnasium (what would be the Bell Center), it was decided not to invest in refurbishing the existing facility. The administration felt that it was unnecessary for the new gym to include an alley, since

San Antonio offered multiple state-of-the-art complexes near Trinity for recreational bowling.[34]

Rumors that the alley would be closed persisted throughout the 1980s, but hard-core bowlers continued to enjoy the lanes in spite of their warped surfaces and unpredictable pin setters until Bell Center was built, which signaled the end of bowling on campus. Mourning the loss, senior Martin Hoffman commented, "When I found the bowling alley, it was like uncovering a lost treasure."[35]

The Fight Over "First Year"

A seemingly innocuous policy was passed in 1986 to encourage nonsexist language, which prompted a name change: the Freshman Seminar became First-Year Seminar. Animated discussion ensued. The *Trinitonian* reported on the debates and pledged to abide by the new approach. An unsigned editorial called the resolution an important step: "The trend towards non-sexist language is already here, but making it official affirms Trinity's recognition of its responsibility in dealing with an issue that is of particular importance to any academic institution. After all, as universities are important influences in the way people think and talk, it is of monumental importance that such issues [should] be at the heart of liberal education."[36]

English professor Scott Baird, who taught a course in language and behavior, called the term *freshman* anachronistic: "When you say *freshmen* that means freshwomen are not included. The word is a reminder that over 200 years ago women could not go to college." History professor Don Clark disagreed, saying the new term was inconsistent and a "politically correct, made-up word."[37] An MBA student wrote a letter to the editor about the specter of censorship and referenced an infamous senator's actions during the Communist Red scare of the 1950s: "Shades of McCarthy! Are we to have an official blacklist of forbidden 'sexist' words?"[38] The school gradually replaced the former term with *first-year* in most references from that point forward.

A children's book debate also played out in the student newspaper and sparked what would become known as "The Giving Tree controversy" in the final semester of the 1980s. Jill Jackson, a member of the newly formed Women's Interest Center and a frequent *Trinitonian* columnist, suggested a pernicious intent behind the seemingly innocent parable of a tree giving everything to a boy. Author Shel Silverstein uses female pronouns when referring to the tree, who by the end is only a stump. Jackson and fellow activists deemed the story an accurate portrayal of "our patriarchal society's perverse notion that a woman's desires and needs are subordinate to a man's" and said it "warps the values of loving and giving." As one might imagine, both issues evoked emotions from all corners and were spoofed in April Fool's editions of the *Trinitonian*.[39]

As the decade wrapped up, one major sign of progress under Calgaard was captured in the October 1989 *US News and World Report*, which recognized Trinity as the best regional university in the West. This would be the first of many regional rankings, which were based on the school's record for quality of student body and faculty, financial resources, student retention, and academic excellence. Calgaard, whose goal since 1979 was to move Trinity into this loftier academic space, said he was gratified but told the *Trinitonian*, "All such ratings are in a sense arbitrary, perhaps capricious. We're pleased that our peers think of us as having a strong academic program."[40]

The school's 1986 self-study addressed the state of athletics by detailing intramural successes, listing future goals of involving more off-campus students, and documenting the added facilities and equipment for the intramural programs. It also mentioned plans to upgrade facilities for intercollegiate sports, expand women's athletics, and add more sports to the varsity programs. The report writers concluded: "The student athletes who participate in the intercollegiate athletics program at Trinity University are well prepared academically and highly motivated. They participate for the sheer pleasure of competition and for the satisfaction of self-improvement. A dedicated group of coaches are committed to the intercollegiate program and the university's administration provides active support and direction."[41]

By the end of the decade, two star volleyball players were recognized as Academic All-Americans, showing that the shift was working. Tami Gash, a National Merit scholar, a Trinity Trustees' scholar, and perennial dean's list honoree, was carrying a 3.76 GPA in chemistry and biology while leading the 1989 volleyball team with aces and kill shots. Her cocaptain (and season MVP) Patti Boulanger led in passing accuracy while logging a 3.49 GPA in elementary education. She was named a President's Scholar and inducted into the Kappa Pi education honor society. "They're obviously an asset to the team," Jenkins said. "But they're also a terrific plus to the athletic program and the school as a whole."[42]

Summing up the sense of shared optimism after a gloomy decade, Oklahoma State University golf coach Ann Pitts characterized the '80s as the time spent fighting Title IX and saw the '90s as the time dedicated to building women's sports.[43]

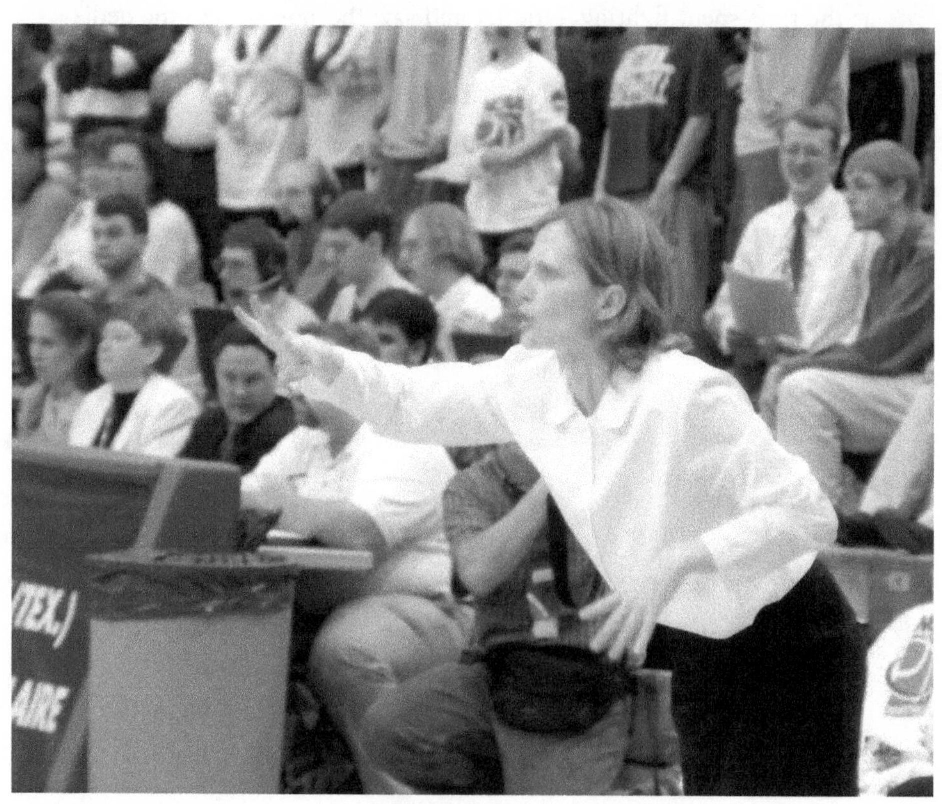

Head basketball coach Becky Geyer

CHAPTER 12

Promises Fulfilled

1990–95

Dr. Calgaard was the one person who changed
the dynamics of Trinity athletics.

—BASKETBALL COACH BECKY GEYER

When it comes to social progress, it seems that every decade has fans and detractors. But historian Daniel T. Rodgers wasn't particularly sentimental about the 1990s. He said the final years of the twentieth century inspired him to title his book *Age of Fracture*. His assessment? "Over years of academic introspection, splintering language, and fierce opposition, the solidarity and broad coalition of the 70s fractured into a morass of identity politics."[1]

However, one "year of change" would feature a historic increase in female representation in US Congress, a celebration of Title IX's anniversary, and progress for women on other fronts.

In San Antonio, Trinity sports fans would fracture over another scholarship-themed controversy, this time affecting the previously untouchable tennis program. But in a few short years, Skyline campus residents would recover, as emotions abated.

At Trinity, Calgaard's promises came into focus in the form of academic excellence and a commitment to a Division III philosophy that attracted students willing to compete in the sports arena and in the classroom. Equity between Trinity's male and female sports reached a level never seen before at the university. All varsity teams would benefit from dedicated and experienced coaches, a coed conference of peer academic institutions, and a new athletic director who would begin a long and successful career.

Looking Back on a Decade of Emergence

The 1989–90 academic year marked the halfway point of Calgaard's two-decade tenure at Trinity, and a variety of official and unofficial reports commemorated the tenth anniversary of his presidential appointment. Two provide a clear snapshot of the school's status heading into the 1990s.

A public relations brochure titled "A Decade of Emergence" documented milestones met in Calgaard's quest for improving Trinity's national reputation, including a growing endowment, increased faculty size, more innovative curriculum, and new residence halls.[2] The student newspaper joined the celebration chorus in a feature titled "Wonder Years: Calgaard Celebrates Decade on Hill," which quoted the president's goal to provide "the best undergraduate education money could buy in the Southwest."[3] Strengthened admissions standards were paying off; the incoming freshman class in 1984 included a record 120 National Merit Scholars. The average combined SAT scores for the class that entered in 1979 (Calgaard's first year) was 1080, but it rose to 1230 for students entering in 1987.

Calgaard's vision for a complete collegiate experience included making life outside the classroom "a stronger component of the university." The *Trinitonian* predicted that the president's residential focus might include "an increased commitment to intercollegiate athletics, significant work on the university swimming pool, and a renovation of the Sams Center." In fact, plans were already under way for all those goals.[4]

Although neither the brochure nor the student newspaper stories specifically addressed it, the idea of the 1980s as a decade of emergence could also apply to women's athletics, which seemed on the cusp of fulfilling the promise of Title IX. This potential was foreshadowed in the 1986 accreditation report detailing future plans for Trinity sports programs.[5] In a decade of sometimes controversial decisions, all of these goals would be achieved. But first, a 1990 decision would signal a setback for a legendary program.

Closing the "Country Club"

The decision to eliminate tennis scholarships shouldn't have been a surprise. Official comments in the late 1980s exposed a clash of opinions about the sport. Trinity's 1986 Self-Study Report stated that "the future of Division I tennis is also under review and the development of the program must be closely monitored."[6] In contrast, that same year, a subcommittee on athletics recommended continuing Trinity's commitment to Division I sports and its first-class tennis program.[7]

An early 1990 *Trinitonian* story about scholarships at another school seemed eerily familiar.

Sportswriter Chris Hart wrote that by abolishing athletic scholarships and leaving the NAIA, Southwestern University was effectively phasing into NCAA Division III competition. He correctly noted that the school was joining Trinity as one of only two schools bravely "blazing the way for collegiate level, non-scholarship sports in the great state of Texas." He educated any "foreigners" who might not be privy to the quasi-religious aspect of sports in Texas: "[T]he move to put academics on equal footing with the almighty ballgame is no less significant than if a long, tall Texan were to trade in his or her Cowboy hat and boots for a Yankees baseball cap and a pair of Nike cross trainers. It's just not normal for that to happen."[8]

Southwestern's decision wasn't unusual for NAIA schools in the early 1990s, as many left in droves after weighing incentives offered by the organization's mammoth competitor. Now flush with funds from a $1 billion television contract, the NCAA could provide lucrative perks like catastrophic-injury insurance for athletes and an expansion of championships for men and women in all three divisions.[9] A retired Southwestern administrator later praised the change, especially for the college's female athletes, since NCAA Division III institutions typically funded programs across a variety of sports instead of just football and basketball.[10]

In the moment, however, Southwestern students agreed with Hart that dropping athletic scholarships was "not normal." Glada Munt, who worked closely with Southwestern president Roy Schilling, later called it "one of the most divisive issues in [her] 45 years at Southwestern." There was another catalyst for the move, one certainly unknown to Hart or other casual observers. According to Munt, Calgaard helped convince his presidential colleague to make the decision, so there would be at least one other academically minded Division III school in Texas.[11]

Hart correctly predicted that Southwestern's shift marked the dawn of nonscholarship competition with other smaller schools in Texas. Indeed, more Texas schools would join Division III in the coming decades.[12]

A women's fall tennis preview in the *Trinitonian* noted that the Division I team benefited from the "fresh outlook" provided by new coach (and former player) Lee Elliott Henson. It also included a prediction from training director Janet Bristor that the 1990–91 team would qualify for nationals.[13]

A few weeks later came the ground-shaking announcement: Trinity's men's and women's Division I tennis players would no longer receive athletic scholarships and would join the school's other teams in Division III. This was consequential in Calgaard's quest to establish a higher-level mission for the university. According to Douglas Brackenridge, "This decision spelled the end of Division I tennis, Trinity's only scholarship sport, bringing to a close a tradition that had endured for more than four decades."[14]

That tradition was already in decline. While the scholarship teams achieved many top rankings, and Emilie Burrer Foster's women twice finished second at the national championships, the status of Trinity tennis had diminished from its peak in the 1970s. In fact, neither the men's or women's teams ranked in the top ten or had qualified for the national tournament the previous season.[15] The problem wasn't lack of coaching prowess. It was the increasing difficulty of recruiting top prospects, many of whom were drawn to larger universities where tennis was a higher priority sport. Also, Calgaard said he was troubled by the trend of high school players attending special athletic academies "to the detriment of other types of learning."[16] When Trinity coaches managed to sign prospects, more often from overseas, some didn't stay long before moving on to other collegiate programs or professional circuits. In

A cartoon racquet illustrates reaction to 1990 demotion of Trinity tennis.

short, these players didn't fit the president's vision of student-athletes who came to Trinity to earn a degree.

In his argument to a board of trustees committee, Calgaard said most institutions similar to Trinity in size, type, and quality competed at the Division III level and shared his philosophy "that athletics should be an extracurricular activity and that scholarships and admission to the university should not be awarded on the basis of athletic ability." The committee forwarded his recommendation, and the trustees planned a vote at their annual meeting on October 5, 1990.[17]

The first sour note was detected the day before the trustees' meeting, when athletic director Gene Norris joined the men's and women's coaches to break the news of the imminent vote to the varsity players. According to the *Trinitonian*, the news came as a shock. "Rumors have circulated since long before coach Emilie Foster's 'leave of absence,'" the editors wrote, "but the swiftness of Calgaard's action caught everyone off guard." Norris confirmed that neither men's coach Butch Newman nor Henson knew the decision was coming so quickly, suggesting they wouldn't have recruited players for that season had they known. However, the athletic director admitted, "There was never a good time to do it."[18]

The players learned their fate in that team meeting. If the vote passed the next day, the four seniors on scholarship would be able to keep the

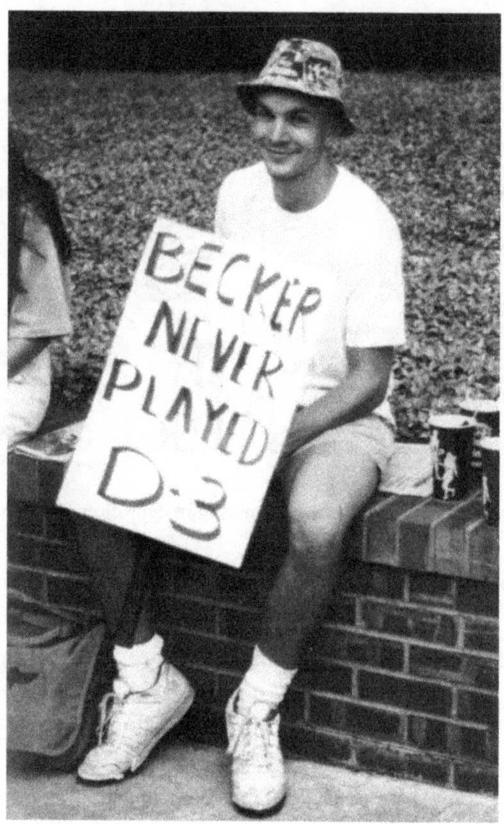

Protestor evoking pro tennis player Boris Becker to make a point

aid and play until their graduation. But the remaining ten players were offered three options: keep their scholarships at Trinity but not play tennis; give up their athletic scholarships and continue to play tennis at Trinity and apply for financial aid; or transfer to another university.[19]

The players soon learned they weren't alone in their anger. In the hours following the coaches' meeting, campus residents sprang into action, forming a resistance strategy in hopes that their raised voices might change the outcome—although vice president for academic affairs Ed Roy told students he was "99 percent sure that the board would approve the proposal." In short order, the Student Association Senate passed a resolution at 8:30 that night claiming "student rights were violated," they made signs at 10:30 p.m., and protested at 8:30 the next morning at Miller Fountain prior to the board meeting. A petition was quickly circulated, stating that "the tennis program is an integral and important aspect of Trinity University" and protesting the fact that students weren't consulted. It got nine hundred signatures.

In what the *Trinitonian* referred to as "a storm of protest," players camped out on the tennis courts that night. The next morning, trustees were pelted with tennis balls as they moved through a gauntlet of students to their meeting. Regardless, Roy was right—the board voted unanimously in favor of the proposal. Students held a candlelight vigil in front of Calgaard's home on Oakmont Court that evening, chanting "Rights are rights and Ron is wrong" and reading aloud their grievances in a letter destined for the American Civil Liberties Union.[20]

The protests on the normally low-key campus, as well as outrage across the local sports community, rattled many administrators. Almost a decade later, vice president for student affairs Coleen Grissom said she still had vivid recollections of students in the atrium screaming and shaking their fists.[21] Another casualty of the protests was the celebration held that week to dedicate the new south campus sports complex, an event drowned out by the reaction.

Days later, Roy sent a memo to students, faculty, and staff outlining the reasons for the board's decision. These included Trinity's recent entry into a nonscholarship conference of peer institutions (the Southern Collegiate Athletic Conference), in which tennis could not participate as a scholarship team, and pressure on the NCAA to eliminate the one-sport scholarship loophole to create a clear distinction between Division I and Division III institutions. In addition, money saved from tennis scholarships could be used to expand the size and quality of Trinity's other intercollegiate offerings, and the decision's timing would give the players enough time to consider their future alternatives.[22]

One line in Roy's memo provided an accurate prognostication, although it's certain few agreed with it at the time: "Within a few years, we believe Trinity can develop one of the best Division III tennis programs in the country."[23]

Local media covered the vote and reaction in depth, and the topic dominated the October 12 *Trinitonian*. The unanimous vote was announced with a large front-page headline cleverly using tennis scoring terms. The twenty-eight-page publication included an overview of the

The Trinitonian

Volume 88, Number 7 The Campus Newspaper of Trinity University • San Antonio, Tx 12 October 1990

Division I falls 24-love

Trinitonian **on tennis controversy, October 12**

decision, descriptions of players' reactions ranging from "emotionally devastated" to "bitter," multiple editorials decrying the outcome, a two-page spread of protest photographs, and a student's invitation to trustees to visit her dorm room and resolve their differences over pizza. Based on two letters published in that issue, some alumni were equally offended, with one 1963 graduate calling the decision "short-sighted and philosophically unsound." Another couple who attended in the late 1950s said they were "appalled at the thought of dismantling the last source of Trinity's sports pride: the tennis program." The paper also reported that players contacted the Trinity Tennis Foundation, which had been founded in 1983 to support the program, and the foundation reached out to alumni to ask their support in maintaining Division I teams.[24]

A headline in that year's *Mirage* was "Academic Reputation or Tennis Tradition? Trustees Choose Academics." The yearbook summary of the events concluded with a quote from men's coach Butch Newman: "It's the end of one era, but the beginning of a new one."[25]

Scottish player Michele Mair, who had earned her country's number one ranking the previous summer, said she didn't like any of the options. "I came to Trinity to play tennis and get a good education and they're giving me an either/or." The junior joined South African teammate Karen van der Merwe in transferring to William and Mary to continue playing at the Division I level. Aimee Shoemaker, a player who decided to stay at Trinity, acknowledged the difficulty Trinity had recruiting talented players who also had good academic standards. But she still called the timing of the decision "tactless."[26]

Trinity's largest campus protests in the last half of the twentieth century were related to the athletic scholarships rather than national issues. In contradictory assessments, the introduction to the 1991 *Mirage* applauded campus residents for finally shedding the "apathy that had hung so heavily for several years as students rose up and made their feelings known about a variety of causes." But just a few pages later, a story about the student response to military involvement in the 1990 Gulf War read, "Trinity's political brow remained fairly unfurrowed last September as in previous years when apathy ruled."[27]

That doesn't mean Trinity students didn't express strong opinions about other issues, such as the administration's position on condoms or alcohol and drug use, as well as thoughts on abortion, racism, and even the army's use of goats in medical training.[28] But nothing compared to the outrage that followed the 1971 and 1990 scholarship decisions. Although many theories could explain the student uproar, Student Association president Andrew Mansfield hinted at the true cause. "If I had had input beforehand, I don't think I would have stood up for scholarship athletics," he said. "They [the administration] made it into an issue."[29] The response from Grissom was unequivocal. "What we need you to understand is this is not a democracy," she said. "The Board of Trustees owns the university and hires the president and the senior executive officers."

Was "Trinity University Country Club" now a thing of the past? The short answer is yes. In the same issue that focused on the scholarship decision and resulting outcry, the *Trinitonian* reported that—for the second straight year—*US News and World Report* ranked Trinity first among 112 colleges in the West region in its annual rankings of America's Best Colleges. Student president Mansfield pointed to the top rating as a demonstration of "the good things Calgaard has done for Trinity."[30] The magazine article about the rankings stated that the honor "represents a remarkable turnaround for a school once considered little more than an educational country club for the children of rich Texans."

This nickname had appeared in Trinity publications since the 1970s, sometimes in derision and often in jest. The retrospective celebrating Calgaard's first decade summed up the change well: "In the past, Trinity University has held a 'country club school' image. With the arrival of University President Ronald Calgaard, that image began to reverse, and today Trinity is one of the most respected schools in the nation."[31]

Certainly, Calgaard's elevation of academic standards had more influence on the national rankings than the demotion of the tennis program. Even though teams hadn't captured any recent championships,

"Tennis Tech" reputation spurred a nearby bookstore to sell "Trinity University Country Club" shirts and jerseys in the 1970s.

the reputational breadcrumbs left by titles won in the 1960s and 1970s remained, and the students and local tennis community were reluctant to let go. But the article about the school's top regional ranking illustrates that at the same time the athletic programs were under perceived attack, Calgaard's academic vision was coming to life and garnering the national recognition he craved.

The immediate aftermath of the board decision was especially difficult for the players left behind. After four male and two female team members transferred before the start of the spring season, Henson hosted a "walk-on" tournament in February, offering the winner a position on the women's varsity team.[32] After leading her depleted team to a final 3–15 season in Division I, she moved to Houston, leaving a hole in the women's coaching ranks.[33]

Butch Newman had been coaching the men's team since 1986 and made the "crazy" suggestion to Norris that he lead both teams out of the ashes of the Division I demotion, a dual role he held until 2008.

Women's and men's tennis coach Butch Newman, 1990.

The former Trinity men's player—and younger brother of 1970s coach John—immediately faced recruiting challenges. "People thought we had dropped the program," he told a local sportswriter. He also had to recruit a high-quality athlete who didn't need a scholarship and could meet the school's lofty academic standards as well.[34] One solution was to recruit from his own intermediate tennis class.[35]

Aimee Shoemaker, who played under three coaches at Trinity, joined the new version of the women's varsity squad. She appreciated Newman's focus on academics over tennis and said he didn't pressure them, which allowed them to enjoy tennis but still play to the best of their abilities.[36] Newman's consequential contributions were later recognized with his 2005 induction into Trinity's Athletics Hall of Fame, and the tennis center was renamed in 2011 in his honor.

After the sport had settled into the Division III philosophy, general consensus about the decision began to shift. Rushing, who was physical education department chair at the time and an original sponsor of the women's tennis program, believes it was the right decision since the teams began playing at an equally high level in Division III. But she sympathized with the talented players whose careers were interrupted. She also felt the decision was easier for Calgaard because he hadn't been on campus during the sport's heyday in the 1960s and 1970s.[37]

The country club T-shirt ads and derisive references eventually subsided and the projected benefits materialized. One was the redeployment of $200,000 from tennis into other programs over the next two years, an investment Grissom felt "created equity in women's as well as men's athletics."[38]

For the next few years, the scars remained visible. In a 1991 story highlighting a new twenty-five-person all-kazoo band, the "Grand Kazoomba" explained why the musical group had formed: "We're trying to fill a void the tennis team left. They're a hard act to follow, but I think we can do it."[39]

1992: A Year of Change

After a tumultuous start to the decade, editors for the 1992 *Mirage* tried to put things in perspective, titling that year's edition "Year of Change." The yearbook's introduction mentions the negative reactions to the elimination of scholarship tennis programs but ends on a hopeful note: "Students can appreciate the reasons for the decisions, in retrospect, and some have even more strongly embraced the new ways."

Over the two decades since Title IX's passage, the number of women earning law degrees increased from 7 percent to 44 percent, and the number of women getting medical degrees went from 9 percent to 41 percent.[40]

Also, the resolution of *Franklin v. Gwinnett County Public Schools* opened up a new source of legal recourse for women's rights. The sexual harassment lawsuit, filed in the late 1980s on behalf of a sixteen-year-old Georgia female high school student against a male teacher, exposed a loophole in the original Title IX legislation. After the student lost in narrow lower-court opinions, the Supreme Court took the case. In their February 1992 decision, the justices forcefully rejected arguments from the lower courts and the George H. W. Bush administration. They ruled that the girl not only had the right to sue for damages in federal court; she also had the right to "all appropriate remedies," and a federal court could order "any appropriate relief," unless Congress said otherwise. Although this decision was unrelated to athletics, historian Welch Suggs saw the judgment as a turning point for women's sports, writing that "for the first time, colleges began taking Title IX seriously."[41]

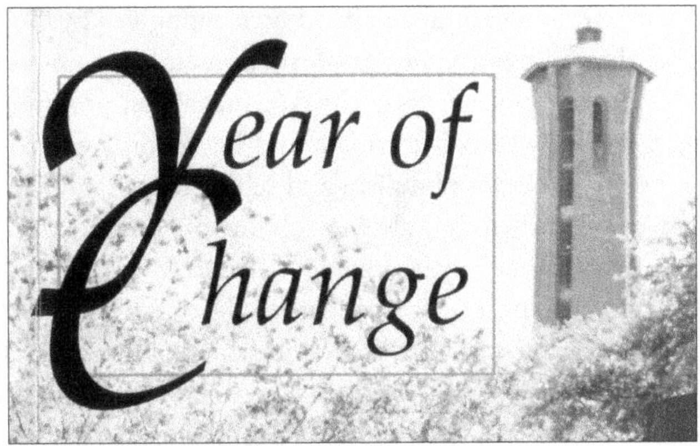

1992 *Mirage* cover set the tone for the annual review.

The unprecedented outcome of the midterm congressional elections compelled some national headline writers to call 1992 the Year of the Woman. The groundswell of support for female candidates was considered a reaction to contentious confirmation hearings for Supreme Court nominee Clarence Thomas the previous year. The televised spectacle featured explosive testimony from Anita Hill about Thomas's alleged sexual harassment. It also forced recognition that no female senators sat on the Judiciary Committee that was questioning the law professor's credibility and claims.[42] That year voters elected more women to Congress than ever before, tripling the number of female senators from two to six and increasing the number of women in the House from 29 to 47. Not everyone appreciated the headlines, however. Sen. Barbara Mikulski of Maryland exclaimed, "Calling 1992 the Year of the Woman makes it sound like the Year of the Caribou or the Year of the Asparagus. We're not a fad, a fancy, or a year." To her point, the number of women in Congress doubled again in the next decade.[43]

This notable progress didn't mean the fight for women's rights were in the past. Conversations at the national level continued as both men and women wrestled with their evolving roles. In his essay, "A Vision of Biblical Complementarity," John Piper declared, "We are adrift in a sea of confusion over sex roles." Piper used scripture to make the case that men could not flourish under personal directives from female superiors. As an example, he said it was inappropriate for a woman to act as umpire, calling balls and strikes for male players, "not necessarily owing to male egotism, but to a natural and good penchant given by God."[44] The response to the Supreme Court confirmation hearings moved writer Rebecca Walker to pen an essay for *Ms.* magazine, prompting what some call the third wave of feminism and broadening the concept to include a "deep respect for pluralism and self-determination."[45]

The gender role debate was also percolating on Trinity's campus. The Women's Interest Center invited students to use a discussion board at the Coates Center to post their responses to the question "What is feminism?" While the intent was to foster healthy dialogue, not all replies were respectful. One *Trinitonian* editorial began, "Nothing draws a battle line faster than the use of the word 'feminism,' as the Women's Interest Center well knows by now.... Sadly the board reveals much of the misogyny, and reverse misogyny, on campus." Although many comments were supportive, the more vehement responses prompted the editorialist to declare "We have not come a long way, baby—men nor women."[46]

The next fall, the WIC sponsored a *Trinitonian* column, "Feminist Viewpoints," aimed at providing space for male and female students to continue dialogue around the fraught term. The columns ran for more than a year, until the university withdrew WIC funding by designating it a "special interest group." Steering committee member Julie Lundquist defended her organization and asked the administration to "ignore the rumors that no one in the group shaves their legs or dates men," but the WIC dissolved in 1994. Two years later Students for the Advancement of Gender Equality formed what the leaders described as a more gender-balanced club.[47]

Meanwhile, national efforts to level the playing fields for female athletes were still lagging. A study released by the NCAA Gender Equity task force on the twentieth anniversary of Title IX registered "disappointing results" toward its goal of equity in intercollegiate athletics. Although undergraduate enrollment in its member schools was almost evenly divided by sex, the task force found that participation numbers and resources landed overwhelmingly in favor of men's programs.[48] A separate 1992 study of Division I athletics validated these results, noting that—even after removing the disproportionate numbers from football—male participants still outnumbered females by almost 50 percent. The budget discrepancies were even greater: men's programs disbursed $1.80 to every $1 spent on women's.[49]

In 1992, seven female athletes sued the University of Texas for lack of varsity programs. Although the UT student body was 53 percent male and 47 percent female, the ratio of 304 men to 90 women in intercollegiate athletes didn't match up; in fact, just the number of male football players exceeded the sum of all female varsity participants. Also, the women's $4.4 million budget paled in comparison to the men's $15.6 million allotment. It was apparently those trends that frustrated UT women's athletic director Donna Lopiano, who resigned to take a position with the Women's Sports Foundation and left the legal challenge in the hands of successor Jody Conradt. The school settled the lawsuit, elevating the club sports of rowing, soccer, and softball to varsity programs. The agreement also spurred construction of dedicated facilities for UT women's softball, soccer, and track and field.[50]

Ironically, the rise of women's intercollegiate sports spurred a depletion of women coaches and administrators. In 1972, 90 percent of women's collegiate teams were coached by females. By 1992, it was only 48 percent.[51]

Some observers considered the snail-paced compliance of schools a continuation of what Libby Johnson called "archaic thoughts." Said one sports historian at Title IX's twenty-year anniversary, "Instead of championing them, female student-athletes are still viewed by a generation of male leaders as half-invited, troublesome stepdaughters who are depleting men's resources."[52]

Thanks to continuing support from the top, Trinity's female athletes rarely found themselves at the center of the contentious conversations occurring at other schools.

One on-campus group that had to adjust to the winds of change was the physical education department, which found that incoming Division III student-athletes weren't seeking degrees in their field, focusing instead on other academic disciplines.[53] As a result, the physical education and athletics major was eliminated. Students were allowed to pursue a minor in the subject, which eventually morphed into the program of sport management. Julie Jenkins approved of the change, saying her players were not attending Trinity to major in physical education. She elaborated: "They're here for pre-med or engineering."[54] The days of women needing a physical education major to play varsity sports were no more.

A highlight in the *Mirage*'s Year of Change was the moment both Trinity men's and women's tennis teams won conference crowns in their first SCAC season. The 1992 Spring Sports Festival marked the first time in the conference's thirty-year history it hosted championships for both men's and women's teams. The event was held at Millsaps College in Jackson, Mississippi, where the athletic director and host was Bob King.[55]

New Facilities, New Conference, New Personnel

Trinity's most visible commitment to campus recreation culminated in 1992 with the major renovation of existing facilities and the construction of new ones. The driving force behind the construction was the need to accommodate ever-increasing intramural participation and provide spectator opportunities at club and varsity contests for students now expected to live on campus.[56]

Sports reporter Chris Hart hoped that new construction would match the ubiquitous red brick, which he considered an integral part of the Trinity experience. Using as evidence the "utterly pale" Sams Center, the "barren baseball field," and the "unendowed" E. M. Stevens Stadium, Hart tied the architectural style to athletic performance, alluding to the losing seasons of many teams: "Is it any wonder that the three native Trinity facilities without any relationship to red brick are the very places where this school is regularly at its worst?"[57]

Dedicated on October 4, 1990, the $11 million Jesse H. Jones Recreational Area was the first major manifestation of the years of planning, development, controversy, and investment from Trinity trustees and other university partners.[58] The project filled the previously acquired six-acre residential tract on the south end of campus and was anchored by the Meadows Pavilion, which functioned as a gathering place and satellite intramural office. Surrounding the pavilion was a softball diamond, soccer field, outdoor basketball courts, sand volleyball court, intramural fields, and a soft-surfaced jogging trail.

After almost two decades of practicing on a "scruffy little grass patch" and playing all games off campus, the Trinity softball team finally had a first-class stadium to call home.[59]

The next necessary construction project was to replace the 1960s-era

Softball team finally got a field and stadium to call their own in 1990.

Sams Center with what would be the Bell Center, an update many in the community felt was long past due. According to Norris, "When the Sams Center was built, Trinity had no women's athletics and the health craze was not near the size it is today." Dean of students Coleen Grissom called the building a "pit" and "an embarrassment to the university."[60] Although it wasn't the primary objective of the $13 million investment, Norris also felt that the Bell Center would bring more and better athletes to Trinity.[61]

The project, which would add 38,000 square feet to the former footprint, created a year-long disruption. To make way for the demolition of the Sams Center in spring 1991, physical education department offices were moved to a nearby house on Kings Court. Gymnastics, bowling, and racquetball classes were cancelled, and other classes were held at alternate campus locations. Both basketball teams and the women's volleyball team had to travel east across Skyline Drive to the Alamo Stadium gym to host home games in the high school complex.

The *Trinitonian* heralded the 1992 opening of the sleek facility in

Trinity hosts NFL Houston Oilers for summer camp.

a headline comparing it to another highly anticipated landmark still under construction downtown: "Forget the Alamodome—Bell Center Unveiled as Answer to All Athletic Problems." The story summarized the many new amenities and quoted Norris, who said, "They really did it right."[62] Ironically, the first customers for the Bell Center weren't students; Trinity had agreed to host the preseason camp for the NFL Houston Oilers, who took advantage of the rooms, meeting areas, and weight room that summer.[63]

The complex's official christening ushered in an era of improved practices and conditioning, hosting of competitive tournaments, "Midnight Madness" basketball pep rallies, and rousing playoff games. Named for recently deceased trustee William H. Bell, the 185,000-square-foot facility offered two gymnasiums, racquetball and squash courts, a fitness center, a training room, a swimming pool, dance and aerobics studios, classrooms, meeting rooms, and offices. The eight locker rooms meant that, for the first time in their history, Trinity's female varsity athletes had their own place to prepare for practices and home games. The new natatorium allowed for the establishment of the school's first intercollegiate swimming and diving program.

That same year, the university also resurfaced the football field and tennis courts and upgraded the outdoor swimming pool with improved locker rooms and a border of "Trinity red brick." (Presumably Chris Hart approved.)[64]

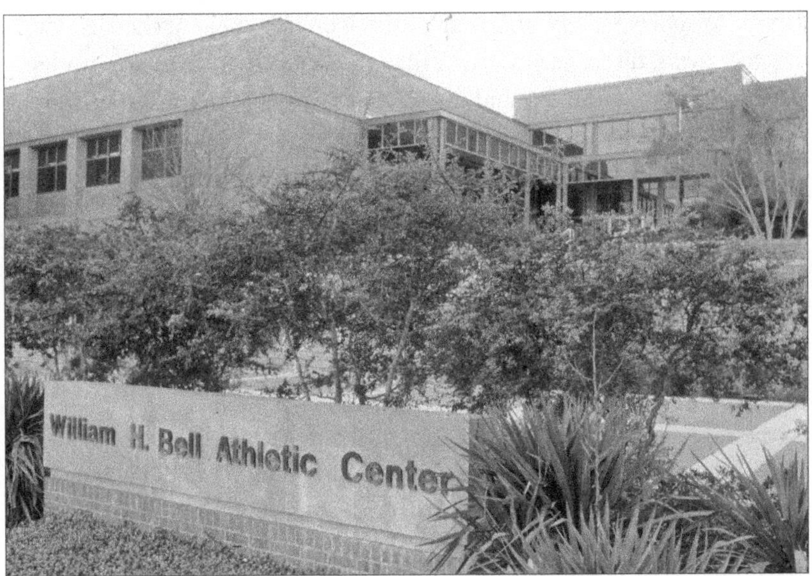

Bell Center, dedicated in 1992

The lower-campus transformation enhanced Trinity's national reputation; not only was the school a haven for academic excellence, but it now also provided access to first-class athletic facilities and support. In addition to Norris's prediction about bringing "more and better" athletes to Trinity, the changes also sweetened the recruiting pitch for coaches and administrators. When Bob King decided to apply for the open athletic director position, he said one of the primary attractions was the new facilities, describing them "as fine as any in the country of this size institution."[65]

Norris also hoped the upgrades would attract more sporting events to campus. Since Trinity was still the only Division III school in Texas, few schools in the nonscholarship division traveled to the "isolated" San Antonio campus.[66] Julie Jenkins immediately used the sparkling new facilities to attract top-ranked competition. At the 1992 Final Four, she was able to recruit coaches from elite Division III programs to come to Trinity for an invitational tournament the next fall. After that first Trinity-hosted event, Jenkins said the ability to hold NCAA tournaments "made a tremendous impact" on their recruiting.[67] And, in fact, the school would accommodate future NCAA playoff matches in a variety of sports.[68] Non-sports activities were also held at the Bell Center; the 1970s disco group The Village People performed for students the same day a swimming and diving meet was held in the natatorium.[69]

And finally, an inclusive training center greatly expanded physical conditioning opportunities for male and female players in varsity athletics, club sports, and intramurals. The program introduced a new approach for the athletes, according to volleyball All-American Amy Waddell. She said the facility provided athletes access not only to training resources but also to a weight room that introduced strength-building as a regular part of Trinity's volleyball program.[70]

As new facilities were opening up, one older one was neglected. The E. M. Stevens track that had inspired the pioneer female distance runners of the 1970s was falling into disrepair. A preview of the 1994 track and field season was eclipsed by the escalating dispute about its safety. It had become hard asphalt and was causing shin splints and other injuries for runners. It also lacked proper amenities for field events, such as sand pits for the long or triple jump.

In the absence of a usable track, Bob Hockey scheduled some cross country workouts on the jogging trail at the northeast corner of campus.[71] Paul McGinlay often moved his track and field practices to Alamo Stadium, as part of an arrangement that allowed San Antonio Independent School District softball teams to use their new field in exchange. While it wasn't an ideal situation, Alamo Stadium was the venue for many events staged that spring and hosted by Trinity.

Trinitonian sports editor Curtis Ruder commented on the situation, noting that the size of the track and field team was second only to football: "They, like the other athletes at Trinity, deserve the best facilities we can give them."[72] The administration would eventually find the funds and remedy the situation in time for the 1996 season.

While just a structure, the Bell Center was the gateway into a new conference and the catalyst for a cascade of personnel changes.

Tiger squads spent almost ten seasons competing against mostly superior scholarship teams as the only Division III Texas school. But in 1989, the school finally shed its independent status to join the College

Logo for coed Southern Collegiate Athletic Conference, renamed in 1991

Athletic Conference (CAC), founded in 1962 as an alternative to the big-time athletics that organizers felt had "permeated academic culture."[73] In fact, unlike many other conferences where geography was the key criteria for membership, the CAC welcomed private universities whose primary focus was academics. Almost all members hosted Phi Beta Kappa chapters, some were featured in annual best-college rankings, and most had stringent entrance requirements similar to Trinity's.[74]

The exit of two CAC members created the opening for Calgaard, who had been conference shopping since leaving the TIAA. The reaction from Trinity's coaching staff and physical education department was exceedingly positive. After a decade of independent play, Norris felt the conference would help his players get more recognition and provide goals for each season. "All the games are important, as either you are playing for a conference title yourself or trying to beat someone who is," he said.[75] The longtime football coach also expressed appreciation for Calgaard's administration, which he said was "philosophically and financially committed" to improving the program, and said he believed the change would make Trinity a "force to be reckoned with."[76]

Since its inception, the CAC had offered only men's sports, but Calgaard made a commitment to adding women's programs.[77] Again, he kept his promise, spearheading a movement with fellow conference members to add women's sports in 1991. Renamed the Southern Collegiate Athletic Conference to reflect its regional representation, the alliance gave men's and women's teams equal opportunities to compete for championships with a chance to advance to Division III national postseason play. Head volleyball coach Julie Jenkins considers the conference expansion the "turning point" for women's athletics at Trinity. "Joining the SCAC is truly what put Trinity athletics on the map," she said, pointing out that in that first year the women's volleyball and soccer teams received their first NCAA postseason bids.[78]

By spring 1992, any lingering doubts about exiting Division I were supplanted by optimism, now that all Tiger teams were competing with peers in a nonscholarship conference. In a story presenting the positive aspects of Division III, the *Trinitonian* noted that the establishment of a "good, solid" intercollegiate athletic program didn't just happen. After pointing out the substantial improvements to facilities and the elevation of coaches to full-time positions (including a new swimming coach), athletic director Gene Norris said, "You only have to look around to see the full support of the administration."[79]

Trinity was the largest school in the SCAC, which also included Tennessee schools Fisk University, Rhodes College, and University of the South (Sewanee), as well as Centre College in Kentucky, Hendrix College in Arkansas, Millsaps College in Mississippi, and Oglethorpe University in Georgia. A minimum number of members had to field a varsity team for a sport to be eligible for conference championships, delaying the introduction of softball and swimming and diving until 1998.[80]

When the conference accepted women's sports, Trinity was still the lone Division III Texas school, but Southwestern University entered the SCAC in the 1992–93 academic year. Norris predicted that more schools would join in the coming years as the cost of maintaining athletic scholarship programs escalated.[81]

Gene Norris, who had been on staff since 1961 and was promoted to athletic director in 1984, had recently stepped down from his position as head football coach.[82] Not long after the new facilities were dedicated, he became director of facilities, a job that provided oversight and scheduling for all activities in the Bell Center, plus the south campus fields, the football and baseball fields, and both swimming pools. Norris called it "an enormous change of direction" in his career but was confident he was up to the task.[83]

As athletic director, Norris was an ardent advocate for women's intercollegiate sports, working with the administration to find and hire female coaches, and he fought to increase funding for team budgets and coaching salaries.[84] Soccer star Suzanne Anderson remembers him as being very supportive of women's sports and of her personally, "both as an athlete and as a coach."[85] Norris stayed at Trinity until 2001. He died in 2013.

Hiring Julie Jenkins introduced a model to Trinity for how a dedicated, specialized coach could transform a program. Jenkins kept her faith in the promises Calgaard made in her 1985 job interview through the seven difficult seasons when she was leading volleyball, track, and junior varsity tennis. Her patience and coaching skills were finally rewarded in the 1990 season—and for the rest of the decade. After not posting a winning record her first five years, the volleyball team turned the corner with a 28–10 record, marking the beginning of an impressive run of winning streaks and exemplary seasons. With the arrival of high school standout Amy Waddell and the imminent prospect of participating in a conference with peer institutions, Jenkins declared, "The tide has turned."[86] Indeed, after a second-round playoff loss ended the 1993 campaign, Jenkins complimented Waddell and fellow seniors Kerry Eudy and Jenny Kafka. "In the last four years, they have brought me my first winning season [four in a row], the first SCAC championship [three], and the first NCAA bids for Trinity [two]."[87]

A second promise fulfilled by Calgaard—a new facility—allowed Jenkins to host regional and national tournaments, exposing the program and players to a higher level of competition and national recognition. Her first season in the Bell Center featured thirty wins (matching the mark set in 1983 under Carol Higy), Waddell's second All-America honor, and the program's first top-ten national ranking. In the facility's second year, Trinity hosted the first round of the NCAA Division III volleyball playoffs.

Finally, Jenkins's 1991 promotion to assistant director of athletics marked a major milestone for women's intercollegiate sports at Trinity. In the 1970s, Libby Johnson held the title of assistant athletic director—in charge of women only—adding to her multiple duties but limiting the range of her responsibilities. Because other expert coaches were hired, Jenkins could focus on her two primary roles under the athletic director: head volleyball coach and NCAA and SCAC compliance officer.[88]

Jenkins has led and observed tremendous success across all Trinity sports for almost forty years. Her sphere of influence has not been limited to women's sports, as she has been recognized as an excellent

Spotlight on Amy Waddell

The 1990 recruitment of elite high school player Amy Waddell marked a historic turning point for the volleyball program. Even some of Julie Jenkins's peers were impressed with the talented player. Glada Munt, who coached the Southwestern University volleyball teams to the NAIA national championship in the 1980s, called Waddell one of the first "elite" Division III players.

Waddell not only raised the level of play for the Tigers; she was also the first Trinity athlete, male or female, to be named to a Division III All-American team. Jenkins joined Waddell and her mother to receive the honor in St. Louis. Later Waddell said, "It was as much an award for Julie as it was for me."

At the end of the 1993 season, *Trinitonian* sports editor Curtis Ruder reflected on Waddell's contributions. After watching a team that won only three games in 1988 transform itself "onto the brink of a dynasty" with a 30–6 record, he suggested that the program's critical moment was when the 5'9" star set foot on Trinity's campus. "In a couple of years," he added, "when the team has continued to be the powerhouse that it is today, the name of the building may still be the Bell Center, but it will also be The House That Waddell Built."

Waddell fondly looks back on those early conference years, recalling the snowball effect that set the stage for success: "We had a handful of girls who played club volleyball who were amazing athletes, and Julie continued to do a good job of recruiting up." She added, "We had a lot of talent, and we also had a lot of fun."

The All-American was inducted to the 2007 Trinity Athletics Hall of Fame based on her school record in career kills and her status as the only three-time conference player of the year in SCAC history. She graduated with a bachelor's degree in English, was selected as one of Trinity's seniors for Who's Who, and had a successful career as a teacher and financial advisor.

Amy Waddell with her mother, Linda, at the 1991 All-American ceremony.

mentor and communicator who is committed to enhancing Division III athletics. She continues in that position to the present day.

Athletic trainer Levi "Knock" Knight retired after thirty-five years of working mostly with the men's teams. A highly respected campus fixture, he was one of the first African American trainers to work at a predominantly white university when he joined the Trinity staff in 1946. He is one of only four non-Trinity graduates inducted into the school's Athletics Hall of Fame.[89]

The 1991 appointment of Janet Bristor as Trinity's first full-time certified athletic trainer guaranteed professional treatment and conditioning for *all* of its student athletes. Bristor had become interested in the field after a trainer successfully treated a back injury she suffered in high school volleyball. Her job entailed managing the training room to accommodate both male and female athletes, coordinating information on student-athletes' physical examinations and insurance coverage, and compiling injury and illness records during the intercollegiate seasons.[90] Her first task, though, in setting up the expanded program was to design state-of-the-art facilities for the Bell Center, a responsibility she approached with expertise and enthusiasm. During construction, she operated out of the concession stand next to the football stadium. Despite cramped quarters and initial lack of air-conditioning, she said the steamy conditions weren't too bad.[91]

Bristor also established a student trainer program to support both intercollegiate and intramural programs. By 1994, it boasted fourteen participants from all classes certified in first aid and CPR. They were made available during any practice, intramural contest, or intercollegiate game and coordinated care in the event of an injury.[92] Players and coaches alike sung their praises, including the men's club lacrosse team. After hosting a tournament on the lower campus fields, Gabriel Gilligan wrote a letter to the *Trinitonian* on behalf of the team, praising the training director: "Janet Bristor has quietly built an excellent training and support facility and staff. Although our opponents were impressed with the quality of our fields, they were more impressed by the support they received from our trainers."[93] Similar compliments were commonplace throughout Bristor's tenure. Students, coaches, and administrators expressed appreciation for her work ethic and ability to inspire.

Yanika Daniels said Bristor was the key to her recovery from reconstructive knee surgery. The basketball player, an Ivy League prospect before a knee injury prematurely ended her high school career, knew it was going to take a lot of work to get back to the level of play she was accustomed to. She told Bristor her goal was to play the final game of her first season without a knee brace. The trainer delivered. Although Daniels said Bristor worked her "to tears," together they completely rehabilitated the knee. The freshman played the season's last game without her brace and never needed it again. Bristor's impact on the athlete extended beyond her college years. "A lot of my major life lessons took place in that training room," Daniels said later.[94]

A footnote on the training program shows that not all female athletes had access to the same resources. Shelley Story, a pitcher and catcher for the Tiger softball team in the early 1990s, was injured during a game when an opposing player cut her hand while wearing illegal metal cleats in a play at the plate. Her parents had traveled from out of town and arrived late. Instead of watching their daughter play, they had to drive her to the emergency room. "If my parents hadn't been there with me that night, I'm not sure what would have happened. I don't remember seeing a trainer," she said.[95] The French major did find her way back to the diamond to support Teresa Machu's team later that season.

Perhaps the most transformational moment in the history of modern Trinity athletics was the 1993 appointment of Bob King as athletic director. King, who met Calgaard while representing Millsaps College in the SCAC, was asked to apply for the Trinity job when Norris was reassigned to oversee the Bell Center.

King brought extensive educational and professional experience to Trinity, including graduate work at the University of North Carolina and the University of Southern California. He'd been a graduate teaching assistant at Idaho State University and worked as a high school football coach in Jackson, Mississippi. He returned to Millsaps, where he had earned his undergraduate degree while excelling in football and basketball. In his four years there, King was a busy athletic director, reorganizing the athletics office, implementing a recruiting strategy, upgrading the women's sports programs, and spearheading plans for a $10 million athletic facility. He considers himself an early supporter of Title IX, which passed before his playing days at Millsaps. He recalls taking classes about the law and said its implications made a significant impact on his perspective.[96]

When the thirty-nine-year-old met Calgaard at the SCAC meeting in San Antonio, they hit it off. King remembers, "I was impressed by Ron as a leader." Not surprisingly, when he set eyes on the new Bell Center, he thought, "Wow, you can really do something with this place."[97]

King had grown up watching coaches leading multiple sports, teaching classes, and doing "whatever else the university wanted you to do." But a new approach began to evolve in Division III, and King jumped on the leading edge, becoming the first Millsaps athletic director not expected to juggle teaching and coaching duties. Calgaard allowed him to bring the same model to Trinity. Decades later, Shirley Rushing referred to bringing King to Trinity as the final puzzle piece in Calgaard's vision. For the first time in her long career, she could say that the school had an "athletic director for both men and women."[98]

As a Division III veteran, King built on the balanced philosophy at Trinity, but his immediate goal was to "get every team at a higher competitive level" and win the SCAC's all-sports President's Trophy. He waited only a year before the teams delivered the honor. His longer-term goals were to upgrade every aspect of the athletic program (including intramurals, which were now under his purview) and to interact with campus, local, regional, and national communities.[99] His first semester, he was greeted with an incoming varsity recruiting class twice as large as in previous years.[100]

Another of King's top priorities was to address Title IX discrepancies in Trinity's budget. "There's nothing you can fund like football," he admitted, "but the rest of the sports we tried to fund the same." King described Calgaard's approach as "hiring quality coaches and spending a dollar on the females for every dollar we spent on the males."[101] That said, nobody pretended that petitioning for money from Calgaard would be easy. King had to work constantly to get travel expenses approved and funding for assistant coaches. Calgaard often accused him of trying to bankrupt the university, but King had a winning argument, which was to remind him that he wanted to create a competitive athletic program. "In my mind that meant we needed to be one of the best schools in Division III," King said. "And when you say 'best' you are always asking for money and support."[102]

Upon arrival, King faced two existential problems—the hangover from the unpopular demotion of the legendary tennis program to Division III and an inherited discrimination charge concerning a Midnight Madness basketball event.

Of lingering dissent over the contentious 1990 tennis decision, King said, "That was already decided and in place when I arrived. I didn't grasp the significance of it until I became athletic director. Then it became clear to me." In one symbolic move at the end of the decade, he implemented Calgaard's concept of an Athletics Hall of Fame and used it to honor the historic achievements of many of those players.

Midnight Madness is a pep rally sponsored by the Association of Residence Hall Students that begins at midnight of the first day allowed by the NCAA for preseason basketball practice. This event was becoming a college tradition across the country and was the second for Trinity in the new gym. Sophomore Yanika Daniels noted, however, a significant but familiar oversight: it only featured the men's team. The women's varsity basketball player expressed her anger in a letter to the *Trinitonian*:

> I was infuriated by the blatant and very arrogant display of unjust treatment toward the women's basketball team through the production of last Sunday night's "Midnight Madness." We were ignored and greatly disrespected. I refuse to tolerate such disrespect as long as I am a vital part of this university's athletic program. I sacrifice my physical well-being and enormous chunks of my valuable time for the sake of representing Trinity. Both were voided of any value at the Midnight Madness. Since when has Trinity had one "Trinity Basketball Team" as referred to on all the publicity posters and flyers and by the M.C. of the event? From what I understand, there are two teams, a women's team and a men's team, who spend equal amounts of time and effort representing Trinity in the classroom and on the basketball court. But somehow only one was honored in the season opening pep rally and the other was not even acknowledged, much less allowed to play. It is obvious we deserve much more respect than what is being given us, first as women and secondly as athletes.[103]

Daniels received an almost immediate response from King. Although the event had been planned before he arrived, he assumed responsibility and wrote a letter publicly validating Daniels's objections and assuring her that plans were already in place to include the women in next year's event. He concluded, "I can assure you that I am extremely sensitive and supportive of issues dealing with gender equity."[104] He kept his promise to Daniels, and the women players joined the men's squad in the 1994 Midnight Madness festivities. A crowd of about 750 showed up to watch intrasquad games, with the men's scrimmage coached by Calgaard and the women's by vice president for student affairs Coleen Grissom.[105]

Despite his trial by fire, King quickly aligned his leadership to the pursuit of the Division III philosophy for the next few decades at Trinity. According to him, the approach allows campus residents to be both students and athletes by offering a "broad-based intercollegiate athletic program that provides equal opportunity for students to excel on the field and in the classroom." He believes that the program gives students every opportunity to be successful, without being "owned" by an athletic department.[106]

To better prepare for conference competition, King created a model to attract experienced full-time coaches who would have time for recruiting. He said the school's recruiting process before his arrival was just getting "whoever came through San Antonio." Once teaching obligations were removed, his coaches had time to better target prospects with the right academic profiles for Trinity's competitive classrooms.[107]

Thus ended the revolving door of part-time and volunteer coaches that hindered the women's programs and hampered recruiting from the now broader pool of experienced female prospects. Even full-time coach Julie Jenkins saw her schedule change from three classes a semester to one. "When Bob King came in, that's when the wheels started," she said.[108]

Publicity Waxes and Wanes

One of the most notable casualties of the tennis demotion was the subsequent decrease in local coverage and publicity for Trinity's varsity teams, although on-campus publication coverage improved. The *Trinitonian* increased staff and expanded its size to more than forty pages in the 1990s. The additional pages allowed the weekly paper to publish more game details, and reporters had access to more comprehensive statistics from the sports information director and the SCAC. The existence of a conference and end-of-season championships also provided meatier material for the budding sportswriters. The yearbook staff became more adept at summarizing team results over the full year, as the introduction of electronic publishing allowed *Mirage* editors to better cover winter and spring sports.[109]

The improved on-campus coverage helped offset waning support from the local media, a subject covered in depth in the full-page *Trinitonian* story "Women's Athletics Not Getting Coverage It Deserves." Sports editor Rachel VanArsdale mentioned Jenkins's complaints that neither of the daily newspapers covered her 1991 volleyball team, even after winning twenty games for the first time in school history. When the River City Classic tournament featured local teams such as Trinity, St. Mary's, and Incarnate Word, no scores were published. "It's really frustrating to see a program that has been turned around not get covered," Jenkins said. "We use the write-ups as recruiting tools since we are nonscholarship. Without them, recruiting becomes very difficult."

Jenkins received a response from Tim Kelly, executive sports editor of the *San Antonio Light*: "We're not adequate, but it was abysmal before." He said sports editors of the past "were all fifty-five-year-old men wearing polo shirts they got free from some golf club." Kelly shouldered some of the blame, suggesting that editors could strive for more inclusive coverage, but he also diverted some culpability back to the universities, saying that if the sports information staff wasn't feeding information about the women's teams to his writers, coverage would suffer.[110] His *Light* colleague Jeff Cohen agreed with Kelly's assessment, calling coverage of women's sports "horrendous" in most daily newspapers but claiming that their paper was "better than average" because they talked about the issue a lot.

To further exacerbate the problem, the three daily newspaper editions (two morning and one evening) were consolidated into one when the *San Antonio Light* closed its doors in 1993. Eventually the surviving *Express-News* trimmed its staff and published just one morning paper, severely limiting space for game coverage, aside from the rare season preview or random player feature.

The scarcity of coverage, along with a dose of misogyny, still prevailed in many corners of the sports landscape. VanArsdale's story captured sentiments from national female athletic leaders, such as the University of Tennessee athletic director who described the publicity situation in metaphor-laden terms: "We're at midcourt now in women's athletic coverage. The key to getting a dunk is in our court, and we can't afford to double dribble or walk with the ball."[111]

A backward glance shows incremental progress for women on many fronts in the early 1990s. In addition to the congressional seats gained during the "Year of the Woman," President Bill Clinton appointed Janet Reno as the first female US attorney general, the Family Medical Leave Act and the Violence Against Women Act passed Congress, and Take Our Daughters to Work Day was launched to expose girls to workplace opportunities and help them build self-esteem. The enforcement of Title IX got another legislative nudge when Congress passed the Equity in Athletics Disclosure Act in 1994, requiring institutions of higher learning to annually report data about their men's and women's athletic programs.[112]

Even more than twenty years after Title IX, however, some doors remained closed. When Trinity athlete Halie Bricker was still in high school in the early 1990s, her sky-high ambitions were quickly grounded at a career day. The Air Force representative told her she couldn't be a fighter pilot because she was a girl.[113]

In 1995, Glada Munt still encountered "archaic thoughts," as her former coach called them, on a playoff trip with the Southwestern baseball team in Wisconsin. Munt recalls, "I was going up in the bleachers and these men asked me if I was the wife of the coach. I said, 'No, I'm the director of athletics' and one of them said, 'How did a girl like you get to be an athletics director?'" After mulling over a range of potential responses, she replied, "I earned it."[114]

Also in 1995, the Physical Education and Athletics Department watched one of its most passionate advocates dance off into her own retirement. Department chair Shirley Rushing discussed the many changes she'd observed in the past thirty-five years in a *Trinitonian* interview. She recounted her two most memorable moments—accompanying the four tennis freshmen when they won the national championships in 1973 and attending an international ballroom dance competition with her students in Cambridge, England. Rushing had instructed a wide variety of activities, including bowling, tennis, team sports, and country-western dance. It was fitting that an all-school country-western dance was held in her honor in the Bell Center ballroom.[115]

Southwestern University athletic director Glada Munt

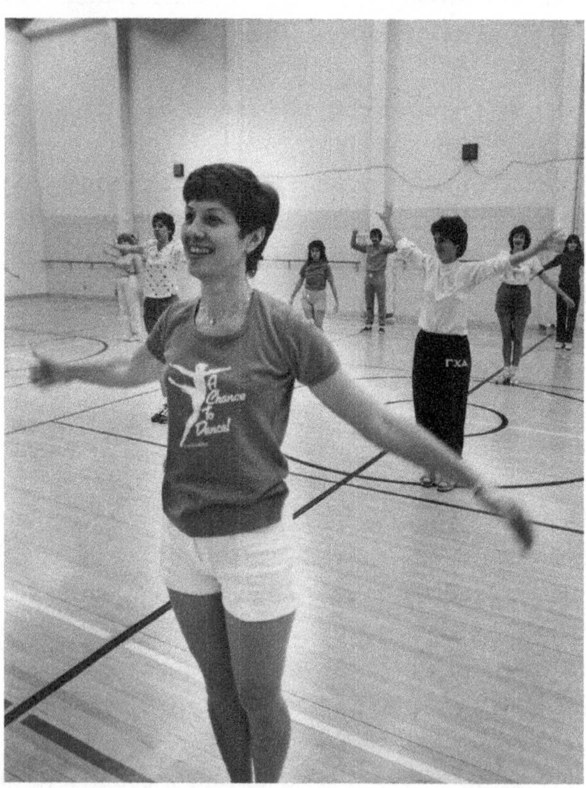

Shirley Rushing leads one of her many dance classes.

While Rushing considered her Trinity career "a total joy from beginning to end," her plan wasn't to retire to a recliner. "I retired early because I wanted to do other things in my life while I still could," she said. When she got a call asking if she'd teach ballroom dancing on a cruise ship, she jumped at the chance and spent the next few years teaching and sailing.[116] Even when she no longer taught, her activism never abated; she has continued to be a mentor to her many students over the years and was a catalyst and contributor to the women's sports history project that inspired this book. Her early contributions to women's sports were recognized in 2022 when she was inducted into the Athletics Hall of Fame. Trinity's women athletes would have to soldier on without Rushing's influence and advocacy, but those who followed her would ensure that her legacy remained intact.

Athletic director Bob King

CHAPTER 13

Leaving the Sidelines

1996–2000

Equity has been achieved.

—TRINITY'S 1996 SELF-STUDY

For Trinity athletics, the pieces were falling into place, including new facilities, an equitable budget, a peer institution athletic conference, dedicated coaches and trainers, and a full-time athletic director. Starting under athletic director Gene Norris and continuing under Bob King, Trinity expanded its intercollegiate program to eighteen sports, added new club sports, and expanded intramural and recreation programs.[1] Trinity teams were poised for success. The school established an Athletics Hall of Fame to recognize outstanding achievements and began to collect and publish more individual and team statistics for the women's teams, providing a more reliable record for the sports summaries of the 1990s and beyond.

Women's tennis and volleyball would shine, and one team would even bring home a title. Although two untimely deaths rocked the athletic community, women's intercollegiate athletics had finally arrived at Trinity.

Positive Reports on Trinity Sports

According to Trinity's 1996 institutional self-study, intercollegiate athletics had made substantial progress since the 1986 report, and the future looked even brighter. In addition to hiring a dedicated athletic director, full-time coaches were employed in almost all varsity sports, with the exception of softball, track and field, and cross country. The athletic budget (at $649,300) had tripled since 1981, increasing by 31 percent in the previous five years, and adequate funds were available to cover team travel expenses. The authors proclaimed that, beginning with the 1996–97 budget, the supplies and expenses for men's and women's individual sports were equitable.[2]

Other improvements listed were the addition of club sports (men's volleyball and men's and women's lacrosse) and an outdoor activities program. The report also noted the resolution of earlier issues, including full-time coaches in soccer and swimming and diving, increased attendance at games, and more mascot performances at athletic events. There were recommendations for better female and minority representation in athletic departments, addition of full-time assistants for several varsity teams, and more competitive programs for cross country, track and field, softball, and golf.

The self-study authors were especially enthusiastic about membership in NCAA Division III and the SCAC. In fact, the lead sentence in the intercollegiate athletics section stated that Trinity "endorses the philosophy, principles, and objectives of a program of nonscholarship intercollegiate athletics, believing that a broad-based athletic program with adequate funding, facilities, and staffing can be competitive and successful at a highly selective liberal arts institution." Also noted were "dramatic gains" in team success, recruiting, facilities, coaches, and budget, likely referring to the two years when Trinity brought home consecutive SCAC President's Trophy honors.

The report endorsed the philosophies of the governance organizations: "As a member institution, the University believes that Division III of the NCAA provides the best framework for achieving the academic-athletic mission of the institution. [B]y recruiting only qualified student-athletes with intellectual curiosity, the student-athlete concept remains strong, and academic success is obtainable." Their conclusion? "By sustaining current successes...intercollegiate athletics will create spirit on campus and recruit academically competitive student-athletes to Trinity University."[3]

In December 1996, Bob King used the *Trinitonian* platform to sum

Spotlight on a Rhodes Scholar

Named Soccer Player of the Year at her high school in Corpus Christi, Texas, all-SCAC midfielder Ana Unruh was a member of the conference championship team every year in her college career. As a senior, she was one of only thirty-two college students in the country to be named a Rhodes Scholar in the 1993 academic year. The chemistry major and geosciences minor also volunteered for the Alpha Phi Omega service organization, served as president of the Chemistry Club and Mortar Board honor society, assisted a local girl's club soccer team, and helped design a chemistry demonstration program at the San Antonio Children's Museum. To cap off her undergraduate career, Unruh was asked by Calgaard to speak at her own commencement ceremony.

She applied her scholarship toward a doctorate in earth sciences from Oxford, which springboarded her into a career in Washington, D.C., in energy and environmental policy. She was named Trinity's Outstanding Young Alumni for 2007–8. And in 2017, she was invited a second time to speak on the Trinity commencement stage. Unruh is currently the only Trinity graduate to receive a Rhodes scholarship.

Anna Unruh, Rhodes scholar

up the fall sports season, his fourth on campus. After expressing his appreciation for the Spirit Committee, cheerleaders, Pep Band, and Tiger Dancers for their support, and the newspaper staff for their "vast and accurate coverage" of events, he addressed the fans: "By attending athletic contests, your enthusiastic show of support has helped the University's athletics teams achieve SCAC championships, NCAA tournament invitations, and NCAA national rankings." Implicit in that statement was the just-completed volleyball season, as that team posted a 31–6 record, won the conference title, made their fifth consecutive trip to the playoffs, and earned coach Julie Jenkins SCAC Coach of the Year honors. King concluded, "I hope you will continue to be a part of one of the finest NCAA Division III athletic programs in the nation."[4]

A Division with a Distinction

According to the NCAA website, its three divisions were created to "align like-minded campuses in the areas of philosophy, competition and opportunity."[5] The website refers specifically to the distinctive nature of Division III, which was formed in 1973 just a year after the signing of Title IX. It uses the division's "unwavering commitment to the academic success of every student-athlete" to explain why its members don't award athletic scholarships. The overview alludes to a familiar debate: "The opportunity to play sports in college is a privilege, but we often forget taking part in collegiate athletics is also a choice. When high school seniors decide to be Division III student-athletes, their choice illustrates their passion for the sport and pursuit of an education. Division III student-athletes compete not for financial reward, but quite simply, for the love of the game."[6]

The NCAA decision to offer three divisions allowed it to segregate its larger, sports-minded institutions from smaller schools without the interest or financial resources to support athletic scholarships. Even the one-sport scholarship exemption was eventually abandoned, one reason Trinity cited for moving tennis to Division III.

What was missing in Trinity's early Division III alliance was inclusion in a conference of like-minded institutions, but that was soon resolved by joining CAC, which then became SCAC, who added women's sports. Many attribute this achievement to Calgaard's persuasive personality. Jenkins recalls, "This wasn't an easy move because the women's sports

Official logo for the NCAA Division III

from the CAC schools were members of different conferences. Calgaard was the driving force for getting both programs on board and forming the SCAC."[7] In the view of sports information director Justin Parker, the entry into this compatible conference and expansion to include women's sports "turned it around," for Trinity, leading to the unprecedented success of the school's intercollegiate program in the years since.[8]

The inclusion of women's teams wasn't an instant SCAC success, according to commissioner Dwayne Hanberry. At first the members' mostly male athletic directors wrestled with the concept of sharing coaches, facilities, and resources, and some harbored ingrained opinions about the viability of female athletes. Hanberry recalls a few of them treating their women's program like intramurals, so they could "check the box" about adherence to NCAA policy. It took the steadfast efforts of advocates like Bob King and Glada Munt to convince their colleagues that women's sports needed to be treated the same. After two decades working with Munt, Hanberry said, "She was really our conscience for women's sports." Despite the speed bumps, the commissioner felt that the SCAC was far ahead of the equity curve compared to other conferences.

One byproduct of those ingrained opinions of female athletes was a delay in admitting softball and swimming into conference competition until 1998. When women's teams joined the SCAC in 1991, Trinity was the only school that offered a fast-pitch softball program. Hanberry said that Rhodes had a club team and the other schools just had "plans." Finally, after members commissioned a feasibility study in 1996, Rhodes and Southwestern added club teams, and softball became an official SCAC varsity sport two years later.

SCAC leaders didn't just talk about a balanced experience; they built and maintained a framework to ensure that student-athletes didn't feel like prisoners to their sport. "One of our founding principles is keep

SCAC commissioner Dwayne Hanberry.

kids in class," Hanberry said. "Professors don't care that you are the leading basketball scorer."[9] The conference mitigates classroom conflicts through shorter seasons, strict time limits on practices, and a scheduling model that reduces midweek competition. Trinity's athletic department was fully engaged with this approach, and practices were scheduled with class attendance in mind. Norris admitted, "If we force them to choose, they will go to class and get off the team."[10] The athletic director's recognition of this new type of athlete was validated in the 3.0 grade point average carried by the 266 intercollegiate athletes in 1992. "They are very self-motivated people," he said.[11] Teresa Machu echoed Norris's observation, noting that she didn't have to remind her players to keep up with their studies on road trips.[12]

The scheduling platform was an especially welcome change for Trinity coaches, who had spent the previous ten years scrambling to fill fifteen to twenty slots each season. Once the school was no longer operating as an independent, it could rely on the conference to arrange its games.[13]

Another unique element of Division III is students' ability to participate in more than one varsity sport—a benefit unheard of for athletic scholarship recipients. SCAC removed seasonal overlap among sports, which allowed Jennifer Warren, Kathy Bieser, and Halie Bricker to

Multisport athlete Halie Bricker.

compete on both the varsity volleyball and basketball teams. Bricker and Bieser would also contribute outstanding performances for Trinity's track and field squad in SCAC competition. Of course, even without overlapping seasons, participating in three varsity sports during a school year is a huge undertaking. How do students manage? Bricker explained, "It's never really been a question for me. It's never been 'Can I do this?' It's always been 'I'm going to find a way to do this.'" Basketball coach Becky Geyer felt the expanded opportunities fit neatly into the nonscholarship program. "A big part of Division III philosophy is participation," she said. "And we, as coaches, are going to work together to help them do that."[14]

After his 1993 arrival, King found he could oversee the newly dominant teams of the 1990s without loosening academic standards, and he had the support of a conference that went beyond recognizing athletic performances. In 1997 Hanberry added an annual academic honor roll for students who were regular varsity members of an SCAC-sponsored sport and maintained a minimum 3.25 GPA.[15] Indeed, as Trinity athletic successes soared in the 1990s, so too did the academic averages of its varsity players. Over the decade, graduation rates were higher and retention rates better among student-athletes compared to the general student population. In a study conducted during the highly successful

1999–2000 sports year, the GPAs of the general population and the student-athlete population were virtually the same, differing by less than one-tenth of a percent.[16]

Elsewhere, in 1997, the all-Texas TIAA dissolved after twenty-one years of operation. Two of the members, Austin College and University of Dallas, joined the SCAC in 2006 and 2011 respectively.[17]

The focus on academics did require a different recruiting approach. At Southwestern, Munt said she had to first find prospects with great SAT scores and then convince them to pay $50,000 a year to play for her school.[18]

Trinity coaches adapted to this academics-first approach, but that didn't mean they settled for lesser-skilled athletes. Jenkins said she finds Division I–caliber athletes who are academically inclined and looking for a small college setting: "There aren't a lot, but they're out there." She peddles the Division III combination of athletic opportunity and academic challenge: "You can make the varsity and not jeopardize your GPA."[19] But she doesn't lower her standards. "If they are not good enough to play in Division I, they are not good enough to play here."[20]

State volleyball champion and blue-chip recruit Amy Waddell had turned down Division I offers because she didn't want an athletic department to own her. She'd visited a campus where the coach arranged for her to stay with players, who took the high school senior to parties featuring alcohol. Jenkins, however, did her research. Realizing Waddell was active in the Christian youth program Young Life, she arranged for her to meet fellow members and attend their leadership training during her Trinity visit. "It felt like this place could be my home," Waddell said, and added her appreciation for Jenkins: "She cared about who I was, not just as a volleyball player."[21]

Coach Butch Newman found he adjusted not only his recruiting style but also his team goals in the wake of tennis's move to Division III. Noting that Division I required a minimum grade point average of 2.0 for varsity players, he focused on the annual honors given by the International Tennis Association to teams whose average was above 3.2. "We had a goal every year to have our team be academic All-Americans even if they weren't player All-Americans," he said. "That fostered what Division III philosophy is all about."[22]

While the SCAC's approach accommodated the academic element, it also created space for students to become involved in other aspects of campus life. Hanberry described Division III as the "landing spot" that would assure students had the opportunity to experience everything college can offer. "Coaches shouldn't be asking more of you than if you wanted to participate in student government or glee club," the commissioner said.[23]

What did the coaches think about this new type of athlete? Several said they preferred to work with academically focused students. Calling the change from Division I "refreshing," Newman felt that his players had a hunger to learn and didn't arrive with delusions of becoming professional tennis players. "They came in knowing there was going to be a life after tennis," he said.[24] Women's soccer coach Nick Cowell was "disenchanted" with the players' attitudes he'd coached in Division I. "They thought they had already made it," he said. "At Division III they are willing to learn and have a very good idea of where athletics fit in."[25]

While dozens of athlete opinions about the benefit of Division III can be found in student publications, this one from Tulsa tennis recruit and NCAA singles champion Lizzie Yasser seems to sum it up: "I like the idea of Division III because it's still really competitive, but it doesn't take over your life."[26] She found time off the court to host a show on the Tiger TV cable channel, earn accolades for a stage act at Parents Weekend in 2000, and serve as cohost for the popular variety show the following year.[27]

When King first mentioned a goal of winning the All-Southern Collegiate Athletic Conference Trophy, it's likely that few, if any, *Trinitonian* readers knew what he was talking about.[28] But it wouldn't take long for them to become familiar with the President's Trophy (a.k.a. the Bell). The 300-pound brass bell, donated to the SCAC by the Norfolk and Western Railroad, is presented each spring to the school with the best overall sports program.[29] King liked that the award "makes the golfer and the football player the same." For several years, one member institution hosted a Spring Sports Festival where teams competed for their respective conference crowns. After the festival scores were added to the fall teams' results, the winner was recognized.[30]

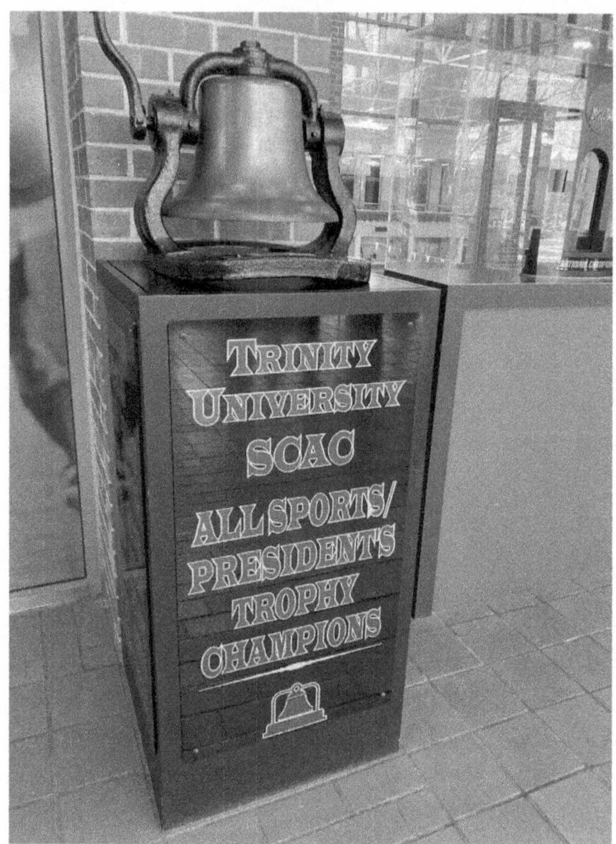

The SCAC trophy in its "perennial" location at Bell Center

The almost instant successes of Trinity teams in their first years of SCAC play might have surprised even Calgaard, who had envisioned conference achievements but not beyond. King said, "We took it to another level to compete nationally."[31] In the first year of conference play, the men's and women's tennis teams captured a 1992 SCAC title, jump-starting a thirty-year tradition of dominance over their conference opponents. Also, the 1992 volleyball and women's soccer teams received their first NCAA Division III postseason bids. The combined successes in the 1993–94 seasons helped King win the SCAC President's Trophy his inaugural year at the helm.[32]

Although it's supposed to be a rotating award, the trophy has resided in the appropriately named Bell Center with few interruptions since

1994. Trinity has won the honor twenty-two times, including eleven straight as of 2022. Only the Tigers of DePauw University in Indiana have housed the award in the off years. Since DePauw left the conference in 2010, Southwestern University has been a frequent runner-up.[33]

As Trinity racked up multiple championships and President's Trophies, sports editor Ron Nirenberg (and future San Antonio mayor) highlighted the athletes of the class of 1997, who he said would "be remembered for bringing Trinity into the national spotlight" after bringing home the all-sports award every year of their four-year sports careers. He added, "The trophy is all that Trinity sports should—and does—stand for. It crosses gender lines, it disregards a few bad games, and makes each sport just as significant as the other. What's important is not one team's season, but the whole University's. Nine months, 15 sports, scores of athletes. Everyone pulls the same rope."[34]

Two years later, sports editor Niki Herbert declared: "The SCAC bell belongs at Trinity," explaining that it was as much a part of the family as "common curriculum, powerful guest speakers, outstanding professors, and Abercrombie kids."[35] Later, summarizing the success of the most recent sports festival, ensuring Trinity's sixth award, Herbert proclaimed, "The bell will continue to ring."[36]

In her 1999 farewell column, soccer standout and cocaptain Sarah Newland provided *Trinitonian* readers with a player's up-close perspective on the value of competing against some of the country's best teams. After listing the soccer team's accomplishments since joining the SCAC, the geosciences major praised the entire athletic progam at Trinity. She added, "The bell trophy is more than something that I tap every time I walk past it; it represents the efforts and dedication of every Trinity athlete, and also the support given by our fans."[37]

While most SCAC athletes are highly competitive in both the arena and the classroom, SCAC leaders are alert to the danger of a win-at-all-cost mentality. Hanberry explained, "Everything we do is about being the best. We need to make sure priorities are in line and that's where we have safety nets."[38] An NCAA vice chair warned that the desire to win can lead schools "to gain competitive advantage in ways that are antithetical to [NCAA] philosophy."[39] Noting that no player wins all the time, Newman's perspective on competition comes down to this: "If you win, you grow. If you lose, you learn."[40]

Spotlight on Teresa Machu

Teresa Machu was both a player and coach at Trinity in the difficult 1980s. She had a variety of campus connections, including her high school basketball coach Jill Harenberg. As a student at Alamo Heights, Machu had an extensive athletic resume: she was selected as an American High School Athlete and chosen for multiple all-district and all-city teams in basketball and volleyball—but none in softball since the school didn't sponsor a team. Her slight stature (5'2") hampered chances for an athletic scholarship, and she chose to stay close to home. She commuted to campus and held down two jobs for her work-study grant, while also meeting classroom obligations and playing four varsity sports.

Machu starred in basketball under Lynn Walker Luna and Carol Higy, and led all players with 356 career free throws. Considering her prolific softball statistics, her freshman coach Gerald Smetzer still considers Machu one of the best all-around female athletes in Trinity history. The *Trinitonian*'s Dorian Martin wrote about Machu's penchant for grape soda and M&Ms and suggested that her teammate's career goal to coach basketball might be too limited: "With her all-around ability and enthusiasm, she could probably coach anything." Indeed, Machu returned for four years to teach and coach Trinity softball and basketball while assisting Jenkins

Norris's forecast about the potential growth of Division III was on target. When it was formed in the 1972–73 academic year, the division boasted 232 schools; by 1996 there were 401 members, most of which had migrated from the NAIA. The exodus continued into the twenty-first century, almost halving NAIA membership and making Division III NCAA's largest.[41]

Teams of the 1990s

Most players and coaches adapted well to the new conference environment and enjoyed the improved facilities. But some programs would take longer to find their footing. Teresa Machu's still independent basketball team played its first home game of the 1989–90 season at the Alamo Stadium gym, since the Bell Center was under construction. Machu wasn't around for conference play or Bell Center improvements. After two difficult campaigns, she left in the summer of 1992. According to Norris, Machu was burned out.[42] She spent the rest of her career teaching and coaching at a local high school.

Teresa Machu, 1990

in volleyball. Although those would be some of the most difficult years in the brief life of both programs, it didn't affect the coach's positivity. "Machu was a little ball of energy," pitcher Shelley Story recalled. "She wasn't the kind of coach who would get mad when you lost."

The workload took its toll, however, and in 1992, she left. It was also the year the state's high school governing body added fastpitch softball to its girls' athletic programs. She found her calling at Churchill High School, where she established and led a highly successful softball program to postseason play in nineteen of her twenty-two seasons.

Looking back, Machu felt that her collegiate decision was the right one. "Trinity was great for me because I loved all sports," she said. It seems Machu was also great for Trinity, and they honored her as an inductee in the school's Athletics Hall of Fame in 2022.

Becky Geyer, a South Dakota native who relocated from Augustana College in Illinois, served as Machu's successor. At Augustana she was head volleyball coach and assistant to the men's basketball coach. Yanika Daniels called Geyer's arrival "pivotal" to the basketball team's success, citing the coach's attention to organization.

Geyer's 11–11 second season was one of the most successful in recent history and marked the first time since 1979 that the women's basketball team had recorded at least eight wins.[43] The following year they compiled a 13–2 record with a perfect 5–0 in SCAC play, thanks to Kathy Bieser, Halie Bricker, Daniels, Jennifer Warren, and Tara Alexander.[44] Geyer recalled the synergy between Daniels and Warren the year they played together: "Yanika could find Jennifer no matter where she was on the court." Describing Daniels, the coach said, "She was just a competitor. She didn't stop."

By the end of the 1992–93 season, Geyer's team won its first SCAC basketball title, was ranked sixth nationally, and made the school's first appearance in the sport's Division III playoffs.[45] Her team compiled

Spotlight on Yanika Daniels

Yanika Daniels was a high school basketball star, but her senior year was cut short by a serious knee injury. As a result, she lost an athletic scholarship from Yale University and then rebuffed other schools that didn't meet her high academic standards. One offer did get through, when her DeSoto High School coach partnered with Teresa Machu to recruit Daniels to Trinity. Machu's plan was to use the player's Division I–level talent to rebuild her team, but she left before her recruit's arrival.

After she unpacked her dorm room and bid her parents goodbye, Daniels made a beeline for the Bell Center to meet with the coach who had convinced her to attend Trinity. To her surprise, she was told by Norris that Machu had not returned and the administration was seeking a replacement. "They had a wonderful new gym," Daniels remembers, "but no coach." Becky Geyer filled the gap, leading the team to playoff runs in Daniels's final two seasons.

In her last home game in front of an appreciative Bell Center crowd, Daniels ended her career in grand style, posting fifteen points and five steals against Southwestern in a 69–64 victory. After their playoff run ended in the first round, Daniels barely trailed Kathy Bieser for the team's point lead (12.9 to Bieser's 13.0 per game average) and was named to the all-conference second team. *(continued on next page)*

records of .500 or better the rest of the decade, including nineteen wins in three seasons.

Geyer was also saddled with Machu's former softball duties. Even though her players finally had a field to call their own, they weren't part of the conference and retained their independent status for most of the decade. Geyer faced the same obstacles as her overworked predecessor, delegating practice to assistant coaches when the pre-season overlapped with basketball. Shelley Story recalls that she and her fellow softball players were cognizant of the challenges during basketball season: "I think we just knew at the time that she had more responsibility than a human being should have to have." The program continued to founder, and in 1994, the season was cancelled when too few players—and no pitchers—showed up for tryouts.[46]

When the SCAC added softball to its lineup, the team could finally file away the bad memories from the past decade. In the first season of conference play since exiting the TIAA in 1982, the 1999 spring

Yanika Daniels, 1993

Daniels found her voice beyond basketball—and Midnight Madness. She was a member of the Alpha Phi Omega service club and president of the Black Student Union. She wrote news and sports stories as a reporter for the *Trinitonian*, and also had an exquisite singing voice. According to Geyer, when Daniels sang the "Star-Spangled Banner" for the team, "chills would go down your spine."

After her graduation in 1996, Daniels studied history and secondary education at North Carolina A&T State University and later earned a law degree while raising four children and coaching youth sports. In 2021 the Plano resident was studying at Southern Methodist University for a master of divinity degree.

Daniels still considers Geyer an important figure in her life, citing the former coach's generosity to her throughout her professional career.

squad welcomed (still part-time) coach Lana Rutledge, an NAIA All-American who played four years for the successful St. Mary's University program. The team posted its first winning campaign since 1976 and hosted the first SCAC softball championship on their home field. They swept their opponents to win the title and watched Rutledge receive SCAC Coach of the Year honors. The next season (Rutledge's last at Trinity), she again earned the conference coaching award after guiding her team to an 18–19 record (11–1 in conference) and a second conference title. They qualified for the Division III playoffs, which was a first for an SCAC team, only to be ousted in the elimination round. The underclassmen from that national qualifying team completed their careers in 2002 with four consecutive SCAC titles and a twelve-game conference tournament victory streak.[47]

The 1991 women's soccer season featured a coaching handoff from former player and part-time coach Suzanne Anderson to Nick Cowell,

Tanya Zwick *(left)* with Nick Cowell, who led women's soccer for most of the 1990s

the program's first full-time hire. Cowell and new men's coach Paul McGinlay were British natives with experience at several levels of soccer competition, including Division III conference championships at Wooster College in Ohio.[48]

In his first season, Cowell led the 1991 Tigers to a 10–9–1 record and a notable turning point: their September 28 loss to Rhodes College was the last time Trinity would lose in SCAC play until DePauw broke their forty-six-game conference winning streak in 1999. His 1992 players captured their first SCAC trophy and qualified for nationals for the first time in Trinity women's soccer history. Tara O'Dowd was named SCAC Player of the Year, and Cowell received Coach of the Year accolades.[49] The team's 1995 sweep through the conference tournament put a cap on an amazing run for that team's seniors; defender and two-time All-American Tanya Zwick noted that she and her fellow seniors were graduating without a single SCAC loss.[50] During the 1996 campaign, Cowell captured his hundredth career coaching victory.[51]

In 1997, the Tigers posted a 14–2–1 regular season record, outscored their competition 59–9, and swept all SCAC opponents for their fifth conference championship. Senior goalkeeper Deb Hutcherson allowed only five goals, shutting out all SCAC opponents.[52] In a playoff game on their home field, Jennifer Hesselmeyer's unassisted goal ensured a 1–0 victory and earned the Tigers a national quarterfinals slot.[53] But their season ended with a 2–0 loss to defending national champion University of California San Diego.[54]

During his Trinity tenure, Cowell led the team into SCAC dominance and vaulted the program into the elite ranks of Division III women's soccer. After the 1999 season, he returned to Division I at Baylor University and later moved to coach Division II at St. Edward's University in Austin. Upon Cowell's departure, McGinlay led both teams for one season before handing women's coaching duties over to assistant coach Greg Ashton.[55]

The new swimming and diving program attracted a coach who would almost match Julie Jenkins's long tenure at Trinity. When the Bell Center opened in 1992 with a world-class natatorium, John Ryan left his head coaching job at Division III Wesleyan University in Connecticut to fill the position of aquatics director at Trinity. The job included establishing the intercollegiate program and teaching advanced swimming and lifeguard training for the physical education department. While serving in the US Army in the 1970s, Ryan helped coach athletes at the nearby Fort Sam Houston training facility for the modern pentathlon.[56] He left the city and the service to coach high school and college programs elsewhere but was happy to return to San Antonio.

Like his softball peers, his teams wouldn't be included in conference competition until later in the decade since not enough SCAC schools sponsored swimming and diving programs. Meet titles were rare, as Ryan was hampered by the team's small size and the lack of a diving program or coach, problems that would be resolved in his first few seasons. Later he and fellow SCAC coaches would host an informal championship before joining formal conference competition in the 1998–99 season.

Ryan oversaw extraordinary careers for several swimmers, including Sarah Scott, a four-time national qualifier and three-time All-American.[57] He expertly guided the program into the new century, winning all but one SCAC championship over the next seventeen years. He was honored as 2000 SCAC women's Coach of the Year by his fellow conference coaches.[58] After he stepped down as aquatic director in 2017, Ryan continued to serve the school as assistant to the head coach.

Swimming stars Shelley Wheeler and Sarah Scott

Dormant in the 1980s, the women's track and field program was revived in time for the first SCAC championships in 1991, as intramural director Jim Potter once again recruited intramural stars to field a team. The next few years the female runners labored under mostly part-time or volunteer coaches, including head soccer coach Paul McGinlay, assistant football coach Scott Williams, and local high school coach Johnny Gonzales. They also had to plan training and meets around the poor condition of the track. In fact, sophomore Stephanie Mestyanek won her 1993 SCAC 10,000-meter championship at nearby Alamo Stadium, since the deteriorating conditions on Trinity's track were not suitable for the conference meet.[59] In 1996, the E. M. Stevens track was finally replaced with a safer polyurethane surface.[60]

Gonzales guided the women to three conference championships in five years and was named 1999 SCAC Coach of the Year for both the men's and women's teams. Several of his athletes posted record-setting performances, some of which still stand; these include Jennifer Graves (triple jump), Julie Grahn and Christal Seahorn (javelin), Aisha Carter (200-meter dash), and Kathy Bieser (shot put).[61]

Carter carved her name in both Trinity and SCAC record books. More than two decades after her graduation, her times in the 100- and

200-meter dash still appeared in Trinity's top five lists. She was later named to the SCAC's fifteenth all-anniversary team for being the only athlete in conference history to win three consecutive conference championships in both events, which was also a record for Trinity women's track and field.[62]

The coach's final season also featured a first for Trinity, when Beth Swearingen became the first Trinity athlete—male or female—to compete in the pole vault at the indoor track and field championships. Already an accomplished runner, the first-year athlete began to experiment with the relatively new event her senior year in high school. The Seattle native, who also ran for Gonzales's cross country team, finished tenth overall at the NCAA meet.[63]

After multiple false starts by mostly male students in the 1980s, cross country arrived for good in 1990. Almost fifteen years had passed since an ice storm prevented me from being the school's first female participant in the fall sport, and only a few prospects showed up to join Bob Hockey's first small squad.[64] A student newspaper article might have given pause to potential recruits not accustomed to distance training. The story listed four types of weekly practice sessions: "There is an economy run of five to seven miles (four to six miles for women), a tempo run of four to five miles for men and three to four for women, intervals (where runners try for fast times on each mile they run, followed by a short rest), and a long run of seven to twelve miles for men and six to ten for women." The good news was that students could work out on their own if they had scheduling conflicts.[65]

The 1991 admission of women's sports into the SCAC breathed life into the nascent program, but Hockey was still struggling to field a strong team. However, experienced runner Karen Hilton made history that season when her third-place SCAC finish made her Trinity's first female runner to qualify for individual regional competition.[66] In 1997, sophomore Laura Fuchs helped her team return to the regional meet and then became the school's first female runner to advance to the Division III national championships. Teammate Tom Pillow joined her at the championships.[67]

After the 1999–2000 academic year, former assistant Jenny Breuer became head coach of the men's and women's teams in both cross country and track. She coached track for eight years and cross country for twelve, providing much-needed stability. Breuer led the teams to success at the conference, regional, and national levels in the years to come.

More than twenty years after Gene Norris attempted to form a women's golf team, Bob King announced that Trinity would sponsor a female golf squad for the first time in its history. He appointed women's soccer coach Nick Cowell to get the program under way in 1994, and the team ended its inaugural campaign on a high note with a 1995 SCAC championship. Stacey Nicholson, a first-year player who was also a starting guard on the women's basketball team, won the individual title and earned all-SCAC team and women's Golfer of the Year honors. Cowell was named women's golf Coach of the Year.[68]

In 1998 golf got a welcome upgrade when King hired Carla Spenkoch, a teaching professional at the nearby Quarry Club. Spenkoch had been named most valuable player for the UT women's golf teams in 1975 and 1976, and *Golf for Women* magazine called her the favorite golf teacher in Texas.[69]

The coach with perhaps the most daunting task was Butch Newman, who shepherded the previous scholarship-sponsored men's and women's tennis teams to Division III competition. As a Division I player himself, the 1967 graduate compiled a Trinity record 53–2 mark, was named captain of the US Junior Davis Cup team, and won fourteen national titles in singles and doubles play. The 1990 shift to Division III completely altered Newman's approach to recruiting, but he embraced the transition and continued at Trinity for years to come. His women's squad won every conference title in the decade, and the men's team captured seven SCAC crowns during that span. Since joining the conference, he was honored six times as either men's or women's CAC or SCAC Coach of the Year and was named 1994 NCAA Division III men's Coach of the Year. To honor his playing and coaching career, he was inducted into the Texas Tennis Hall of Fame in Dallas in 1996.[70]

The most stable women's program with the longest-tenured full-time coach was volleyball. Julie Jenkins was the first to leverage her skills into the best campaign for any Trinity women's varsity team in the 1990s. With increasing support, first-class facilities, and a competitive conference, her teams compiled an impressive run of winning streaks and successful season records. During this time, they advanced seven consecutive years into the NCAA Division III playoffs, won six of the first nine SCAC championships, and ended the decade at the top of the collegiate game, competing in the national championship finals match. Jenkins took home six SCAC Coach of the Year awards. Home games drew large numbers of vocal spectators who got caught up in the excitement of a winning program that—unlike other women's teams—didn't have to compete for attention with a similar men's program.

After Jenkins set a personal milestone with her two hundredth victory in 1994, she received praise from an unlikely source. Referee Will Vick, who had been officiating in the city since 1972, said, "There is no better brand of volleyball played anywhere in San Antonio than here at Trinity."[71]

But another controversy arose at the end of the decade in the form of dueling letters between a female varsity competitor and her baseball colleagues. Kyle Schumacher started the skirmish with a letter to the *Trinitonian* comparing the superior condition of the men's field to the poor condition of the softball diamond. Players had dubbed the unpacked dirt infield "the beach" because of its loose texture. Schumacher added her frustration about temporary fencing and the perceived lack of support from the school's sports information staffers. She concluded with a reference to Title IX. Crediting the law, which had been mandating equal opportunity for more than twenty-five years, she wrote, "While Trinity may conform to the legal requirements of Title IX, it does not embody the real spirit of equality and still needs to level the playing field between men's and women's sports."[72] Two male players responded a week later "on behalf of TU baseball." They wrote that there was no equality of sports at Trinity and gave the reason that "all sports are different." They concluded with an all-caps declaration: "WINNING WILL ALWAYS LEVEL THE PLAYING FIELD."[73]

Clearly, there was more work to be done to level the real and metaphorical playing fields in the years to come.

From Heartbreak to Celebration

The final years of the century wrapped up with emotional lows and competitive highs.

Janet Bristor's sudden death in 1997 shocked campus residents. The popular athletic trainer poured passion into her support of all athletes—intramural and intercollegiate, male and female. She had built strong relationships in her six years, and her passing was greatly mourned. Soccer coach Paul McGinlay said all of the coaches respected her, adding, "The intensity with which she approached her efforts was fabulous. Her job was her life." Niki Estes, a senior who was a student trainer under Bristor all four years, said, "She was the kind of person that it was impossible to be in a bad mood around, because she simply wouldn't allow it. The world just lost a wonderful person." After her death, the basketball teams wore black ribbons on their uniforms in her memory.[74]

In what should have been a seminal season for Ryan's swimming and diving team—their first as an official member of the SCAC—expectation turned to tragedy. On December 16, 1998, sophomore swimmer Alex Row drowned in the Bell Center pool. He had been attempting to swim three underwater laps when he passed out, and his teammates weren't aware of the situation until several critical minutes elapsed. Their attempts at resuscitation were unsuccessful, and Row was transported by ambulance to the hospital where he was pronounced dead. A graduate of Churchill High School in San Antonio, Row was memorialized by friends, classmates, teachers, and coaches at an emotional service in the university chapel. The athletic department offered the option of canceling the season, but team members chose to continue, dedicating the season as a tribute to Row.[75]

After seven consecutive years of making the playoffs but being rebuffed in the regional round, Julie Jenkins's volleyball team advanced to the 1999 finals. An early victory over Washington University—a perennial playoff rival that had defeated the Tigers in their previous seven matches—signaled the reversal of fortune. The Tigers carried their momentum into a conference tournament sweep for their sixth SCAC crown in the decade and then to their first regional championship title. The team continued its playoff winning streak to the quarterfinals

Swim relay team at 1999 SCAC meet. Left to right, Lynn Lyons, Erika Chow, Sarah Armstrong, and Christy Jayne. The initials on Jayne's arm are in memory of fallen teammate Alex Row.

(against Ithaca College) and semifinals (vs. Muskingum College of Ohio), advancing to the NCAA national championship match in New York City.[76] With two of the country's best players, defending champion Central College of Iowa topped Trinity in straight sets, 15–8, 16–14, and 15–7. Sophomore middle blocker Lauren Hamilton led the Tigers with nine kills and six blocks.[77]

Softball player Noelle Stockman began a *Trinitonian* piece on Jenkins by describing the effect she had on volleyball in the fifteen years of her Trinity career: "[T]he program has exploded." She went on to recount the six SCAC championships, which resulted in Jenkins being named SCAC Coach of the Year six times. She noted that the team advanced to the Sweet 16 five times, was ranked third in the nation, and finished conference play undefeated with a 1–0 record. "This is the best season in Trinity's history," she declared.[78]

Senior Alishia Farley was named SCAC Player of the Year, All-Final Four, and an All-American. Junior Desiree Pratt joined her teammate with All-America honors and remains the school's all-time leader in assists. Jenkins was honored by the Division III South Region and the American Volleyball Coaches Association as Coach of the Year. The Tigers ended the season with a best ever 38–3 record, setting the stage for success in the new millennium.[79]

Butch Newman's tennis squads continued their SCAC dominance and almost annual national qualifying traditions through the 1990s. In 1997, his women's team had a breakthrough at nationals in Claremont, California. After five straight years of making it to the Division III semifinal match, the Tigers reached the finals at last by edging out the defending champions from Emory 5–4. The season ended in a 6–3 loss to top seed Kenyon College.[80]

After two more years of playoff frustration, both the women and men finally reached the pinnacle of Division III. The 1999–2000 women's team compiled an undefeated record in regular season play against their division opponents and won their ninth consecutive SCAC championship, and the men won their own conference title. Both teams advanced to the 2000 NCAA Division III championships.

Then, on one landmark day in May, the two teams clinched their respective Division III championships, fulfilling the goal they had strived to attain after entering the division a decade earlier. After continuously knocking on the national championship door, the portal opened for both of Newman's teams, culminating in a rare double-championship and the first tennis titles at Trinity in more than two decades. It was also the first time any SCAC school had won a national title in the organization's thirty-eight-year history.

Gustavus Adolphus, a small college in Minnesota, played a role in both of Trinity's championship titles. The men came back from a 3–0 deficit to defeat Gustavus Adolphus 4–3 in Kalamazoo, Michigan, for the national team crown.[81] Thirty minutes later on the Gustavus Adolphus campus, the Trinity women defeated the University of California San Diego 5–4 for their own national championship. Trailing 2–1 after doubles competition, Lizzie Yasser, Lindsay Smith, Abbe Ulrich, and Laura Cumming won their singles matches, while Ulrich and Cumming teamed up to win the lone doubles point. In addition to the critical point in doubles, it was freshman Ulrich's comeback singles victory (2–6, 6–4, 6–1) that decided the consequential team title.[82] Other team members were Lindsey Baldwin, Amanda Browne, Kristin Law, and Nadine Nitisusanta.

Newman viewed the accomplishment as finally putting to rest the disappointment Trinity students, alumni, and fans had experienced following the move from Division I to Division III. "Winning these

Double shot of success:

Men's and women's tennis bring home national titles

***Trinitonian* announcement of historic double tennis titles in 2000**

two national championships," he said, "has gotten us past that period of tumultuous transition." It also had a positive effect on recruiting, giving the veteran coach hope for future teams.[83]

In her recap of Trinity's tennis program in 2001, a *San Antonio Express-News* writer reflected on the 1990 decision: "Many believed it was the end of successful tennis at Trinity. That belief was wrong."[84]

Closing Out the Century

By the late 1990s, great strides had been made in terms of educational opportunities for women. The twenty-fifth anniversary of Title IX inspired a summary from the Department of Education, the federal agency responsible for oversight of the law:

> Twenty-five years after the passage of Title IX, we recognize and celebrate the profound changes this legislation has helped bring about in American education and the resulting improvements in the educational and related job opportunities for millions of young Americans....In 1971, 18 percent of female high school graduates were completing at least four years of college compared to 26 percent of their male peers. Today, that education gap no longer exists. Women now make up the majority of students in America's colleges and universities in addition to making up the majority of those receiving master's degrees. Women are also entering business and law schools in record numbers. Indeed, the United States stands alone and is a world leader in opening the doors of higher education to women.[85]

Several developments in women's sports marked positive national trends. For female basketball players, the 1996 Olympics in Atlanta sparked a sea change for professional prospects. The previous third-place finish of the women's team, made up mostly of collegiate players, prompted a call to women cagers who were competing overseas in the absence of a stateside professional league. With financial aid from the men's National Basketball Association, many came home—for less pay—to represent their country. The team reclaimed the gold medal, but perhaps more importantly, the NBA partnership inspired another attempt at a US league. This one stuck. The Women's National Basketball Association began play in 1997. Also, the Women's Basketball Hall of Fame opened in Knoxville, Tennessee, in 1999.[86]

Soccer was experiencing its own renaissance in the United States, as the number of females playing high school and collegiate soccer exploded.[87] Internationally, the US team participated in the first women's World Cup in 1991. (Men's teams had been competing since 1930.) Women's soccer was finally added to the Olympic slate in 1996.

Court challenges continued, including a Title IX–based decision that protected one domineering organization from legal challenges. In *NCAA v. Smith*, the Supreme Court ruled in 1999 that the intercollegiate governance group didn't have to abide by Title IX rules. Although the NCAA collected money from and ran tournaments for its members, the fact that the organization didn't directly receive federal funds excused it from having to abide by the equity guidance.[88]

At Trinity, the vehement opposition to the tennis scholarship decision early in the decade had morphed into an acceptance—and even endorsement—of the move. And an unscientific word scan of student newspaper and yearbook articles shows that the use of the term *feminist* seemed to wane, virtually disappearing from the campus vocabulary by 1999.

A special issue of the *Trinitonian* published the last month of the decade, however, seemed to resurrect sexist views of the past. In what some readers may have considered a tone-deaf edition, the editors ran a feature listing the "sexiest" students from each class. In their introduction, they wrote this defense: "All of the people chosen were based entirely on whatever the person nominating them thought was sexy.... We hope that everyone takes this section in the nature it was intended. We hoped it would be seen as an amusing aspect of the last paper for this semester. Whether you chalk this up as stupid or cut out the pictures and paste them on your walls, we had a good time putting this section together."

The senior honoree for the "Lovely Ladies" category was varsity track

Aisha Carter *(second runner from left)* practices off the sprint starting blocks.

and field star Aisha Carter. One of her voters commented, "There's just something about a woman who can kick any man's butt."[89] Regardless of the intent of the frivolous piece, one could argue that the recognition points to evolving perceptions about women athletes. An English and education major, Carter was involved in student government, was named outstanding senior by the Mortar Board national honor society, and served as president of the Black Student Union.[90] To top off an outstanding collegiate career, Carter was chosen by her senior peers to be the student speaker at their 1999 commencement ceremony.[91] Perhaps the word *sexy* had a different definition at the end of the millennium.

Another significant campus change was occurring in the school's executive suite. Years earlier, President Calgaard had advised Trinity's board of trustees that he would step down at the end of the decade. True to his word, he retired in 1999 and was replaced by John R. Brazil.[92] Asked about his most satisfying accomplishment, Calgaard answered, "Developing and implementing an institutional mission to have a nationally prominent, primarily undergraduate, mostly liberal arts institution. We have made rather dramatic progress in that direction, and I find that personally most satisfying."[93]

Calgaard had the infrastructure in place and the right people employed to see his vision fulfilled. After twenty years of progress, he left behind a significant academic and athletic legacy that continues to this day. According to athletic director Bob King, "Ron Calgaard really set the tone." He added, "I think we fulfilled his mission."

Julie Jenkins agreed. In her speech at the 2017 dedication of the Ron and Genie Calgaard gym at the Bell Center, the assistant athletic director said, "Here's the thing: every facility throughout this campus could be named in Ron and Genie's honor. That's how highly regarded these two are to Trinity, and what an impact they have made on this entire university." In her remarks, Jenkins recalled her arrival in 1985, when only men's sports had full-time coaches, women endured a revolving door of leadership, and the school didn't sponsor women's varsity teams in golf, track and field, cross country, or swimming and diving. She thanked Calgaard for the significant increase in budgets, which covered full-time coaches, travel expenses, and even the purchase of a twenty-five-passenger bus to take her players to the airport.[94] In a *Trinitonian* interview, she acknowledged the role of athletics in the president's higher-level vision. "President Calgaard wanted to raise admission standards to better our reputation," she said. "He decided the school was not going to make exceptions for athletes like they had been doing. This whole restructuring changed the national image of Trinity."[95]

Future championship coach Becky Geyer also praised Calgaard's support. "He came to every game. He loved all of the programs. We had the resources. He always provided for us," she said. "In my opinion, Dr. Calgaard was the reason for our success."

In addition to Shirley Rushing's earlier retirement, another notable departure occurred in 2000, when Jim Potter left after thirty-five years as intramural director.[96]

Trinity's rising reputation as a regional leader in academics with successful intercollegiate Division III teams presented a problem few probably complained about. In the 1998–99 academic year, many of the recruits who came out for varsity teams had to go through tryouts. "In some ways, it's sad," King said, as he welcomed the biggest pool of recruits in the school's history. Of the 650 incoming students, 121 expressed interest in playing in the SCAC, forcing some coaches to consider junior varsity squads.

The sports editor reporting on the historic turnout put the issue in perspective, admitting that it might be difficult to show newcomers how Trinity athletics has changed in the 1990s. "[T]he University recently has gone from a has-been to a must-have for a record number of high school graduates," Ron Nirenberg wrote. "As Trinity climbs toward provenance in Division III athletics, the cost of success is that players aren't guaranteed a spot on the team. But a Trinity degree is something they all can attain."[97]

In spring 1999, Trinity hosted the SCAC Spring Sports Festival. Tiger titles in softball, baseball, women's tennis, men's tennis, women's track and field, and men's track and field provided the razor-thin edge over rival DePauw. For the sixth straight year, the 300-pound President's Trophy remained in the Bell Center.[98] By decade's end, Trinity men and women had captured ten SCAC championships, with teams from six sports qualifying for NCAA playoffs. In the 1999–2000 season alone, eight teams qualified for NCAA playoffs, setting a new school record.[99] Of course, the dual tennis championships of 2000 would mark a major turning point for Trinity's next century.

The significant progress Calgaard, King, Jenkins, and others had spearheaded was recognized in 1999, when the school placed ninth (among more than three hundred Division III schools) in the Sears Cup rankings for the most successful sports programs in the nation. The normally low-key Bob King boasted, "Without question, we are one of the best in the country. We've said it all along and now we have this to prove it."[100]

MOMENTUM

FOR A NEW MILLENNIUM

South view of athletic fields in distance, with Murchison Tower in foreground, 2019

CHAPTER 14

Two Decades of Steady Progress

2000 and Beyond

> Title IX has enhanced, and will continue to enhance, women's opportunities to enjoy the thrill of victory, the agony of defeat, and the many tangible benefits that flow from just being given a chance to participate in intercollegiate athletics.
>
> —NINTH CIRCUIT COURT OF APPEALS JUDGE CYNTHIA HOLCOMB HALL

After half a century, the impact of Title IX is evident in every corner of US society. Women have more options for graduate and post-graduate degrees, can pursue previously male-dominated professions, have carved out more representation in the political arena, and have increased their participation in sports at every level. For once, forward progress was maintained without significant disruption, stagnation, or retreat.

According to retired Trinity educator Shirley Rushing, the twenty-first century also marked the unofficial end of the pioneering and building phase of women's intercollegiate athletics, or as she said, "We didn't have to fight anymore."[1] The momentum forged in the late 1990s carried into the first two decades of the century, as most programs continued their conference dominance and earned postseason victories. One even won an NCAA national title in 2003.

Libby Johnson's hopes for the future of women's intercollegiate athletics—unfulfilled during her lifetime—finally came to fruition, thanks to her foundational efforts and those of pioneering peers like Rushing, Emilie Foster, Glada Munt, and Julie Jenkins. By 2019, when the university celebrated its 150th anniversary, Trinity sponsored eighteen nonscholarship intercollegiate sports, equally divided between men and women. In addition, 23 percent of Trinity students were participating in varsity sports. Not only did student-athletes of this era participate on competitive teams and earn national recognition; they also maintained high academic standards and remained active in campus activities and service organizations. This balanced approach signals the manifestation of the Division III athletics philosophy becoming an integral part of the overall campus experience.

Best of the (Division III) Best

In 2000, director of athletics Bob King and his teams were coming off an unprecedented year of success. It could have been these achievements that inspired two national periodicals to highlight Trinity. One unlikely compliment came from the business-oriented *Wall Street Journal*: "Few of the 400+ DIII schools pull it off better than Trinity where learning and playing are in near perfect balance"[2] But it was *Sports Illustrated for Women*'s listing of Trinity as one of the Best Colleges for Women Athletes in 2000 that placed King's program in the upper echelon of Division III schools for serious female student-athletes, recognizing Trinity as a "top place to pursue all things athletic and academic." The ranking was the result of a magazine poll that considered a school's overall records, successes in varsity sports, intramural and club activities, and fan support. Among Trinity's noted strengths were support for all sports and for building momentum for the successes in tennis, volleyball, and soccer the previous year.[3] An unsigned *Trinitonian* editorial celebrated the honor:

> Ranking third among all the Division III schools for the best women's athletics program . . . is no small feat. In this era where, unfortunately, sexism, racism and all the other -isms exist, it is comforting to know that Trinity does not uphold barriers. Assistant Director of Athletics for Student Athletes Julie Jenkins, Director of Athletics Bob King, the coaching staff and all female athletes past and present should be commended for making Trinity's program the success that it is. Title IX opened the doors for

High jumper Christyn Schumann won four national titles from 2004 to 2006.

> women's athletics, but it takes the perseverance of those involved to make programs successful. We, as a community, should support the women's athletics as fully as we do the men's. These ladies have excellent programs, and they can teach us all about the strength of women.[4]

A follow-up *Trinitonian* story featured coaches and players praising the quality of the athletes, increased fan support, and improved funding that allowed Trinity teams to compete with the best schools nationally and provided more support staff so that coaches could recruit. Softball player Sheila Deane said, "You may think that Trinity is just a small school in Texas, but we're outplaying big-name schools."[5]

Early in the century, four of the 2002 fall teams came tantalizingly close to their respective finals. The women's volleyball team reached the NCAA championship semifinals, and both women's and men's soccer teams advanced to their own semifinal rounds, with just one goal preventing each from advancing to the title match. The Tiger football team reached the 2002 national championship game. While none captured a national title, being in the "Final Four" capped their remarkable seasons.[6]

The second semester of that academic year was undoubtedly the best ever for women's basketball, when Becky Geyer's team won the 2003 NCAA Division III national championship, the first non-tennis championship in school history. (Eight months later, the undefeated men's soccer team hoisted its own national trophy.)

That year King's programs earned another significant honor, fourth place out of 450 schools for the 2002–2003 Director's Cup, awarded by the National Association of Collegiate Directors of Athletics. Trinity finished behind Williams College, a college that fielded thirty-one teams to Trinity's eighteen. That fact didn't dilute King's enthusiasm, however. "We have achieved two goals in one process by competing athletically at the top with schools that we are competing against academically," he said.

Considering the school's focus on academic success, King was equally proud of another first for Trinity in 2003: the average GPA of his 425 athletes was higher than the average of the rest of the student body. "That's just phenomenal," he said. "These players are the true definition of student-athletes."[7]

National recognition for Trinity athletics early in the century wasn't just marking an arrival; it was denoting a milestone in a continuing journey, as this quote from *Sports Illustrated for Women* concludes: "Bottom line: After 25 years of women's sports, the momentum is still building."[8]

Grading the Impact of Title IX

Decades of progress for women was chronicled in a number of national retrospectives, including several published on Title IX's fortieth and forty-fifth anniversaries, in 2012 and 2017. Although most reports heralded the increase in female college graduates entering the workforce, some noted societal gaps yet to be filled. One area of concern was wage equality. According to the ACLU Women's Rights Project, "Even though now women have supposedly equal access to educational opportunities, they still earn less than men regardless of educational attainment, and women, in fact, have to attain a Ph.D.—basically the highest degree possible in academia—in order to match the lifetime earnings of men who have bachelor's degrees."[9] The disruption of parenting, especially in the prime earnings years, also left its mark. Ann Crittenden, in *The Price of Motherhood*, estimated that the typical college-educated woman lost more than $1 million in lifetime earnings and retirement benefits after opting out to raise children and then trying to reenter the workforce.[10]

The Department of Justice's "Equal Access to Education: Forty Years of Title IX" report began with the good news. During that time, graduation rates increased from 59 to 87 percent for women with a high school degree, and from 8 to 28 percent for women with a college degree. The 2012 report concluded that "women now have higher graduation rates, lower high school dropout rates, take more advanced placement exams and earn more advanced degrees than their male counterparts."

Since the Department of Justice was the federal organization responsible for enforcing Title IX, most of its report unsurprisingly listed examples of the agency's advocacy for plaintiffs who reported violations. The summary also documented the expansion of protection beyond the law's original intent, including against sexual harassment and assault of—and by—teachers and students, as well as new areas of protection for gender orientation and harassment against students who didn't conform to gender norms. Several cited cases zeroed in on sports-specific disparities, such as inferior facilities and disparate scheduling. Many of the judgments forced schools to develop or modify policy, training, and preventive measures to create a safer environment for these new protected classes of students.[11]

Five years after the Department of Justice review, the NCAA published their own take on what they called Title IX's forty-five-year "roller-coaster ride" and pointed out that congressional supporters of the original legislation didn't consider it a "sports law" when voting for its 1972 passage. Of course, the NCAA spent most of the 1970s ferociously fighting the legislation.[12] When considering the objectives articulated in the sports section of Title IX, statistics confirmed that many goals were being met. In 1972, girls comprised 7 percent of all participants of high school sports. In 2017 that number rose to 43 percent. College participation exploded from fewer than 30,000 female athletes in 1972 to more than 215,000 in 2018.[13]

The authors conceded that the NCAA's introduction of women's national championships in 1982 was considered a "hostile takeover" by AIAW leaders.[14] The NCAA report's candid conclusion? "Title IX has survived in the face of repeated challenges and resistance. The historical record proves that it has often been difficult for the male-dominated world of sport to share participation opportunities, resources, and power with girls and women. Title IX also faces a growing complacency about the need for the law after 45 years, since some contend that girls and women have 'made it' in sport and no longer need the support of a federal law."[15]

Two professors presented their own comprehensive research on the state of women's sports. "If you build it, they will come" was the sunny perspective of a 2014 follow-up study by Vivian Acosta and Linda Jean Carpenter. The Brooklyn College researchers spelled out several statistics that captured progress made at the interscholastic and intercollegiate levels in the decades since Title IX: "The high school participation gender ratio increased from 1 girl for every 12 boys in 1971 to 1 girl for every 1.39 boys in 2013. Total varsity sports participation that year was 4.5 million boys and 3.2 million girls, a significant improvement from the 1971 numbers of 3.6 million boys and fewer than 300,000 girls."[16]

Colleges were also fielding more teams for women across all NCAA divisions, doubling from an average 2.5 teams per school in 1970 to 5.6 teams just seven years later. In 2014 the number had grown to 8.83 teams per school, and Division III's average was even better at 9.06. The researchers noted that "the real level of growth is not just from 2.5 to 8.83 teams per school, but 8.83 teams at many more schools, schools that didn't have any teams for women when Title IX was enacted 42 years ago." In fact, the quickening pace toward the end of the century meant that one out of three women's college teams had been established since 1998.[17]

The most popular intercollegiate women's sport in 2013 was basketball, which was offered in 99 percent of all NCAA schools that fielded women's varsity teams. Basketball also had the highest percentage of female coaches, at 60 percent.[18] The fastest-growing sport was soccer, which increased its intercollegiate presence from 3 percent of colleges in 1977 to 90 percent in 2014.[19]

A lighthearted fortieth anniversary observance was held at the Charles Schultz Museum in Santa Rosa, California. Schultz, the cartoonist behind the popular *Peanuts* comic strip, had formed a friendship with Billie Jean King and became a trustee for her Women's Sports Foundation in 1976. Three years later he ran a series of strips featuring sports-happy Peppermint Patty as "a fierce, informed advocate for Title IX" sharing gender equity statistics with her *Peanuts* pals. *Leveling the*

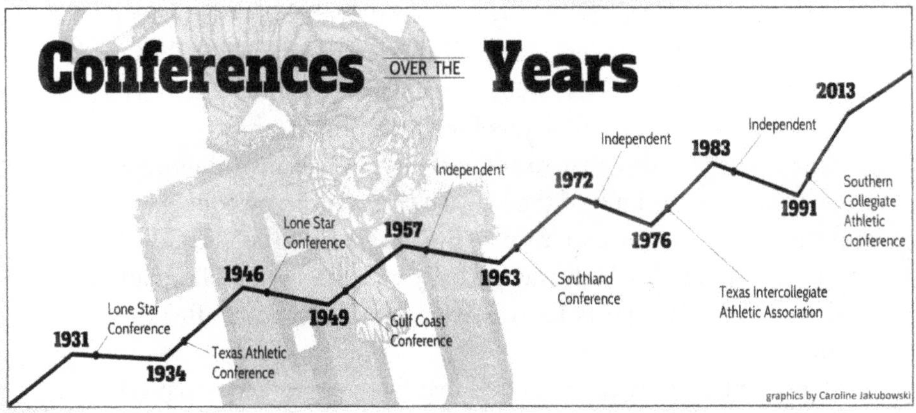

The 2014 "Athletes and Scholars" series included an illustration of the path of Trinity's conference memberships—and gaps of independent play—over the past eighty years.

Playing Field, a 2012 exhibition highlighting the special series, posthumously honored the cartoonist's advocacy for women's sports.[20]

Women were not the only beneficiaries of these advances. All three reports provide proof that men also came out ahead. Male students are also included under the law's protections against harassment, retaliation, sexual assault, and gender stereotypes; and general participation levels for male high school and college athletes also increased over the decades. The studies all conceded, however, that male student athletes continue to have more opportunity and access to more resources in college athletics, and progress was yet to be made for true equality.[21]

In 2014, *Trinitonian* managing editor Lydia Duncombe published "Trinity Revealed," an ambitious four-part series about the state of intercollegiate sports on campus. In one segment, "Trinity Sportsmen and Women: Athletes and Scholars," she reported that not only had the caliber of the teams improved over the years; the number of participants had more than doubled, from 200 to 485, in the prior decade. (It was 560 by 2017.) In fact, a survey of incoming students revealed that one of the top five reasons they chose Trinity was because of its intercollegiate athletic programs. In response, the school's admissions office employs staff dedicated to these prospects.[22]

Duncombe dug into details of the athletic department's share of Trinity's $100 million budget, which showed that King's department was allotted almost 4 percent ($3.9 million) of the school's overall 2014 plan. In contrast, Julie Jenkins recalls her early experience: "All of the money going into athletics went to tennis and nothing else.... We had no money to recruit good players for all the other teams."

The series revealed that to support eighteen teams (nine men's and nine women's), the bulk of the 2014 budget went to personnel costs for fifteen head coaches and twenty-five assistants. The second-highest expense was travel, which was partially affected by the elimination of the annual SCAC sports festival, which ended in 2008 after forty-six years.[23]

Duncombe's research confirmed that fifteen years and two presidents after Calgaard's retirement, student-athletes continued to enjoy support from the top. In a nod to the simon-pure mantra of the 1970s, President Dennis Ahlburg, who served from 2010 to 2015, expressed his appreciation for the approach of Division III schools, which weren't trying to make money off their sports teams. He denounced the way larger schools treated their athletes, "like they are gods, instead of students who are particularly good at athletics." He added, "I would have much less of a problem with this if they treated talented poets, actors, musicians the same way." Duncombe offered insight from players and coaches who agreed that the Division III philosophy provided the right balance. Basketball player Libby Kruse briefly considered attending a Division I school but didn't because, as she explained, "Sports are all you do; it's a job that's more important than school."[24] Coach Cameron Hill felt that his Trinity athletes benefited from the opportunity "to have three aspects of their college life—academics, athletics and social."

But unaddressed in the series was the existential crisis the SCAC had confronted just two years earlier, when the conference was forced to reorganize after seven schools broke away to form their own more geographically focused group. This forced the SCAC to recruit two other schools to meet the NCAA's seven-team minimum.[25] Commissioner Dwayne Hanberry credits two athletic directors with Trinity roots in saving the conference. Glada Munt and Bob King leveraged their strong reputations and lobbied their professional network to convince other Texas schools to leave established conferences and join the SCAC in 2012. "If I didn't have Glada and Bob on my side, I don't know if we could have pulled off what we did," Hanberry said. The nine-member SCAC now features mostly Texas institutions.[26]

Building New Legacies

Commissioner Hanberry cites athletic director Bob King's long tenure and hiring decisions since 1993 as two reasons the school consistently performs at the top of the conference. He noted the extraordinarily long careers of many coaches under King. Golf coach Carla Spenkoch and Jenkins boasted almost sixty years of Tiger team coaching between them before Spenkoch retired in 2021. "It's hard to discount how important that continuity is," Hanberry said. "When you're at the Division III level, it's really easy for someone to use it as a steppingstone to go to Division II or Division I." He thinks the reason King and his coaches have stayed is that Trinity takes care of them: "They found good people and have kept them."[27]

Volleyball

Julie Jenkins chose to spend her career in Division III and is the longest-serving coach in Trinity history. In 2017 she became the first SCAC coach in any sport to win three hundred conference matches. On October 1, 2021, the sweep over host Centenary College in Shreveport, Louisiana, made her the third coach in NCAA Division III history to achieve a thousand victories.[28]

In a local newspaper story, Jenkins reflected on her journey: "I felt the picture, down the road, was going to be to our advantage because I felt we could build something." She admitted that having never been to Texas before 1985, she'd never had huevos rancheros and wasn't familiar with local cuisine. She explained: "I didn't know how to pronounce *fajita*—put it that way."[29]

After the 2021 season, the SCAC bestowed Coach of the Year honors on Jenkins for the fourteenth time, as she led her team to the national quarterfinals. At the end of the previous season, her overall record at Trinity was a superlative 985–422 (.700 winning percentage), including a 358–38 record (.902) in the SCAC since the team joined in 1991.[30] The high point of Jenkins's career (so far) was the 1999 NCAA finals match. Over her thirty-six seasons, Jenkins's squad has qualified for NCAA

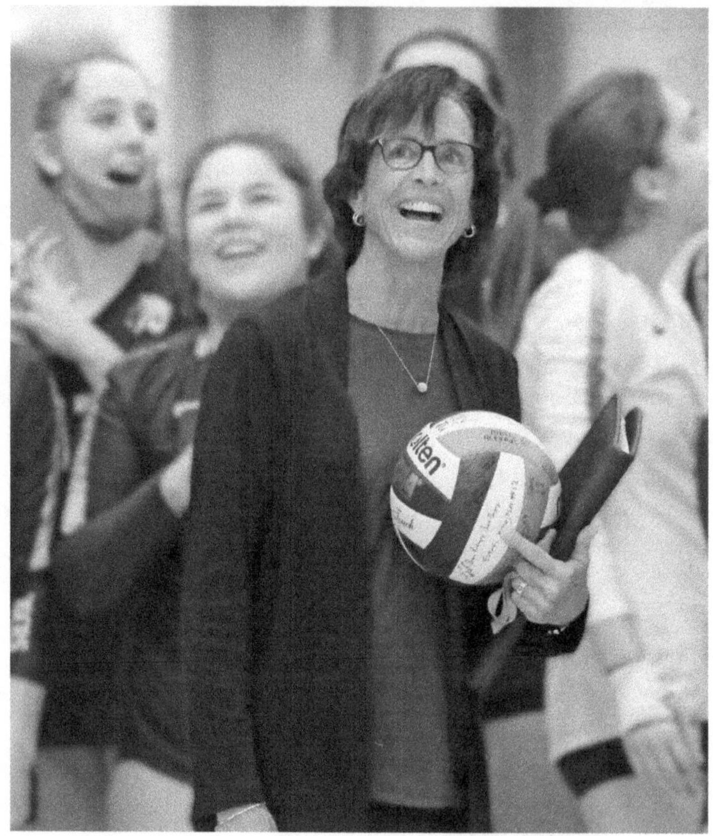

Julie Jenkins in 2021, holding autographed ball presented by Bob King to commemorate her thousand career victories

postseason play twenty-five times, advancing six times to the Division III quarterfinals and four times to the semifinals.

Tennis

Both tennis teams entered the 2000–2001 academic year as defending NCAA Division III champions, and the women again advanced to the title match before a loss ended their season. In the years since moving into Division III, the female netters have won thirteen conference titles and advanced to the postseason fourteen times under seven coaches. Butch Newman relinquished his head coaching duties in 2008 to become director of tennis.

Basketball

The women's basketball squad had floundered for a decade, but in 2003, the Tigers finished the season on a 23–1 run, earning them a playoff invitation that led to their first postseason wins. They surprised third-ranked Washington University, who had won four of the previous five NCAA championships. And fourth-ranked Hardin-Simmons University was undefeated that season before falling to the Tigers. A 63–54 semifinal win over the University of Rochester earned Geyer's team a spot in the title game in Terre Haute, Indiana.

"Slipper Fits Trinity in DIII Title Game" topped the *Express-News* article about the extraordinary win. Junior Allison Wooley scored the title-winning basket with eleven seconds left to lock down a 60–58 victory over Eastern Connecticut State University. Wooley, who led the team with eighteen points in the defining game, was named tournament MVP.[31] Standouts from that campaign include Megan Selmon—who earned All-America honors and was named to the All-Tournament Team—and Jenna Smith, a transfer student who would shatter every Trinity steals record. Also in that game was sophomore Tara Rohde, who later became the fourth player to exceed five hundred points in a season. In 2005, she became the only Trinity player to be awarded the Jostens Trophy, designating her as the Division III Women's Basketball Player of the Year. Rohde was inducted into the Trinity Athletics Hall of Fame in 2019.

Also in 2005, Geyer left her thirteen-year career at Trinity for a Division I position. She had been twice named SCAC Coach of the Year, captured three conference titles, and took the Tigers to the postseason four times. She was also honored as Sportswoman of the Year in 2003 by the *San Antonio Express-News*.

Amie Bradley steered the Tigers to 117 wins and two postseason appearances over seven seasons before Trinity graduate Cameron Hill took over in 2012. In the 2021–22 campaign, Hill guided his top-ten team to the quarterfinal round of the Division III playoffs.

In the 2019–20 season, All-American Abby Holland wrapped up her storied career after breaking several records, not only at Trinity but for SCAC, and she finished as the second leading scorer in the school's history.

Soccer

Greg Ashton's 2000 soccer squad, led by two-time All-American Becky King, opened the century by earning the school's first appearance in the NCAA national semifinals. That feat was repeated in 2002 with the record-setting performance of senior Erica Adelstein. Lance Key replaced his former Tiger teammate as coach in 2004 and led the team to seven SCAC championships and eight NCAA appearances before reaching the zenith of postseason play. His 2013 squad advanced to the finals and hosted the Division III championship match at Toyota Field in San Antonio. There they suffered their only defeat of the season, a 2–0 loss to William Smith College, a team that posted shutouts in all six of its playoff victories. One of that year's Tiger superstars was Emily Jorgens, who was named 2013 Division III Midfielder of the Year and received the NCAA Elite 90 Award (presented to the athlete with the highest GPA competing in the semifinals). Jorgens earned All-America honors every year of her college career. Kelsey Falcone's performance that season and the next made her the only Trinity player to exceed twenty goals twice in a college career.[32]

Since 2015, coach Dylan Harrison—another former Trinity men's soccer player—has maintained the team's conference dominance and playoff streak. His career record against SCAC foes was a perfect 55–0–0, and the team's invitation to the 2021 playoffs marked its twelfth consecutive postseason appearance.

Softball

Softball started the new century with a second SCAC title under Lana Rutledge. Successor Roland Rodriguez guided his team to five twenty-win seasons and another four conference crowns. His 2005 team finished third at the NCAA West Regional, the best finish in school history.[33]

From 2005 to 2007, pitcher Erin Mulvey was the dominant player, winning three SCAC Pitcher of the Year awards and breaking nearly every pitching record in her three seasons at Trinity. To date, she is the only Tiger pitcher to throw three no-hitters in her career; she still holds the career record of 463 strikeouts in her three seasons.

Nicole Dickson Smith returned to her former south campus diamond to coach the Tigers to another SCAC title in 2007 before the team fell into a decade-long slide.[34] In that difficult period, Trinity—and almost every other SCAC competitor—played second fiddle to a juggernaut Texas Lutheran University team that captured six conference championships and won the NCAA Division III national crown in 2019.

Track and Field and Cross Country

Women's track and field vaulted to national prominence early in the century, thanks to the talents of four-time NCAA champion high jumper Christyn Schumann. Her first crown in 2004 marked Trinity's first individual NCAA title (men's or women's) since 1983, when Louise Allen and Gretchen Rush claimed the women's Division I doubles tennis title. Schumann was inducted into the Trinity Athletics Hall of Fame in 2019 and remains the only four-time NCAA champion in school history.[35]

Long-distance runner Emily Loeffler, an eleven-time NCAA qualifier in cross country and track and field, was named to four All-American teams, Trinity's first female cross country athlete to do so. She paced the 2008 team to a sixth-place finish in the national championships, and concluded her illustrious career by earning All-America honors in both indoor and outdoor track and field events in spring 2009. Her Trinity women's track and field records include the 1,500- and 3,000-meter runs and the 3,000-meter steeplechase.

After graduation and marriage, Emily Loeffler Daum earned a master's from Texas A&M and entered the coaching ranks at Trinity in 2012. She replaced head coach Jenny Breuer after her own successful twelve-year tenure and has guided her cross country squads to nine SCAC championships in her six seasons as head coach (six for the women and three for the men). Daum also guided the women's team to a top-five regional finish for five consecutive seasons and has mentored five individual NCAA qualifiers. Molly McCullough became Trinity's first two-time All-American in cross country in 2017 and 2018 under Daum, and she broke her coach's school records in the 5K and the 6K.

Golf

Long-time coach Carla Spenkoch led the women's golf team back to relevance in the 2010s, capturing four conference titles in seven seasons, including the 2021 SCAC championship in her final season with the team. She was named SCAC women's golf Coach of the Year following each of her conference crowns in 2014, 2016, and 2017. She also coached the men's team to two runner-up seasons.

Swimming and Diving

Seven years after Stan Randall arrived to coach divers, two of his female competitors burst onto the national scene. Lindsay Martin and Hayley Emerick won Trinity's first NCAA Division III individual diving championships in 2010. Martin claimed the one-meter title, and on the three-meter board, she finished second to her Tiger teammate Emerick, who became the most decorated student-athlete in the Trinity program. She was the only Trinity swimmer or diver to earn All-America honors every year of her career. Emerick was also a finalist for the NCAA Women of the Year Award in 2011, a recipient of a NCAA postgraduate scholarship, and a 2022 inductee into the Trinity Athletics Hall of Fame.

The following season Ruth Hahn took advantage of Emerick's graduation and won her own three-meter crown, becoming the third Trinity diver in three years to win a national championship. Hahn, who was also a member of the Society of Women Engineers, finished fourth in both events in 2013, ending with six All-America honors in her career.

Both the men's and women's swimming and diving teams have dominated in the SCAC, with the women capturing twenty-one conference titles, eight of them consecutive.

All athletic programs were upended in January 2020, when COVID 19 spread across the world. Games and tournaments were abruptly suspended or postponed to the following fall—and then postponed again. Finally, with no spectators allowed, all eighteen Tiger teams squeezed their compressed schedules into one chaotic spring season in 2021. Despite the circumstances, several Tiger teams enjoyed success. Under Dylan Harrison, the women's soccer squad posted an unblemished record of 10–0 (7–0 SCAC) to win their conference crown, and the women's cross country team ran to another title under Daum. Men's and women's teams in swimming and diving, golf, and track and field won their SCAC crowns.[36]

Renovating and Modernizing

Central to team successes has been world-class facilities. Calgaard's building boom that started in the 1980s continues to this day. The community residential plan initiated in 1989 and expanded in 1992 is still in place. Today students must live on campus their first three years, and seniors have the option of the recently acquired apartment housing facing the new Trinity entrance off of Hildebrand Avenue.[37]

One lower-campus field honors Jim Potter, the man who encouraged physical activity for many athletes through his immensely popular intramural program. In 2017, the grassy plot used for many intramural contests was renamed Potter Field in honor of his thirty-three-year Trinity career. Potter was recognized as Outstanding Professor in 1971, inducted into the Athletics Hall of Fame in 2003, and given the Alumni Association's Spirit of Trinity award in 2006.[38]

Thanks to a former tennis player who helped usher in Trinity's early championship era, both the upper and lower tennis complexes have been renovated. The four upper courts were improved and rededicated in 2011 to Al G. Hill, who played under Clarence Mabry after the complex opened in 1959. The lower Delavan courts were also updated with the help of Hill's generosity and renamed for his former doubles partner and current tennis director Butch Newman. A 2008 upgrade to the lower courts included another red brick building that serves as tournament headquarters and a press box for tennis matches and softball games, appropriately named Mabry Pavilion.[39]

In 2017 Bob King spearheaded a $15 million update to the Bell Center, the facility that had attracted him to Trinity twenty-five years earlier. The building was expanded to include an 8,000-square-foot fitness center, an enlarged sports medicine area, and enhanced locker rooms. The renovation also included updates to the Sams Gymnasium's seating and scoreboards and a chance to rebrand the gym as the Ron and Genie Calgaard Gymnasium. Calgaard and his wife remained grandstand fixtures at Tiger contests until his death in 2020.[40]

The soccer field was improved in 2011 and renamed for the long-time men's (and sometime women's) varsity soccer coach. The Paul McGinlay soccer field provided expanded seating and was updated with a red brick structure for game administration.

(top) The intramural field was named for former intramural director Jim Potter in 2017.
(bottom) A spectator's view of the Butch Newman Tennis Center

(top) **A panorama of the Paul McGinlay soccer field**
(bottom) **Updated (and renamed) Multipurpose Stadium**

Since 2012, enhancements to the Multipurpose Stadium (formerly the E. M. Stevens Stadium) include a resurfaced polyurethane track, an updated high-resolution videoboard/scoreboard, installation of artificial turf, and an expanded press box to accommodate coaches, staff, and broadcast crew for the Tiger Network and visiting videographers. A field competition area, including a hammer throw cage, was constructed on the newly acquired Oblate property west of campus.

Trinity was formally listed as a modernist historic district in 2019 by the National Register of Historic Places in honor of its architecture, the only Texas campus with this designation, and one of just three colleges in the country.[41]

As of 2022, King was leading an effort with Trinity committees and staff members to implement a Lower Campus Athletics Master Plan.[42]

Two Dominant Decades Conclude

Trinity's time in the SCAC has featured unprecedented success. Bob King's teams have carved their names in the SCAC record books, lifting more than 235 CAC and SCAC trophies. This is more than any other conference school, even though Trinity joined the league thirty-seven years after its founding.

Evidence of Trinity's commitment to academics can be seen in the SCAC's Honor Roll of varsity athletes who maintain a minimum 3.25 GPA. Trinity led with 287 names in 2021, followed by Colorado College (243) and Southwestern University (237).[43]

Undoubtedly King successfully implemented the vision Libby Johnson and Ron Calgaard had for a balanced campus experience. According to SCAC commissioner Dwayne Hanberry, "Trinity has been the gold standard of the SCAC."

After winning his third Athletic Director of the Year award in 2015, King was profiled in a local paper, where the model for his success was summed up: "He treats all 18 of Trinity's athletic teams equally."[44]

In their almost half century of intercollegiate competition, Trinity women have won twenty-six team and individual national titles. Several of these champions have emerged from Trinity just since 2000. Dozens of female athletes have earned Division III All-America designations, but five took home the prestigious honor every year of their college careers: Lizzie Yasser for tennis (1999–2002), Lindsay Smith for tennis (2000–2003), Ashley Farrimond for volleyball (2001–4), Hayley Emerick for diving (2008–11), and Emily Jorgens for soccer (2011–14).[45]

To honor Trinity athletes' accomplishments over the years, Calgaard and King initiated the Athletics Hall of Fame in 1999. Since then, Trinity has inducted eighty individuals and ten teams. Of those, twenty-one individual women and seven women's teams have been honored. The five women's Division I tennis national title teams (1968, 1969, 1973, 1975, and 1976) and the 2000 Division III tennis champions entered the Hall of Fame in 2005 and 2013 respectively.

The only non-tennis women's team in the Hall of Fame is Geyer's 2003 national basketball champions. Two other members relevant to the progress of women's varsity programs are Butch Newman, who led

The logo for the Trinity Athletics Hall of Fame

the tennis program into the nonscholarship Division III era, and Calgaard, the architect for the Division III philosophy in his twenty-year term.[46]

In closing, one contemporary controversy provides perspective. While not directly associated with Trinity or Division III, a historic event for women's intercollegiate sports was hosted just three miles south of the Skyline Campus. The finals of the NCAA Division I women's basketball championships had been scheduled for March 2021, at the Alamodome in downtown San Antonio.[47] Ordinarily the sixty-four teams (men's and women's) would play elimination rounds spread out across the country and the final four for each would go to one city for the semifinals. Unfortunately, the global pandemic was still surging, and the NCAA had to make a difficult decision: instead of hosting just the final four teams, all women's teams would play in San Antonio, and all of the men in Indianapolis. Players would be restricted to team bubbles to stop the spread of the virus.

That meant organizers in the two cities had to locally stage more than thirty games over three weeks, prepare for more than two thousand people (just from the teams and traveling squads), and accommodate the highly restricted conditions mandated by the NCAA. I was a local volunteer for the women's tournament and watched as the controversy unfolded.

During early rounds in the women's tournament, an Oregon player posted an online video of the weight room assigned to these premier college players, which consisted of a tiny stack of barbells and short pile of yoga mats. Her male counterparts, on the other hand, enjoyed expansive facilities.

The concurrent staging of the tournaments provided a unique real-time opportunity to compare the inequalities. The viral video spread faster than COVID, inspiring participants to share similar disparities with meals, facilities, and promotional swag bags provided to male and female players. The conclusion: even half a century after Title IX, male competitors were still favored with superior facilities and marketing support from NCAA leadership.

The hoopla over the video forced difficult conversations and public relations backlash that didn't end when Stanford coach Tara VanDerveer won her second women's collegiate title over upstart Arizona. One reporter faulted NCAA leadership for their failure to note the disparity: "Nobody looked at that space and said, 'Something's not right here.' It took someone posting on social media to bring attention to the issue."[48] The discussion extended to similarly inadequate facilities at the 2021 Division I women's volleyball and softball championships.

After their initial pushback, NCAA executives ordered a gender equity study to address the issues. In August 2021, the study's first phase was released and echoed the unsatisfactory report in 1992. One positive finding from the third-party report was that Division III exhibited much more equality than its revenue-producing sibling in Division I. The NCAA's reaction to the study was to officially brand both men's and women's basketball championships as March Madness.[49]

Only time will tell if this was a superficial gesture or a sign of sincere progress. Thus, the conversations continue.

Epilogue

For readers who have reached this point, I have a question: did you see the handoffs that led to the headlines? Did you notice that—as in a track meet or torch relay—some exchanges were performed in the blink of an eye, and others demanded a slower transition, sometimes even from a standing start?

Since my few athletic talents were best displayed in running events, and the instigator of this project was a member of our 1975 state qualifying mile-relay team and fellow torch-bearer, I've found the lens of the relay race to be helpful while assembling this story of generational progress. The participants spanned eras, attitudes, and experiences. Shirley Rushing, Emilie Burrer Foster, Glada Munt, Libby Johnson, and Julie Jenkins help us appreciate those who first bore the flame for women's sports. There were also the many athletes who directly advanced the cause through those handoffs highlighted in the previous pages, such as Mary McLean to Glada Munt; Nancy Spencer to Val Franta; and Libby Johnson to Jill Harenberg to Teresa Machu to Yanika Daniels. All these women either coached or played for the other in a cascade of learning, teaching, and mentoring

Of course, more than once since 1869, a baton was dropped. And facilities may have hindered rather than enhanced performance, not unlike the shin splints I suffered from running on an outdated surface in the 1970s. These mishaps of history might have slowed progress, but they didn't stop it for Trinity's female athletes, who always moved forward, no matter the pace.

Many observers will say the race isn't yet won, pointing to some troubling trends of the twenty-first century, including the rise of youth sports specialization and diminishing diversity in sports leadership ranks.

The increase in athletic scholarships available to high school girls ushered in the first unwelcome trend: the pressure on girls to focus their entire youth career on one sport, sometimes even before they reach puberty. In 2016, Christine M. Riordan, the president of Adelphi University (a Division III school) wrote that this culture "leads to unrealistic expectations and excesses that follow athletes and their parents into intercollegiate play." She added,

> Years before college, young athletes—particularly those in the middle and upper-middle classes—are increasingly pressured to specialize in a single sport in order to increase their opportunity to play college athletics and receive an athletics scholarship. They join year-round, sport-specific organizations requiring season after season of demanding participation (and significant financial commitment) in order to stay in the player-development pipeline. Parents devote their lives to taking their kids to practices and tournaments year-round in the belief that athletics provides a likely vehicle to fund their child's college education.[1]

Riordan explains that the facts don't support this assumption. The most recent statistics from the NCAA show that only 7 percent of the 7.2 million high school athletes play varsity sports at any level of the NCAA; of those few who do continue, 40 percent enroll in nonathletic scholarship Division IIII schools. Only 2 percent of those continuing to play for the other two divisions are awarded some form of athletic scholarship to compete in college, and if those athletes aren't playing football or basketball, the subsidy rarely represents a full ride. Finally, only 2 percent of those scholarship recipients move to the professional ranks. Riordan further points out that the amount available for academic scholarships (more than $50 billion) dwarfs the amount available for athletic aid ($3.6 billion).[2]

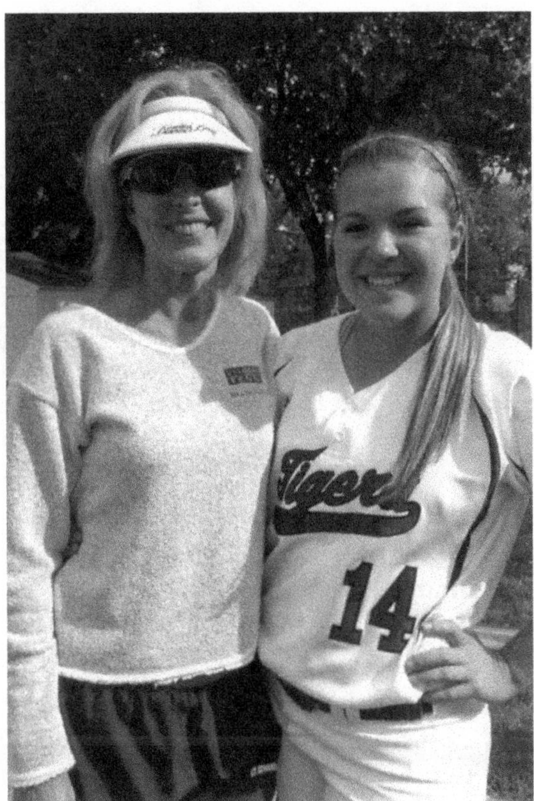

Two star Trinity pitchers, Julie Roba and daughter Katie Castillon, 2014

Several Trinity athletes who became parents or coaches have experienced this challenge up close. Julie Roba, a softball, bowling, and junior varsity tennis standout from the late 1970s, introduced her two children to a variety of sports to match her own varied youth experiences. But once her daughter Katie showed promise as a softball player, she was encouraged to give up all other activities in the ninth grade. Her life became centered around select team softball, and her schedule was dominated by lessons, games, and travel—routines foreign to her mother. "We never took lessons. We just played," Roba said of her own childhood. Katie followed in her mother's footsteps as a starting pitcher for the Tigers, this time on a true home field.[3]

Former Trinity soccer player and coach Suzanne Anderson knew she was fortunate that her private high school allowed her to play multiple team sports in the late 1970s and felt that the variety gave her confidence to try new things. She's concerned that current club team trends could be limiting experience and excluding aspiring soccer players from what she feels is becoming an "elitist" sport. Anderson feels that those who can't pay for a trainer, the best equipment, and the right club are "really hamstrung." She added, "It should be a sport for all, and everybody should have the same opportunity."[4]

Kerry Eudy, one of Julie Jenkins's stellar volleyball players, faced a similar dilemma as a Houston-area high school athlete in the early 1990s. She wasn't able to join club or select teams, and her school offered only two team options for girls: volleyball or basketball. In her senior year, school officials forced Eudy to choose between volleyball or cheerleading. Eudy went in front of the Santa Fe school board and argued against the limitations imposed on her and other girls. To her distress—but to Trinity's benefit—she lost the argument and selected volleyball.[5]

As a high school coach, Teresa Machu encouraged students to play in a variety of sports, especially after observing injuries caused by overuse, including ACL knee injuries common in youth basketball.[6] She believes that a multisport approach helps girls build knowledge and a more competitive edge. After talking with Division I coaches at summer softball camps, however, Machu realized that the pressure wasn't coming from the colleges but from parents. Her personal philosophy after forty years in girls' and women's sports: "Kids need to be kids."[7]

The second distressing development in the decades after Title IX is what one sports historian called the "gradual extinction of advocates of women in sport."[8] The problem? The decline of female leadership. Once the NCAA forced the female-led AIAW out of existence in 1982, the percentage of women in charge, both in administration and coaching, dropped precipitously. As a result, female voices were muted and role models for girls and young women diminished. The most disturbing statistic was the plunge in female head coaches leading women's intercollegiate teams, from 90 percent before Title IX to 42.7 percent by 2021.[9]

A number of factors have been blamed for this setback. "Historically, coaches for women's teams came from the ranks of physical educators

Teresa Machu's Churchill High School team celebrates her final softball game after twenty-two years over the program, 2015.

who were also teaching," reported Acosta and Carpenter. "Prior to Title IX, few of the female coaches were paid for their coaching duties." This model held little attraction for male coaches, who could make a living in the more established men's athletic departments of the day without taking on the multiple roles of coach, teacher, and laundry attendant.[10] After 1972, coaching a women's team became more inviting, as pay increased and other obligations were removed.[11]

A similar trend unfolded at Trinity. Libby Johnson and Shirley Rushing personified the spread-too-thin model of early coaching and sponsorship. Johnson's successors were mostly female and part-time to their sport; and they had to juggle a variety of roles. In the 1990s, men began filling the gaps. The gender ratio began shifting back in the twenty-first century, however, as Trinity's budget became more equitable and

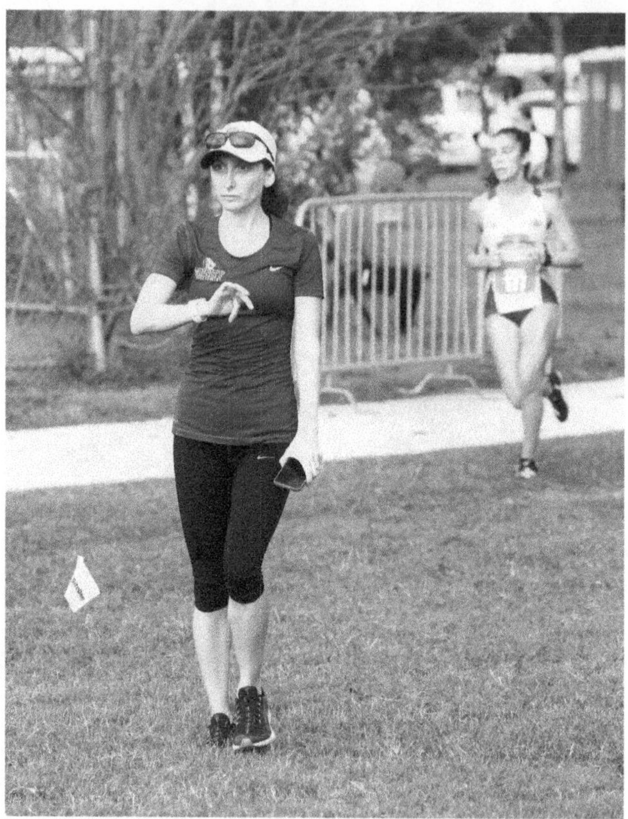

Emily Loeffler Daum, Trinity men's and women's cross country coach

coaches more specialized. In 2022, the five female coaches for Trinity's nine women's teams (at 55.6 percent) exceeds the 44.5 percent average for all Division III schools.

A second contributing factor to this decline in female leadership is the male domination of athletic department leadership. In their 2020 report, Acosta and Carpenter found that only 24 percent of all athletic directors were female, even though nearly half of all college athletes were women. Division III led the NCAA with 32 percent.[12] The presumption is that males are more inclined to hire males. In fact, the researchers identified a correlation that tied the athletic director's gender to the percentage of female coaches. In the Division III example, if a school's athletic director was female, the rate of its female coaches was 53.9 percent; if an athletic director was male, the percentage dropped to 44.4 percent.[13]

Women's sports pioneer Donna Lopiano suggests that this discriminatory treatment is not intentional: "It happens because people are not educated in the importance of ethnic, cultural and gender diversity and simply do the easiest and most comfortable thing: hire people they are comfortable with, know and associate with—people just like them." She adds, however, that "it is hard for those in the majority to understand how hurtful these stereotypes are to minority groups."[14]

Even the NCAA posed the question "Where Are the Women?" in *Champion*, their member magazine. After interviewing several female coaches for the 2017 article, the author confirmed that the rise in coaches' salaries led to more men applying for these positions. But some women pointed to persistent gender bias, lack of mentorship and professional networking, and the difficulties of balancing the demands of the job with marriage or motherhood.[15] Adding fuel to the fire was the fact that the ubiquitous select club and travel teams for single-sport high school athletes are typically overseen by male coaches. In her decades at Southwestern University, Glada Munt observed that incoming female athletes often expressed a preference for male coaches, since many grew up with them.[16]

Regardless of the causes, the results reinforce a vicious cycle that prevents girls and young women from having female role models. One researcher considers this trend "detrimental to development." The Department of Justice's forty-year Title IX report emphasized the importance of women moving into leadership: "The equal educational opportunities for which the Department advocates will better prepare women for success in the workplace and society at large, and will enable them to take on leadership roles in the public and private sectors. Additionally, as women achieve increased visibility in positions of leadership, more young women will benefit from these inspiring female role models."[17]

Another stubborn statistic of note is the lack of diversity among sports information directors, who decide which teams and players to publicize; as of 2021, statistics show that these directors are predominantly white males. According to Richard Lapchick, president of the Institute for Sport and Social Justice, this can create a conundrum. "The Sports Information Director has the opportunity to highlight coaches of color, student athletes of color, and women, and if we have overwhelmingly white men as we have had in that position, then who are they going to end up highlighting, even if it's not conscious?" he asked.[18] While Justin Parker has held Trinity's sports information director position since his own graduation in 2000, he follows the lead of his athletic director and focuses on a balanced view when providing coverage for male and female Tiger teams.

One still evolving issue is that of transgender women competing in sports. Sports and educational governing organizations are adapting to the advancing science in developing criteria that best provides fair competition. Trinity's stated focus on diversity, equity, and inclusion underscores its commitment to a welcoming environment for all students, and the university will continue to update its participation policies based on criteria from the governing entities.

One final question: was it worth the effort?

Despite these trends, most evaluations of the post–Title IX era remain positive for women's education overall and women's sports in particular. Those of us working on the Trinity Women's Intercollegiate Athletics History project were especially impressed (but not surprised) by the wide range of experiences athletes encountered after Trinity. Their accomplishments range from raising and fostering children to earning academic, medical, and law degrees. Their professions include nonprofit directors, children's clothing entrepreneurs, Presbyterian pastors, Alaskan adventure outfitters, pediatric psychiatrists, FBI supervisors, academic administrators, and emergency room physicians. A few pursued athletic-focused careers: Glada Munt (1974), Mary Walters (1979), and Teresa Machu (1984). Also, not interviewed for the book but equally impressive for their contemporary sports leadership are former basketball player Portia Lowe Hoeg (2001), the current executive director of the Division III Centennial Conference; and intramural star Erin O'Donnell (2007), one of only four women serving as a general manager in the thirty-team AAA minor league baseball system after her 2021 appointment.

Regardless of their ultimate life experiences, the former athletes who were interviewed for this project repeated some common lessons learned from sports: discipline, teamwork, leadership, self-confidence, communication, and time management. A few personal statements stood out from the dozens of interviews conducted.

For Emilie Burrer Foster (1969), her broad youth and collegiate sports experience presented unique opportunities for her coaching and consulting career, such as sharing tea with the prime minister of Ireland and speaking to a group of five thousand in Argentina. She said the self-confidence she gained through her athletic career made a big difference.

Alison Taylor (1977) believes that her Trinity softball experience helped her work well with people from all backgrounds, a lesson she carried into a career in health care and nonprofit work. She also felt that her playing days taught her about the importance of teamwork: "We had no outside support. We had to learn to rely on each other."

Sarah Scott Mayo (1973), whose advocacy for an official tennis team in 1971 set the stage for a future national championship, said that Bob Strauss's motor learning labs helped in her entrepreneurial career.

Jill Harenberg O'Neill (1978) is glad she expanded her participation: "I really thought that my life would be tennis but I learned so much more with the other sports that I played."

FBI supervisor Terri Hailey (1981) said that the discipline derived from participating in sports transferred to her academic life at Trinity. She also felt that working under a coach on three teams—and learning about listening to direction, engaging with people, and working for someone else—helped her transition to post-college life. "It's not about you; it's about the team," she said.

Nonprofit director Suzanne Anderson (1984) believes that competing as an independent against formidable teams helped her become adept at dealing with adversity and how to lose graciously. But she also appreciated another benefit of sport: learning to have fun.

Volleyball All-American Amy Waddell Stewart (1994) took advantage of the unique opportunity to assume an early leadership role in a venue where she didn't consider herself a leader. She also felt that her time being a "big fish in a small pond" instilled in her deep confidence.

Kerry Eudy (1994) found that balancing workouts, games, and schoolwork helped her succeed at Trinity and in her postgraduate education (psychology and law) and extended into adulthood. "Now I like to have a lot of things going on at the same time," she admitted. Something else stuck too—when she's late to something, she's still afraid she'll have to run laps.

Discipline was key for Shelley Story (1994), who says it comes naturally to her in her work as dean of students at Southwestern University. But she's not sure which came first. "Does athletics teach you discipline or is it the other way around?" she pondered.

Julie Jenkins is a firm believer that participation on a team develops character, and she went on to list her players' many qualities: "They know how to get along with people, and how to bite their tongue, and be tolerant, and not sweat the small stuff, and get along. They learn how to handle conflict and are also better equipped to perform under pressure."

Statistics from the corporate world back up Jenkins's assessment. A 2017 report showed that women still lagged in participation in the executive ranks, but of those who had advanced to the company C-suite (CEOs, CFOs, etc.), 94 percent played high school sports and 52 percent played college sports.[19]

The story of Trinity women's collegiate athletics isn't just about the stars, of course. In fact, many of the relay runners in this race were much more accomplished as students than as athletes. Others brought scant experience but an openness to risk. And still others had to perform under the burdens of scarce support and uneven competition. Their successes weren't measured by championships. These women—like Ana Unruh, Betty Meadows, and Dorian Martin—would be graded on the values instilled in them to prepare them for life after sports. These attributes can be summed up in the CASH acronym Jenkins uses with her players; Jenkins believes that if she's successful in helping her athletes develop character, they graduate feeling Confident, Ambitious, Strong, and Happy.

In spite of the hurdles, female athletes at Trinity kept their gaze forward and their priorities balanced. According to athletic director Bob King, the decision to forego athletic scholarships was the right one. "We're in a good place," he said in 2020.[20]

Or, put another way, Libby Johnson was ahead of her time.

ACKNOWLEDGMENTS

In January 2020, when the Trinity University Women's Intercollegiate Athletics history project members asked me to convert our years of research and interviews into a book, it made sense on many levels. Writing is second nature to me. My first job out of Trinity was as a daily newspaper sportswriter, and I recently retired from decades of corporate communications. Also, I'm a sports fan and frustrated athlete who had some brief moments in the sun before age and injuries slowed me down. And I am forever linked to Trinity. It is my favorite institution, the place where I not only received my journalism degree but also met my husband of more than forty years.

I had never written a book, and my years lost in corporate life separated me from the extraordinary success story of Trinity women's athletics following my own softball and running exploits of the 1970s. It didn't help that a global pandemic precluded on-campus visits and relegated fact-gathering and interviews to videoconference calls.

So I needed a lot of help. Here are some—but certainly not all—of those who are really responsible for the creation of this book.

Trinity's administration has been a stalwart sponsor of this project on many levels, including Dee Johnson, former vice president of academic affairs, who helped Douglas Brackenridge with initial expenses related to archival research and oral history interviews; Mike Bacon, vice president of advancement, who saw the promise of this effort and provided seed funding to get it started; and Celeste Mendoza and Karla Hagen Phillips of Alumni Relations and Development, who picked up the torch and procured the funds needed to publish this book.

The support of the Athletic Department through Bob King, director of athletics, was invaluable, and sports information director Justin Parker contributed the bulk of the facts and narrative for the final chapter. Two Trinity Board of Visitors members, Linda Kay Peterson '66 (past) and Leslie Hollingsworth '88 (current), provided our team much needed insight and inspiration on our storytelling journey.

The research and oral history portion of this multiyear project wouldn't have been possible without early Trinity Coates Library support from Meredith Elsik and Jes Neal. Current archivist Abra Schnur valiantly picked up the in-progress oral history project in 2020 at the outset of the COVID-19 pandemic, secured funding, and provided leadership for the creation of the online platform complementing this book. Other college library professionals helped Douglas Brackenridge with his early research, especially at Texas Woman's University in Denton, where decades of material related to women's athletics and governance is archived. Author and professor emeritus at Baylor University Nancy Goodloe provided early support. Diane Saphire contributed her sharp inquiry skills at the Texas Woman's University archives and in other ongoing contributions. Student support came from Mellon grant interns Ardi Saunders, Sam Henry, Hope Walker-Tamboli, and Zoe Grout, who did a fabulous job of creating the Playing Field website in summer 2021.

And this story couldn't have been told without the more than forty athletes and coaches who participated in oral history interviews, personal visits, or phone calls. Honest conversations about these mostly halcyon but sometimes difficult days brought us such joy and appreciation for the privilege of accessing living history. Special thanks go to Glada Munt, Yanika Daniels, and Emilie Foster, who tolerated many repeat phone calls to confirm details or flesh out stories. Also, sincere appreciation for those who reviewed specific sports sections—Emilie Foster, Julie Jenkins, Becky Geyer, and Teresa Machu—thank goodness for your sharp memories. A special shout-out goes to Munt for reviewing the entire draft before Trinity University Press began its process.

Your unbelievably quick turnaround and priceless feedback have made this a much better product. I am also grateful to Jody Conradt, who accepted Shirley Rushing's invitation to write a Foreword and read the manuscript during the UT Longhorn's 2022 playoff run.

I must extend my kudos to the many student publication editors and reporters who tried their best with their still-developing skills to tell the women's sports stories of this past half-century. Also, I enjoyed the efforts of the trail-blazing female sports editors who bravely intruded upon the previously male-dominated world of intercollegiate athletics in the formative years—Carolyn White, Carolyn Kluttz, and Dorian Martin. If I missed someone, please pass on my appreciation.

Many thanks go to the professionals at Trinity University Press who patiently guided me through the process—Tom Payton, Steffanie Mortis, Sarah Nawrocki—and their BookMatters partners, Dave Peattie and Tanya Grove, who worked their magic to make this book much more visually and intellectually interesting.

Six more people deserve praise before I bow out. Of course, the inspiration for telling this story was Peggy Kokernot Kaplan. Even when she and I ran together casually in a noontime group or officially on Trinity's first women's track team, I could never keep up with my speedy friend. I'm so happy she didn't let her curiosity falter. She lit this torch, and I am so grateful she can now find her national qualifying 880 time in Trinity's online archives! Another constant presence behind the proverbial curtain was my husband, co–sports editor, and best friend, Dave Pasley '77, who not only provided daily encouragement but also drove across the city during the Covid shutdown for curbside groceries and way too many takeout meals. He also let me co-opt his forty-five-year-old "Trinity University Country Club" T-shirt for motivation.

Finally, four others have walked almost every step of this journey. The project's two on-campus shepherds were Jacob Tingle in sport management and Angela Breidenstein in the education department. They enthusiastically kept this project moving while dealing with the unprecedented pandemic that upended campus life. They were making an almost-overnight transition from classroom content delivery to an unfamiliar video platform.

From the beginning, Shirley Rushing Poteet and Douglas Brackenridge kept the flame afire for this project. As a student, I never had either as a professor, but I am so grateful to have benefited from their wisdom and guidance at this later stage of my life. Shirley was a steadfast supporter and reliable source for information and contacts over half a century. Douglas dedicated countless hours to research, and the knowledge gained from writing his own Trinity history book in 2004 was invaluable.

A special cheer goes to the women and men listed below, who agreed to be interviewed for this history project. Many of the formal interviews and related transcripts can be found on the Trinity Playing Field website.

Alison Taylor '77
Amy Brown St. Clair '76
Amy Waddell Stewart '94
Becky Geyer
Betsy Ascani Henderson '77
Betsy Gerhardt Pasley '77
Betty Meadows '70
Bob King
Butch Newman
Christy Jayne Curtis '02
Donna Stockton Roup '76 (through Robin Dreier)
Dwayne Hanberry
Emilie Burrer Foster '69
Emily Loeffler Daum '09
Erin Rice Patterson '98
Gerald Smetzer
Glada Munt '74
Halie Bricker Benson '97
Herb Stumberg
Jana Steinmetz '76
Jill Harenberg O'Neill '79
Julie Jenkins
Julie Roba Castillon '80
Justin Parker '00
Kerry Eudy '94
Lynn Walker Luna '77
Mary McLean Wilson '67
Mary Walters '79
Monica Flores '76
Nancy Spencer '71
Pam Steinmetz '74
Peggy Kokernot Kaplan '75
Rindy Lobdell White '72
Sally Goldschmeding Branch '68
Sarah Scott Mayo '73
Shelley Story '94
Shirley Rushing
Sue Bachman Henderson '77
Susan Davis Carter
Suzanne Anderson '84
Suzy Gray '82
Teresa Machu '84
Terri Hailey '81
Yanika Daniels '95

SELECT BIBLIOGRAPHY

This book relies heavily on research conducted at the Trinity University Coates Library, the Texas Woman's University Archives in Denton, Texas, and archival materials obtained online. Included in the Trinity Special Collections and Archives are presidential papers, athletic council records, oral history interviews with former women athletes, photographs dating from the early 1900s to the present, and other records relating to women's intercollegiate athletics. Student publications accessible online include the *Trinitonian* newspaper from 1900 to 2022 (missing years in the 1930s), the *Mirage* yearbook from 1919 to 2022, and the *Course of Study Bulletin* from 1869 to 2022. Texas Woman's University houses many papers from the Women's Recreation Association and the Texas Association of Intercollegiate Athletics for Women.

Here are some other useful references.

Acosta, R. Vivian, and Linda Jean Carpenter. "Women in Intercollegiate Sport. A Longitudinal, National Study, Thirty-Seven Year Update. 1977–2014." www.acostacarpenter.org.

Bell, Richard C. "A History of Women in Sport Prior to Title IX." *Sport Journal* 10, no. 2 (2008). http://thesportjournal.org/article/a-history-of-women-in-sport-prior-to-title-ix/.

Brackenridge, R. Douglas. *Trinity University: A Tale of Three Cities*. San Antonio, TX: Trinity University Press, 2004.

Festle, Mary Jo. *Playing Nice: Politics and Apologies in Women's Sports*. New York: Columbia University Press, 1996.

Fields, Cheryl. "Appeals Court Rejects Charge That NCAA Forced Women's Group Out of Business." *Chronicle of Higher Education*, May 30, 1984.

———. "NCAA Urged to Withdraw Its Women's Sports Plan." *Chronicle of Higher Education*, May 27, 1975.

———. "They Don't Trust Jocks." *Chronicle of Higher Education*, May 12, 1975.

———. "Women's Athletics: Struggling with Success." *Chronicle of Higher Education*, May 22, 1978.

———. "Women's Sports Group Plans for Possible Dissolution." *Chronicle of Higher Education*, January 20, 1982.

Francis, David R. "Changing Work Behavior of Married Women." National Bureau of Economic Research, November 2005, www.nber.org/digest/nov05/changing-work-behavior-married-women.

Gerber, Ellen W., Jan Felshin, Pearl Berlin, and Waneen Wyrick. *The American Woman in Sport*. Boston: Addison Wesley, 1974.

Goodloe, Nancy R. *Before Brittney: A Legacy of Champions*. Victoria, Canada: Friesen Press, 2014.

Hill, Jessica. "Fact Check: Post Detailing 9 Things Women Couldn't Do Before 1971 Is Mostly Right." *USA Today*, October 28, 2020. www.usatoday.com/story/news/factcheck/2020/10/28/fact-check-9-things-women-couldnt-do-1971-mostly-right/3677101001.

"History of Women in Sports," Elmira College, https://faculty.elmira.edu/dmaluso/sports/timeline/index.html

Howell, Reet. *Her Story in Sport: A Historical Anthology of Women in Sports*. New York: Leisure Press, 1982.

King, Billie Jean. *All In: An Autobiography*. New York: Knopf, 2021.

LeBlanc, Diane, and Allys Swanson. *Playing for Equality: Oral Histories of Women Leaders in the Early Years of Title IX*. Jefferson, NC: McFarland, 2016.

Miller, Char. *San Antonio: A Tricentennial History*. Austin: Texas State Historical Association, 2018.

NCAA. "45 Years of Title IX: The Status of Women in Intercollegiate Athletics." June 2017, www.ncaapublications.com/p-4510-45-years-of-title-ix.aspx.

Oliphant, Judith Lee. "Title IX's Promise of Equality of Opportunity in

Athletics: Does It Cover the Bases?" *Kentucky Law Journal* 64, no. 2 (1975): 432–64.

Riordan, Christine M. "In Praise of Division III Athletics." *HuffPost*, April 7, 2016. www.huffpost.com/entry/in-praise-of-division-iii_b_9636666.

Texas Lone Star Network. "Longhorn Women's Sports 1949–1977." https://www.texaslsn.org/women-sports-leaders-the-early-years.

US Department of Justice. "Equal Access to Education: Forty Years of Title IX." June 23, 2012. www.justice.gov/sites/default/files/crt/legacy/2012/06/20/titleixreport.pdf.

Women's Sports Foundation. "History of Title IX." Aug. 13, 2019. www.womenssportsfoundation.org/advocacy/history-of-title-ix.

Wushanley, Ying. *Playing Nice and Losing: The Struggle for Control of Women's Intercollegiate Athletics, 1960–2000*. Syracuse, NY: Syracuse University Press, 2004.

IMAGE CREDITS

Unless otherwise noted, Trinity photos and illustrations are from the Coates Library Trinity University Publications Collection. Files from the Publication and Digital Collections are searchable through the library's special collections tab on its website at https://lib.trinity.edu/.

Frontis, Trinity University Athletics

Page 7, 1903 *Trinitonian* Annual Number, p. 49, Coates Library Special Collections and Archives (SCA), Trinity University, San Antonio, Texas. Hereafter, SCA

Page 8, Tehu_009; page 10, Tehu-152; page 12, unknown image no., Tehuacana Collection; page 14, Tehu-142; page 33, awaxbldgs5; page 42, awoodbuildings5; page 56, 87-8c-004; page 57, 98-18-001; page 63, Sky-Pool; page 64, Sky-Sams; page 67, 0219_bowling_feb_73.tif; page 80, askyathletics5; page 81, 88-38-85-001; page 103, UA-91-17-6_001; page 211, UA-85-03b-153_001; page 255, Bell Center; page 268 (Rushing), UA-85-01c-158_002; page 283, UA-90-06b-68_001. All from Digital Collection, SCA

Page 11, *Cumberland Presbyterian*, July 12, 1888

Page 16, V2#9, June 1902, page 180, SCA

Page 18, public domain

Page 20, TCHU055, Tehuacana Collection, Folder: Group Scenes Students, Photograph Collection, SCA

Page 22, courtesy Frank W. Shiels, class of 1980

Page 25, 1928 *Mirage*

Page 28, Photograph Collection, Waxahachie Collection: Folder Personalities Female, SCA

Page 40, 1914 (page 199) and 1920 (page 169) *Mirage*

Page 46, courtesy AAGBPL Archives and Memorabilia

Page 47, 1951 *Mirage*

Pages 49 and 58 (page 63), 1952 *Mirage*

Page 51, courtesy Shirley Rushing

Page 52, Olga Fallen Papers, Box 18, Folder 5, Texas Collection Library, Baylor University

Page 53, 1951 *Mirage* (page 31)

Page 59, 1956 *Mirage*

Page 62, 1963 *Mirage*

Pages 65 and 116, Photograph Collection, Skyline Collection: Folder E. M. Stevens Stadium, SCA

Pages 66, 236, 247, 270, 286, 301, 305, and 328, courtesy Trinity Athletics Department

Page 69, 1963 *Trinitonian*

Page 73, courtesy Emilie Burrer Foster

Page 74, courtesy Wayland Baptist University athletics department

Page 75, Neal Barr Photography

Page 82, Paul Popper, Popperfoto Collection, via Getty Images

Page 86, courtesy Mary McLean Wilson

Page 88, 1967 *Trinitonian*, page 7

Page 90, courtesy Becky Vest

Pages 91 and 327, © San Antonio Express-News/ZUMA Press

Page 95, 1973 *Mirage*

Pages 95 and 111, 1971 *Mirage*

Page 100, courtesy Paul Ridings

Page 105, 1978 *Mirage*

Page 106, New York Historical Society, Archive Photos, via Getty Images

Pages 113, 155, 161, 166, and 189, 1976 *Mirage*

Page 115, 1972 *Mirage*

Page 117, 1975 *Mirage*

Page 119, *Totem*, yearbook of McMurry College, 1962, courtesy McMurry University Library, Abilene, Texas

Pages 122, 135, and 163, 1975 *Trinitonian*

Pages 127 and 268 (Munt), courtesy Southwestern University

Page 139, US House of Representatives, History, Art, and Archives

Pages 142, 146, 159, and 170, courtesy Jana Steinmetz

Pages 147, 174, 253, 280, 318, and 319, courtesy Betsy Gerhardt Pasley

Pages 156 and 183 (page 2), 1978 *Trinitonian*

Page 158, courtesy Mary Walters

Pages 164, 178, and 181, 1976 *Trinitonian*

Page 165, 1978 *Mirage*

Page 167, courtesy Peggy Kokernot Kaplan

Page 172, © Diana Mara Henry, www.dianamarahenry.com

Page 175, 1977 *Mirage*, page 65

Page 177, 1977 *Trinitonian*, page 9

Pages 195, 202, and 216, 1980 *Trinitonian*

Pages 198, 302, and 312, Trinity Strategic Communications and Marketing

Page 204, courtesy University of Texas Athletics

Pages 207 and 213, 1982 *Mirage*

Page 209, courtesy Carla Brundage

Page 217, 1981 *Trinitonian*

Pages 219 and 223, 1985 *Mirage*

Page 222, 1990 *Mirage*

Page 226, 1986 *Trinitonian*

Page 228, 1988 *Trinitonian*

Page 229, 1986 *Mirage*

Pages 232 and 242, 1991 *Mirage*

Page 241, 1991 *Trinitonian*, page 17

Page 244, 1990 *Trinitonian*

Page 246, 1997 *Trinitonian*, page 10

Page 249, 1992 *Mirage*
Page 254, 1991 *Trinitonian*, page 21
Pages 257 and 276, courtesy SCAC
Page 260, courtesy Amy Waddell Stewart
Pages 273 and 285, 1993 *Trinitonian*
Page 275, © 2022 National Collegiate Athletic Association
Page 277, 1995 *Trinitonian*
Pages 288 and 293, courtesy John Ryan
Page 295, 2000 *Trinitonian*
Page 297, 1997 *Trinitonian*
Page 309, 2014 *Trinitonian*
Page 321, TrinityTigers.com
Page 325, *Trinity Magazine,* July 2014

NOTES

Introduction

1. Gerber et al., *American Woman in Sport*, 4, 68–69.

2. Goodloe, *Before Brittney*, xv.

3. Brackenridge, *Tale of Three Cities*, 180, 311.

Chapter 1. No Time for Sports

1. "The Synod of Texas," *Cumberland Presbyterian*, Sept. 25, 1890, 1.

2. Gerber et al., *American Woman in Sport*, 12.

3. Supreme Court of the United States, "U.S. Reports: Bradwell v. The State," Library of Congress 83, 1872, www.loc.gov/item/usrep083130/.

4. Brackenridge, *Tale of Three Cities*, 28–30.

5. Howell, *Her Story in Sport*, 249.

6. Trinity University Coates Library Special Collections and Archives (SCA), Minutes of Trinity University's Board of Trustees, June 3, 1884.

7. SCA, "A Letter to the Girls," *Trinity Exponent* 1, no. 5 (Nov. 1888): 6.

8. Bell, "History of Women in Sport." For an introduction to the history of American sports, see John A. Lucas and Ronald A. Smith, *Saga of American Sports* (Philadelphia: Lea & Febiger, 1978).

9. Patricia Vertinsky, "Exercise, Physical Capability, and the Eternally Wounded Woman in Late Nineteenth Century North America," *Journal of Sport History*, 8.

10. History of Women in Medicine, https://www.uab.edu/medicine/diversity/initiatives/women/history.

11. Howell, *Her Story in Sport*, 356.

12. Ibid., 362.

13. Brackenridge, *Tale of Three Cities*, 21.
14. Ibid., 35–38.
15. *Trinity University Catalogue*, 1886–87, 26–27.
16. Brackenridge, *Tale of Three Cities*, 109.
17. Ibid., 53–69.
18. *Trinitonian*, Dec. 1901, 62–63. Indian clubs are wooden clubs shaped like a large bottle or bowling pin that are swung for gymnastic exercise.
19. Ibid., June 1902, 180.
20. Ibid.
21. Brackenridge, *Tale of Three Cities*, 61. The NCAA Division III football championship is the Amos Alonzo Stagg Bowl, a game Trinity participated in (and lost) in 2002.
22. Ibid., 61–62.
23. Welch Suggs, "Historical Overview: At Play at America's Colleges," in *New Game Plan for College Sport*, ed. Richard Lapchick (Westport, CT: Praeger, 2006), 4.
24. Howell, *Her Story in Sport*, 365.
25. Bell, "History of Women in Sport."
26. Gerber et al., *American Woman in Sport*, 69.
27. Ibid., 62.
28. "Women's Basketball Historical Timeline," Women's Basketball Hall of Fame, www.wbhof.com/about/history; Howell, *Her Story in Sport*, 419–22.
29. Gerber et al., *American Woman in Sport*, 62, 77.
30. Ibid., 91–135.
31. "Longhorn Women's Sports 1949–1977."
32. *Trinity University Catalogue*, 1901, 14.
33. Howell, *Her Story in Sport*, 245.
34. Letter from Robert Bone to his parents, c. 1900, typescript copy in Trinity Archives.
35. SCA, "Trinity University," *Cumberland Presbyterian*, Apr. 19, 1902, 465.
36. SCA, "Church News" *Cumberland Presbyterian*, Aug. 30, 1901, 427; *Trinity University Bulletin*, Aug. 1911, 4.

Chapter 2. A Small Step Forward

1. Suggs, "Historical Overview," 3.
2. Brackenridge, *Tale of Three Cities*, 97–102.
3. "National Collegiate Athletic Association," Wikipedia, last modified June 2, 2022, https://en.wikipedia.org/wiki/National_Collegiate_Athletic_Association.
4. "Woman's Place in the World," *Trinitonian*, Oct. 1902, 55–57. The *Trinitonian* replaced the *Trinity Exponent* in 1900, which replaced the monthly *Trinity Herald* in 1883.
5. Luther H. Gulick, "Athletics from the biologic viewpoint," *American Physical Education Review* 11 (1906), 158.
6. *Trinity University Bulletin* 1, no. 3 (Dec. 1904).
7. *Trinity University Catalogue*, 1906, 75.
8. *Trinity University Bulletin* 7, no. 4 (1910): 4–5; SCA, Minutes of Board of Trustees, June 3–4, 1911; Brackenridge, *Tale of Three Cities*, 97–86.
9. *Trinity University Catalogue*, 1903, 10; 1906, 10, 75.
10. A. C. Scott, "The Importance of Physical Education," *Trinity University Bulletin* 8, no. 6 (1911): 5–6.

11. Brackenridge, *Tale of Three Cities*, 103.
12. *Trinitonian*, Oct. 1902, 44–45.
13. "Longhorn Women's Sports 1949–1977."
14. *Trinitonian*, Nov. 1902, 73.
15. "Longhorn Women's Sports 1949–1977."
16. Brackenridge, *Tale of Three Cities*, 104–5.
17. Howell, *Her Story in Sport*, 179–80.
18. Brackenridge, *Tale of Three Cities*, 104–5.
19. Howell, *Her Story in Sport*, 179–80.
20. Suggs, "Historical Overview," 9.
21. Brackenridge, *Tale of Three Cities*, 101–2.
22. Suggs, "Historical Overview," 9, 10.
23. Goodloe, *Before Brittney*, 7, 364; "Longhorn Women's Sports 1949–1977"; *Mirage*, 1927, 89.
24. Howell, *Her Story in Sport*, 432–33, 437, 576.
25. Suggs, "Historical Overview," 8; Howell, *Her Story in Sport*, 437, 247.
26. Bell, "History of Women in Sport"; Gerber et al., *American Woman in Sport*, 72.
27. Gerber et al., *American Woman in Sport*, 71. The "temporary unfitness" mentioned in item 11 is an obvious reference to the monthly menstrual cycle.
28. Howell, *Her Story in Sport*, 437, 451.
29. LeBlanc and Swanson, *Playing for Equality*, 30.
30. *Mirage*, 1924, 124; 1926, 89, 106. Trinity faculty minutes, May 1, 1924.
31. *Mirage*, 1924, 124; 1930, 123.
32. Ibid., 1922, 22; 1927, 22.
33. *Trinity University Catalogue*, 1927, 68–69.
34. *Mirage*, 1928, 103–4.
35. Gerber et al., *American Woman in Sport*, 63.
36. Ibid., 63–65.
37. Ibid., 65–66, citing M. M. Duncan, *Play Days for Girls and Women* (New York, n.d.), 80.
38. Brackenridge, *Tale of Three Cities*, 127; Goodloe, *Before Brittney*, 5.
39. "Longhorn Women's Sports 1949–1977."
40. *Mirage*, 1927, 89.
41. Gerber et al., *American Woman in Sport*, 19.
42. Ibid., 21.
43. Ibid., 66.
44. "Longhorn Women's Sports 1949–1977."
45. *Mirage*, 1929, 15, 19.
46. Festle, *Playing Nice*, 26.
47. Howell, *Her Story in Sport*, 591.
48. "Longhorn Women's Sports 1949–1977."
49. Howell, *Her Story in Sport*, 591.
50. "A Strike," *Trinitonian*, 1911 Commencement Number, 450–56. A similar story, "When a Maid Stoops to Conquer," *Mirage*, 1912, 54–55, describes how a talented female athlete is unable to attract the man she loves until she reverts to traditional feminine passivity.

51. Bell, "History of Women in Sport."

52. Donald E. Everett, *Trinity University: A Record of One Hundred Years* (San Antonio: Trinity University Press, 1968), 122.

Chapter 3. Wartime Holding Patterns

1. Brackenridge, *Tale of Three Cities*, 147–50.

2. Everett, *Record of One Hundred Years*, 122. Miller and Calvert would also serve on Trinity's board of trustees.

3. Miller, *Tricentennial History,* quoting from Green Peyton's *San Antonio: City in the Sun* (1946).

4. *Trinitonian*, Oct. 20, 1942, 2.

5. Ibid., March 12, 1943, 4.

6. SCA, Minutes of Board of Trustees, May 18, 1943.

7. Women's Recreation Association (WRA) Photographic Collection, 1910–1965, Oregon State University Special Collections and Archives Research Center, scarc.library.oregonstate.edu/findingaids/?p=collections/findingaid&id=2796.

8. Manuel Grajales, "Fischer, Alva Jo [Tex]," *Handbook of Texas Online*, accessed March 27, 2020, www.tshaonline.org/handbook/entries/fischer-alva-jo-tex; and "Lessing, Ruth Elizabeth [Tex]," accessed April 12, 2022, www.tshaonline.org/handbook/entries/lessing-ruth-elizabeth-tex. "Alva Jo Fischer," aagpbl.org/profiles/alva-jo-fischer-tex/390.

9. Jeneane Lesko, "League history," AAGPBL Players Association, 2014, www.aagpbl.org/history/league-history; Emma Span, "Is Softball Sexist?" *New York Times*, June 6, 2014.

10. Brackenridge, *Tale of Three Cities*, 158–60.

11. *Course of Study Bulletin*, 1947, 94.

12. *Mirage*, 1949, 178.

13. Bell, "History of Women in Sport," citing Gerber et al., *American Woman in Sport.*

14. *Mirage*, 1948, 132–33.

15. Ibid., 1949, 177; *Trinitonian*, Oct. 21, 1949, 2.

16. Gerber et al., *American Woman in Sport,* 65–66.

17. *Trinitonian*, April 1, 1949, 4.

18. Ibid.

19. Interview with Shirley Rushing, July 7 and 15, 2020.

20. *Mirage*, 1992, 35 (plate 18).

21. Brackenridge, *Tale of Three Cities*, 167.

Chapter 4. Progression and Regression

1. Robert D. Putnam and Shaylyn Romney Garrett, *The Upswing: How America Came Together a Century Ago and How We Can Do It Again* (New York: Simon & Schuster, 2020), 300.

2. *Mirage*, 1992, 35 (plate 18); 1951, 4.

3. Miller, *Tricentennial History*, 124–25.

4. Brackenridge, *Tale of Three Cities*, 171–97. For more background, see Mary Carolyn Hollers George, *O'Neil Ford, Architect* (College Station: Texas A&M University Press, 1992).

5. Ibid., 182–202.

6. *Mirage*, 1952, 63; 1953, 128; 1956, 201; 1958, 156.

7. *Course of Study Bulletin*, 1955, 165–66; *Mirage*, 1955, 159.

8. Cady would complete a long and distinguished physical education career at Sam Houston State University where she served for thirty-two years before her retirement. For more information see www.shmfh.com/obituaries/Ruth-Cady/#!/Obituary.

9. *Trinitonian*, Nov. 7, 1958, 3.

10. Ibid., Nov. 19, 1954, 1.

11. Ibid., April 8, 1960, 2

12. Ibid., March 29, 1961, 1; Feb. 16, 1962, 6; Brackenridge, *Tale of Three Cities*, 245–46.

13. Festle, *Playing Nice*, 20–21.

14. Ibid.; "Longhorn Women's Sports 1949–1977." Hiss was hired at UT in the 1919–20 academic year.

15. Putnam and Garrett, *The Upswing*, 300.

16. Kate Cruikshank, "Birch Bayh: Biography," Indiana University Modern Political Papers, https://libraries.indiana.edu/birch-bayh-biography.

17. Putnam and Garrett, *The Upswing*, 300.

18. Rushing interview, July 7 and 15, 2020.

19. D. Harold Byrd Jr. obituary, www.dignitymemorial.com/en-ca/obituaries/dallas-tx/d-byrd-10026191.

20. Brackenridge, *Tale of Three Cities*, 205; SCA, Memorandum John H. Moore to J. Noman Parmer, Vice President for Academic Affairs, Aug. 7, 1979, Calgaard Presidential Papers, Box 84–27, Folder Sports–Track Athletics, 1979–89.

21. *Trinitonian*, Sept. 27, 1963, 6.

22. Gerber et al., *American Woman in Sport*, 66.

23. *Trinitonian*, July 31, 1970, 7; Rushing interview, July 7 and 15, 2020.

24. Brackenridge, *Tale of Three Cities*, 245.

25. "Longhorn Women's Sports 1949–1977."

26. Rushing interview, July 7 and 15, 2020. Some school names changed since the 1960s; Incarnate Word College is now the University of the Incarnate Word, and Texas Lutheran College became Texas Lutheran University.

27. *Trinitonian*, Nov. 19, 1965, 5; communication with Emilie Burrer Foster, Dec. 1, 2020.

28. *Trinitonian*, Dec. 18, 1963, 6.

29. Ibid., Nov. 19, 1968, 6.

30. Ibid., Nov. 27, 1969, 7; Texas Association of Intercollegiate Athletics for Women (TAIAW) Collections, Kitty McGee papers footnote, MSS 77, Box 7 folder 46, Volleyball, District IV 1969–70 tournament, Texas Woman's University (TWU) Archives. The tournament was for District IV in the TCIAW.

31. *Trinitonian*, Oct. 4, 1963, 6.

32. Ibid., Jan. 13, 1968, 6.

33. Gerber et al., *American Woman in Sport*, 74–75; Goodloe, *Before Brittney*, 33. The major wording changes were made by leaders of the Division for Girls and Women's Sports.

34. Festle, *Playing Nice*, 80–81.

35. Goodloe, *Before Brittney*, 9.

36. "Longhorn Women's Sports 1949–1977"; Festle, *Playing Nice*, 100.

37. Gerber et al., *American Woman in Sport*, 39–40.

38. Foster communication, Aug. 16, 2021. Foster noted that she didn't realize the game

she and the neighborhood boys were playing had a name. Only later did she learn it was called stickball.

39. Joseph W. McCarley obituary, http://porterloring.tributes.com/obituary/show/Joseph-W.-McCarley-102527754.

40. Karl O'Quinn, "Burrer Wins Crown in Straight Sets," May 9, 1965, and "Burrer Looked Good on Eastern Net Tour," Sept. 10, 1965, *San Antonio Express-News*; Interview with Emilie Burrer Foster, Jan. 18, 2018.

41. O'Quinn, "Burrer Wins Crown in Straight Sets" and "Burrer Looked Good on Eastern Net Tour"; Foster interview, Jan. 18, 2018.

42. Festle, *Playing Nice*, 37.

43. Foster communication, Aug. 16, 2021.

44. Communication with Emilie Burrer Foster and Janis Rinehart Brown, Feb. 17, 2022.

45. Gilbert Rogin, "Flamin' Mamie's Bouffant Belles," *Sports Illustrated*, April 20, 1964; Rogin, "Bouffant belles, Texas Track Club"; "Longhorn Women's Sports 1949–1977."

46. Festle, *Playing Nice*, 93.

47. Kit Fox, "How Big Hair Got These Runners on the Cover of Sports Illustrated," *Runner's World*, Nov. 3, 2015.

48. "The Real Story of Kathrine Switzer's 1967 Boston Marathon," *Runner's World*, April 2007; King, *All In*, 133.

49. Festle, *Playing Nice*, 45.

50. Communication with Nancy Spencer, Feb. 14, March 14, and Nov. 14, 2021.

51. "Betty Friedan, Who Ignited Cause in 'Feminine Mystique,' Dies at 85," *New York Times*, Feb. 5, 2006.

52. H. W. Brands, *American Dreams: The United States since 1945* (New York: Penguin, 2010), 175–76.

53. Festle, *Playing Nice*, 106.

54. Ibid, 94; communication with Susan Davis Carter, Aug. 2021.

55. Gerber et al., *American Woman in Sport*, 75–76.

56. Leona Holbrook, "Sport: An Expression for Human Quality," American Association for Health, Physical Education, and Recreation, 1968.

Chapter 5. The Unique Status of Women's Tennis

1. The photo was taken at the dedication of the school's first varsity tennis courts on Nov. 5, 1959. The complex was donated by trustee Arthur A. Seeligson Sr., a longtime supporter of tennis in San Antonio. In photo foreground John Newman makes the first official serve on the courts, while Coach Clarence Mabry watches from the left. Other players are Jimmy Moses, Rod Susman, and Chuck McKinley.

2. "June Ebert Byrd," www.porterloring.com/obituaries/June-Ebert-Byrd?obId=18168244.

3. *Trinitonian*, Oct. 5, 1955, 2.

4. Brackenridge, *Tale of Three Cities*, 243–44.

5. "About the WTA," www.wtatennis.com/about. Women's (paid) professional tennis didn't begin until the WTA was established in 1970.

6. Marilyn Montgomery Rindfuss obituary, *San Antonio Express-News*, Feb. 12, 2006.

7. *Trinitonian*, Sept. 14, 1962, 9–10; Oct. 6, 1961, 4. See also "From the Archives: July 8,

1962: Susman Triumphs at Wimbledon," *San Diego Union-Tribune*, July 8, 2018; John Sarkis, "Young Champ," July 7, 2018, http://girardmeister.com/tag/karen-hantze-susman.

8. King, *All In*, 176.

9. Interview with Sally Goldschmeding Branch, Aug. 24, 2018.

10. Rushing interview, July 7, 2020.

11. Branch interview, Aug. 24, 2018, and Sept. 21, 2021; *Mirage*, 1996, 120.

12. Facebook "Tales from the Court" seminar, June 25, 2019.

13. *Trinitonian*, April 7, 1966, 7; April 22, 1966, 6; Facebook "Tales from the Court." The 1966 state tournament was hosted by the Texas Recreational Federation of College Women. Also, there's a question about Goldschmeding's participation in 1966; it's possible that her involvement as pledge mistress for her large Gamma sorority class kept her from tennis team activities. The *Trinitonian* names her as a member of the 1966 team, but other women listed on that squad recall little official competition that year.

14. *Trinitonian*, March 3, 1967, 6; March 17, 1967, 6; Feb. 9, 1968, 9; Rushing interview, July 7, 2020. These are more examples of the still interchangeable terms like *varsity* or *extramural* since teams from the 1950s had also been called varsity. Also, some players refer to "the" tournament that year, suggesting Rushing couldn't find more than one.

15. *Trinitonian*, March 10, 1967, 6; April 7, 1967, 7; interview with Mary McLean Wilson, Oct. 16, 2017.

16. *Course of Study Bulletin*, 1968, 226. The tennis entry continued to 1973–74. After that date, women's tennis became a scholarship sport and was no longer considered a student activity.

17. TAIAW Collections, Kitty Magee, MSS 77, Box7 folder 44, Shirley Rushing to Kitty Magee, April 23, 1969, TWU Archives. The governing group at the time was the Texas Recreational Federation of College Women.

18. Ibid., Letter, Shirley Rushing to Kitty Magee, June 17, 1970, TWU Archives.

19. Karl O'Quinn, "Back Home Again," *San Antonio Express-News*, Sept. 16, 1967.

20. *Trinitonian*, Sept. 22, 1967, 7.

21. Rushing interview, July 7 and 15, 2020.

22. *Trinitonian*, Sept. 22, 1967, 7.

23. This book-sharing relationship was repeated a half century later, when Rushing shipped Foster the newly released Billie Jean King autobiography in 2021.

24. Facebook "Tales from the Court."

25. Foster interview, Jan. 18, 2018.

26. "College Tennis and National Girls and Women in Sports Day," *College Tennis Online*, Feb. 3, 2004, www.collegetennisonline.com/Tennis/NewsDetail.aspx?nwId=7042.

27. "Gals Get Job Done," *San Antonio Light*, June 23, 1968.

28. *Mirage*, 1968, 59–60, 65. An article featuring Becky Vest made no mention of the championship, since it probably occurred past the print deadline.

29. "Gals Get Job Done."

30. O'Quinn, "A Unique Problem." According to O'Quinn's 2016 obituary, he always had strong opinions about women in sports. His stepdaughter said, "He was an 'empower women' guy before anyone had put the two words together." Mary Mills Heidbrink, "O'Quinn Had a Long Career as Sports Journalist," *San Antonio Express-News*, Feb. 23, 2016.

31. "Burrer Wins Tennis Title," *San Antonio Light*, June 22, 1969.

32. "Emilie Burrer," Trinity University Athletics, www.trinitytigers.com/history

/halloffame/hof2001/EmilieBurrer. The other four-time champion is high-jumper Christyn Schumann (2004–6).

33. *Trinitonian*, June 1, 1969, 6.

34. Harold Scherwitz, "Tribute to Emilie," *San Antonio Light*, June 25, 1969.

35. "Rebecca Louise Vest," Biographies of Female Tennis Players, last modified Aug. 8, 2015, https://tennisforum.com/62174305-post3689.html; interview with Becky Vest, Aug. 7, 2018.

36. Interview with Betty Meadows, March 7, 2018.

37. Jan Felshin, "The Dialectic of Woman and Sport," in Gerber et al., *American Woman in Sport*, 189–96.

38. While it seems ironic that a tobacco company would sponsor athletes, the industry had money to spare after being banned from broadcast advertising in 1971. Despite her reservations, Billie Jean King felt the sponsorship was "the greatest in the history of sports. They never asked us to smoke, and never asked us to endorse their product." King, *All In*, 177, 179. The ad campaign launched the popular phrase "You've come a long way, baby," and sponsorship would continue until 1995.

39. Interview with Sarah Scott Mayo, Feb, 18, 2018.

40. *Trinitonian*, April 24, 1980, 7; May 8, 1970, 8; Mayo interview, Feb. 18, 2018.

41. Rushing interview, July 7 and 15, 2020; Mayo interview, Feb. 18, 2018.

42. Rushing interview, July 7 and 15, 2020.

43. Ibid., April 6, 2019.

44. Ibid.

45. Rushing interview, July 7 and 15, 2020.

46. Spencer communication, Dec. 1, 2020.

47. *Trinitonian*, March 17, 1972; April 7, 1972, 10; *Mirage*, 1972, 134.

48. Spencer communication, Feb. 14, 2021.

49. Women wouldn't compete in the NCAA postseason until women's championships were added in the 1981–82 academic year.

50. Spencer communication, Feb. 14, 2021.

51. *Trinitonian*, Sept. 29, 1972, 10.

52. Ibid., March 16, 1973, 11; communication with Glada Munt, Oct. 26, 2021.

53. Communication with Donna Stockton Roup through Robin Dreier, Dec. 20, 2020.

54. Interview with Shirley Rushing and Douglas Brackenridge, Jan. 10, 2016.

55. *Trinitonian*, Feb. 23, 1973, 7.

56. Rushing interview, July 7, 2020.

57. Johnny Janes, "Another Trinity Tennis Title in the Works?" *San Antonio Light*, April 15, 1973.

58. There were nine tie-break points at the time; it is now seven.

59. Facebook "Tales from the Court."

60. "Tigerettes Cop Crown," *San Antonio Express-News*, June 16, 1973, 26.

61. *Trinitonian*, June 29, 1973, 6.

62. "Tigerettes Cop Crown"; *Trinitonian*, Sept. 7, 1973, 11. The student article erroneously says the women won the NCAA title, although it was the USTA collegiate championship.

63. Rushing and Brackenridge interview, Jan. 10, 2016.

64. Rushing interview, July 7, 2020; *Trinitonian*, Sept. 7, 1973, 11.

65. *Trinitonian*, Jan. 18, 1974. Nielsen numbers quoted in the Billie Jean King autobiography state that participation exploded in the early 1970s, when surveys showed Americans playing tennis increased from 10 million to 34 million between 1970 and 1974. King, *All In*, 268.

66. The organization dropped the word "Lawn" from its title after 1974, becoming the United States Tennis Association.

67. *Trinitonian*, Sept. 26, 1975, 10; "John Newman," University of Incarnate Word Athletics, https://uiwcardinals.com/sports/womens-tennis/roster/coaches/john-newman/273.

68. SCA, "Marilyn Rindfuss," Texas Tennis Museum and Hall of Fame, www.texastennismuseum.org/rindfuss; Marilyn Rindfuss, Box 01-05, Sports, Tennis, Women.

69. Joel Drucker, "TBT, 1881: The birth of USLTA, when the game was called lawn tennis," *Tennis*, May 21, 2020.

70. *Trinitonian*, June 29, 1976, 7; "Rindfuss Was Top-ranked Tennis Player, Longtime Teacher," *San Antonio Express-News*, Feb. 9, 2006.

71. Kevin O'Keeffe, "Val Franta Remembered," *San Antonio Express-News*, Nov. 1, 1984.

72. Bill O'Bryant, "Emilie Burrer Foster 'Back Home' as Trinity Coach," *San Antonio Light*, June 18, 1978.

73. Ibid.

74. Foster communication, Dec. 1, 2020; *Trinitonian*, Feb. 22, 1985, 11.

75. *Trinitonian*, Sept. 28, 1978, 14; Foster interview, Jan. 18, 2018.

76. *Trinitonian*, Oct. 10, 1980, 12.

77. Ibid., Aug. 31, 1990, 20.

78. "Trinity University's Hall of Fame," Trinity University Athletics, www.trinitytigers.com/history/halloffame/index.

79. *Trinitonian*, April 18, 1983, 6.

80. "Emilie Foster Returns to Trinity as Volunteer Assistant Tennis Coach," Jan. 15, 2020, Trinity University Athletics. www.trinitytigers.com/sports/wten/2019-20/Releases/200115_foster.

81. Communication with Pam Steinmetz, June 9, 2021.

Chapter 6. Building a Bridge to Equality

1. Lapchick, *New Game Plan for College Sport*, 128.

2. John Darnton, "Antiwar Protests Erupt Across U.S.," *New York Times*, May 10, 1972; *Trinitonian*, Nov. 10, 1978, 5.

3. Jill Lepore, *If/Then: How the Simulmatics Corporation Invented the Future* (New York: Liveright, 2021), 302.

4. This quote is repeated in a number of articles and blogs, including Sherry Boschert, "Media amplify Title IX controversies," 37WordsMedia, Sept. 21, 2016, www.sherryboschert.com/media-amplify-title-ix-controversies.

5. Donna Lopiano, "Gender and Sport," in Lapchick, *New Game Plan for College Sport* 127–28.

6. "Until 1968, a Married Texas Woman Couldn't Own Property or Start a Business Without Her Husband's Permission. This Dallas Attorney Changed That," *Texas Monthly*, Jan. 5, 2021, www.texasmonthly.com/being-texan/until-1968-married-texas-woman-couldnt

-own-property-start-business-without-husbands-permission-dallas-attorney-changed -that/.

7. NCAA, "45 Years of Title IX," 2, https://www.ncaapublications.com/p-4510-45-years -of-title-ix.aspx.

8. Linda Napikoski, "1970s Feminist Activities," ThoughtCo, Sept. 11, 2019, www .thoughtco.com/1970s-feminist-activities-3529001.

9. "'Y' Faces Hot Topics," *San Antonio Light*, April 12, 1970.

10. Brackenridge, *Tale of Three Cities*, 231, 309, 296; *Trinitonian*, May 8, 1970, 1.

11. Communication with Shirley Rushing, Jan. 2021.

12. "St. Mary's Wins Volleyball Title," *San Antonio Express-News*, Oct. 30, 1970. According to the school's athletics timeline, Johnson took the team to a 12-3 match record in 1970. St. Mary's University Athletics, https://rattlerathletics.com/sports/2012/12/22 /timeline.aspx.

13. *Trinitonian*, Nov. 19, 1971, 11; Dec. 3, 1976, 9.

14. Ibid., Dec. 3, 1971, 11.

15. Ibid., March 5, 1971, 10.

16. "Coed Cagers End Season," St. Mary's University *Rattler*, 1972, issue and page unknown.

17. Brackenridge, *Tale of Three Cities*, 259.

18. *Trinitonian*, Jan. 24, 2014, 3. Blystone's comments are in an article reporting on Wimpress's death.

19. Ibid., Sept. 17, 1971, 4.

20. Brackenridge, *Tale of Three Cities*, 258.

21. *Trinitonian*, Oct. 22, 1971, 11; Oct. 1, 1972, 4; March 30, 1973, 7.

22. Brackenridge, *Tale of Three Cities*, 262.

23. *Trinitonian*, Sept. 3, 1971, 4. The term "simon-pure" is defined as "complete genuine, authentic or honest." According to the Collins English dictionary, it was used for a Quaker character in the play *A Bold Stroke for a Wife* (1718), who must prove his identity against an impostor's claims.

24. *Trinitonian*, April 2, 1976, 12, 13. "Simon Pure" appears dozens of times in *Trinitonian* sports pages during the 1970s with some later reappearances, but it doesn't seem to have been adopted in other collegiate or sport settings, aside from a handful of references in sport journalism.

25. Brackenridge, *Tale of Three Cities*, 262.

26. *Trinitonian*, March 30, 1973, 7.

27. *Mirage*, 1972, 145.

28. *Trinitonian*, March 17, 1972, 12.

29. *Mirage*, 1972, 145.

30. *Trinitonian*, March 30, 1972, 7.

31. Ibid., April 2, 1976, 12, 13.

32. Ibid., Feb. 11, 1972, 1.

33. Ibid., Sept. 8, 1972, 4.

34. Joe Jares, "When It Comes to Winning, He's the Most," *Sports Illustrated*, Oct. 2, 1972.

35. "Athletic Group Named Southland Conference," *San Antonio Light*, April 6, 1963.

36. *Trinitonian*, March 30, 1973, 7.

37. Ibid., Oct. 13, 1972, 7.

38. Ibid., Jan. 19, 1973, 7.
39. Ibid., March 30, 1973, 7.
40. Ibid., Feb. 8, 1974, 11.
41. Brackenridge, *Tale of Three Cities*, 264.
42. Information derived from articles in the *Hamlin Herald*, local newspaper from online sources; printed copies in the Trinity University archives.
43. Ibid; "Louie Pearl Brewer Johnson," Find a Grave Memorial, Feb. 14, 2011, www.findagrave.com/memorial/65636241/louie-pearl-johnson.
44. "Miss Johnson in New Roles," St. Mary's University *Rattler*, undated, c. spring 1969, St. Mary's University Archives.
45. Goodloe, *Before Brittney*, 81. Results of the team's success or Johnson's contributions at the district competition were not recorded.
46. "St. Mary's University Adds P.E. Instructor for Women to Expanding Faculty," News Release, Aug. 15, 1967, St. Mary's University Archives.
47. "Miss Johnson in New Roles."
48. Karl O'Quinn, "Miss Coach," *San Antonio Express-News*, April 17, 1969.
49. Ibid.
50. Libby Johnson application, Jan. 6, 1970, St. Mary's University Archives, Folder, Libby Johnson materials, St. Mary's University Archives.
51. Interview with Terri Hailey, *The Woman, the Myth, the Legend: Libby Johnson*, https://spmt3314.coateslibrary.com/exhibits/show/libby-johnson/interviews/terri-hailey.
52. Rushing interview, July 7, 2020.
53. Letter, J. W. Langlinais to Libby Johnson, May 8, 1972, Folder, Libby Johnson materials, St. Mary's University Archives.
54. "History of the Boston Marathon," Boston Athletic Association, www.baa.org/races/boston-marathon/history.

Chapter 7. Signing and Defining Title IX

1. Goodloe, *Before Brittney*, 43–44. For history of changes in Title IX, see www.womenssportsfoundation.org/advocate/title-ix-issues/history-title-ix.
2. This national governance model for collegiate sports was inspired by the Texas Commission for Intercollegiate Athletics for Women (TCIAW, later TAIAW), which was established in 1968.
3. "NCAA releases new report as Title IX turns 45," NCAA, June 21, 2017, www.ncaa.org/news/2017/6/21/ncaa-releases-new-report-as-title-ix-turns-45.aspx.
4. Bil Gilbert and Nancy Williamson, "Sports are unfair to women," *Sports Illustrated*, May 28, 1973. It's apparent the statistic is from before 1973 and the AIAW policy reversal.
5. Goodloe, *Before Brittney*, 14–15.
6. "TCIAW Raps Wranglers' Scholarships," March 21, 1971, *Odessa American*.
7. Rushing communication, Jan. 2021.
8. O'Quinn, "A Unique Problem."
9. O'Quinn, "Burrer Looked Good on Eastern Net Tour"; Rushing communication, Jan. 2021.
10. Span, "Is Softball Sexist?"
11. Robert Carle, "The Strange Career of Title IX," *Academic Questions* 29, no. 4 (2016).
12. Interview with Jill Harenberg O'Neill, May 30, 2019.

13. Foster interview, Jan. 18, 2018.

14. Carla Lowry obituary, *Austin American-Statesman*, July 25, 2015.

15. Carla Lowry, "Leaders' Functions, Sources of Power, and Sources of Group Attraction Involved in Women's Intercollegiate Team Sport Groups," Doctoral Dissertation, Texas Woman's University, May 1972.

16. Ibid.

17. Munt communication, Dec. 14, 2020.

18. "Southwestern's Munt Reflects on the 40th Anniversary of Title IX," SCAC, June 21, 2012. www.scacsports.com/news/the_gift_of_equity.

19. "Carla Lowry," Southwestern University, www.southwesternpirates.com/general/halloffame/bios/lowry.carla?view=bio.

20. Adam Clymer, "Birch Bayh, 91, Dies; Senator Drove Title IX and 2 Amendments," *New York Times*, March 14, 2019.

21. Vanessa Grigoriadis, "Bernice Sandler: The Godmother of Title IX," *Politico*, Dec. 29, 2019, www.politico.com/news/magazine/2019/12/29/bernice-sandler-the-godmother-of-title-ix-088277.

22. Iram Valentin, "Title IX: A Brief History," *WEEA Digest* (Aug. 1997).

23. Clymer, "Birch Bayh, 91, Dies."

24. "Mink, Patsy Takemoto," History, Art, and Archives: U.S. House of Representatives, https://history.house.gov/People/detail/18329.

25. Clymer, "Birch Bayh, 91, Dies."

26. Women's Sports Foundation, "History of Title IX."

27. Goodloe, *Before Brittney*, 44.

28. Wushanley, *Playing Nice and Losing*, 63. The lawsuit's official name was *Kellmeyer, et al. v. NEA, et al.*

29. Ibid, 66.

30. Ibid.

31. TAIAW Women's Collections, MSS 77, Box 9, Folder 10, District VI, TWU Archives.

32. Letter, Sue Garrison to Directors, Aug. 27, 1973, TAIAW Collections, Sue Garrison Papers, MSS 77, Box 9, Folder 13, TWU Archives.

33. Munt communication, Dec. 14, 2020; April 21 and May 27, 2021.

34. Letter, Libby Johnson to TAIAW members, Nov. 13, 1973, TAIAW Women's Collections, Sue Garrison Papers, MSS 77, Box 9, Folder 8, TWU Archives.

35. Wushanley, *Playing Nice and Losing*, 66.

36. Goodloe, *Before Brittney*, 16–19.

37. Wushanley, *Playing Nice and Losing*, 70.

38. Oliphant, "Title IX's Promise," 462.

39. Ibid, 434.

40. Ibid, 460; Wushanley, *Playing Nice and Losing*, 88.

41. Festle, *Playing Nice*, 132, 133.

42. Oliphant, "Title IX's Promise," 461.

43. SCA, Duncan Wimpress Presidential Papers, Box 01-13, folder Intercollegiate Athletics.

44. *Trinitonian*, Feb. 4, 1977, 9. Quotation taken from the *Daily Texan*, UT student newspaper.

45. Goodloe, *Before Brittney*, 217–18

46. Letter, Sue Garrison to Charles Samson, April 5, 1974, TAIAW Women's Collections, Sue Garrison Papers, MSS 77, Box 9, TWU Archives.

47. *Trinitonian*, April 2, 1976, 14. This comment is almost identical to one included in "Sport Is Unfair to Women," *Sports Illustrated*, May 28, 1973.

48. Interview with Amy Brown St. Clair, June 1, 2018.

49. Interview with Glada Munt, Dec. 17, 2017.

50. *Trinitonian*, Jan. 24, 1975, 7. The NCAA was formed in 1906.

51. Fields, "They don't trust jocks" and "NCAA Urged to Withdraw Its Women's Sports Plan."

52. Wushanley, *Playing Nice and Losing*, 95.

53. In addition to being a member of the NCAA, Trinity would briefly join the NAIA, since it was a requirement for TIAA schools when the conference was established in 1976.

54. L. Leotus Morrison letter to NAIA member presidents, Feb. 28, 1975, TAIAW Women's Collections, Sue Garrison Papers, General Correspondence, MSS 77, Box 9, Folder 13 TWU Archives.

55. Fields, "They don't trust jocks," 3.

56. Wushanley, *Playing Nice and Losing*, 99–101.

57. July 24, 1975, Congressional Record, Senate P24635.

58. "Mink, Patsy Takemoto."

59. Oliphant, "Title IX's Promise," 435.

60. Ibid, 456.

61. Ibid, 455; Fields, "They don't trust jocks."

62. Oliphant, "Title IX's Promise," 454.

63. Ibid, 464.

Chapter 8. From Intramural to Intercollegiate

1. *Trinitonian*, Feb. 4, 1972, 9.

2. Ibid., Feb. 9, 1973, 6.

3. *Trinitonian*, Sept. 8, 1972, 6; Sept. 21, 1973, 10; Sept. 20, 1974, 5; interview with Betsy Gerhardt Pasley, Nov. 1, 2017.

4. *Trinitonian*, April 25, 1980, 17; April 26, 1974.

5. Ibid., Sept. 29, 1972, 11; Oct. 6, 1972, 7.

6. Ibid., Nov. 2, 1973, 11.

7. Ibid., Nov. 7, 1975, 10; April 4, 1975, 9.

8. Ibid., Feb. 9, 1973, 6.

9. Ibid., March 12, 1976, 6.

10. Ibid.

11. Ibid., April 26, 1974, 9.

12. Interview with Terri Hailey, Jan. 12, 2018.

13. Interview with Alison Taylor, Dec. 18, 2018; *Trinitonian*, Sept. 29, 1978, 13.

14. *Trinitonian*, Oct. 7, 1977, 2; interview with Julie Roba Castillon, April 10, 2019.

15. O'Neill interview, May 30, 2019; interview with Betsy Ascani Henderson, May 2, 2018.

16. Taylor interview, Dec. 18, 2018.

17. Interview with Suzy Gray, Oct. 30, 2018.

18. Hailey interview, Jan. 12, 2018.
19. Ibid.
20. SCA, Memorandum, Committee on Intercollegiate Athletics, April 1976, Box 01-22, Bruce Thomas Papers, Folder Athletics.
21. Ascani Henderson interview, May 2, 2018.
22. *Trinitonian*, Oct. 15, 1976, 10.
23. Communication with Terri Hailey, Jan. 2021; Steinmetz communication, June 9, 2021; communication with Betsy Ascani Henderson, Sept. 1, 2021.
24. April 1976 memorandum, Committee on Intercollegiate Athletics; Hailey interview, Jan. 12, 2018.
25. *Trinitonian*, Sept. 28, 1973, 10; Oct. 28, 1977, 2.
26. Interview with Lynn Walker Luna, Dec. 7, 2017
27. LeBlanc and Swanson, *Playing for Equality*, 105; *Trinitonian*, April 2, 1976, 2; interview with Mary Walters, May 17, 2019. The comment "or worse" refers to the common suspicion that a girl interested in sports was a homosexual, an unwelcome designation in this era of legal discrimination.
28. Munt interview, Dec. 17, 2017.
29. *Trinitonian*, Feb. 17, 1978, 12.
30. Ibid., March 23, 1973, 11.
31. O'Neill interview, May 30, 2019.
32. Interview with Rindy Lobdell White, Sept. 8, 2021.
33. "Six-on-six basketball," Wikipedia, last modified May 22, 2022, https://en.wikipedia.org/wiki/Six-on-six_basketball.
34. *Trinitonian*, Nov. 10, 1972, 9; Nov. 19, 1976, 9.
35. Steinmetz communication, June 9, 2021.
36. Hailey interview, Jan. 12, 2018.
37. O'Neill interview, May 30, 2019; Ascani Henderson interview, May 2, 2018.
38. O'Neill interview, May 30, 2019.
39. *Trinitonian*, Jan. 25, 1974, 10.
40. *Baylor Lariat*, Jan. 23, 1974, 8; Feb, 22, 1974.
41. TIAIW score sheet for the 1978 state tournament held at San Angelo State University on March 2, 3, 4, 1978, TAIAW Collections, MS 77, Box 16, Jody Conradt Folder, TWU Archives.
42. *Trinitonian*, Nov. 19, 1976, 9.
43. Ibid., March 12, 1976, 6. In 1974, TCIAW changed its name to TAIAW and its divisions from Districts to Zones.
44. Hailey communication, Jan. 2021; interview with Sue Bachman Henderson, Dec. 7, 2017.
45. Walker Luna interview, Dec. 7, 2017.
46. *Trinitonian*, March 3, 1978, 13.
47. TCIAW changed its name to TAIAW in 1974.
48. Letter from Libby Johnson to Sue Garrison, Sept. 24, 1973, TAIAW Collections, Sue Garrison Papers, MS 77, Box 11, Folder 32, TWU Archives.
49. Letter from Sue Garrison to Libby Johnson, Oct. 13, 1972, TAIAW Collections, Sue Garrison Papers, MSS 77, Box 9, Folder 10, TWU Archives.

50. Letter from Libby Johnson to Sue Garrison, Oct. 13, 1972, TAIAW Collections, Sue Garrison Papers, MSS 77, Box 9, Folder 8 District IV, TWU Archives.

51. Rushing and Brackenridge interview, Sept. 17, 2017.

52. Communication with Monica Flores, May 19, 2021.

53. Walker Luna interview, Dec. 7, 2017; Hailey interview, Jan. 12, 2018; Hailey communication, Jan. 2021.

54. "Volleyball at Its Prime," *The Woman, the Myth, the Legend: Libby Johnson,* https://spmt3314.omeka.net/exhibits/show/libby-johnson/a-look-at-women-s-sports/volleyball; Steinmetz communication, June 9, 2021.

55. Walters interview, May 17, 2019.

56. Munt interview, Dec. 17, 2017.

57. Hailey interview, Jan. 12, 2018; *Trinitonian*, Jan. 14, 1977, 10; Jan. 28, 1977, 6.

58. Hailey interview, Jan. 12, 2018.

59. Bachman Henderson interview, Dec. 7, 2017.

60. Steinmetz communication, June 9, 2021.

61. Munt interview, Dec. 17, 2017.

62. Steinmetz communication, June 9, 2021.

63. Munt interview, Dec. 17, 2017.

64. Walters interview, May 17, 2019. Walters was inducted into the University of Dallas Hall of Fame in 2007.

65. Interview with Theresa Machu, May 13, 2020.

66. O'Neill interview, May 30, 2019; Flores communication, May 19, 2021.

67. *Trinitonian*, Dec. 12, 1975, 12.

68. Ibid., 7.

69. O'Neill interview, May 30, 2019.

70. *Trinitonian*, Oct. 1, 1976, 11; Oct. 22, 1976, 11.

71. SCA, Minutes of Trinity University Athletic Council, Nov. 26, 1974, Wimpress Presidential Papers; Kaplan interview, Jan. 22, 2018; Davis Carter communication, June 28, 2021. The noontime group ran out of the Sams Center for decades and included Trinity professors Douglas Brackenridge, David Oliver, Scott Baird, Hal Barger, Ken Hummel, and John Donahue, as well as several Presbyterian ministers and a local dentist.

72. Davis Carter communication, June 28, 2021.

73. Pasley interview, Nov. 1, 2017.

74. Spencer communication, Feb. 14, 2021; Munt communication, Oct. 26, 2021.

75. *Trinitonian*, Sept. 20, 1974, 5. TCIAW became TAIAW in March 1974 as TCAIAW realigned its structures to be compatible with AIAW at the national level. At this point, the policy of allowing athletic scholarships enabled Trinity teams to be ranked intercollegiate rather than extramural. See Goodloe, *Before Brittney*, 32–36.

Chapter 9. New Hurdles Emerge

1. Janet Nguyen, "5 things to know about the inflation crisis during the '70s," Sept. 5, 2018, www.marketplace.org/2018/09/05/5-things-70s-inflation/. Ironically, this worldwide price spike helped Trinity, refilling the university's depleted endowment since it was heavily invested in oil and gas ventures. Brackenridge, *Tale of Three Cities*, 276.

2. Daniel T. Rodgers, *Age of Fracture* (Cambridge, MA: Belknap Press, 2011), 150, 164.

3. *Trinitonian*, Nov. 18, 1977, 4, 5.

4. Edith Grinnell, "The Last Mile: 1977," www.jofreeman.com/photos/Houston remember.html.

5. Kokernot's Feb. 28, 2007, letter, can be viewed at http://dianamarahenry.com/stamps /PegKokernotKaplanendorsement.htm.

6. SCA, Minutes of the Trinity Intercollegiate Athletic Council, Nov. 26, 1974, and April 2, 1976; Wimpress Presidential Papers; Jeré Longman, "At Texas A&M, a Long Journey to the Final Four," *New York Times*, March 30, 2011.

7. *Trinitonian*, April 29, 1977, 8.

8. *Mirage*, 1976, 113.

9. *Trinitonian*, Dec. 3, 1976, 9.

10. Ibid., Sept. 10, 1976, 11.

11. Ibid., April 2, 1976, 12, 13.

12. SCA, Letter from Duncan Wimpress to Hugh Meredith, April 2, 1975, Wimpress Presidential Papers.

13. *Trinitonian*, Sept. 10, 1976, 11.

14. SCA, Minutes of the Combined Meeting of the Administrative Council and Board of Directors of the Texas Intercollegiate Athletic Association, April 14, 1978, Thomas Presidential Papers, Box 01-22, Folder Intercollegiate Athletics.

15. *Trinitonian*, Feb. 20, 1981, 13.

16. Brackenridge, *Tale of Three Cities*, 262–64. The conference had problems getting underway. See *Trinitonian*, Sept. 10, 1976, 11.

17. SCA, Minutes of the Trinity Intercollegiate Athletic Council, Nov. 26, 1974 and April 2, 1976, Wimpress Presidential Papers.

18. *Trinitonian*, Feb. 4, 1977, 9. Pasley may have intended to reference junior Tommy Toler in the article.

19. Ibid.

20. SCA, Memorandum Moore to Parmer; 1976 Self-Study, 123, 268–69.

21. Hailey interview, Jan. 12, 2018.

22. *Trinitonian*, Feb. 4, 1977, 9.

23. Ibid., April 25, 1980, 17.

24. Ibid., April 2, 1976, 14.

25. Ibid., July 3, 1975, 3.

26. Ibid., April 2, 1976, 14. Garcia actually wrote that Johnson "yells exasperatedly" in her response, although there's no confirmation that was her demeanor at the time.

27. Hailey interview, Jan. 12, 2018.

28. SCA, Memorandum, Committee on Intercollegiate Athletics, April 1976, Box 01-22, Bruce Thomas Papers, Folder Athletics.

29. Fields, "Women's Athletics."

30. *Trinitonian*, Sept. 15, 1978, 2.

31. Ibid., Dec. 9, 1977, 10.

32. Ibid., Oct. 20, 1978, 2.

33. Ibid., Jan. 27, 1978, 11.

34. Festle, *Playing Nice*, 249.

35. *Trinitonian*, Feb. 4, 1977, 10.

36. Ibid., Sept. 10, 1976, 9.

37. Ibid., April 2, 1976, 14.

38. SCA, Memorandum Moore to Parmer.

39. *Trinitonian*, Feb. 1, 1980, 15.

40. Hailey interview, Jan. 12, 2018.

41. Festle, *Playing Nice*, 191.

42. Edward Jaworski, "Women's Sports Are Doing Just Fine," *New York Times*, Aug. 6, 1978.

43. *Trinitonian*, Feb. 16, 1979, 23.

44. U.S. Department of Justice, "Equal Access to Education."

45. Wushanley, *Playing Nice and Losing*, 111.

46. *Trinitonian*, Sept. 23, 1978, 10.

47. Ibid., Sept. 21, 1979, 14.

48. Ibid., Oct. 19, 1979, 18.

49. Ibid.

50. Hailey interview, Jan. 12, 2018.

51. Brackenridge, *Tale of Three Cities*, 314.

52. Trinity University, *Trinity University: Honoring the Past, Shaping the Future* (San Antonio: Trinity University Press, 2019), 126.

53. Parmer would lead the charge for stricter admission standards; by 1979 Trinity was second only to Houston's Rice University in average SAT scores of incoming freshmen. Brackenridge, *Tale of Three Cities*, 286, 316–18.

54. *Trinitonian*, March 18, 1977, 9.

55. At the time of Moore's 1979 report, the decade's only substantive improvement in facilities was the conversion of the "Slab" to the Pittman courts in 1977. This provided a third set of tennis courts for the women's Division I team to practice on, especially when conditions were windy. *Mirage*, 1977, 79; Foster communication, Dec. 1, 2020.

56. SCA, Memorandum Moore to Parmer; 1976 Self-Study, 123, 268–69.

57. *Trinitonian*, April 25, 1980, 17.

58. Ibid.

59. Ibid.

60. Ibid., Feb. 1, 1980, 13.

61. Interview with Shirley Rushing, Trinity University Athletic Histories, April 29, 2016, https://spmt3314.omeka.net/exhibits/show/libby-johnson/interviews/shirleypoteet.

62. *Trinitonian*, Feb. 1, 1980, 13.

63. Douglas Brackenridge communication with Gerald Smetzer, Nov. 10, 2016.

64. *Trinitonian*, Feb. 1, 1980, 13. The Student Senate subcommittee on intercollegiate sports was formed to "investigate the problem" and included female athletes Joy Scharf and Dorian Martin.

65. Ibid., 2, 13.

66. Ibid., Feb. 12, 1980, 2.

67. Ibid., Oct. 19, 1979, 19; April 18, 1980, 14.

68. St. Clair interview, June 1, 2018.

69. *Trinitonian*, Oct. 15, 1976, 10.

70. Hailey interview, Jan. 12, 2018.

71. Libby Johnson obituary, *San Antonio Light*, June 14, 1991. She was survived by her brother, Donald E. Johnson, who died in Fort Worth, Texas, on Nov. 20, 2011.

72. Munt interview, Dec. 17, 2017.
73. Machu interview, May 13, 2020.

Chapter 10. Transition Woes

1. Hill, "Fact check." This article addressed a common social media thread about the "9 things women couldn't do in 1971." The authors fact check each point and list the legislation that provides resolution of the issue.
2. Cruikshank, "Birch Bayh: Biography." Bayh's state of Indiana was the last to ratify the ERA, in 1977, before the extended deadline—which he helped negotiate—expired in 1982.
3. Festle, *Playing Nice*, 196.
4. Rodgers, *Age of Fracture*, 149.
5. *Trinitonian*, Jan. 22, 1982, 2.
6. *Trinity Magazine*, spring 1986, 9.
7. Goodloe, *Before Brittney*, 213.
8. "Title IX: Legislation that leveled the playing field," *Golf Week*, June 23, 2012.
9. *Newsweek* quotations are lifted from a story in the *Trinitonian*, Oct. 17, 1980, 18.
10. *Trinitonian*, Oct. 17, 1980, 18.
11. Suzanne C. Willey, "The Governance of Women's Intercollegiate Athletics: Association for Intercollegiate Athletics for Women (AIAW), 1976–1982," Doctoral Dissertation, Indiana University, Dec. 1966, 17–20.
12. Wushanley, *Playing Nice and Losing*, 134, 194.
13. Bell, "History of Women in Sport."
14. Goodloe, *Before Brittney*, 29.
15. Wushanley, *Playing Nice and Losing*, 139; Festle, *Playing Nice*, 203. Much of the NCAA's revenue came from sponsorships, while the AIAW's was primarily from membership fees.
16. Fields, "Appeals Court Rejects Charge."
17. Goodloe, *Before Brittney*, 30.
18. Goodloe, *Before Brittney*, 31. Mulkey would return to her home state in 2021, leaving Baylor for Louisiana State University
19. Fields, "Women's Sports Group."
20. Goodloe, *Before Brittney*, 32.
21. Festle, *Playing Nice*, 225.
22. *Trinitonian*, Dec. 5, 1980, 17.
23. "NCAA Graduation Rates: A Quarter-Century of Tracking Academic Success," NCAA, www.ncaa.org/about/resources/research/ncaa-graduation-rates-quarter-century-tracking-academic-success.
24. *Trinitonian*, Dec. 5, 1980, 17, 19.
25. Ibid., Feb. 5, 1982, 5. "Home and home" is a reference to the requirement that each school plays its conference football opponent twice in a season—once on their home field and once on the opponent's. This made scheduling difficult but provided a fair approach in a sport where home-field advantage is often significant.
26. Ibid., March 26, 1982, 10.
27. Brackenridge, *Tale of Three Cities*, 327.
28. *Trinitonian*, Feb. 11, 1982, 2.

29. Ibid., Feb. 5, 1982, 2.

30. SCA, Letter from Ronald Calgaard to Harry Fritz, Aug. 4, 1982, Calgaard Presidential Papers, Box 02-27, Folder NCAA Correspondence/Reports; *Trinitonian*, Feb. 6, 1982, 5.

31. *Trinitonian*, Sept. 26, 1980, 15.

32. Box 88, folder 38, "Personalities," Robert V. Hockey, Trinity University Archives.

33. During an unrecorded conversation between Douglas Brackenridge and Ron Calgaard before his death in 2020, Calgaard did not remember any specific reason for not filling the position other than an effort to centralize authority in physical education and athletics. Hockey also brought a broader resume to the position, including a doctoral degree and specialties in fields other than coaching.

34. Hailey interview, Jan. 12, 2018.

35. Walker Luna interview, Dec. 7, 2017.

36. *Trinitonian*, Feb. 20, 1981, 13.

37. Hailey interview, Jan. 12, 2018.

38. *Mirage*, 1981, 206.

39. *Trinitonian*, Sept. 4, 1981, 9.

40. Ibid., Nov. 6, 1981, 10; Nov. 16, 1981, 10. See also, *Mirage*, 1982, 204–5. Technically, Trinity was required to compete in regional playoffs in order to gain a Division III national bid, but no Division III teams in Arkansas or Louisiana competed in volleyball. In effect the TAIAW state tournament served as a regional tournament.

41. *Mirage*, 1984, 213–14.

42. *Trinitonian*, Feb. 19, 1982, 8; *Mirage*, 1982, 215.

43. Ibid., Jan. 16, 1983, 10.

44. Ibid., March 26, 1982, 9.

45. Ibid., Sept. 19, 1980, 14; Oct. 10, 1980, 12.

46. Ibid., Sept. 9, 1983, 15.

47. Ibid., Nov. 21, 1980, 18.

48. *Course of Study Bulletin*, 1980, 260; *Trinitonian*, April 18, 1983, 7, 10.

49. Personal recollection of Douglas Brackenridge.

50. Hailey interview, Jan. 12, 2018.

51. *Trinitonian*, Sept. 30, 1983, 16–17.

52. Interview with Suzanne Anderson, July 6, 2020.

53. *Trinitonian*, Oct. 10, 1980, 13.

54. Anderson interview, July 6, 2020.

55. *Trinitonian*, Feb. 10, 1984, 19.

56. *Mirage*, 1985, 64.

57. *Trinitonian*, Dec. 2, 1983, 25.

58. *Mirage*, 1985, 64.

59. *Trinitonian*, Feb. 1, 1985, 1.

60. *Mirage*, 1985, 134.

61. *Trinitonian*, April 13, 1984, 21.

Chapter 11. Hope on the Horizon

1. Julie Jenkins speech at September 13, 2017, dedication of Ron and Genie Calgaard Gym.

2. *Trinity Magazine*, spring 1986, 13.

3. *Trinitonian*, Oct. 19, 1984, 10–11; April 25, 1986, 9. The reference to "letters" might have been proverbial, since in an April 2022 communication McCabe doesn't recall receiving any.

4. Jenkins interview, May 27, 2017.

5. *Trinitonian*, Nov. 7, 1986, 10.

6. Ibid., Sept. 18, 1987, 9.

7. Harry Page, "Trinity Alums Ready to Help," *San Antonio Express-News*, April 12, 1987.

8. *Trinitonian*, April 16, 1987, 7; April 24, 1987, 13.

9. Ibid., Nov. 20, 1987, 11.

10. Ibid., March 27, 1987, 12.

11. Ibid., Feb. 12, 1988, 16.

12. Ibid., April 1, 1986, 6. The headline over both fake game recaps was "Trinity falls just short."

13. Festle, *Playing Nice*, 219.

14. *Grove City College v. Bell*, www.oyez.org/cases/1983/82-792.

15. U.S. Department of Justice, "Equal Access to Education"; "Civil Rights Restoration Act of 1987," www.govtrack.us/congress/bills/100/s557.

16. Ibid.

17. Irvin Molotsky, "House and Senate Vote to Override Reagan on Rights," *New York Times*, March 23, 1988.

18. "The 14th Amendment and the Evolution of Title IX," www.uscourts.gov/educational-resources/educational-activities/14th-amendment-and-evolution-title-ix.

19. Fields, "Appeals Court Rejects Charge."

20. *Trinitonian*, Sept. 6, 1985, 9.

21. Ibid., April 8, 1988, 32; *Mirage*, 1987, 116–17.

22. *Trinitonian*, April 8, 1988, 32; Nov. 11, 1988, 22.

23. *Mirage*, 1985, 85.

24. *Trinitonian*, Sept. 13, 1985, 11.

25. Ibid., Sept. 12, 1986, 10, 11; Dec. 5, 1986, 12; *Mirage*, 1987, 126–27, 221.

26. Jenkins interview, May 27, 2017, and Feb. 20, 2020.

27. *Trinitonian*, Sept. 30, 1988, 8.

28. Ibid., April 1, 1989, 4.

29. Brackenridge, *Tale of Three Cities*, 359.

30. *Trinitonian*, Sept. 11, 1987, 6. Boerne High School paid for the relocation expenses.

31. The facilities most commonly used by the softball team were Rusty Lyons, Tony Martinez, Lambert Beach, and Olmos fields. Communication with Teresa Machu, Jan. 2021.

32. *Mirage*, 1988, 48; *Trinitonian*, Feb. 3, 1989, 16; April 28, 1989, 12.

33. *Trinitonian*, April 1, 1988, 19.

34. Unrecorded telephone interview, Douglas Brackenridge with Ronald K. Calgaard, Jan. 20, 2018.

35. *Mirage*, 1989, 54.

36. *Trinitonian*, Feb. 21, 1986, 4; April 22, 1988, 17.

37. *Trinitonian*, Feb. 14, 1992, 2.

38. Ibid., Feb. 28, 1986, 3.

39. Ibid., April 1, 1989, 4. The authorship of the faux column was attributed to Gloria Steinem.

40. *Trinitonian*, Oct. 13, 1989, 1.

41. SCA, "Report of the Institutional Self-Study for the Commission on Colleges of the Southern Association of Colleges and Schools," 1986 Trinity University Self-Study, 238–39; Ghent, *Calgaard's Calling*, 10.

42. *Trinitonian*, Jan. 26, 1990, 24.

43. "Title IX: Legislation that leveled the playing field."

Chapter 12. Promises Fulfilled

1. Rodgers, *Age of Fracture*, 178.

2. *Trinitonian*, Sept. 7, 1990, 4.

3. In Ron Calgaard's first decade, graduate degrees offered at Trinity declined from ten to three.

4. *Trinitonian*, April 28, 1989, 1, 5, 8.

5. 1986 Trinity University Self-Study, 238–40. See also *Trinitonian*, Sept. 9, 1988, 4; Nov. 1988, 12; Sept. 8, 1989, 4; Oct. 27, 1989, 7.

6. 1986 Trinity University Self-Study, 240.

7. *Trinitonian*, Feb. 12, 1986, 16.

8. Ibid., Feb. 23, 1990, 21. During Southwestern University's history with the NAIA, the NAIA had one division; it added a second in 1992 after Southwestern's decision to drop scholarships and leave the organization. Also, the university did not have a men's football program between 1951 and 2013.

9. Suggs, "Historical Overview," 19. The organization that once had more than 450 institutions had just 249 in 2020, many of which switched to NCAA Division II or III.

10. William B. Jones, *To Survive and Excel: The Story of Southwestern University, 1840–2000* (Georgetown, TX: Southwestern University, 2006), 520–24.

11. Munt communication, Dec. 14, 2020; April 21 and May 27, 2021.

12. "List of college athletic programs in Texas," Wikipedia, last modified June 8, 2022, https://en.wikipedia.org/wiki/List_of_college_athletic_programs_in_Texas#Division_III. As of 2022 there were sixteen Division III schools in Texas.

13. *Trinitonian*, Sept. 7, 1990, 24.

14. Brackenridge, *Tale of Three Cities*, 357.

15. The men and women were ranked twenty-fifth and twenty-second respectively in 1990.

16. Ghent, *Calgaard's Calling*, 6.

17. *Trinitonian*, Oct. 12, 1990, 1. At the time this was only true of schools outside of Texas, since Trinity was the state's sole Division III member in 1990.

18. *Trinitonian*, Oct. 12, 1990, 1.

19. Brackenridge, *Tale of Three Cities*, 357–58.

20. *Trinitonian*, Oct. 5, 1990, 1; Oct. 12, 1990, 1, 12, 14; Brackenridge, *Tale of Three Cities*, 357–58.

21. *Trinitonian*, April 9, 1999, 2.

22. Ibid., Oct. 12, 1990, 1.

23. Ibid.

24. *Trinitonian*, Oct. 12, 1990; *Mirage*, 1991, 18.

25. *Mirage*, 1991, 21.
26. *Trinitonian*, March 27, 1992, 23, 25.
27. *Mirage*, 1991, 2–3, 10.
28. Ibid., April 28, 1989, 15.
29. Ibid., Oct. 12, 1990, 4.
30. Ibid., Oct. 12, 1990, 3.
31. Ibid., Sept. 1, 1989, 6.
32. Ibid., Feb. 22, 1991, 22; Feb. 1, 1991, 17.
33. Ibid., April 12, 1991, 21.
34. Bellis, "Back on Top."
35. Interview with Butch Newman, March 5, 2019.
36. *Trinitonian*, April 24, 1992, 34.
37. Rushing interview, July 7 and 15, 2020. Later Calgaard told a student that he questioned the myth of national recognition from the program after those decades, asking attendees at a board meeting if they knew the most recent men's Division I tennis champions. "Who can tell me?" he asked. "Not a soul," he remembered. Ghent, *Calgaard's Calling*, 6.
38. *Trinitonian*, April 10, 1992, 24; April 9, 1999, 2. While the full impact is unknown, this figure probably doesn't take into account lost donations from local benefactors who supported the Division I program.
39. *Trinitonian*, Sept. 20, 1991, 23.
40. "Bridging the Gender Gap: The Positive Effects of Title IX," Athnet, www.athleticscholarships.net/title-ix-college-athletics-3.htm.
41. Suggs, "Historical Overview," 22.
42. This wasn't a surprise, since only two female senators served in the hundred-person chamber—the same number present the year Title IX legislation was signed, and also on its tenth anniversary in 1982.
43. "Year of the Woman," U.S. Senate, Nov. 3, 1992, www.senate.gov/artandhistory/history/minute/year_of_the_woman.htm.
44. John Piper & Wayne Grudem, *Recovering Biblical Manhood and Womanhood: A Response to Evangelical Feminism* (1991), 38, 63.
45. R. Claire Snyder-Hall, "Third Wave Feminism and the Defense of Choice," *Perspectives on Politics* 8, no. 1 (2010): 255–61.
46. *Trinitonian*, March 20, 1992, 11; March 27, 1992, 14. The Women's Interest Center was formed in 1988 to give students an opportunity to "foster an open and receptive atmosphere for thoughtful women and men at Trinity," where feminism is taken seriously rather than being "flippantly written off." Another objective of the center was to encourage the addition of a women's studies program; that goal was met in 1989 with the first offering of a minor in women's studies. *Trinitonian*, April 22, 1994, 11, 13; Feb. 24, 1989, 4.
47. Ibid., Jan. 21, 1994, 11–13; April 22, 1994, 13.
48. Ratios favoring men's athletics—despite equal enrollment—included participation 70/30; operating budget 77/23; scholarship funds 70/30; and recruiting funds 83/17. Final report of the NCAA Gender Equity Task Force, 1993, 80. "Achieving Gender Equity: A Basic Guide to Title IX and Gender Equity in Athletics for Colleges and Universities" (Overland Park, KS: NCAA, n.d.); *NCAA News*, Aug. 4, 1993, 1, 14–16.

49. Malcolm Moran, "Campus Changes Coming, Like It or Not," *New York Times*, June 22, 1992.

50. Amy Shipley, "Playing Field Levels at Texas," *Washington Post*, July 6, 1997.

51. Festle, *Playing Nice*, 273.

52. Festle, *Playing Nice*, 280.

53. Brackenridge, *Tale of Three Cities*, 357–58.

54. *Mirage*, 1993, 92; Jenkins interview, Feb. 20, 2020.

55. "Top 20 Moments, Baseball," SCAC, May 20, 2011, https://scacsports.com/inside_athletics/anniversary20/top20_bsb_a.

56. King interview, June 25, 2020.

57. *Trinitonian*, April 6, 1990, 2.

58. Ibid., Aug. 31, 1990, 19.

59. Brackenridge, *Tale of Three Cities*, 359–60; *Trinitonian*, Feb. 8, 1991, 22.

60. *Trinitonian*, April 29, 1989, 80.

61. *Mirage*, 1991, 25.

62. *Trinitonian*, Aug. 22, 1992, 39.

63. Ibid, Sept. 4, 1992, 26.

64. *Mirage*, 1991, 25; *Trinitonian*, April 17, 1998, 15.

65. *Trinitonian*, Aug. 28, 1993, 44.

66. Although Southwestern University made its decision to exit the NAIA in 1990, it hadn't yet completed its transition to Division III as the second Texas team in the division.

67. Jenkins speech at Calgaard Gym dedication; Terrence Thomas, "Volleyball Coach Trinity's Big Winner," *San Antonio Express-News*, Oct. 20, 2017.

68. *Trinitonian*, April 23, 1993, 25.

69. Ibid., Jan. 28, 1994, 10.

70. Interview with Amy Waddell Stewart, May 20, 2020.

71. *Trinitonian*, Sept. 8, 1995, 24.

72. Ibid., March 25, 1994, 27, 30.

73. Interview with Dwayne Hanberry, Nov. 12, 2020.

74. "Southern Collegiate Athletic Conference," Wikipedia, last modified May 18, 2022, https://en.wikipedia.org/wiki/Southern_Collegiate_Athletic_Conference.

75. *Trinitonian*, Sept. 2, 1988, 13.

76. Ibid., Aug. 31, 1990, 20.

77. Ibid., Sept. 2, 1988, 13.

78. Jenkins speech at Calgaard Gym dedication.

79. *Trinitonian*, April 24, 1992, 33, 36.

80. *Trinitonian*, Sept. 20, 1991, 23.

81. Ibid., March 27, 1992, 23.

82. Ibid., Jan. 26, 1990, 23.

83. Ibid., Oct. 30, 1992, 22.

84. Ibid., Jan. 26, 1990, 23; Oct. 30, 1992, 22–23.

85. Anderson interview, July 6, 2020.

86. *Mirage*, 1991, 74.

87. Ibid., Nov. 19, 1993, 19; Aug. 27, 1994, 4.

88. *Course of Study Bulletin*, 1991, 234.

89. The others are Clarence Mabry in 1999, Ron Calgaard in 2005, and Shirley Rushing

in 2022. Trinity University's Hall of Fame, https://trinitytigers.com/history/halloffame/index.

90. *Trinitonian*, Oct. 4, 1991, 24; SCA, "Report of the Institutional Self-Study for the Commission on Colleges of the Southern Association of Colleges and Schools," 1996 Trinity University Self-Study, 209.

91. *Trinitonian*, Sept. 6, 1991, 28.

92. Ibid., Dec. 2, 1994, 23.

93. Ibid., Feb. 14, 1992, 10; Dec. 2, 1994, 23. Bristor claimed that Trinity was one of the few schools that also provided trainers for intramural competition.

94. Interview with Yanika Daniels, May 14, 2020.

95. Interview with Shelley Story, May 29, 2020.

96. Interview with Bob King, June 25, 2020.

97. Tom Orsborn, "Trinity's King excels at his 'pretty cool' job," *San Antonio Express-News*, June 16, 2015.

98. Rushing interview, July 7 and 15, 2020.

99. *Trinitonian*, April 16, 1993, 8; *Mirage*, 1993, 92.

100. *Trinitonian*, Aug. 25, 1993, 44.

101. Orsborn, "Trinity's King excels."

102. King interview, June 25, 2020.

103. *Trinitonian*, Nov. 5, 1993.

104. Ibid., Nov. 12, 1993, 10.

105. Ibid., Nov. 4, 1994, 21.

106. King interview, June 25, 2020.

107. Ibid.

108. Jenkins interview, May 27, 2017.

109. *Mirage*, 1998, 256.

110. *Trinitonian*, Dec. 6, 1991, 23.

111. Ibid.

112. "Title IX turns 45."

113. Interview with Halie Bricker Benson, June 8, 2020.

114. "Munt Reflects on the 40th Anniversary"; Munt communication, Oct. 26, 2021.

115. *Trinitonian*, April 7, 1995, 21.

116. Rushing interview, July 7 and 15, 2020.

Chapter 13. Leaving the Sidelines

1. Brackenridge, *Tale of Three Cities*, 357–58.

2. Supplies and expenses (S&E) is a common reference used in all Trinity department budgets; it excludes any salaries or special funding.

3. SCA, 1996 Trinity University Self-Study.

4. *Trinitonian*, Dec. 6, 1996, 32.

5. "Our Three Divisions," NCAA, www.ncaa.org/about/resources/media-center/ncaa-101/our-three-divisions.

6. "Division III," NCAA, www.ncaa.org/sports/d3.

7. Jenkins speech at Calgaard Gym dedication.

8. Interview with Justin Parker, June 25, 2020.

9. Hanberry interview, Nov. 12, 2020.

10. *Trinitonian*, March 27, 1992, 28.
11. Ibid., 23.
12. *Trinitonian*, April 3, 1992, 7.
13. Parker interview, June 25, 2020.
14. *Trinitonian*, Feb. 3, 1995, 22.
15. "SCAC Academic Honor Roll," SCAC, https://scacsports.prestosports.com/awardsHonors/all_academic/index. The names of recipients of this award from its 1997–98 commencement to the present are archived on the SCAC web page.
16. Brackenridge, *Tale of Three Cities*, 360. The retention rate compares the advancement of first-year students to second-year status.
17. "Texas Intercollegiate Athletic Association (1976–1997)," Wikipedia, last modified April 21, 2022, https://en.wikipedia.org/wiki/Texas_Intercollegiate_Athletic_Association_(1976–1997).
18. Munt communication, Dec. 14, 2020; April 21 and May 27, 2021.
19. *Trinitonian*, March 27, 1992, 23, 28.
20. Ibid., Sept. 15, 2000, 16.
21. Stewart interview, May 20, 2020.
22. Newman interview, March 5, 2019.
23. Hanberry interview, Nov. 12, 2020.
24. Newman interview, March 5, 2019.
25. *Trinitonian*, April 28, 2000, 29. Despite his expressed disenchantment, Cowell left Trinity after the 1998–99 season to lead the Division I Baylor University soccer program. After four years he would return to coaching Division III at SCAC rival Sewanee, and then at St. Edwards University in Austin.
26. *Trinitonian*, Sept. 15, 2000, 16.
27. Ibid., April 7, 2000, 14; March 30, 2001, 16. Tiger TV was launched in 1996 when a cable network was installed across campus. It included a dedicated channel for student-oriented and hosted programming. *Trinitonian*, Aug. 24, 1996, 18.
28. Ibid., April 16, 1993, 8.
29. "SCAC President's Trophy," SCAC, March 10, 2022, https://scacsports.com/awardsHonors/presidents_trophy.
30. The SCAC spring festival would be discontinued in 2017.
31. King interview, June 25, 2020.
32. SCAC, https://scacsports.com/landing/index.
33. "SCAC President's Trophy Results," SCAC, May 18, 2022, https://scacsports.com/awardsHonors/presidents_trophy_results.
34. *Trinitonian*, April 25, 1997, 16.
35. Ibid., April 23, 1999, 31.
36. Ibid, Aug. 27, 1999, 26.
37. *Trinitonian*, April 16, 1999, 23.
38. Hanberry interview, Nov. 12, 2020.
39. Riordan, "In Praise of Division III Athletics."
40. Newman interview, March 5, 2019.
41. Jones, *To Survive and Excel*, 522–24.
42. *Trinitonian*, Feb. 28, 1992, 30.
43. Ibid., Feb. 5, 1993, 19.

44. Ibid., Jan. 20, 1995, 24–25; Jan. 27, 1995, 20.

45. Ibid., Feb. 3, 1995, 20; Feb. 17, 1995, 20.

46. Story interview, May 29, 2020; *Trinitonian*, Feb. 25, 1994, 22.

47. *Trinitonian*, Jan. 19, 1999, 16; "Trinity Softball Coach Resigns," Trinity University Athletics: Softball, May 7, 2010, www.trinitytigers.com/sports/sball/2009-10/releases/5-7-2010_Coach_Resigns; "SCAC Softball, Past Champions," SCAC, https://scacsports.com/sports/sball/past_champions/main; "Top 20 Moments, Softball," SCAC, https://scacsports.com/awardsHonors/anniversary20/top20_sball.

48. *Trinitonian*, Sept. 6, 1991, 34.

49. Ibid., Sept. 4, 1992, 28; Nov. 6, 1992, 20; Nov. 13, 1992, 23. Also "Top 20 Moments, Women's Soccer," SCAC, Dec. 17, 2010, https://scacsports.com/awardsHonors/anniversary20/top20_wsoc.

50. *Trinitonian*, Nov. 10, 1995, 20.

51. Ibid., Oct. 11, 1996, 31.

52. *Mirage*, 1997, 132.

53. "Top 20 Moments, Women's Soccer."

54. *Trinitonian*, Nov. 15, 1996, 25.

55. Ibid., April 28, 2000, 29.

56. "Modern pentathlon," Wikipedia, last modified June 5, 2022, https://en.wikipedia.org/wiki/Modern_pentathlon.

57. *Trinitonian*, March 20, 1998, 18.

58. Ibid., Feb. 5, 2000, 17.

59. *Trinitonian*, March 25, 1994, 27; Oct. 29, 1993, 33; "SCAC Women's Track and Field, Past Champions," SCAC, www.scacsports.com/sports/wtrack/past_champions/main.

60. Ibid., Dec. 1, 1995, 3.

61. "Trinity Tigers Records," Trinity University Athletics: Track and Field, www.trinitytigers.com/sports/track/Records/WTF_Records.pdf.

62. "Sewanee's Stone highlights Southern Collegiate Athletic Conference's 15th anniversary track and field team," SCAC, https://scacsports.com/inside_athletics/anniversary15/wtrackfield.

63. *Trinitonian*, March 17, 2000, 20.

64. Ibid., Aug. 31, 1990, 20.

65. Ibid., Oct. 5, 1990, 23.

66. Ibid., Oct. 25, 1991, 23.

67. Ibid., Nov. 21, 1997, 22; "NCAA Division III National Cross Country Championships," Pitzer Athletics, Nov. 22, 1997, www.sagehens.com/sports/wxc/HistoriansReport/Results/1997women.htm.

68. *Trinitonian*, April 8, 1994, 22; Sept. 9, 1994, 24; SCAC, scacsports.com/sports/wgolf/archive/index. King had been working on adding golf to the SCAC, starting when he was athletic director at Millsaps College.

69. *Trinitonian*, Aug. 28, 1998, 31, 38; Sept. 11, 1998, 18.

70. Ibid., Feb. 16, 1996, 22.

71. Ibid., Sept. 23, 1994, 20.

72. Ibid., March 31, 2000, 24.

73. Ibid., April 7, 2000, 11.

74. *Trinitonian*, Feb. 14, 1997, 20.

75. Ibid., Jan. 22, 1998, 4.

76. Ibid., Dec. 3, 1999, 20.

77. "Top 20 Moments, Women's Volleyball," SCAC, Nov. 12, 2010, www.scacsports.com /awardsHonors/anniversary20/top20_wvball.

78. *Trinitonian*, Dec. 3, 1999, 20

79. Ibid., Aug. 19, 2000, 30.

80. "Top 20 Moments, Women's Tennis," SCAC, June 2, 2011, https://scacsports .prestosports.com/awardsHonors/anniversary20/top20_wten.

81. *Trinitonian*, Aug. 19, 2000, 25.

82. "Trinity's 2000 National Championship Tennis Teams," Trinity University Athletics, www.trinitytigers.com/legends/2000_national_championships/.

83. Ibid., Sept. 17, 1999, 19; "Top 20 Moments, Women's Tennis."

84. Bellis, "Back on Top."

85. "Title IX: 25 Years of Progress," U.S. Department of Education, June 1997, https:// webarchive.loc.gov/all/20210210090718/https://www2.ed.gov/pubs/TitleIX/index.html.

86. Festle, *Playing Nice*, 276–77. The Olympic pay was $50,000, while many players could earn $300,000 overseas.

87. "USA, An Overview of American Women's Soccer History," RecSportsStatistics-Foundation, https://www.rsssf.org/usadave/am-soc-overview-wom.html.

88. Maggie Mertens, "The Title IX Loophole That Hurts NCAA Women's Teams," *Atlantic*, April 1, 2021.

89. *Trinitonian*, Dec. 4, 1998, 14.

90. Ibid., Jan. 29, 1999, 7.

91. Ibid., March 31, 1999, 3.

92. Brackenridge, *Tale of Three Cities*, 371.

93. Ibid., 372.

94. Jenkins speech at Calgaard Gym dedication.

95. *Trinitonian*, Jan. 24, 2014, 10.

96. Ibid., April 28, 2000, 31.

97. Ibid., Aug. 28, 1998, 34.

98. Ibid., July 27, 1999, 26.

99. Brackenridge, *Tale of Three Cities*, 360.

100. *Trinitonian*, Jan. 21, 2000, 19.

Chapter 14. Two Decades of Steady Progress

1. Rushing interview, July 7 and 15, 2020.

2. "Tiger Athletics."

3. "Division III Schools," *Sports Illustrated for Women*, Sept.–Oct. 2000.

4. *Trinitonian*, Sept. 15, 2000, 8. The 2000 Summer Olympics in Sydney, Australia, didn't begin until Sept. 15.

5. Ibid., April 27, 2001, 20.

6. Brackenridge, *Tale of Three Cities*, 382.

7. *Trinitonian*, Aug. 22, 2003, 24. Trinity was listed in the NACDA top ten rankings in the 1998–99 and 1999–2000 academic years. King's programs would again finish fourth in 2004–5 and in the top ten the following year.

8. "Division III Schools."

9. Kate Stringer, "No One Would Hire Her. So She Wrote Title IX and Changed History for Millions of Women. Meet Education Trailblazer Patsy Mink," *The 74*, March 1, 2018, www.the74million.org/article/no-one-would-hire-her-so-she-wrote-title-ix-and-changed-history-for-millions-of-women-meet-education-trailblazer-patsy-mink/.

10. Ashley Fetters, "4 big problems with the Feminine Mystique," *Atlantic*, Feb. 12, 2013; "The Gender Pay Gap Widens with Age," National Bureau of Economic Research, July 2017; Claire Cain Miller, "The Gender Pay Gap Is Largely Because of Motherhood," *New York Times*, May 13, 2017.

11. U.S. Department of Justice, "Equal Access to Education." The report cited one case that addressed retaliation of a male Alabama high school coach who was removed from his position after he complained about unequal funding for his girls' basketball team.

12. The uncomfortable fact that the NCAA was a strong opponent to Title IX—and even filed lawsuits to stop it—wasn't overlooked in its own report, which said "the reactions to Title IX's application to athletics were intense."

13. "The Status of Women in Intercollegiate Athletics as Title IX Turns 40," NCAA, June 2012, www.ncaapublications.com/p-4289-the-status-of-women-in-intercollegiate-athletics-as-title-ix-turns-40-june-2012.aspx; Jaeah Lee and Maya Dusenbery, "Charts: The State of Women's Athletics, 40 Years After Title IX," *Mother Jones*, June 22, 2012, www.motherjones.com/politics/2012/06/charts-womens-athletics-title-nine-ncaa/; "Number of NCAA college athletes reaches all-time high," NCAA, Oct. 10, 2018, www.ncaa.org/about/resources/media-center/news/number-ncaa-college-athletes-reaches-all-time-high.

14. "The Status of Women."

15. Ibid, 12.

16. Acosta and Carpenter, "Women in Intercollegiate Sport," 1.

17. Ibid, 5.

18. Basketball is an outlier in this coaching statistic.

19. Acosta and Carpenter, "Women in Intercollegiate Sport," 1–2.

20. Stanley Kay, "How Peanuts' Peppermint Patty became a fierce advocate for female athletes," *Sports Illustrated*, Aug. 19, 2016, www.si.com/more-sports/2016/08/19/peppermint-patty-peanuts-charles-schulz-female-athletes.

21. "Status of Women in Intercollegiate Athletics as Title IX Turns 40," 10; Acosta and Carpenter, "Women in Intercollegiate Sport," 2.

22. *Trinitonian*, Jan. 24, 2014, 5–6. As of 2022, former tennis player and 2017 graduate Elena Wilson holds the position of coordinator for athletic recruitment and success.

23. Ibid., Jan. 24, 2014, 5–6; Jan. 31, 2014, 5; Feb. 21, 2014, 5–6; Feb. 28, 2014, 5; "2015 SCAC Fall Record Book," Aug. 11, 2015, 32, https://issuu.com/scacsports/docs/2015_half_two. Per Glada Munt, the disparity in conference school facilities required additional rental costs, so the tradition was canceled after forty-six years.

24. *Trinitonian*, Jan. 31, 2014, 5.

25. The conference set this minimum to maintain automatic playoff bids.

26. Hanberry interview, Nov. 12, 2020.

27. Ibid.

28. "Jenkins Earns 1,000th Victory with Sweeps of Austin, Centenary," Trinity University Athletics: Volleyball, Oct. 1, 2021, www.trinitytigers.com/sports/wvball/2021-22/releases/20211001l99b2h.

29. "College volleyball; Still going strong after four decades; Under Jenkins, Trinity blossoms into a D-III dynasty," *San Antonio Express-News*, Oct. 20, 2017.

30. "Julie Jenkins," Trinity University Athletics: Volleyball, https://trinitytigers.com/sports/wvball/coaches/Julie_Jenkins.

31. *Trinitonian*, March 28, 2003, 1, 18.

32. Paige Mullin, "Herons win National Championship with 2-0 victory over Trinity," William Smith Soccer, Dec. 7, 2013, https://hwsathletics.com/news/2013/12/7/WSSC_1207130717.aspx.

33. *Trinitonian*, Feb. 3, 2006, 23.

34. Ibid., Jan. 14, 2011, 10.

35. Emilie Foster also won four national individual titles, but they were in USLTA tournaments, not NCAA tournaments.

36. "Trinity Collects 10th Straight SCAC Presidents' Trophy," Trinity University Athletics, May 21, 2021, https://trinitytigers.com/general/2020-21/releases/20210521k1jscd.

37. *Trinitonian*, March 27, 1992, 1; *Mirage*, 1992, 25.

38. James Hill, "Intramural Field to be Named in Honor of IM Director," Trinity News, June 5, 2017, www.trinity.edu/news/intramural-field-be-named-honor-im-director.

39. "Al G. Hill Jr. Tennis Stadium," Trinity University Athletics, www.trinitytigers.com/facilities/Al_Hill_Tennis_Stadium. The midcampus Pittman courts (on the old "Slab") were closed in 2021 for other use.

40. "Evolution of the Athletic Center," Trinity News, April 29, 2019, www.trinity.edu/news/evolution-athletic-center.

41. "Historic District Designation," Trinity News, May 30, 2019, www.trinity.edu/news/historic-district-designation.

42. "Bob King," Trinity University Athletics, www.trinitytigers.com/information/directory/bios/B.Kingadminbio09-10.

43. "SCAC Announces 2020–21 Academic Honor Roll Recipients," SCAC, June 25, 2021, https://scacsports.com/inside_athletics/2021_HonorRoll.

44. Orsborn, "Trinity's King excels."

45. These women join Division I tennis stars Carrie Fleming (1976–79), Louise Allen (1981–84), and Gretchen Rush (1983–86) as the only other female Trinity athletes in this exclusive club.

46. "Trinity Hall of Fame."

47. For the second year in a row, no NCAA Division III men's or women's national championships were held because of the pandemic.

48. Maggie Mertens, "The Title IX Loophole That Hurts NCAA Women's Teams," *Atlantic*, April 1, 2021.

49. Alanis Thames, "N.C.A.A. to Use 'March Madness' Slogan for Women's Basketball, Too," *New York Times*, Sept. 29, 2021.

Epilogue

1. Riordan, "In Praise of Division III Athletics."

2. "NCAA Recruiting Facts," NCAA, last modified Aug. 2020, https://ncaaorg.s3.amazonaws.com/compliance/recruiting/NCAA_RecruitingFactSheet.pdf; "Scholarships and Grants for College Students," Debt.org, last modified Feb. 23, 2022, www.debt.org/students/scholarships-and-grants/.

3. Castillon interview, April 10, 2019.

4. Anderson interview, July 6, 2020.

5. Interview with Kerry Eudy, May 19, 2020, and email communication Sept. 30, 2021.

6. "NCAA College sport association racial and gender report card," www.tidesport.org/college.

7. Machu interview, May 13, 2020.

8. Suggs, "Historical Overview," 140; Festle, *Playing Nice*, 225.

9. "2020–21 Women in College Coaching Report Card," WeCOACH, wecoachsports.org/resources/research.

10. Munt interview, Dec. 17, 2017.

11. Acosta and Carpenter, "Women in Intercollegiate Sport," 18.

12. "Women Leaders in College Sports, in Partnership with Arizona State University Law Program Directors, Announce NCAA Division I, II and III Athletic Director Research Findings," Women Leaders in College Sports, Nov. 17, 2020, www.womenleadersincollegesports.org/WL/about/press-releases/women-leaders-asu-law-ncaa-athletic director-research-findings.aspx. As of 2020, Division I had 15 percent female athletic directors and Division II had 21 percent.

13. Acosta and Carpenter, "Women in Intercollegiate Sport," 18, 28, 37.

14. Lopiano, "Gender and Sport," 141.

15. "Where Are the Women?" *Champion* (NCAA), Winter 2017.

16. Munt communication, Dec. 14, 2020; April 21 and May 27, 2021. Trinity's sports information director confirms that the department receives similar feedback from Tiger female teams.

17. Longman, "Number of Women Coaching." Quote is from Nicole M. LaVoi, a codirector of the Tucker Center for Research on Girls and Women in Sport, and U.S. Department of Justice, "Forty Years of Title IX," 13.

18. Lois Elfman, "TIDES Report Shows Increased Diversity in College Sports Is Slow," Diverse: Issues in Higher Education, Feb. 25, 2021. https://diverseeducation.com/article/206038.

19. Christine Brennen, "45th anniversary of Title IX cause for celebration," *USA Today*, June 22, 2017, www.usatoday.com/story/sports/columnist/brennan/2017/06/22/title-ix-45th-anniversary/418751001/.

20. King interview, June 25, 2020.

INDEX

Page references in *italics* refer to figures and photos

Betsy Gerhardt Pasley is a 1977 graduate of Trinity University. A collegiate athlete, she was active in sports information and student publications as a student and became the first female sportswriter at the *San Antonio Light* after graduation. She has more than thirty years of experience in corporate communications for technology, manufacturing, and financial services companies. She lives in San Antonio, Texas.

Jody Conradt coached women's college basketball for thirty-eight years, retiring in 2007 after serving as the head coach for the University of Texas for thirty-one years. In 1998 she became the second woman inducted into the Naismith Memorial Basketball Hall of Fame and was inducted in the inaugural 1999 class for the Women's Basketball Hall of Fame. She remains a passionate leader for women's opportunities in sports and education as the special assistant to the athletic director at the University of Texas.

The publisher and Trinity University thank the following donors, who helped make publication of this book possible.

Trinity University Board of Visitors
Rick and Peggy Kaplan
Jennifer Zinn

Seth and Brooke Asbury
Ronald and Leslie Boerger
Debbie Brackenridge and
Tim Hayes
Laurel Brackenridge
R. Douglas Brackenridge and
Diane G. Saphire
Angela Breidenstein
Molly Mohr Bruni and Justin Bruni
Mary Bueno
Norma Elia Cantú and Elvia Niebla
Jeanette and Eugene Clark
Andries Coetzee
Bethany Coetzee
David J. Deering
Georgia Erck
Jan Fluitt-Dupuy
James Garner
Becky Geyer
Marlyn and Larry Gibbs
Martha Giles
Teresa and Richard Giles
Rick and Dawn Gray
Cameron and Tim Hayes
Alfonso Hernandez
Leslie K. Hollingsworth
Julie B. Jenkins and Terri Hailey
Patti and Harry Jewett
Vanessa Kimble
James Laurie
Ann and Carl Leafstedt
Sally L. Lloyd
Barbara and Mark McBryde
D. Rozena McCabe
Bridget and Matthew McGregor
Celeste Guzmán Mendoza and
Michael Mares Mendoza
Joseph and Karen Motes
Glada Munt
Sandra Nicholson
Jill H. O'Neill
Elizabeth and David Pasley
Thomas Payton and Arturo Ordoqui
Linda T. Peterson
Karla and Lorne Phillips
Gail and Marc Raney
Phil Reed
John Rowland
Shirley Rushing-Poteet and
John Poteet
Amy St. Clair
Brad Samuelson
Kimberly Sayles and Josef Webster
Mary and Mark Simon
Rachel Simon and Tex Pasley
Tara Simpson
Jane Polk Sinski
Steffanie Mortis Stevens and
John Stevens
Burgin Streetman and
William Lambrecht
Jacob and Jennifer Tingle
Elizabeth and Jesse Walker
Mary Walters
Jennifer Warren
Lou N. Williams
Elena Wilson
Allison Wolff
Daniel N. Zinn
Ann and David Zuk